ALLEN LANE

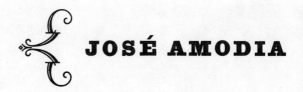

JOSÉ AMODIA

FRANCO'S POLITICAL LEGACY

FROM DICTATORSHIP TO FAÇADE DEMOCRACY

43675

ALLEN LANE
Penguin Books Ltd
17 Grosvenor Gardens
London SW1W OBD

First published 1977
Copyright © José Amodia, 1977

ISBN 07139 0488 7

Printed in Great Britain by Billing & Sons Ltd,
Guildford, Surrey

Phototypeset in Great Britain by
Filmtype Services Limited, Scarborough

CONTENTS

43675

43872

LIST OF TABLES

PREFACE

'*L'Espagne, dont tout le monde a parlé et que si peu de gens connaissent.*'[1]
By the middle of the nineteenth century, when these words were written,
the French traveller in Spain had recognized a situation which still exists
today. After the distorted image given to Spain by French romanticism,
there has appeared a new image, just as distorted though less artistic,
in the brightly-coloured brochures which entice the tourists to Spain.
And of the millions of foreigners who visit the country every year, very
few know her well. In the political field, opinions on Franco's Spain vary
between two oversimplified extremes. There are those who still see her,
as in the early forties, a fascist regime, turned now into a museum piece,
an anachronism; and those who think that with a slight touching-up,
once Franco has disappeared, Spain will take her place in a democratic
western Europe.

On a more scholarly level, British political scientists have not felt inclined to spare the subject much time. One only has to glance through
the politics section of any British library to realize how little has been
written in this country on Franco's Spain. This work cannot aspire to
fill that gap which is so large that it requires the combined efforts of
many specialists on Spanish affairs. I hope, however, that it will make a

contribution by providing an overall view of the Spanish political system at a key point in its history, when Franco's life is nearing its end and the structures of government he has created will have to stand by themselves. The period when this book was written should also be borne in mind. Apart from some minor adjustment it was concluded during the winter of 1974–5.

Although the formal approach adopted in this study is institutional, the aim is not a detailed analysis of the various institutions of government, but an overall critical assessment of the Spanish political system, sustained throughout the book by a common thesis: the struggle condensed in the dichotomy evolution–involution. I have paid a great deal of attention to the legal development of the regime, particularly at a constitutional level. In view of the lack of reliable information at other levels and the non-availability of many sources, I consider this approach, for the time being at least, as good as any, and better than most. My opinion is here supported by two very different but equally respected authorities in the field of Spanish politics, R. Fernández Carvajal and J. J. Linz. 'It seems to me that we desperately need more studies on constitutional law in our country, and that, contrary to a widely held view, this need is greater than that for pure sociological or political analysis of different events and situations'[2] wrote the former, and the latter: 'the official legal texts often are very revealing and deserve more attention of political scientists than a one-sided behaviourism would lead us to expect'.[3]

In order to keep to a minimum quotations from the Fundamental Laws and to facilitate the consultation of their content I have added as an appendix my own translation of the Spanish constitution. However, I have tried to provide a second dimension by going beyond a purely formal and theoretical analysis of legal texts to support my own interpretations and conclusions with events and opinions extracted from the political reality of Spain.

On balance the conclusions of this work are not very flattering to the Franco regime. I have reached them as a result of my personal experience as a Spaniard and through a careful study of available sources. My intention has been to offer an objective presentation of the fruits of that experience and that work, and I want to make this clear to all those who may find it difficult to accept the opinions expressed.

I cannot conclude without acknowledging the help received in various ways from several friends and colleagues in Spain. Although I am solely responsible for the opinions and judgements this book contains, their names had better remain anonymous. I should like to give my thanks to my students in Bradford, whose cooperation, criticism, and stimulus in tutorials and seminars have made a much greater contribution than they realize; also to the staff of the Social Sciences Library at the University of Bradford, in particular to Mr J. J. Horton, whose help in the search for source material has been so useful. My thanks too to Miss S. Embleton, the patient typist of the various drafts of this work.

1 ❧ INTRODUCTION

The Second Republic

The Spanish Second Republic was a failure, a total failure. The jubilation that inundated the centre of Madrid, from Cibeles to the Puerta del Sol, during the uncertain hours of 13 and 14 April 1931 was but the short sparkle of a dream which would never become a reality. It was not the fall of the Monarchy that the people were celebrating, nor were they joyously saluting the arrival of the new Republic; their demonstration was the spontaneous welcome – based more on hope than reason – given to the incipient regime which was expected to be 'their' regime, the regime of the people. At long last Spain was to be ruled by a government that would apply the simple but just method of taking away from the rich to give to the poor. The era of oppression had come to an end. The new republican leaders would make sure that the old reactionary forces: Church, army, aristocracy, landowners, etc. had their powers and influence curtailed, in favour of those who, until then, had been the oppressed and deprived. This kind of thought must have filled the elated minds of those who were shouting *¡Viva la República!* in the streets of Madrid.

History was being made in those crucial hours of mid April, the political pendulum was swinging almost dramatically from right to left, and it was all happening in an uncharacteristically Spanish manner: violence played no part. The results of the local elections held on 12 April 1931 had, in all the major cities, gone in favour of the republican candidates. It might have been true that, taking the country as a whole, the elected monarchist councillors outnumbered republican ones four to one;[1] but the King was wise enough to realize that the big urban centres, the industrialized areas, had a considerable demographic weight which was under-represented in the results, when compared to less populated areas of the country, and that in those areas political awareness and commitment were at their highest.

It was not only the working classes that were filled with joy and hope at the arrival of the Second Republic. Some of Spain's most brilliant minds and illustrious figures lent their support to the new regime. Machado, Ortega y Gasset, Pérez de Ayala and many others expressed, in their own different ways, the faith and expectations they had placed upon them, to this day, last attempt at liberal democracy in Spain. And yet, little more than five years later, in the middle of 1936, civil war broke out in the country bringing to a bloody end the whole republican experiment. In spite of its violence, the war did not represent a sudden and soul-destroying collapse of the hopes and expectations of 1931, because many of them had already been lost, or at least badly shaken by the time the war started. The history of the Spanish Second Republic follows a clearly descending line from hope to despair, from trust in reason to trust in violence, and, if it were applied to the spring and early summer of 1936, one can almost accept as a truism the title of Gil Roble's memoirs 'Peace was not possible.'[2]

It is in this light that the failure of the Second Republic must be interpreted. Its inability to fulfil the many high hopes it had awakened justifies the use of the term failure. But whereas the reality of this failure is not in question, the allocation of responsibility for it has been disputed by all those who participated in or lived through the ideological struggle that shook and split up the Europe of the thirties. Time and new generations are providing the necessary perspective to see the republican years with certain detachment. Historical impartiality has not asserted itself yet – the irreconcilable attitudes of mutual hatred of both victors and vanquished in the Spanish Civil War are to be blamed for this postponement of truth – but as the dust of the struggle settles and the wounds are healed, one is more able to discern what happened and why it happened.

In a general view of the Second Republic three major aspects seem to stand out. First, the Republic was founded upon a number of ideals which, however misguided or clumsily implemented, were well meaning, were largely necessary for the country, and aimed at creating a more just society. Secondly, the republican ideals never turned into tangible realities, because one section of the community – comprising large sectors of the working classes – was not willing to sit out patiently the slow process of reform, and because the forces of reaction bluntly opposed the changes implied by those ideals and openly rejected the regime that stood by them. Finally, in the war that put a tragic end to the republican experiment the forces of reaction won and tried to justify that war, and the regime it produced, in the failure of the Second Republic, a failure for which they were very largely responsible.

To elucidate the full significance of all three aspects, it would be necessary to follow in detail the history of the Republic and of the Civil War, a task well beyond the limits of this introduction.[3] Certain points, however, must be underlined, since a clear understanding of the republican system is essential to comprehend Franco's regime which is in many ways modelled as a negation of the former.

The Spanish Second Republic has often been called a republic of intellectuals, an epithet complimentary for some, pejorative for others, but always appropriate. By and large the intelligentsia of Spain were behind the Republic in 1931. As the life of the country unfolded along a path of frustration and disorder, many intellectuals became disappointed with the system and openly expressed their discontent and even their disapproval. Nevertheless, when the outcome of the Civil War put before them the tragic choice of staying in Spain with the victors or following the Republic into exile, the majority opted to leave. As if the losses in human life had not been enough, Spain suffered at the end of the Civil War a brain-drain possibly as serious as any country has ever known.

But the adjective intellectual has greater significance when applied to the actual founders of the Republic. They were mostly men of letters, journalists, university professors, lawyers who saw the problems of Spain largely through the eyes of the writers of the 1898 Generation, and hoped to halt the process of national decadence that had been such an obsession for those writers. They were, however, sadly lacking in political experience and more often than not they tried to operate at too abstract a level, setting up schemes which, though clear in their minds, were totally divorced from the social reality of a poor country concerned more with immediate results than with grandiose prospects or eloquent politicians. And these men, with all their intellectual virtues and political failings, were confronted in 1931 by a gigantic task. Spain had to be reconstructed. The diagnosis of decadence given by the 1898 Generation may not have been sociologically sound, but it was, nevertheless, pointing in the right direction. It was not necessary to be a social scientist to see what was wrong; most Spaniards were aware of the gravity of the situation, even if they could not agree as to the solution.

'An archaic economy and weighing upon it the agrarian problem and the predominating role of the big banks; a powerful Church whose spiritual power had so often over the centuries mingled with the temporal power; an army which had, during the first thirty years of the twentieth century, drifted towards militarism; regions with marked national characteristics (Catalonia, Euzkadi, Galicia) in need of freedom to develop; intellectual minorities whose knowledge was in sharp contrast to the cultural backwardness of the majority of the population; and an old, rickety State, as anachronistic as the social classes it served, which had to be constructed anew to render it effective and, what was most important, to create institutions that would make uninterrupted development towards a democratic life possible.'[4] A fair summary of the ailments Spain was suffering from, as expressed by one of the best-known contemporary Spanish historians. The Second Republic had to find a cure for all of them.

The State they brought in to replace the exhausted and discredited monarchy of Alfonso XIII was a republic, with all the makings of a liberal democracy. Right from its inception on 14 April 1931 the provisional government proclaimed the principle of the rule of law and the submission of all its activities to the future approval of the Constituent Cortes.[5] The constitution prepared by the Cortes, or Parliament, elected in June, followed. It was a liberal constitution leaning towards the left. It could not be otherwise. The republican government was supported in Parliament by a socialist majority;[6] besides there can be no doubt that the solution to the problems of Spain at that crucial moment lay in a leftward direction. The constitution was approved on 9 December 1931, after months of stormy debates, with the favourable vote of all the deputies present in the Cortes. However, the constitutional text had obvious weaknesses which became more evident as the months went by and the increasing opposition of political extremists multiplied the difficulties of government.

The two most controversial points in the constitutional law were the articles dealing with the relations between Church and State, and those concerned with regional autonomy. The former were too drastic, the latter too ambiguous.

Spain was and still is a Catholic country.[7] But the Catholic Church was and had been, from at least the beginning of the nineteenth century, aligned with the forces of reaction. Its grip on Spanish education had to be lessened, if not broken, to achieve a fairer society. Some changes in matters of religion were, then, unavoidable. To believe, as Sr Madariaga does,[8] that those changes could be achieved under the 1851 Concordat, still in force at the beginning of the Republic, is, to say the least, naïve. On the other hand, the constitution, and its sequel in these matters, the Law on Religious Confessions and Congregations of May 1933, adopted an attitude which was too extremist and yet in practice not terribly effective.[9] It alienated from the Republic many middle-of-the-road Catholics, who might perhaps accept that 'the Spanish State had no official religion',[10] but could not endure what they considered to be the discriminatory nature of articles 26 and 27 of the constitution. These articles determined that the Catholic Church, the same as any other Church, should be subject to a special law of associations, should not receive any subsidy from the State, should be subject to taxes, and should not be allowed to teach. The way was also prepared in a rather indirect manner for the dissolution of the Jesuit Order.

From our vantage point more than forty years later, it is difficult to imagine the impact of those articles on the Spain of the time. They smacked of nineteenth-century anticlericalism. By the time they were drafted and approved, the republican government and the Church hierarchy had already shown each other their mutual dislike; Cardinal Segura, the Cardinal Primate of Spain, had had to be exiled by the provisional government of the Republic during May 1931, for his overtly pro-monarchist activities, and some extremists had already burnt down a number of churches and convents, in Madrid first – the burnings started on 11 May – and later in the provinces. In this matter, as in so many others, the left-wing founders of the Republic were aiming correctly but they missed their target. They did not loosen the stranglehold of the Catholic Church on Spanish society. An attempt at curtailing the intervention of the Church in temporal matters was made to look like an attack on the spiritual essence of Roman Catholicism. In this misplacement of emphasis, the arrogance of some republican speeches – like the famous one of Manuel Azaña, 'Spain is no longer a Catholic country, even though there may be many millions of Spanish Catholics'[11] – was not so much to blame as the attitude of the forces of reaction, impatiently waiting to gather the ammunition necessary to overthrow the Republic. Here, in the sensitive area of the relationship between Church and State, they were to find a well-stocked arsenal.

The constitution suffered from ambiguity in the question of regional autonomy. Republicans were committed to granting some measure of independence in internal affairs to those regions with individualizing features, Catalonia, the Basque country and, to a lesser degree, Galicia. The promise to Catalonia had been made in San Sebastián in the summer of 1930 when a group of leading republicans – most of them later formed the provisional government of the Second Republic – met, as a kind of conspiratorial Fronde, to plot and prepare for the downfall of the Monarchy, which appeared imminent. On the other hand, when the Second Republic came into being, the Catalans had to be dissuaded from setting up a separate state as their old leader Maciá seemed to desire. Confronted with separatist inclinations in Catalonia and with the moral obligation to provide autonomous administration for certain regions, the Constituent Cortes opted for an ambiguous solution. They did not call Spain a 'nation' in order not to hurt the feelings of Catalan and Basque nationalists. In its place they gave a curious definition: 'Spain is a Republic of workers of all kinds' (article 1). They also kept away from federalism, availing themselves of the formula of the integral State. Wavering between extremes, they were able to find a middle path to regional autonomy. The Catalan Statute passed by the Cortes in September 1932 represented the main success of the republican efforts. The Basque country, with its more conservative form of nationalism, did not gain its statute of autonomy until after the beginning of the Civil War. Here again, those displaced by the Republic found a suitable front to attack. The Republic would be accused of going against the interests of the nation, of trying, under the cover of autonomy, to split up the national territory, of attempting to undo what Ferdinand and Isabella, the Catholic monarchs, had achieved back in the fifteenth century.

The same story could be told of all the other Republican attempts at social or political reform, whether they affected agriculture, the army or the educational system. In some instances, the opposition arose out of fear of losing privileges; the big landowners felt threatened by the programme of land redistribution – weak and limited though it was – for the *latifundio* areas of southern Spain. In other cases, as in Azaña's reform of the armed forces, the door was opened to intrigue and conspiracy. During the dictatorship of Primo de Rivera, the army had evolved towards conservatism and was, from the beginning, a potential enemy of the Republic.[12] Not surprisingly, many officers did not welcome Azaña's plans, as War Minister in the provisional government, to reduce the army to its proper role and to put an end to militarism. And they moved even further to the right, becoming only too receptive to pleasing compliments – the equation Army = *Patria* was a favourite – and to incitements to intervene in politics coming from those who stood to gain by the overthrow of the Republic. Before the final *coup d'état* in 1936, the army had tried to get rid of the Republic by force, in the summer of 1932, and with the support of members of the aristocracy and of some big landowners.[13]

The great tragedy for the men who founded the Second Republic was not, however, the enmity their plans aroused among large sections of the upper classes, the army and the Church. They expected this and would have coped with it had they enjoyed the support of the working classes, but this, for the most part, they were unable to muster. They found themselves between two fires. Their projects of reform went too far for some, and not far enough for others. The extreme right would not entertain any idea of change, while the extreme left wished to change everything and change it quickly, lest their opportunity ran away.

Anarchism, usually a doctrine of extremist minorities, had become a mass movement in Spain. The CNT (*Confederación Nacional del Trabajo*), the anarcho-syndicalist organization, founded in 1911, had by 1931 a tremendous numerical force, not far from the one million mark,[14] and its activities were to a large extent dominated by the most militant group, the FAI (Federación Anarquista Ibérica). The uncompromising attitude of this organization, whose philosophy openly rejected the established order and refused to accept the authority of the Second Republic,[15] led to violent strikes and all kinds of direct action, and in turn to confrontation with the police: the major problem of the Republic, the maintenance of public order, thus appeared. It was a game impossible to win. Disorder and chaos in the streets would not only make running the country impossible, but it would give the right-wing forces grounds to criticize and oppose all the proposed reforms as dangers to national stability, and it would even provide a justification for the army to intervene. On the other hand, repression would make the working classes believe that, after all, the Republic was no better than its predecessors had been. As it happened, the Republic failed on both counts, unable, as it was, to satisfy either side.

The socialists cannot be absolved from blame for the lack of public order. In a way, their responsibility is much greater. The republicans could not expect much support from the anarchists, but they relied on the socialists for survival and they were badly let down. The national elections of 1933, which gave the victory to the parties of the centre and the right, represented a sudden halt in the path to reform. From that moment onwards, a rift split the socialist movement. There were those who hoped to return to the republican experiment as it had been before 1933, and those who no longer had any faith in a socializing republic led by bourgeois intellectuals.

Mussolini was riding high in Italy, Hitler had come to power in January 1933, Dollfuss violently suppressed socialism in Vienna a year later . . . The fascist threat was hovering over most of Europe, and it was reflected in Spain in some of the activities of the Catholic party CEDA, three of whose members entered the government in October 1934, and even more so in the foundation of Falange Española at an electoral meeting held in a Madrid theatre on 29 October. Falange, whose founder and leader was José Antonio Primo de Rivera, would become the Spanish prototype of fascism.

These two facts put together, the disillusion with the Republic and the fear of fascism, partly explain the drift of many socialists towards violent activism.[16] The chasm between moderate socialists led by Indalecio Prieto and followers of Largo Caballero, who would be satisfied with nothing short of a proletarian revolution, became larger as the Civil War neared. To say as Madariaga has said that 'the circumstance that made Civil War inevitable in Spain was the civil war inside the socialist party'[17] may be a stylistic hyperbole; nevertheless, it was a major factor contributing to the ultimate disaster of July 1936, and the eventual downfall of the Second Republic.

Finally, the Civil War. In February 1936 elections to the Cortes were held once more – the third national elections under the Second Republic.[18] The results favoured the left, as they had in 1931. The Popular Front coalition won and a return to the early Republican reform was expected and partly attempted, but the extreme right would not allow it. Some generals started to plot soon after the Popular Front's victory and they were not lacking in encouragement and support from the expected quarters: the landowning aristocracy, bankers, certain sections of industry . . . In many ways, the military uprising resembled a nineteenth-century *pronunciamiento*, only this time it came up against the unyielding opposition of the militant working classes and what was to be an overnight putsch turned into a three-year civil war.

To try to ascertain now whether the Spanish Civil War was inevitable is futile. It is there, as a bloody landmark in the history of Spain, and as the starting point – a tragic one, indeed – of Franco's regime. The Second Republic was a failure, and everybody involved in its history must bear some responsibility for that failure. People, according to their viewpoints and convictions, have in the past, and will in the future, distribute the weight of responsibility in different ways. Two facts, however, stand out, I think, unquestionably clearly. The Civil War was a terrible disaster for Spain. It was initiated and won by the forces of reaction, who have since run the country.

The Legitimacy of Franco's Regime

'Time cures everything,' reads a Spanish proverb, and the day will come when the years 1936–9 will be distant enough to put on the Civil War a historical patina that will diffuse its tragic colours. In a way, this process is already happening and would have been greatly accelerated if the regime had not celebrated the memory. This was one of its gravest errors. The Civil War finished officially with a communiqué signed by Franco on 1 April 1939. Some kind of a dictatorial system might have been unavoidable after such a long period of fighting. The victors were quick to impose such a system, but not to heal the spiritual wounds of the nation. No compromise with the defeated was accepted. The fate imposed on the losing republicans varied from prison and execution to exile and oblivion. It was a negative attitude that hoped to create the 'new' by totally eradicating the 'old'. Franco's regime tried to find legitimacy in denigrating the Second Republic and glorifying the Civil War.

When comparing the Second Republic with Franco's regime, whether in an overall view or in any particular aspect, one is always struck by their antithetical nature. As they are separated by a civil war, antagonistic positions are understandable. But need the new regime have been the exact opposite of the previous one? A fascist-like dictatorship took the place of a liberal democracy; a monarchy of sorts eventually replaced the Republic; political parties were banned and a single-party system imposed; trade unions were banned; the Catholic Church was given back the temporal powers lost under the Second Republic; the army more than regained its militaristic role . . . The list could be made almost endless.

Falangist doctrine, in a diluted form, lies behind these reversals. It is futile to argue whether this doctrine was cause or effect of the radical change of direction in Spanish political life. It existed at the time of the Civil War and Franco's side adopted its tenets as their ideological basis. This question will be discussed later in some detail,[19] but one point must be underlined here as essential to understanding the present-day political situation in Spain. Franco's regime rejected the ideological principles of the Second Republic and embraced the falangist doctrine so wholeheartedly that now it cannot evolve within those narrow limits. Even if the desire for radical change existed, progress would be made very difficult by the heavy shackles remaining from early days. To shake them off would amount to a revolution.[20]

Let us now return to the question of legitimacy. Like so many other terms in political science, legitimacy is a very elusive concept. Fraga Iribarne, Professor of Politics at the University of Madrid and for some years Minister of Information and Tourism in Franco's cabinet, defines it in the following way: 'The legitimacy of a political regime is in essence a historical reality, which consists basically of the people accepting a political system as the most appropriate for their social conditions, at the present moment, in relation to past experiences, and as a hope for the future.'[21] From this definition he goes on to try to establish the legitimacy of origin and the legitimacy in practice of the Spanish regime. The former is to be found in the failures and excesses of the Second Republic, and the latter in the peaceful progress of Spain since the Civil War.

As regards the legitimacy of origin, the condemnation of the republican experiment combined with the falangist inheritance gave birth to a curious collection of political myths to legitimize and prove the validity of Franco's regime. At best these are half-truths and rest upon a one-sided interpretation of history, and at worst they are simply that, myths. The whole of Spanish history from the beginning of the nineteenth century to 1936 is condemned as a continuous process of national disintegration. If anything, the only elements worth saving from that period are nineteenth-century carlism and the dictatorial years (1923–30) of General Primo de Rivera. The rest were attempts at importing foreign ideologies – liberalism, socialism, anarchism – which were in conflict with traditional Spanish values. That is why Franco's regime found its roots much further back in history, in the glorious days of the sixteenth century; an idea expressed by Franco in rather nostalgic terms in 1942: 'Given the choice of a period in Spanish history, which one would we choose? Undoubtedly we would not hesitate to choose that of Isabel la Católica, Cisneros, Charles I and Philip II.'[22] This theory met, in different ways, with the approval of both carlists and falangists and it is to this day a recurrent theme in official speeches and writings.

The Second Republic is presented as the culmination of the process of national decline initiated in 1808. It is here where Francoist propaganda has applied its most cruel blows, in the way the republican history has been presented – and in its two corollaries, the communist bogy and the transformation of a civil war into a crusade. Whether in the rhetorics of politicians or in the drier prose of legal texts, whether in learned works of historians or in more elementary books for schools, the years of the Second Republic have been put to the Spanish people as an epitome of social, economic and political vices without a trace of virtue. The multitude of examples which substantiate the above statement makes quotation almost unnecessary.[23] In more recent years this campaign has abated somewhat, and the publication of some works presenting a less distorted picture allowed, but the echoes of the previous period are still audible, as in the following incredible summary found in a book recommended by the Ministry of Education for eight- and nine-year-old children:

'In 1931 Alfonso XIII, the last King, had to leave the country and the Republic was established. This Republic was ruled by freemasons, socialists and communists. They burnt many churches and convents and persecuted Catholics, there were many strikes, people were killed and there was a great deal of disorder. The communists, who always do what they are ordered by the Russians, wanted to turn Spain into a communist republic.

'Then all good Spaniards, with the best of the armed forces, and led by General Franco, rose in arms to restore order and to free Spain from the communists.

'The war of liberation lasted three years because the communists, the reds, were greatly helped by the Russians and by communists from other nations, who sent them arms and soldiers.'[24]

This lengthy quotation clearly links the interpretation given to the history of the Second Republic with the two other political myths behind the legitimacy of origin of Franco's regime: the communist threat to Spain and, in fact, to all western Europe, and the view that the war waged by Franco's nationalist forces was a crusade to save the country and Christianity. For many years – while all dissident voices inside Spain were gagged – official propaganda poured out, accompanied by 'documentary evidence', to prove that the Civil War had been inevitable in the face of communist plans to turn Spain into a Russian satellite. Time has discredited this theory and the forged nature or non-existence of the documents on which it was based has been denounced,[25] and even admitted,[26] although it has not died away altogether. The importance of this political myth in building up a legitimate image of the regime was considerable. Those of us who were brought up and educated in the Spain of the forties and fifties are witness to it. The line of argument followed here should not be confused with the part played by communists on the republican side during the war. Shameful as this was in many aspects – according to the most reliable sources – it provides no basis whatsoever for legitimizing Franco's regime.

The communist bogy was to have other uses. During the years of the Cold War it provided the United States of America with an excuse to cast aside political scruples and to reverse its attitude towards Franco's Spain. Even today, in spite of the contacts Spain has established with some communist nations, it is frequently used to explain away workers' or students' unrest, no longer linked directly to Russia, but still given the abstract label of 'subversive communism'.[27]

The estimates of the number of deaths during the Civil War and the purge that followed are between 400,000 and 600,000 – a frightening toll to pay for the disorders and murders which had littered the life of the Second Republic. To this loss of human life we have to add the thousands who had to go into exile, and the material devastation of the country after three years of bitter fighting. No, it was not possible to justify it all with the myths. Something more decisive had to be found, something which transcended material values; that something was the title of Crusade applied to the Civil War. The only befitting expression, Civil War, was tacitly banned, and replaced by War of Liberation, and Crusade, to generate the idea that Franco's followers had gone into battle like medieval crusaders to fight the enemies of God, this time not in the Holy Land but at home. They were fighting to save Christianity, and when spiritual values are at stake, material losses become irrelevant. The connivance of the Catholic Church, both in Spain and in Rome, was in this respect all-important. No better document can be found to illustrate the attitude of the Church towards the Civil War than the pastoral letter signed by the majority of Spanish bishops and dated 1 July 1937. The war was, by then, nearly one year old and the vision of it gained by the Spanish prelates during that period could not be much more distorted. All right was with the nationalists and all wrong with the republicans. The 'with-God' were fighting the 'without-God'. Pro-Russian communists were the great villains in the plot against Spain. Crimes – described by the bishops with some lurid details – were only happening on one side; on the other side there were just 'a few excesses, committed by error or by auxiliary personnel'. The Church, said the bishops, had always stood for social justice, the working classes were strongly protected by the law and the nation was well on the way to a better distribution of wealth – one has to assume that the bishops were referring to the pre-republican days![28] With this official backing from the Church, the myth of the Crusade gained momentum and pervaded with a kind of inquisitorial zeal Spanish life during the post-war years. The Spanish Church has come to regret these attitudes,[29] while the word Crusade has been included in the text of the Principles of the National Movement as a 'permanent and immutable' reminder of the legitimacy of origin of Franco's regime.[30]

The doctrine of legitimacy does not become redundant once a regime has been successfully set up. The regime must foster an atmosphere of general consent amongst the people. The principles upon which the new political order rests have to be acceptable, or – what is more important – made to look as if they are acceptable, to the majority. In the Spanish case the problem arising out of legitimacy was twofold. First, it was necessary to show that the regime enjoyed the support of Spaniards – not too difficult a task in a dictatorial situation. Second, Franco's regime had to be legitimized in the eyes of foreign powers, which became particularly hostile after the defeat of the Axis in the Second World War. These two goals have been the main guidelines of political development in Spain over the last thirty years. The change from dictatorship to what might be called façade democracy has been determined by the desire for some resemblance of popularity at home, and some degree of acceptance abroad. And the regime seems to have succeeded on both fronts. The image of a regime in constant mutation has been encouraged in official circles in Spain. The regime wants to be viewed as an evolutionary entity, as a body endowed with sufficient flexibility to adapt itself to a changing reality, in short, as a movement. As we shall see in later chapters this mutability applies to all the institutions from the head of State to the Cortes and from the party to the syndicates. Everything changes. Once the totalitarian solution was seen to be unviable soon after the Civil War, the evolutionary theory gained force. It was a question of survival, to change or to die. But, what kind of change?

The Spanish regime started by rejecting the principles of liberal democracy and adhering to the fascist doctrine of Falange. Later it found that it had to co-exist with countries governed according to the democratic principles and a formula to combine these apparently self-excluding realities became necessary. Without giving up its original principles the regime started to change, eradicating its most blatant birth-marks, and purifying their linguistic guise. New institutions were created to cover up the isolated figure of the dictator. A 'democracy' was founded on very much the same principles used to establish a totalitarian state. The dictator, the single party, the state-controlled syndicates, the rump parliament, the mass rallies, the one-sided referenda served to create a democracy of sorts, as they would have served a fascist regime in different historical circumstances. The nature of all these institutions could not have been the same in both cases, but their continued existence seems to suggest that the change has not been as great as it first appears.

Other arguments and myths have been frequently used to enhance the aura of legitimacy surrounding Francoism. The regime as provider of peace and prosperity was an image fully exploited during the sixties. The originality of Spanish democracy was another one. At the end of the evolutionary road, finding it impossible to move any further towards liberal democracy without repudiating most of its original principles, the regime decided on another justification. The idea that Spain is different can be found, at least in latent form, throughout the life of the regime. Until quite recently it was epitomized by the most popular of tourist slogans: 'España es diferente'. Here was the answer. Spain was not the same as other nations, and therefore had a democratic system which suited her idiosyncracies. Spanish democracy is not a form of liberal democracy, but that does not make it any less democratic.[31] The Spanish character is bedevilled by certain failings – *demonios familiares* as Franco would call them – such as individualism, lack of solidarity and extremism, that make it incompatible with liberal democracy as understood in Western Europe. The democracy Franco has given Spain is tailor-made to fit the temperament of her people. Certainly, it is not a complimentary assessment of the Spanish temperament and does not stand up to close examination, but it is there as the latest myth in a long process of self-justification.

The Diachronic Evolution of Spain

The uneven progress of different sectors of society or the inability to maintain well-balanced development in social, political and economic matters is not new to Spain. The Second Republic offers a good example. Its political structure was far ahead of the socio-economic infrastructure, and the republican attempts to raise the latter to the level of the former did not meet with much success. The problem had recurred before and it has become acute during the Franco years.[32]

Since the end of the Civil War the face of Spain has changed. Materially the improvement has been staggering, both in quantity and speed. The figures produced by the INE (Instituto Nacional de Estadística) or by the yearly reports of the major banks show a fast rate of increase of GNP and a Spain moving towards the threshold of affluence as measured in income *per capita*. There are more cars, more television sets, more washing-machines; luxury apartment blocks are sprouting everywhere; better education, better transport, more social security are now available to Spaniards. The whole picture is outlined under glowing statistics in the latest Plan for Economic and Social Development.[33] In its first chapter, entitled 'Spanish society and the Spanish economy in 1970', a summary is given of the quantitative economic progress of Spain during the sixties. The impression left is a most pleasant one. In purely economic terms, the country is developing fast, 'the cake is getting bigger'.

Has all this extraordinary economic development been accompanied by a similar social development? If we consider the economic development to follow a careful plan, then we have to conclude that nothing comparable has been done in the social sphere. The development plans have all had in their heading the adjectives 'economic' and 'social', in that order. 'Social' appears as an afterthought without much impact on the plans' actual contents.[34] However, it is impossible to achieve a considerable economic development without altering the social situation. Here, too, Spain is very different from what she was in 1950 or even in 1960. The increased mobility of the population, the migration from rural areas into urban conurbations, the higher standard of living and education, etc. have all contributed to alter the social habits of the Spaniard. However, we cannot talk of social development as the result of a carefully-worked-out plan. The social transformations, some progressive, some regressive, have a certain fortuitous appearance and it is appropriate to refer to them as social changes.

The diachronic nature of the evolution of Spain during the Franco years is more apparent in her political face. The *desfase* – to use a term common nowadays in Spanish publications – of the political regime in relation to the nation's economic development and social change is considerable. (*Desfase* has no exact English equivalent: it means 'not kept pace with' or 'out of step with' in the sense of lagging behind.) This is not to say that Spain has experienced no political alteration over the last three decades. But the regime has been unable, or has not wanted, to keep pace with socio-economic evolution. What changes there have been have had neither the aim nor the effect of giving Spaniards a greater share and a freer hand in running their own country – an essential condition for real political development. On the contrary, the regime has evolved within a narrow authoritarianism, allowing progressive moves that improve its façade, provided that they do not endanger its monopoly of power or put in question the ideology justifying it. This process is best followed through the series of Fundamental Laws issued over the years to form what might now be called the Spanish constitution. From the first Fundamental Law, promulgated in 1938, to the latest one, issued at the beginning of 1967, there stretches a long road of constant 'democratization' with the final goal always round the '*next*' corner'. Now the constitutional structure is complete there are no more corners to turn and the promised democracy is nowhere in sight. Political life has become stagnant, and at times even regressive. We can thus summarize the diachronic evolution of Spain in three appropriate headings: economic development, social change, and political stagnation.

Economic Development

In 1939 Franco's nationalist troops won control of a devastated country. Three years of warfare had meant enormous material losses, which a backward and underdeveloped Spain could ill afford. The Second World War and the period of isolation imposed by the Allies on Spain during the late forties made things worse; Spaniards named that decade 'the years of hunger'. Even in the fifties, with the doors of the world open again and with the financial support of the USA, the economic situation did not improve much. The autarchic policies pursued by Franco's governments had been unsuccessful for, in 1957, the national economy was near bankruptcy. And yet, a few years later, during the sixties, someone started to talk of a 'Spanish miracle' in the fantastic growth of the economy. 'Economic miracles' were no novelty. Italy and Japan had their miraculous development too. But for the majority of Spaniards it was new and exciting to find themselves affluent. This was to become one more way of justifying the regime.

It all began with a change of government in February 1957. A new figure, the politically aseptic expert, entered Franco's Cabinet and economic recovery got under way. The devaluation of the peseta – its parity was altered from 42 to 60 pesetas to the American dollar – and a stabilization plan – a practical wage freeze, higher bank rates, reductions in public expenditure, encouragement of foreign investment, increase of taxation – were the first steps. It was necessary to stop the decline before starting to build. As if to prove that economic self-sufficiency had been abandoned, during 1958–9 Spain joined the International Monetary Fund and the International Bank for Reconstruction and Development, and she became a member of the OEEC – later to become the OECD (Organization for Economic Co-operation and Development) – which started to publish yearly reports on the state and prospects of the Spanish economy. In 1962, at the request of the Spanish government, a team of experts of the IBRD carried out a thorough study of the economic situation after the stabilizing measures taken three years before.[35] The recommendations suggested that the moment of development had arrived. And so it was.

Already in February 1962 a new department had been created under the name of Comisaría del Plan de Desarrollo, with the aim of planning and coordinating economic development. From this department, which in 1965 was given ministerial status, emerged the three four-year programmes which have served as the guidelines for the development of the Spanish economy since 1964. The first development plan covered the years 1964–7, the second 1968–71, and the third and present one started in 1972 and stretches to the end of 1975. It is not my intention to cast a critical eye over the details of the success and failure of economic planning in Spain. We can accept as valid the glowing results shown in official statistics and in the speeches of Laureano López Rodó, the man who, as Minister in charge of Economic Development, engineers it all. Some of their figures and quotations will convey a sufficiently clear picture.

Two rather crude indicators of the degree of development of a country are the distribution of the economically active population between agriculture, industry and the service sector, and national income per head. On both counts the transformation of Spain has been outstanding, taking her from an underdeveloped agrarian country up to just below that imaginary line where development and industrial society are supposed to begin. The population of Spain at the end of 1970 was very nearly 34 million people.[36] Out of this total 12.7 million (37.5 per cent) were working. The labour force has increased by about one million people since 1960, when the figure was 11.7 million. Over the development years the economically active population has been drifting away from agriculture in favour of industry and services:

TABLE I[37] – DISTRIBUTION OF THE WORK FORCE BETWEEN ECONOMIC SECTORS (PERCENTAGES)

	1960	*1965*	*1970*
Agriculture	41.3	33.2	29.2
Industry	31.4	34.7	38.1
Services	27.3	32.1	32.7

This follows the trend of western Europe's other countries, although Spain still lags behind. On the other hand, she has left behind other European countries, such as Portugal and Greece, which were her equals fifteen years ago.

During the sixties national production increased at more than 7 per cent a year, with industry making a greater contribution every year. This was reflected in exports. Spain, traditionally an exporter of agricultural produce, was in 1970 selling abroad more citrus fruit and similar produce than in 1960, but its dominance in the trade balance had been considerably reduced, in favour of manufactured goods. In 1960 agricultural produce accounted for 53.8 per cent of total exports. By 1970 that percentage had been brought down to 34.9, even though agricultural exports had more than doubled.[38] Economic growth and increased exports were accompanied by greater demand at home, and the level of imports went up considerably. In fact, the trade gap that had been wiped out by the stabilization plan has become once more a normal feature in the balance sheet as can be seen in the following table:

TABLE 2[39] – FOREIGN TRADE (IN MILLION DOLLARS)

	1960	1965	1970
Imports	721	3,018	3,951
Exports	725	966	1,856
Balance of trade	+4	−2,052	−2,095

Nevertheless, this commercial deficit has been more than compensated for in the balance of payments by other items such as tourism, the remittances of Spaniards working abroad and the inflow of foreign capital. Not only have they made up for the trade losses in most years during the last decade,[40] but the final totting-up has been showing a good surplus, that has allowed the Spanish treasury to build up reserves.[41] Spaniards have seen their income per head increase steadily, bringing with it material benefits and comforts as the consumer society arrives south of the Pyrenees. This expansion was expected to continue over the next ten years. The third development plan, looking towards the future, well beyond the end of its four-year life, forecast for Spain in 1980 a standard of living similar to the one enjoyed now in the rest of western Europe. Table 3, taken from the third development plan, gives a numerical summary of the 'economic miracle'. This forecast now appears optimistic in the economic recession of the mid seventies.

TABLE 3[42] – INDICATORS OF STANDARD OF LIVING

	1960 (*actual*)	*1970* (*actual*)	*1980* (*forecast*)
Level of income			
Income per capita (dollars)	290	818	2,000–2,100
Food consumption			
Proteins (g/person/day)	75	84	94
Meat (kg/person/year)	19	44.7	52
Eggs (kg/person/year)	6	11.1	15
Sugar (kg/person/year)	17	26.6	38
Milk (kg/person/year)	60	84.7	100
Cultural level			
Degree of illiteracy (per 100 people)	11.2	5.7	0.7
Primary and secondary education (number of pupils)	4,050,000	6,000,000	7,360,000
Higher education (number of students)	71,000	175,000	277,000
Books published	12,038	19,900	30,000
Consumer durables			
Telephones (per 1,000 people)	59	135	320
Cars (per 1,000 people)	9	70	225
Television sets (per 1,000 people)	5	70	400
Fridges (manufactured per 1,000 people)	1	25	72
Washing machines (manufactured per 1,000 people)	3	15	38
Consumption of industrial products			
Steel (kg/person/year)	65	260	475
Cement (kg/person/year)	173	493	720
Electric power (kWh/person/year)	612	1,515	4,130
Petrol (litres/person/year)	32	102	380
Housing			
Houses (per 1,000 people)	257	270	329

The economic development of Spain has not, however, escaped strong and bitter criticism from many different angles. Economists have found all kinds of faults, both in general principles and in matters of detail, in the official development policies.[43] The most frequently used are: that economic planning was started in the wrong way by faithfully imitating the French model without regard for the totally different situation and requirements of Spain; that the development plans were prepared and drafted in an undemocratic manner (what else could be expected?); that they do not tackle the basic structural problems of the economy – agrarian reform, introduction of a progressive tax system, modernization of industrial production, control of financial forces, etc.; that economic growth lacks solidity since it is based upon foreign patents and know-how; that Spain is becoming a colony in economic terms . . .

At the end of the day, the Government is able to drown all these criticisms in a flood of statistics as an irrefutable proof of growth, and to say, repeatedly, through its Minister in charge of Economic Development: 'Never so much was achieved in such a length of time.'[44] Which happens to be the truth, though not the whole truth.

Social Change

Social changes have lagged sadly behind this economic growth, unnoticed and ignored very often amidst the overpowering propaganda of the development plans. An authoritarian regime can, and frequently does, achieve economic growth within certain limits. When that regime is composed of and supported by conservative forces, social evolution is curbed to maintain the stability of the regime and the privileged position of those inside it, but at the same time to allow those changes demanded by the needs of growth. Spain is a perfect fit for this stereotyped pattern of development. She has increased her wealth and has seen her general standard of living rise steadily over the last fifteen years. Her social texture looks somewhat different too; but this transformation has been haphazard and has produced a great deal of human suffering; social objectives have always been subservient to economic goals.

Two question marks hang over the future of Spain. They both arise out of the diachronic development of the country. The first question is concerned with economics. Can Spain sustain her present rate of growth without radical changes in her political as well as in her social structure? There are many who believe that the limits of economic development under authoritarian methods have now been reached and that further development will require much more freedom.[45]

The second question has a greater relevance for us here. Can the Spanish political regime survive the pressures created by new social conditions? To put this question in the right perspective, it must be underlined, once more, that social changes have been an inevitable consequence and not a planned result of economic growth, and that social changes may yet prove the final undoing of the regime.

The main feature of Spain during the sixties has been the movement of population; it has been so great that it dwarfs all other changes. This movement of population has taken three basic forms: migration of peasants into the industrialized urban centres, emigration of Spanish workers to the more affluent countries of western Europe, and massive temporary immigration of foreign tourists. All three were encouraged by the Spanish government because they saw in them some economic gain. The transfer of population from agriculture into industry was essential for development. The remittances of Spanish workers abroad and the revenue from tourism covered the trade gap and built up reserves. What the government did not foresee at all, or at least did not assess properly, in their desire for growth, were the far-reaching consequences of these movements.

The social effects of the population movements during the sixties are, first, the concentration of large numbers of workers in the three main industrial centres in Spain (the Basque Country, Barcelona and Madrid) and in others of lesser importance, such as Saragossa and Navarre; and secondly, the contact between Spaniards and the social patterns of western Europe.[46] The size of these effects can be seen from the figures given in Tables 4 and 5. The change is not only quantitative, it is qualitative too and therefore difficult to assess. How much has contact with other peoples, who enjoy greater freedom, who, in the case of workers, have their own independent unions to look after their interests, affected Spaniards? The impact must have been considerable. Besides, the Spaniards who did not experience the Civil War, either because they were too young at the time or were born after it, now form the majority of the population,[47] and they feel less attached to the regime and its original myths, and more receptive to ideas from abroad. Their attitude shows a reaction against the enclosed environment in which they were brought up. As a result, an ever-increasing section of the Spanish people is questioning the idiosyncracies of the socio-political system and they expect a rational and convincing answer – appeals to traditional values or demagogic slogans along the lines of 'we are different' or 'we are better' no longer satisfy.

TABLE 4[48] – TOURISTS VISITING SPAIN

1966	1967	1968	1969	1970
17,251,746	17,858,555	19,183,973	21,682,091	24,105,312

It is difficult to imagine development which adheres to the economic models of western Europe without at the same time importing their social and political patterns. The attempt is being made, but can it succeed?

TABLE 5[49] – EMIGRATION TO EUROPEAN COUNTRIES

Year	Numbers leaving	Numbers returning	Net emigration
1960	40,189	12,194	27,995
1961	116,524	8,315	108,209
1962	147,692	46,344	101,348
1963	145,859	52,730	93,129
1964	192,299	98,993	93,306
1965	181,278	120,678	60,600
1966	130,700	131,700	−1,000
1967	60,000	85,000	−25,000
1968	66,127	51,653	14,564
1969	92,160	29,600	62,560

The workers in the shipyards of El Ferrol, in the mines of Asturias, in the steel works of Bilbao, in the car factories of Barcelona, in the underground of Madrid, have found the strength of numbers, and are acting like their counterparts in Europe. As their standard of living rises, so does the similarity in behaviour. Only their goals differ. Spanish workers – or at least the most aware amongst them – are struggling to achieve more elementary gains: free unions, the right to strike, a minimum living wage.[50]

The falangist trumpets which announced the end of the class struggle in the thirties had been sounded too soon. The new technocratic tune – economic development will cure all social evils – met with no more success. It would, however, be a blunder to oversimplify the issue to a confrontation between the working class and the regime. There are other ingredients. To begin with, awareness of and protest against the unjust situation is not the monopoly of workers. University students and a few of their teachers, some members of the clergy – particularly the younger ones, certain illegal political organizations, a handful of publications, and other groups share in the burden and risk of denouncing social injustice. All together, they still constitute only a minority, but their voices are getting louder and are beginning to embarrass defenders of the *status quo*.

Education is an area where the pressure of protest is having some effect. The White Paper[51] produced by the Ministry of Education and Science in 1969 contains the most open self-criticism the regime has ever allowed itself, and the Law on Education that soon followed it[52] set out rather ambitious and, by Spanish standards, drastic reforms. It all came about largely as a result of demonstrations and pressure from university students. Their complaints were primarily concerned with the SEU,[53] the officially-imposed student syndicate, which they wanted replaced by free and democratic unions. In the course of the struggle, other grievances emerged. The university was accused of being a middle-class institution, the absenteeism of many professors was exposed, the outmoded and inflexible nature of most courses and the overcrowding and lack of facilities were denounced. Protest in the end yielded fruit. The Minister of Education was replaced and reform got under way.

The picture would be incomplete and misleading if it were simply to convey an idea of official negligence in the face of spontaneous social change. The regime has, over the years and out of a sense of self-preservation, avoided the alteration of the social structure and of social attitudes as far as possible. No other interpretation can be given to their refusal to carry out those economic reforms with the greatest social impact, such as the introduction of progressive taxation.[54] The same intention has to be attached to the denial of free trade unions, since it is well known that in a capitalist society, such organizations provide the lower classes with the only way of securing a fairer share of the national wealth.

Where the regime has proved most proficient at avoiding change has been in its efforts to nurture and keep alive that stratum lying half-way down the social pyramid, between the working class and the bourgeoisie, that some authors have called *clases medias*,[55] and others *el macizo de la raza*.[56] Made up of small landowners, shopkeepers, *rentiers*, tradesmen, and other similar occupations, it is permeated with the most reactionary characteristics: attachment to traditional patterns, mistrust of all that implies renovation, indifference in politics amounting to support for the established order, and an almost grateful subservience to authority. These traditional middle classes have been located by J. Linz and A. de Miguel mostly in the provinces of the central plateau,[57] and recent sociological studies show them to have a remarkable capacity for survival in spite of economic development. The regime has relied on the passive support of this traditional middle class; what is more, it has tried to instil its attitudes in the nation as a whole, encouraging indifference and diverting attention away from the real problems confronting their society. Thus they have succeeded in transforming the country, at least on the surface, into a 'political desert' – to quote, once again, Ridruejo, who, being a poet, had the gift of linguistic precision.[58] Even today, with greater freedom, a higher standard of living and more contact with other peoples, the level of political consciousness is still extremely low, as surveys and polls have shown.[59] The harm done in the last thirty years cannot be cured with quantitative economic growth alone.

Socially, then, the image of Spain is extremely confused, in part because the country is going through a period of transition, with all the painful experiences that implies. But the importance of this factor should not be overestimated, for the real roots of that confusion are embedded in the diachronic development we have been discussing. The country appears hesitant amidst alienating policies of consumption, social paradoxes and uncertainties, and, above all, political stagnation.

Political Stagnation

Since the whole evolutionary process we are considering is under the aegis of economic objectives, it seems appropriate to summon the testimony of López Rodó, the *éminence grise* behind the development plans: 'I see an essential and living parallelism between our Fundamental Laws and the programming of development, and I believe that they cannot be separated.'[60] The remark is as equivocal in the context of the speech from which it is taken as it looks here in isolation. It is not quite clear whether the minister then in charge of development means that Spain has evolved economically as little or as much as she has politically. One has to assume that the latter interpretation was intended, but both are false, for nothing in the political evolution of the regime resembles what has happened in the economic field. The point will be made clear when considering the different political institutions and forces, and how they have altered. But first a few general comments must be made about the political nature of the regime as a whole.

Official sources in Spain prefer to talk of Fundamental Laws. The term constitution is usually avoided,[61] it smacks of the rationalist approach of nineteenth-century liberalism and brings back unwanted memories of the Second Republic. The use of 'Fundamental Laws' – an expression found also in other countries like West Germany – has been primarily explained by saying that the former, with their staggered appearance over a period of nearly thirty years, have been most appropriate for Spain. The constitutional structure was built up little by little, unhurriedly, and taking full account of national needs and demands.

There are seven Fundamental Laws. They are in chronological order of promulgation:

1. The Labour Charter, issued during the Civil War, on 9 March 1938, and substantially modified on 10 January 1967.
2. The Law on the Cortes, issued on 17 July 1942, and modified twice, 9 March 1946 and 10 January 1967.

3. The Charter of the Spanish People of 17 July 1945, modified like the previous one on 10 January 1967.
4. The Law on the Referendum of 22 October 1945.
5. The Law on the Succession, issued on 7 July 1947, also modified on 10 January 1967.
6 The Law on the Principles of the National Movement of 15 May 1958.
7. The Organic Law of the State of 10 January 1967.

The higher platform on which these laws stand in relation to all other legislation was not established until 1947. There had been references to fundamental laws before,[62] but it was in article 10 of the Law on the Succession when, for the first time, certain laws – five in all – were given constitutional status, establishing the requirement of a referendum to alter or to repeal them. After 1947 two more laws were given that same fundamental rank.

The erratic chronology and order of Fundamental Laws is evident; they do not give the impression of a carefully worked out constitutional process which has been claimed. It looks more as if Franco and his legislators never had a clear aim, save their own maintenance in power. The jagged trajectory followed by the Fundamental Laws appears to be based upon expediency and opportunism. The pressures of political events, both at home and abroad, were the main determining factors. Very noticeable, for instance, is the sudden promulgation of three Fundamental Laws during the closing stages of the Second World War and immediately after. Fascism had been defeated and Franco was hurriedly trying to alter the fascist looks of his own regime. Equally noticeable is the lack of logical order. No rational explanation can be found to account for it. The constitutional process was initiated with a law dealing with labour and social problems and from there it meandered aimlessly up to 1967 when the Organic Law of the State tried to fill gaps, update the older laws and put some order into the chaotic development.

The seven Fundamental Laws as a whole do not constitute a harmonious body. They suffer from a gestation which has been too slow and fragmented. All the same, they comprise more or less all the elements that make up a classical constitution. They have a dogmatic part summarized by the Principles of the National Movement. They have a declaration of rights in the two Charters. And they define, in the Law on the Cortes, the Law on the Succession and the Organic Law of the State all the major institutions of government. However, the completion of the constitution and the differences, both in style and juridical precision, that separate the early Fundamental Laws from the more recent ones, do not amount to much more than a formal and exterior change. The authoritarian nature of the regime remains unaltered.

Although Franco's regime has not received much attention from non-Spanish political scientists, it is still included in studies of a more general character. In these it is typed variously, depending on the author's opinion but always within one field – that of authoritarianism. It is undoubtedly a hybrid regime in which we find the crossed threads of a past which wanted to be almost totalitarian and a present which pretends to be democratic. It is difficult to classify, and at least one author has assessed it as unclassifiable.[63] As recently as 1964 M. Duverger placed the Spanish regime, together with the Portuguese, under the common title of fascist dictatorship.[64] This classification looks back rather than forward. The origins of the regime at least serve as a basis for the adjective used. Looking to the future, another French writer, M. Prélot, uses the expression 'constituent dictatorship' though he only applies it to one period in the life of the regime.[65] This describes much better the way in which the regime has developed, although it is losing its force since the constituent process and the life of the dictator are drawing to their end.[66] It seems less accurate to speak of military dictatorship like C. F. Friedrich and Z. K. Brzezinski,[67] or of a military regime, like S. E. Finer.[68] The military element placed a decisive role in setting up the regime and still helps to sustain it, but it is no longer the predominating force, though it could be, once again, at some future date.

The adjective most frequently used of the Franco regime is 'authoritarian'. Many writers coincide on this point.[69] In this category, and almost as a curiosity is the combined form 'clerical-authoritarian', which a fairly recent work applied to it.[70] The term 'clerical', like the term 'military', only defines one aspect of the whole. The other adjective, 'authoritarian', gives a more complete and accurate description.

Juan Linz, professor at an American university, has tried to establish the characteristics of the regime's authoritarianism with greater detail and accuracy than perhaps any other writer.[71] For him, Franco's regime is neither totalitarian nor democratic but belongs to an intermediate category which he calls authoritarian. The principal difference between it and totalitarianism is that it allows a certain degree of pluralism which, compared with that in a democracy, is limited and not representative. Linz also points out that the regime has no objectively formulated ideology but rather what he calls a 'mentality' or 'mentalities' more emotional than rational; that it does not try to mobilize the masses and is quite content with passive support – in fact it prefers its citizens to be politically apathetic; and that the single party is a weak organization which is not the real centre of authority and serves as a tool of those really in control.

Linz's theory still retains its force and is the most accurate definition of the Spanish regime. However, there is another aspect which does not appear in Linz's definition and which, in recent years particularly, has become a real obsession with the holders of power in Spain. This is the democratic mask which the regime has been fashioning solely to appear less authoritarian. This characteristic, which could be considered incidental, has come into the foreground and has become the *raison d'être* of many of the political changes in the country during the last few years. It is the essence of *aperturismo* or democratization, Spanish style. The desire to show the world a democratic face has made the regime abandon some authoritarianism on occasions. The Press Law of 1966 and the introduction of direct elections for nearly a fifth of the members of the Cortes have meant a certain loss of control for the regime. A greater sacrifice than this could not be expected in an authoritarian system. This shows up to what point the centres of power are prepared to go in order to give a democratic varnish to its original authoritarianism. For this reason, when it comes to defining Franco's regime, to put it into a definite category, this pseudo-democratic tendency must be kept in mind. But as authoritarianism still lurks behind the façade and does not hesitate to show itself when it feels threatened, the expression 'façade democracy'[72] seems to suit it well. And it would be even better, bearing in mind its origins, and remembering that the regime does not like to be considered as static, to place it on an authoritarian line which comes from dictatorship and is going towards façade democracy. All the institutions we are now going to examine are somewhere along that line.

2 ❧ THE HEAD OF STATE

'No government which has to depend on Church, army and landlords can secure more than a temporary support in Spain. No government which represents a purely material well-being at the cost of liberty can satisfy Spaniards. And in a country where half the population sits in cafés and criticizes the government no dictator can prosper for long.' These general statements were made by Gerald Brenan[1] about Primo de Rivera's dictatorship, which lasted less than seven years, and they were written in 1942 when Franco had been in power for an even shorter period. Today, more than thirty years later, there are no longer any grounds for such an argument. During all that time Franco has remained as leader of Spain, his dictatorial powers almost intact, his popularity – if one is to judge by the demonstrations of public support staged at crucial moments in the Plaza de Oriente in Madrid – unabated to the end, the continuity of his regime beyond his death carefully planned. Have things changed since Brenan wrote? Or was his prognosis wrong in the first place? The head of the Spanish State for well over three decades was a dictator determined 'to hold on to the helm of the State for as long as God granted him life and clarity of judgement'.[2] How did it all come about? Essential to understanding the reality of the Spanish regime –

and not to prove or disprove Brenan's words – is a clear picture of that centre of authority on which the whole regime rests.

To examine the post of Head of State in Spain it is necessary to differentiate the dictatorial form incarnated by Franco from the constitutional form of the monarchy. The position of Franco, in spite of a considerable lack of legal definition, is unmistakably clear: there, standing in the centre, is the almighty figure of a ruler whose powers have no limits but his own will. Looking towards the future – a future which is almost present, since Franco's age[3] and precarious state of health make the final step towards the succession imminent – the picture is reversed: a legally-defined post, even a successor nominated, but nothing is clear. Confusion and uncertainty surround the future king, inviting the observer to indulge in a certain amount of soothsaying.

The present regime was born out of a revolutionary situation, the 1936–9 Civil War; at first it centred all its powers in one of the generals who had risen against the republican government, General Francisco Franco. And it was from him, as the creative force, that the framework of the new state emerged over more than thirty years. The initial moment of creation must be placed chronologically on 29 September 1936, and geographically in Burgos, historical town in the very heart of Old Castile.[4] A great deal has been written about how Franco was chosen by his fellow generals, and even today it is impossible to ascertain exactly what happened during September 1936 at the meetings of the generals, members of the Nationalist Junta, both at Burgos and Salamanca. Were they looking for a military leader to unite the fragmented nationalist side? Were they appointing a new head of government, a government as yet non-existent? Or was their intention to invest Franco with unlimited powers for an unlimited period of time? All these are questions begging an answer from historians. The lack of reliable sources may impede us from ever knowing.[5] It is nevertheless possible to start the study from two certain premises: a formal one is represented by the text of the decree issued by the Nationalist junta handing its powers over to Franco; the more positive one is inherent in the fact that, whatever the intentions of the generals and their expression of them, General Franco assumed then, and has since exercised, all the powers of the State.

A week after the beginning of the military uprising against the Popular Front government of the Second Republic, on 24 July 1936, the rebel side set up what they called the National Defence Junta, a body of generals headed by the oldest among them, General Cabanellas. This Junta, lacking the most essential tools of government (civil servants, records, etc.) limited itself to military matters. As the war went on, the need for a more unified leadership and government became apparent on the nationalist side. It was necessary to impose some administrative order on those parts of Spain they controlled, and to lay down the foundations of the regime to replace the republican one when victory came. At this juncture power was transferred to Franco, and the decree has the characteristic that qualifies Franco's position as a dictator: ambiguity, vagueness, ill-defined powers amounting to quasi-omnipotence.

The decree states in its first article: '. . . His Excellency, General Francisco Franco Bahamonde is appointed Head of the Government of the Spanish State, and he shall assume all the powers of the new State.' There is a great deal of ambiguity in this article. The boundaries imposed by the expression 'is appointed Head of the Government of the Spanish State' are removed by the sweeping statement which follows: 'he will assume all the powers of the new State'. This statement even seems to make unnecessary article 2 nominating Franco Generalissimo of all land, sea and air forces.

The same ambiguity can be detected in the preamble of the decree: 'All kinds of reasons seem to point out the advisability of turning into one all the powers which will lead us to the final victory and to the establishment, consolidation, and development of the new State.' This often-ignored passage contains in its involved language a great deal of foresight. The concentration of powers led to victory and the all-powerful dictator was to establish over the years, through a process of self-limitation, a new state. Whether this state is the one the generals wanted is another matter.

In the decrees can be seen a state whose institutions emerge over the years from that central source and constantly gravitate towards it, as they depend on it for stability and even for existence. The appearance of these institutions represented a process of self-limitation, though more formal than real. The powers of Franco as undisputed leader have survived amidst all other political forces and institutions. Not even the delimitation of the post of Head of State by the Organic Law of January 1967 affected Franco's position. The post of Head of State, as defined in the latest Fundamental Law of the country, only applies to the King as one of his successors. Because Franco will have not a successor, but successors, no one man can step into his shoes. Franco's position could not and will not be maintained after his death, the post of Caudillo could not be repeated. It could, in fact, be said that the post of Head of State was made to measure, to fit the idiosyncracies of the Generalissimo; and when we separate the two, man and office, we find the office incomplete, almost incomprehensible. This moulding of the highest office of the state to fit the characteristics and wishes of a man has been carried to the extreme of including his name in the Constitution. Article 2 of the Law on the Succession says: 'The office of Head of State is held by the Caudillo of Spain and of the Crusade, Generalissimo of the Armed Forces, don Francisco Franco Bahamonde.'[6] Thus to understand fully the Headship of State with Franco at the helm it is necessary to study the man. This is well outside the scope of this work and readers may refer to any of the many biographies of Franco so far published.[7]

Let us then begin by examining the post of Head of State as it appears at present. Sánchez Agesta considers its major characteristics to be the following: to be personal, in the sense that the post is attributed to one particular person; to hold extraordinary powers; to be an exceptional post, since it is not only attributed to one person, but it is attributed for life; to have its powers negatively defined, that is to say, that all the power that does not belong to any other institution is that of the Head of State.[8]

These features, though acceptable in general lines, could no doubt be simplified and reinforced at one point. The four characteristics could be reduced to two: the post is personal as it is vested in Franco for the duration of his life; the post is endowed with extraordinary powers, ill-defined as Professor Sánchez Agesta says, but only formally limited by the existence of other institutions. With Franco in office, it is difficult to foresee a situation in which he would have to give way to another political institution, unless violent means intervened. Certainly the last thirty years do not offer one single example of such an occurrence.

These extraordinary powers of Franco constitute a whole, they are interdependent, but for the sake of methodology we shall look at them from four different angles: constituent powers; *pluriempleo* powers; powers over the succession; charismatic power.

Constituent Powers

When examining any political facet of present-day Spain it seems un-avoidable to go back to its origin, to the Civil War. The military uprising in July 1936 failed in most of the major cities. Madrid, the capital, remained in the hands of the republican government and therefore the rebels were unable to take over the existing administrative machinery. Besides, their ideology, the ideology of the so-called nationalist side, was antipodean to the republican one. Faced with an institutional vacuum, they concentrated all the powers normally divided amongst several institutions in the hands of Franco. This occurred when the nationalist Junta entrusted Franco with the task of winning the war and of founding a new state.

These constituent powers were corroborated when the first attempts were made, in the laws of 30 January 1938 and 8 August 1939, to set up, next to Franco, some kind of administrative framework. By the first one Franco was given the supreme power to legislate. The second one went a step further, stating that he could legislate without even consulting his Council of Ministers.[9]

These unlimited constituent or foundational powers could perhaps be justified by the initial institutional vacuum. Political power had to be concentrated, since there were no institutions to share it. What is more difficult to explain and justify is the dilatory setting-up of new institutions, and particularly the fact that the creation of the institutional structure in no way diminished Franco's original powers. The Organic Law of the State of January 1967, which was supposed to represent the completion of the constitutional cycle, clearly states that as long as Franco remains as Head of State, he will have the powers granted to him by the Laws of 30 January 1938 and 8 August 1939.[10]

Professor Fernández Carvajal uses an expression very befitting to Franco's position: 'constituent dictatorship'.[11] A very accurate label: dictatorship because powers are concentrated in one person; and constituent because that person was to establish little by little, very little by little, a kind of constitution. The Fundamental Laws, from the Labour Charter of 1938 to the Organic Law of the State of 1967, emerged from the constituent dictatorship. Their process of elaboration differed, owing to the lack of controls over the Caudillo's authority, which accounts for a great deal of unpredictability, and the large chronological gaps between the Fundamental Laws. Their origins in different historical circumstances, and the need, perforce, for each to be based on those already in existence partly account for their diversity. But whatever their differences, whether the original text of the bill came out of the government, the National Council of the Movement or the Cortes, in the last instance it was Franco's authority that gave a new law constitutional status.

The prudence of Franco has often been praised and talked about by his admirers.[12] A man, we are told, who, in spite of his unlimited powers, has always been reticent to use them. A man who can legislate *per se*, without the intervention of any other body, but who has very rarely done so. Numerically this is true. Fernández Carvajal stresses the fact that, since its creation, only on five occasions has Franco legislated without going through the Cortes.[13] A sixth instance was added in 1970 when the Caudillo issued two decree-laws about the National Movement, availing himself, as the preamble of one of them states, of his special powers.[14] And even more recently he issued two more decree-laws as a final attempt to provide some safety for his successor.[15] The number may seem low, but we must not allow it to cloud our judgement. The results are not as meagre as the low figure might suggest. To build up a new state, a whole pseudo-democratic façade, and to maintain behind it, intact, or almost intact, his dictatorial powers, suggests guile rather than prudence, a conservative spirit – in the pejorative sense of the adjective – rather than a creative one.

In 1945, as part of a democratizing campaign, Franco instituted a system of referendum as a brake on his own constituent powers. The system was introduced with the aim of protecting Spaniards 'against the deviation shown in recent political history, when, in matters of utmost importance or public interest, the will of the Nation can be supplanted by the subjective judgement of her rulers'.[16] These words are amusing and paradoxical; they state that the new law is to guarantee the nation against the arbitrary decisions of rulers, yet the law is signed by a man whose powers are practically unlimited.

The holding of the referendum was at first optional, since it was left to the Caudillo to decide whether and when to have a referendum;[17] but the situation was changed in 1947. A kind of supra-legality was established by the Law on the Succession. Certain laws were placed above the rest and were given the name of Fundamental Laws of the Nation, and the holding of a referendum became compulsory to repeal or alter any of them.[18]

That the referendum as a safeguard for people's interests had little effect we shall see in a moment. But let us consider first how this self-imposed limitation upon Franco's constituent powers was no limitation when he decided to ignore it. In May 1958, Franco issued a new Fundamental Law without putting it to a referendum, the Law containing the Principles of the National Movement, the doctrinal basis of the regime. It was issued in the first person – 'I promulgate' – should there be any doubt as to who was giving it force. It could be argued – and in fact the argument has been used[19] – that the referendum is compulsory only to repeal or alter a Fundamental Law and that the Law of the Principles of the National Movement did neither. This is true. But true too is that the referendum was instituted for the Head of State to consult the people about important laws and issues, and could there be a more important law than this? After all, it attempts to summarize the ideology of the regime in a number of principles, and these are said to be 'by their own nature permanent and immutable'. Perhaps the moment when the law was issued, May 1958, was a critical time and the subject too delicate to go into the elaborate and complex ways of a referendum, and that Franco opted for expediency. However, this is not the point in question. The important thing is that when faced with a crisis the dictator did not hesitate to wave aside any formal limitations, to use his constituent powers in full; there is no reason to believe that he would have acted differently if confronted with a similar situation another time. After all, 'this is the quintessence of autocracy: that the autocrat is able to determine by and for himself to what extent he will use his power. Any self-imposed limits – and there always are such – do not alter this criterion, as long as the autocrat retains the power to discard them, whenever he deems it desirable in the interest of the regime.'[20]

Not that the referendum itself was much of a limitation. So far two referenda have been held in Spain. The first one on 6 July 1947 approved the Law on the Succession and the second on 14 December 1966 ratified the Organic Law of the State. On both occasions the referendum suffered from all the evils that this form of direct democracy is prone to. It was blatantly transformed into a plebiscite with Franco as the central figure, and the voters were showered with propaganda which presented them with the alternative of either saying *Sí*, and consequently supporting their virtuous Caudillo and the progress and peace of the Nation, or saying *No* (or abstaining) and throwing away a future of peaceful and prosperous coexistence. This may sound an oversimplification and/or a biased description. A look at the Spanish press in the days leading up to the two referenda will soon counter any accusations of one-sided distortion. One detects a certain difference between the two propaganda campaigns. In 1947 the memory of the Civil War was still vivid and Franco was presented as the military leader, the saviour of his country. Twenty years later the tenor was changed and Franco became the paternalistic ruler who, as many of the published photographs show, loved the company of his grandchildren. There was a change in style but not in essence. The two following examples of propaganda attempt to put across the same message under different covers:

'To vote YES at the referendum means the security of your home, the preservation of your possessions, the defence of your family and, above all, the defence of religion. To vote NO means persecution, proletarian slavery, the destruction of the family, the submission to Muscovite dictators and, what is even worse, to atheist and materialist coercion.'[21]

'Think of your home. Vote for peace.'[22]

In the emotional atmosphere generated by this type of propaganda, with no campaign in favour of the *No* or the abstention being allowed,[23] and with little or no attempt to explain the significance and implications of the Law put to the referendum, it is hardly surprising that the results show an overwhelming percentage of *Sí* votes. In 1947, 88.59% of the electorate voted, and out of this total 92.94% voted *Sí*.[24] In 1966, the results were even more favourable to the regime. 88.85% of the electorate voted, and 95.40% of them said *Sí*,[25] including one man who wrote the *Sí* with his own blood![26]

'Pluriempleo' Powers

The term *pluriempleo* (meaning 'several employments') in this context may seem amusing, even a little frivolous. It is not intended as such. It is used here to define a certain facet of Franco's powers. For many Spaniards *pluriempleo* represents a tragedy. It means having to multiply their efforts to do several jobs in order to keep themselves and their families. In the case of Franco *pluriempleo* means accumulation of posts and the concomitant concentration of powers. Together with the office of Head of State, he held for many years the posts of Head of Government, Leader of the National Movement, and Generalissimo of the Armed Forces.

When the Organic Law of the State was first promulgated at the beginning of 1967, political writers, both in Spain and abroad, stressed that in the legal text the posts of Head of State and Head of Government were defined as separate offices. It was assumed that Franco would soon appoint a man to deal with the day-to-day running of the country. A Spanish newspaper[27] undertook a public poll to find the most popular candidate. But nothing happened. Even the legal separation of the two offices was no novelty. It had already been established in 1957.[28] The 1967 Law made the separation clearer by providing a better definition of both posts and gave it constitutional status. Several years were to lapse before Franco, troubled by his advanced age and ailing health, would finally decide in the summer of 1973 to hand over the day-to-day business of government. Even then the decree appointing a separate Head of Government stated categorically that this in no way curtailed the extraordinary powers acquired by Franco during the Civil War. Furthermore, Franco continued to preside over the meetings of the Council of Ministers at his private residence of El Pardo Palace. This is not to say that the separation of the two most important posts in the Spanish political structure, which had been kept together for well over thirty-five years, was of no significance. The change, if nothing else, clearly indicated the fast-approaching end of francoism with Franco. But even under pressure of time, the dictator has always shown reluctance to relinquish his multiple powers, and only given them up when this became inevitable. The choice of a new Head of Government appears very much as a final attempt to guarantee the survival of francoism without Franco. In the next chapter we shall deal with the appointment of the Head of Government, his powers and specific functions. It is sufficient now to emphasize that this agglomeration of different posts in the hands of a single man, this political *pluriempleo*, has been a concentration of power free from limits or responsibility. Franco, as Caudillo, has not only been the highest representative of the Spanish nation in all important spheres, but also its effective leader. He holds the national destiny in his hands and this supremacy is accompanied by a total lack of responsibility. Franco is only answerable before God and History,[29] and as Head of State his person is inviolable.[30]

Powers over the Succession

The most serious problem confronting any dictatorial regime is the problem of succession. This problem is particularly acute in the Spanish case. A system dependent on a single man for a very long period of time runs the risk of collapsing when he goes. To fill the gap left by a dictator is always a difficult and delicate task; more often than not it fails. The Spanish solution is to be found in the Law on the Succession of 1947. Here, once again, we see that Franco was granted special prerogatives, which belonged to him and only to him. These prerogatives were basically three:

1. to propose to the Cortes the person who will succeed him;
2. to propose to the Cortes the annulment of the previous proposal;
3. to propose to the Cortes the exclusion from the line of succession of any royal person who patently deviates from the fundamental principles of the State, or who acts in a manner that renders him unworthy of his rights to the succession.[31]

In all three cases Franco was to propose to the Cortes and the Cortes would then decide. What would have happened if the Spanish Cortes had not accepted Franco's suggestion? The probability of this occurrence was so remote that it was not even foreseen in the constitution. Fernández Carvajal[32] believes that if the Cortes had opposed Franco's proposal, he would have had to make alternative proposals until one was accepted. Other authors give a different interpretation. Escobar y Kirkpatrick,[33] for instance, thinks that Franco's proposal amounted to a direct nomination and approval by the Cortes was meaningless, since Franco could have changed his mind and revoked a nomination even when the Cortes had accepted it.

These disagreements amongst theoreticians of the regime, and the quiet and bitter quarrels that went on for years in the royal cliques who supported different pretenders to the Spanish throne, were brought to an end in July 1969, when Franco proposed to the Cortes that Prince Juan Carlos de Borbón y Borbón should be his successor; and the Cortes lent their enthusiastic approval to the proposal. In the voting, which took place publicly, with each member of the Cortes standing up in turn as his name was called to express his vote, only 19 opposed the proposal and 9 abstained from a total of 519 present.[34] This overwhelming support was to be expected in view of the composition of the Cortes and particularly the aura of prestige surrounding the Caudillo. This was best expressed by the *procurador* who, when it was his turn to vote, stood up and said: '*Sí, por Franco*'.[35] And this takes us to the final point in the examination of Franco's extraordinary powers.

Charismatic Power

Charismatic power does not, like the other powers mentioned, have a specific area where it manifests itself. The constituent power, the power resulting from his holding several posts, the power over the succession all have a prescribed zone of application. On the other hand, the charismatic power not only covers the area of all the other powers, reinforcing them; it goes well beyond to envelop the whole activity and the entire figure of Franco. He is placed on the highest pedestal, on a pinnacle no other Spaniard can reach, and from there he directs his followers, who, dazzled by such greatness, obey and acclaim their leader, their ruler, their Caudillo. *Caudillo* – the Castilian echo of *Führer* and *Duce* – is the word that epitomizes Franco's charisma and its explanation and justification is to be found in the doctrine of *caudillaje*.

In Franco's charisma we find the *raison d'être* of his unlimited powers and, consequently, of his regime. Franco does not fit perfectly Max Weber's mould of a charismatic leader. But Max Weber himself admits that his trilogy of traditional, legal and charismatic authority is established at a high level of abstraction and that the categories do not exist in pure form.[36] And in Franco's history as leader of the Spanish nation we find more than sufficient elements to justify a charismatic label.

Over more than thirty years a massive propaganda has created an image of Franco towering above all Spaniards as their natural ruler, providently singled out to lead his country to victory in the Civil War and then to peace and prosperity. This almost supernatural image of the Caudillo is not limited to the theory which finds the origin of all power in God. Its most extreme forms tell of the finger of God singling out Franco to save the Spanish nation. This sort of propaganda was rife at the end of the Civil War; in a way it was the natural sequel to the title of crusade given to the actual war. As time went on, and as the regime evolved, there was a tendency to play down this aspect of the *caudillaje*, but it has never entirely disappeared. In the sixties we come across propaganda of this kind: 'Nowadays coins show Francisco Franco as Caudillo of Spain by the grace of God, because this exceptional man has re-awakened the old idea of the divine origin of power. Spanish people, with their deep religious feelings, could not but notice, over and over again, the hand of God protecting the wisdom, the justice, the strength and the temperance of Franco.'[37]

It is not only in propaganda pamphlets, anonymously published, where one finds this theory; the charisma of Franco has been stated and defended in more serious works by university professors.[38] All these tell of Franco as a man of such exceptional qualities that it would be impossible not to appreciate them, and folly to ignore them. All those with a stake in the system contribute to maintaining this image. Over the years all ministers in their major speeches have included a few lines to remind Spaniards how much they owe to their leader and how grateful they ought to be to him.[39] And to prove the response of the people to this call, all public appearances of Franco are supported by large demonstrations, organized to create what a Falange newspaper called 'a permanent referendum'.[40]

Two points require further comment. We have indicated how Franco's charisma was created and maintained over the years without investigating whether this charisma was based on reality. This is largely irrelevant. 'What is alone important is how the individual [Franco in our case] is actually regarded by those subject to charismatic authority, by his "followers" or "disciples".'[41] And there can be no doubt that his followers or disciples do regard Franco, and want Franco regarded, as a charismatic leader. Obviously, and this takes us to the second point, Franco's charisma has changed since the Civil War. It has undergone, to use Max Weber's language again, a process of routinization. It has even weakened, in the sense that it has become less prevalent and covered over by a more paternalistic layer. Nevertheless, the Caudillo has held all the extraordinary powers we have described and his decisions and his actions have been officially above error and outside the reach of criticism all the way to his deathbed.

To pass from this exceptional situation to a more normal one seems extremely hazardous. The succession of a charismatic ruler may not be impossible but it is highly problematic. All the legal safety valves included in the constitution, and the fact that Franco has already named his successor, may not secure the future beyond the Caudillo. One problem is the change of Head of State. There are others equally difficult to solve. But the enormous gap the death of Franco will leave will require bridging with a great deal of care and tact if total collapse is to be avoided. The signs, as we are now going to see, do not augur too well.

The Succession

As well as making the form of succession dependent upon Franco's will – the one in fact used – the law had foreseen the possibility of Franco dying or becoming incapacitated without having appointed a successor. Had this situation arisen the following mechanism would have come into operation. The functions of the Head of State would have been taken over by the Regency Council, composed of three dignitaries: the President of the Cortes, who would also be President of this Council; an Archbishop, member of the Council of the Realm; and the General with highest seniority in the Armed Forces.[42] Within three days of the death of Franco this Regency Council would call on the government and the Council of the Realm to hold a joint meeting, secret and uninterrupted, in order to choose a person of royal blood to propose as king to the Cortes. If the Cortes did not accept the proposal, the Government and the Council of the Realm would propose other names either as king or as regent.[43] This complex mechanism always had a subsidiary nature; it only applied if Franco died without a successor. But, as we know, in 1969, the name of Juan Carlos de Borbón y Borbón had been accepted by the Cortes as his successor. This mechanism, inserted in the constitution as a kind of insurance policy, immediately became redundant. Its possible application would only have been restored had Franco revoked the nomination of the Prince; a highly unlikely event – in spite of some rumours to the contrary during the last few years – for as Franco himself pointed out in his address to the Cortes the day he made the proposal: '. . . and time, taking into account my age, is not likely to provide any new elements to make me change my mind'.

The appointment of Prince Juan Carlos as successor to Franco had a number of consequences:

1. The definitive establishment of a monarchy in Spain,[44] since after Juan Carlos the post of Head of State will become hereditary in accordance with article 11 of the Law on the Succession.[45]
2. Republican hopes, which never had much chance of becoming a reality, were finally destroyed.
3. The Carlist claim to the throne received its *coup de grâce*.[46]
4. The Count of Barcelona, father of Prince Juan Carlos, saw his claim as son of Alfonso XIII, last Spanish king, destroyed too.

The Principles of the National Movement state that the political form of the Spanish Nation is that of a traditional, Catholic, social and representative monarchy. If these Principles are to be, by virtue of their own nature, permanent,[47] how could anybody, within the legal framework, harbour republican hopes? Many arguments have been put forward in favour of the republican solution in Spain – apart from the purely theoretical ones of the universal conflict between monarchy and republic. These arguments have tended to advocate a republican solution in an indirect or roundabout way. An open opposition to the monarchy would be against the Principles of the National Movement, and constitutes a political crime. The provision in the constitution for a regent, if no suitable person of royal blood was found to replace Franco, raised some hopes of a permanent regency – a contradiction in terms, since the regency is, by its own nature, a temporary institution. Others felt that there was not much support in the country for a monarchy, that the high vote for a monarchy in the referenda was not saying yes to the monarchy, but yes to Franco. It was also said, in favour of the republican solution, that to re-establish a monarchy would be against the flow of history. The monarchy is a retreating institution. In the countries where it has not yet disappeared, its powers and prerogatives are constantly being curtailed. Besides – the republican argument concludes – in Spain the monarchy is totally discredited; during the period 1876–1931 Spanish people were alienated from a crown that always gave shelter to the most reactionary ideas.

The republican solution could not, and did not, prosper. The monarchist option was the only one accepted by the Fundamental Laws. But, what kind of a monarchy is it going to be? Although on monarchist issues constitutional terminology and official political oratory in Franco's Spain have borrowed a great deal from the royalist cliques and Frondes, both Carlist and Alfonsine, of the pre-Civil War years,[48] a clear attempt has been made to sever links between the new monarchy and the historical monarchy that had Alfonso XIII as its last king. Franco stressed this fact when he spoke to the Cortes on 22 July 1969, and the *procuradores* reacted enthusiastically to his words: 'The kingdom that we have established with the consent of the people owes nothing to the past; it springs from that crucial episode on 18 July [1936], which is in itself a transcendent historical event and cannot be subject to any conditions.'

Thus, at a stroke, a new monarchy was born, without any formal connections with the past beyond the Civil War. It was, as Franco said, *una instauración* and not *una restauración*. The antithesis is clear cut. The dictionary of the Spanish Academy gives as equivalents of *instaurar*, to establish, to found, to institute; and defines *restaurar* as to bring back a thing to its previous state or estimation. In Spanish history the period from the end of 1874 to 1931 is known as the Restoration, because the Bourbon dynasty was reinstated on the throne in 1874 after six years of exile. Franco must have had this in mind when addressing the Cortes. He did not want another restoration. To make his intention clear, should there be any doubt, he went as far as to change the title of Prince of Asturias. In the new monarchy the former Prince of Asturias has become Prince of Spain.

Franco's objective was really double-fronted. On the one hand he wanted to push aside don Juan, Count of Barcelona, the legitimate heir of Alfonso XIII, had a restoration taken place. His political ideas were somewhat suspect and he was excluded. On the other hand, the Caudillo did not want the new monarchy to receive the Bourbonic inheritance, with its disastrous record from the beginning of the nineteenth century. No, the monarchy was to find its legitimacy in the Civil War, the 'finest hour' of Franco's regime, and therefore an excellent platform from which to launch the new institution.

The nomination of Prince Juan Carlos came as no surprise. It was expected. He had been Franco's favourite since the Count of Barcelona allowed him, in 1948, to take charge of the Prince's education. And by 1969 the Prince had fulfilled all the necessary requirements to be officially declared the successor. He was of royal blood, he was a male, a Spaniard (though born in Rome) and a Catholic, and he had reached the age of thirty.[49] He was considered to have the necessary qualifications for such high office, and the day after his nomination he met the last condition when in the chamber of the Cortes he swore loyalty to the Principles of the National Movement and to the Fundamental Laws of the State.[50]

But all this constitutes the formal side of the succession and, so far, it is the only side that offers any certainty. Juan Carlos's appointment as Prince of Spain does not guarantee continuity for the regime beyond Franco's life. Setting up the new monarchy has been possible only with Franco's support. Without this support the viability of a monarchy is extremely questionable, particularly the type of monarchy that can be conjectured from the Fundamental Laws. A quick glance at Title II of the Organic Law of the State uncovers very worrying premonitions. The future King will not inherit Franco's extraordinary powers; this would be an impossibility. His authority will nevertheless be very wide, much wider than that of his royal contemporaries in the other western European monarchies. It is that of a very powerful monarch. He will not be a purely representative figure, although he will fulfil this function. He will have the powers to act, execute, and participate fully in events. The legislator has made this clear. Next to a King who 'is the highest representative of the Nation', and next to a King who 'personifies national sovereignty', he has defined a King who '*exercises* [my italics] the supreme political and administrative power'.[51]

The absolute power gained and maintained by Franco during more than thirty years could not survive him. To hand it over to the new King would amount to a return to the hereditary absolutism of the *ancien régime*, an impossible task in the developing Spain that looks to the twenty-first century. That is why limits have been imposed on the King's authority. He cannot act on his own; all his actions and decisions require the participation of another institutional body, taking either the elusive form of advice given to the King, or the more tangible reality of a counter-signature or authorization[52] by the Council of the Realm, the President of the Cortes, the Head of Government or a minister. The margins of constitutional interplay between the two elements – the wide powers of the monarch on the one side and the functional limits set to them on the other – have been variously interpreted. There is agreement on the considerable spread and depth of royal power, but some authors see the intervention of a second person or institution in all actions and decisions as a considerable limitation of the King's power, which could reduce the King's role to the level of his counterparts in the other European monarchies.[53] Others believe that according to the Fundamental Laws the King enjoys the monopoly of national sovereignty.[54] In any event the future Spanish monarchy seems to hark back towards the nineteenth century. Whether one calls it a limited monarchy[55] or an Orleanist monarchy,[56] or whether one sees in it the Germanic *Monarchische Prinzip*,[57] what the Spanish constitution defines as a traditional, Catholic, social and representative monarchy appears as a rather anachronistic institution, though perhaps inevitable in the ideological atmosphere in which it was born: an ideology that denies any value to the separation of powers, that is opposed to popular sovereignty, that reduces to a minimum the strength of suffrage, that does not recognize political parties, that has no faith in parliament, and that is hostile, as a matter of principle, to the heritage of liberalism.

Let us now look at some of the powers the King will have. He appoints the Presidents of the Government, the Cortes, the Supreme Court of Justice, the Council of State, the National Economic Council and the Court of Accounts. The method for all these appointments is the *sistema de ternas*, which works in the following way: the Council of the Realm selects and presents a list of three names from which the Head of State picks one. The royal discretion in these appointments is not total, but, as we shall see later, the control exercised by the Council of the Realm could be weak.

Of all the appointments mentioned the most important are those of the Head of Government and the President of the Cortes. The Head of 'State, by the mere fact of appointment, gains a great ascendancy over them, and over the institutions they lead. This ascendancy is made even greater by the power of the Head of State to dismiss them both when he thinks fit, the only condition being that he must have the consensus of the Council of the Realm.[58] The Head of State nominates too the different Ministers, though their names are put to him by the President of the Government.[59] He can, if he so wishes, chair the meetings of the Council of Ministers, thus becoming the effective leader of government policies, with the Council of Ministers in an assisting role.[60]

We reach here the widest and most dangerous point in the extension of royal powers. If the king decides to take an active part in politics, ideal relations between him and the Head of Government would be necessary for a stable future. Any friction would be likely to lead to the dismissal or resignation of the Head of Government and his Ministers, as the weaker side in the conflict. A situation in which the Government and the Council of the Realm seek each other's support to oppose the king is not very probable; and if it did occur it would shake the very foundations of the throne.

All this is pure hypothesis. We are using the constitutional texts as a glass ball, to read the future in them, and the signs that can be discerned are extremely ominous. There are those who see the situation differently. The British press in general, after the nomination of Prince Juan Carlos, have forecast a powerless monarchy, with the king as a puppet in the hands of a quasi-dictator supported by the army.[61] This could happen if the King accepts a passive role, renouncing the powers the constitution grants him. But we must not forget that the King stands in the very centre of sovereignty, and all constitutional authority springs from him. Therefore, if the King clung to his legal powers, Spain could witness a repetition of the Greek experience of 1967. The downfall of his brother-in-law King Constantine, and the proclivity of the Spanish Army to meddle in politics, might damp Prince Juan Carlos's ambitions. Perhaps he might even follow the advice given him by Emilio Romero, for many years editor of the daily *Pueblo*: 'to reign is to set up the game without taking part in it'.[62] A difficult task when the tantalizing call of power is so loud and clear. To avoid temptation the king would have to show a great deal of wisdom and prudence. Unfortunately, the Spanish Bourbons have rarely been endowed with such qualities.

As one reads on through the Fundamental Laws, the image of the powerful king becomes even more apparent. Without overstepping legal boundaries, he could establish a crowned dictatorship when the external security and independence of the nation, her territory or the institutional system of the kingdom are seriously threatened.[63] Once again he would have to listen to the Council of the Realm before taking such a step, but in the last instance he decides whether the gravity and imminence of the danger are such that he must assume exceptional powers. The king will have supreme command of the Armed Forces and he will be the ideological leader as Head of the National Movement and guardian of its principles.[64]

The king's powers extend into the legislative sphere.[65] He sanctions and promulgates laws. This is not a purely formal prerogative. The king can, if he so wishes, return a Bill to the Cortes for further consideration, though to do this he must have the approval of the Council of the Realm.[66] He can also exercise, through the Government and the President of the Cortes, a tremendous influence in the legislative chamber, controlling the composition of committees and the items to be included in the agendas of meetings of these committees and of the plenary sessions of the Cortes.

Finally, the king has his hands on the lever that controls the constitution. To repeal or modify any of the Fundamental Laws a referendum is necessary, but the initiative belongs to the Head of State, so that no constitutional reform is possible without his consent. He may not reform the constitution on his own, but he can certainly oppose attempts to alter or diminish the powers the constitution gives him. And, were this not enough, he is also the supreme judge in constitutional matters. He decides whether a law, a decree or some other regulation violates the Fundamental Laws of the State or the Principles of the National Movement and should therefore be declared void.

This list of royal powers – by no means a complete one – is bound to cause real concern to any Spaniard who takes a serious look at it. The constitution is only a part – the formal one – of the political game. To a large extent, its success or failure will depend upon historical, social and economic factors, and upon the people who incarnate the institutions. This, however, cannot serve as a basis for optimism. There is little reason to believe that a threat which is now theoretical will be less of a threat when put into practice. Setting up a monarchy in the last decades of the twentieth century seems a foolhardy enough undertaking;[67] even worse, that monarchy is to find its legitimacy in one of the saddest and darkest events in Spanish history, the Civil War of 1936–9. The King is given powers that any of his nineteenth-century ancestors would have envied, for, as we shall see, the efficacy of the controls set against those powers appears extremely doubtful.

The Council of the Realm

Spanish political institutions over the last thirty years have shown, at least on the surface, two interrelated evolutionary tendencies. Their superficiality must be stressed because the evolution seems limited, in many cases, to purely linguistic and formal aspects, without really touching the essence of the institutions. The Cortes in their present form are not as they were in the forties; on the other hand, the practical differences are far fewer and less profound than the altered legal texts suggest. The two tendencies are, first, the formal limitation of the powers of the Head of State through the creation of new institutions or the promotion of those already in existence; and, secondly, the raising of the representativeness of such institutions.

The creation and later the reform of the Council of the Realm fit the pattern suggested perfectly. When, in 1947, by popular referendum, Spain became a kingdom and a mechanism to succeed Franco was established, the Council of the Realm was created to assist the Head of State in all matters pertaining to his office. Twenty years later, in 1967, and also with the support of a referendum, the composition and functions of the Council of the Realm were altered in the dual direction earlier indicated. At the beginning the Council of the Realm was made up of fourteen members: the President of the Cortes, who presided over the Council; the highest ranking Prelate in the Cortes; the longest serving Captain General or Lieutenant General in the Armed Forces; the Chief of the Military Staff; the President of the Council of State; the President of the Supreme Court of Justice; the President of the Institute of Spain; four councillors elected by the members of the Cortes; and finally, three more councillors directly appointed by Franco.[68] The lack of representativeness and independence of this Council is self-evident. They formed a coterie of important people who were largely dependent on the Head of State, and therefore unable to exercise any control over him. Out of the fourteen councillors, ten were appointed by the *Caudillo* and the other four, though elected, arrived at the Council through the already dubious channel of the corporative chamber.

From 1947, when Spain was isolated from the rest of the world, to 1967, when she was hoping to join the EEC, many things were changed, and amongst them the composition of the Council of the Realm. The number of members was increased from fourteen to seventeen, reflecting a parallel change in the Cortes. The seven *ex-officio* members remained in the Council, but the number of elected members went up from four to ten, still elected inside the Cortes, from and by the *Procuradores* of the different groups that make up the legislative chamber.[69] In the 1967 Council the *ex-officio* members are outnumbered by those elected, and this formal change suggests greater independence in the functioning of the Council. Reality, however, has destroyed such hopes. The formal change has been nothing but that, a formal change. The councillors are all of them well known for their allegiance to the system and to the Head of State, and the elected ten hold, in most cases, other important posts to which they have been appointed by the Head of State or by his government.[70] Even those who hold a favourable opinion of the Council of the Realm and its future in the system, recognize that the autonomy of its members is highly doubtful.[71]

In its original form, the Council of the Realm was a consultative body. Later, when its composition was modified, so were its powers. And here too the Council seems to have taken a step forward. From 1967 it became a more visible moderating force, though its effectiveness is still very much in question. Fundamentally, it continues to be a consultative body, but in three special cases the decision of the Head of State, in order to be valid, requires a favourable report or the agreement of the Council. Such cases are:

1. the returning to the Cortes of a law for further deliberation;[72]
2. the lengthening of the four-year life of the Cortes;[73]
3. the dismissal of the Presidents of the Government, the Cortes, the Supreme Court of Justice, the Council of State, the Court of Accounts, and the National Economic Council.[74]

The Head of State has to seek the advice of the Council of the Realm in several other cases,[75] but in these the Council's opinion is not binding. The Council of the Realm also intervenes in the nomination of some high offices through the system of *ternas*.

In weighing up the effectiveness of the Council of the Realm as a moderating body, one has to consider its composition and, once again, to differentiate the situation with Franco as Caudillo, from that with a King and a Head of Government. The Council as a moderating or limiting force on Franco has never existed; it has never been more than a group of important figures, to whom Franco would turn for advice frequently, but only follow it when its recommendations coincided with his own judgement. To quote but one example, coming from a far from suspect source: with Franco in power 'it would be naïve to think that the selection of the three names proposed by the Council of the Realm for the post of Head of Government could be anything other than a "prefabrication"'.[76]

The effectiveness of the Council when confronted with the King rather than Franco is also doubtful. Its composition would have to change, and this in turn would require much greater change in the Cortes. Then, the wide powers of the King might reject, or object to, this binding harness in a moment of crisis. Here one is back on speculative ground. In the framework after the succession it will be extremely difficult to strike a balance between the King, the Head of Government and the Council of the Realm. They form an unequal and almost mis-shapen triangle, and it is hard to visualize who will occupy the apex. In the fight for it lies the gravest danger.

Finally, the Council of the Realm plays what seems to be an important part in the *recurso de contrafuero*. This is the appeal or action to be taken against any law, regulation, or decision that contravenes the Fundamental Laws of the State, and therefore is unconstitutional. It is worth looking at it closely, because it typifies the regime, and it certainly endorses what has been said about the relationship between the Head of State and the Council of the Realm.

Until 1967, when the Organic Law of the State was issued, there was
no formal procedure to deal with unconstitutional events.[77] The need
for it had not arisen. The constitution was only half written and Franco's
will was unchallengeable. But the Organic Law brought in, together
with the completion of the Constitution, a system of appeal in the case
of an unconstitutional event. The general principles laid down by the
Organic Law of the State were developed and implemented by another
law a year later.[78]

Political means rather than the courts were chosen to deal with
unconstitutionality. Many arguments have been put forward in favour
of either form of control – and in fact of some hybrid forms too. They are
very often contradictory, and they all command some measure of support.
But it is fair to say that the rights of the individual are better served and
protected through jurisdictional channels on account of the greater
independence and juridical efficiency of legal courts. On the other hand,
control by a political body lends itself more easily to manipulations and
interference by those in power.

The mechanism established now in Spain is extremely curious and of
enormous complexity. At all stages of procedure it brings in people who
took an active part in the elaboration and approval of the law under
examination, and in the end deciding whether there is a case of *contrafuero*
is left entirely to the Head of State. It operates in the following way: the
initiative corresponds to the National Council of the Movement or the
Standing Committee of the Cortes. In theory any Spaniard may raise a
petition denouncing the unconstitutional character of a regulation, but
one of these two bodies decides whether there is a case to be made. If
there is, an appeal is made to the Council of the Realm. This Council
then seeks the opinion of an *ad hoc* committee, and eventually submits a
recommendation to the Head of State. Finally, the Head of State freely
decides on the matter.

The most surprising aspect of the whole process is that in spite of its
apparent complexity, the final decision rests on the discretion of one
person. Besides, behind the complicated process, the juridical guarantees
are somewhat suspicious. The members of the National Council, as
well as those of the Standing Committee of the Cortes, are also members
of the legislative chamber, and, consequently, they first take part in the
making of the law and later judge its constitutionality. The same could
be said of the Council of the Realm. A majority of its members is drafted
from the Cortes, and those who do not sit in the Cortes hold posts
dependent on executive power. Even the objectivity and independence

of the special committee that advises the Council of the Realm are not beyond question.[79]

The appeal for *contrafuero* has, so far, been upheld in only one case. The Government had issued by decree a code of discipline for civil servants.[80] One of its articles made it a serious offence for civil servants to criticize or express disagreement with the decisions of their superiors, and to publish any work directly or indirectly connected with their department without prior authorization. The appeal, initiated by a private person, considered that this article contravened some of the principles contained in the Charter of the Spanish People (articles 3, 12 and 17). After going through all its stages, the appeal was finally confirmed by the Head of State[81] and the relevant sections of the article in question were declared unconstitutional. It was, undoubtedly, a move in the right direction; alas, a rather solitary one. The approval and subsequent application of laws, like the Public Order Law – in its 1971 version – or the Official Secrets Law, which clearly contravene principles proclaimed by the Charter of the Spanish People, have demonstrated how weak is the protection provided by *contrafuero*.

3 ❧ THE GOVERNMENT

Introduction

In a dictatorial situation, such as Spain has been experiencing for more than three decades, the predominance of executive power is sufficiently obvious. The position of Franco as the centre and largely the monopolizer of power was made abundantly clear in the previous chapter, as was the fact that the creation of a number of political institutions over the years had in no way challenged his domineering role. A second feature of any dictatorial experience is the absence of political responsibility, since those wielding power, in this case the Caudillo, cannot be made accountable for their political decisions or actions. Not that these manifestations of the executive power can be attributed solely to Franco; his ministers must have had a considerable, on occasions crucial, influence in decision making. But however influential they may have been – and this influence has fluctuated with personalities, domestic affairs, international events, etc. – their decisions, their policies, and, in the final instance, their ministerial posts have been totally dependent on the will of Franco. Overshadowed by Franco, a minister has been a kind of high-level secretary, lacking political initiative or independence, and responsible for failed policies or changes in the political climate of the country, while the dictator retained discretionary powers and stayed beyond any formal political control.

The Government is now, like most other political institutions in Spain, taking the first steps towards that future in which it will not merely assist a dictator, but it will, together with the King, make up the double-pronged executive foreseen by the Spanish constitution. Next to the King, who is not likely to be purely decorative, there is a government headed by a President also with ample powers. Between both institutions, King and Government, the Council of the Realm tries to achieve political equilibrium at the top. Its maintenance is, on purely constitutional terms, extremely difficult and fraught with dangers, particularly now that the support and control of the dictator's charismatic prestige have finally been removed.

The word 'government' is being used here with the same meaning as the Council of Ministers. This equivalence or terminological confusion occurred in Spanish constitutional law throughout the nineteenth century,[1] and has persisted, as can be seen in Title III of the Organic Law of the State of 1967. 'Government' is used to emphasize the political side of the institution and 'Council of Ministers' brings to mind administrative functions. Again the concept of government is wider than that of Council of Ministers, or, at least, that is the implication of important legal texts, such as the 1957 Law on the Central Administration of the State. Article 86 of the constitution of the Second Republic is relevant here: 'The President of the Council and the ministers constitute the Government.' A very similar definition is found in the first law that, during the Civil War, attempted to deal with the organization of government in that part of Spain controlled by Franco's forces: the law of 30 January 1938, article 16 of which states: 'The Presidency [of the Government] is attached to the Head of State. The ministers, together with him, constitute the national Government.'

Having clarified these points, one can safely ignore the subtle legal differences between the two expressions, 'government' and 'Council of Ministers', and use them as equivalents.

After the initial attempts represented by the Junta de Defensa Nacional and the Junta Técnica del Estado,[2] Franco set up the first formal government of nationalist Spain by the law of 30 January 1938. The government was then composed of eleven ministers, with one of them, the Foreign Affairs Minister, discharging the duties of Vice-President; and Franco kept for himself besides the Headship of State the post of President of the Government. Some changes were introduced in December of the same year, and in the following August, when the post of Vice-President disappeared together with some other ministries. The blatant dictatorial situation of the early years of the regime did not require and was opposed to a meticulous regulation of the executive, and although the initial legislation was supplemented by some other laws and decrees, the legal framework of the Government, as regards both its composition and functions, remained basically the same until the promulgation in 1957 of the Ley de Régimen Jurídico de la Administración del Estado (Law on the Administration of the State), whose drafting was largely due to Laureano López Rodó, Professor of Administrative Law, a then obscure figure taking the first steps of his political career, and to become during the sixties one of the most influential politicians in Spain.

The 1957 Law on the Administration of the State is fundamental in the move towards a regular and systematic framework of government in Spain, but in its administrative aspects rather than its political ones. It restructured the ministerial departments and redistributed their functions; it set up Comisiones Delegadas de Gobierno, or Government Committees, to infuse some agility in handling specialized business; it created, within the Presidency, a department to deal with economic planning and coordination – later to become the Comisaría del Plan de Desarrollo, the ministry from which López Rodó produced Spain's 'economic miracle'; and, in general terms, divided and regulated the powers and attributions of the government, its President and the ministers. For the first time the post of President of the Government was an office separate from that of Head of State; nevertheless this legal distinction had no practical effect since Franco held both for many years after. To explain away this anomaly the Ley de Régimen Jurídico de la Administración del Estado, although including the Head of State amongst the higher offices of the Administration, does not refer to it in any detail – thus avoiding the issue – because, as the preamble says, 'the powers and prerogatives [of the Head of State] must be the object of a special law.'

The legal structure of the executive power was completed by the Organic Law of the State, of which sections 2 and 3 deal respectively with the Head of State and the Government. The constitutional gap was at last closed, although this lengthy delay, like so many others, has never been officially explained or justified. The Law clarified and formalized appointments and dismissals of members of the government. But in practice the anomalous situation continued, due to the exceptional nature of Franco's position, and the secrecy surrounding government activities. All this imposes serious limitations. For the time being, and for various reasons, political analysis of the government of Spain, unless one wishes to indulge in conjectural exercises, is largely a constitutional and juridical study, which can be supplemented by looking at the outstanding political figures who have formed part of successive governments. Examining the Government in any other way is made almost impossible by several important factors: the legal prohibition of political parties, the total inefficiency of the Cortes when it comes to extracting information from the Government; the official control of mass media; the strange silence of Spanish politicians, whose pens have shown great fertility in the writing of theoretical works, but total barrenness in the fields of political memoirs or of books relating the intimacies of power;[3] and, above all, the secrecy of the government, whose contact with public opinion never goes beyond the official note or the unchallenged ministerial speech.

Therefore this study of the Spanish government is limited to different aspects of the appointment, cessation, dismissal, functions, and powers of the President and his ministerial team, in particular the peculiarities and dangers of the established system. Since the legal provisions are only the channel through which the political process flows, and that interpreting and implementing laws are largely in the hands of those who wield power, a look at the most important individuals and groups in Franco's governments will always throw some further light on the situation, adding a few pieces to the jigsaw puzzle. The political responsibility of the executive and its fundamental importance in the democratic evolution of Spain is examined separately.

The President of the Government

Up until 8 June 1973, the date of the official appointment of Admiral Carrero Blanco as President of the Government, Franco had – at least formally – occupied this post together with that of Head of State. There are those who maintain that Franco, with his physical and mental faculties declining rapidly with advancing age, had lost control long before, and that ministers had for some time been exercising his control.[4] However, it seems to us more appropriate to speak of Franco gradually handing over, specific functions first and definite powers later, to his closest collaborators. Carrero Blanco's role is in this context the most important of all, though at times rather imprecise; he led a very retiring and almost obscure life, shying away from the forefront of political life and appearing only occasionally to proclaim his faith in Franco. In the post of Under-Secretary to the President, which he occupied from 1940 – with ministerial status from 1951 – he remained close to Franco and his influence in day-to-day government must have been considerable. But, leaving aside the undoubted ascendancy over Franco of individual figures like Carrero Blanco or Esteban Bilbao, it is in 1962 that the process began which eventually led to the appointment of a person other than the Caudillo for the Presidency. In the ministerial reshuffle in summer 1962 Franco nominated, for the first time since 1939, a Vice-President. The choice fell on Captain-General Muñoz Grandes, a prestigious military figure, one of Franco's old colleagues in the African campaign of the twenties, and leader of the Blue Division which fought against Russia in the Second World War. This appointment could be interpreted – and has been interpreted[5] – as an attempt to enlist the help of the military in closing the ranks when the regime was threatened by a wave of strikes and by serious economic problems at home, while at the same time being rebuffed abroad.[6] Another interpretation is that the appointment was the first sign of Franco's intentions to find himself a dauphin – even if a rather mature one – a possible head of government for the future, and a successor in the eventuality of his unexpected death.[7]

The appointment of Muñoz Grandes had no further repercussions. As already said it was no more than an indication of some vague plan in Franco's mind, a plan which was to get much closer to realization when in 1967 Carrero Blanco, without relinquishing his post as Under-Secretary to the President, took over from Muñoz Grandes as Vice-President of the Government. The Admiral's influence within the Presidency was thus greatly increased. It seems reasonable to assume that from that moment he started to discharge many of the duties and functions pertaining to Franco as Head of Government. Political events from then on carried the mark of Carrero Blanco's rising preponderance. In the summer of 1972 Franco decreed[8] that Carrero Blanco as Vice-President would automatically become President in the event of Franco's sudden death; and less than twelve months later, and once again by a unilateral legislative decision by the Caudillo, Carrero Blanco became the first Head of Government under Franco.

The separation of the offices of Head of State and President of the Government was not to be definitive until Franco's death; as the text of the law appointing Carrero Blanco as President stated categorically, Franco would continue to enjoy all the powers invested in him at the time of the Civil War, and even the separation of the two posts was contemplated as a *suspensión* or interregnum; if it did not work in practice the dictator could take over again. Hence the suggestions, made after Carrero Blanco's assassination, that Franco might resume his duties as President of the Government.

Although the separation of the two posts was based solely upon Franco's will, choosing Carrero Blanco followed the formal procedures established by article 14 of the Organic Law of the State. It was arrived at through the curious system of *ternas*. The system had been used before – for the appointment of the President of the Cortes, for instance – but never at this high level. Under article 14 the Council of the Realm submits a list of three names to the Head of State from which he selects one. With Franco the whole operation could only have been a pure formality; the persuading pressure of his personal prestige and authority must have prevailed. The choice of Carrero Blanco was obvious; his position as Franco's favourite was well known not only to the members of the Council of the Realm, but to the country as a whole. With the sudden disappearance of Carrero Blanco the selection of a new President was not so simple. There was no clear favourite. In any event, given the exceptional circumstances, it is reasonable to assume that Franco's will was once more decisive.

The system has successfully operated on two occasions, and yet this experience is far from sufficient to conclude that it has been tested and proved. For one thing, it is far from democratic. The whole operation takes place at the top of the political hierarchy, so that the connection between the election-cum-designation of the President and the people is so tenuous as to be non-existent; and the same is true, as we shall see later, of his dismissal. But even if the lack of democratic principles is acceptable, the efficiency of the *ternas* is extremely dubious; the question marks hanging over its viability in the post-Franco years are many and profound. Even Fernández Carvajal, whose studies of the Spanish constitution are as scholarly as they are sympathetic towards the regime, admits that the proper functioning of the *ternas* in the future monarchy will depend on a number of fundamentally important conditions concurring – conditions which do not exist at the present moment: 'first, a scrupulous independence separating Government and Council of the Realm, so that the former cannot turn the latter into a kind of docile *alter ego* thus perpetuating the established political line; second, a wise choice by the Council when selecting the *terna*, so as to include in it the names of persons with wide political support in the country, and with the possibility of success in a hypothetical election by the people; third, good judgement on the part of the King to pick the most suitable man from the *terna*'.[9] His conditions are highly idealized and their consequences would have tremendous repercussion. And Fernández Carvajal goes even further when he suggests, referring to his third condition, the possibility that the King, rather than make the choice himself, may put the three candidates submitted by the Council of the Realm to the vote of the people.[10]

This delicate situation affects the continuation of the regime, since the conditions set out by Fernández Carvajal, which are no more than a minimum, would alter its very essence. The independence of the Council of the Realm from the executive power was discussed in the previous chapter. It is notable as an indicator of the recent trend of events, that two of the ministers in the government formed by Arias Navarro in January 1974 were members of the Council of the Realm when he was appointed President.[11] Besides, a genuine independence of the Council from the Government would require greater independence for the Cortes, since a majority of the Council of the Realm come from the ranks of the Cortes; this in turn would entail a democratization of the electoral system and the introduction of an effective system of incompatibilities so that a large proportion of the Cortes members are not, as happens now, controlled by the government.

In the vacuum left by the prohibition of political parties it is difficult to see what acceptable method the Council of the Realm can employ to arrive at the *terna*. It is likely to degenerate towards constant lobbying by the pressure and interest groups that have come to replace political parties, and towards the exercise of personal favouritism without public support or accountability. How can, for instance, the councillors assess the support and popularity enjoyed by different political figures not only in the country as a whole, but even in the chambers of the Cortes? The councillors are in no position to judge when only two of them, out of a total of seventeen, can claim direct electoral links with the people.

Questions of this nature, casting doubts on the system of *ternas*, can be easily multiplied. Is the *terna* going to offer the King three distinct possibilities or three personal variables of the same political solution? Either case needs channels for the formulation of clear political programmes by aspiring candidates. Such channels do not exist at present. The *terna* is secret; official sources announce the final choice but never the other two on the list. It is left to the more or less well-informed guesswork of the press, both in Spain and abroad, to intimate who the contenders were.

Will the King be consulted before the list is drawn up, or will he be in a position to insinuate the name or names he wishes? The King will not, of course, enjoy the powers of persuasion of a charismatic dictator, but his constitutional powers are wide, and if he proves to have a strong political temperament there is every likelihood that he will influence the members of the Council. Going a step further, what will happen in the case, not foreseen legally but all the same a possibility, of the King objecting to all three names in the *terna*?

All these unanswered questions form a condemnatory criticism in themselves. Without taking an excessively pessimistic attitude one cannot but view with concern the mechanism established for the appointment of the President of the Government. The present mechanism has not yet really been tested, and can only operate successfully in an authoritarian system. The stability of the Presidency will depend on the support of palace cliques and right-wing groups inside the regime, with the subsequent dangers of intrigues, concealed tensions, clashes between groups, and all of it in the charged, and at the same time delicate, climate of the post-Franco years.

Once appointed, the President of the Government, as one of the two parts of the bicephalous executive, has ample powers, according to the constitution. He represents the government in its dealings with both the Head of State and the Cortes, he has the initiative in the appointment and dismissal of ministers, although he needs the support of the Head of State in both cases; he chairs the meetings of the Council of Ministers, unless the Head of State is in attendance; he draws up and directs general policy, oversees economic planning, and coordinates the activities of the various ministries. He acts too as Leader of the National Movement by delegation of the Head of State.[12]

Bearing in mind the differences separating the political systems of the two countries, the tandem King and President of the Government in Spain resembles the partnership between President of the Republic and Prime Minister in France. For the dual executive to function satisfactorily, there must be a wide area of consensus between the two parts, otherwise a stalemate or crisis situation is reached which can only be overcome by the dismissal or resignation of the Government or the adoption of exceptional measures, such as a referendum, by the Head of State. The more relevant solution is that in which the President and his Government are dismissed or forced to resign, for it refers to the all-important question of the political responsibility of the executive power. Before going into this subject, however, it seems necessary to discuss the

Council of Ministers, the role of individual ministers, and, above all, the discretionary nature of many of the powers of the executive.

The Council of Ministers

The Council of Ministers comprises besides the President, the Vice-President or Vice-Presidents – the law is vague, there can either be one or several Vice-Presidents – and the ministers. After a very brief existence during the Civil War, the Vice-Presidency was re-created on a personal basis – it would be more accurate to speak of the appointment of a Vice-President rather than of the re-creation of the Vice-Presidency – as part of Franco's plans to find a successor. In 1967 the Organic Law of the State gave the Vice-Presidency constitutional status, and from that date the post has undergone a number of changes. It was first occupied by Carrero Blanco on his climb to the Presidency, then it was in the hands of Torcuato Fernández Miranda, who combined it with the duties of Secretary-General of the National Movement. And finally, after the assassination of Carrero Blanco, the new President, Arias Navarro, decided to have three Vice-Presidents, who are, in order of priority, the Minister of the Interior, the Minister of Finance, and the Minister of Labour, or, in the language of the official press, a political Vice-President, an economic Vice-President, and a social Vice-President. Apart from the temporary role as deputy for the absent or ill President and his higher honorific status, the position of the Vice-President does not differ much from that of the other ministers, and the comments about them which follow equally apply to him.

In its composition the Council of Ministers shows a characteristic feature of our time: the progressive enlargement of the sphere of influence of the administration, and together with it a parallel preponderance of economic policies. Whereas Franco's first government, formed in January 1938, had only eleven members, besides himself the number has now risen to twenty, including the President, and this has brought with it a number of new economic portfolios: in 1951 the Ministry of Industry and Trade was divided into two separate departments; in 1957 the President of the National Economic Council joined for a time the Council of Ministers; in 1962 a *Comisaría* was created to take charge of economic planning; its head became Minister without Portfolio in 1965, and a full member of the cabinet in 1969. As a corollary of all these structural changes, there has been a gradual ascendancy gained inside the Council by those ministers with posts of a financial, commercial and, in general, economic nature.

In the composition of the Council of Ministers can be detected the vestiges of the original nature of the regime, and some of its present authoritarian features. The military still has guaranteed control of three ministries and it has often had more – the Government formed in July 1962 had, including Franco, eight members with military backgrounds. The Ministry of Syndical Relations, separate from the Ministry of Labour, points to government interference, which in practice amounts to total control, in the professional organizations of the working class. The remnants of falangist influence and of the early totalitarian attempts are to be found in the Secretariat of the National Movement, the head of which has ministerial rank. Even the Ministry of Information hides behind its innocuous-sounding name more precise political tasks of censorship and propaganda, though it is true that the other half of this Ministry of Information and Tourism has acquired enormous importance over the last fifteen years, as tourism has become a major source of revenue for the country, and on that basis alone would justify a separate ministry.

Since the Civil War ministers have come and gone for a variety of reasons but the decisive factor has always been Franco's will, both in the dismissal of old ministers and the appointment of new. But now, well into the transitional period leading to the succession and after two governments without Franco as President it is reasonable to assume that changes have occurred. The constitutional system for the selection and appointment of ministers should have come into operation. That is to say, the President of the Government – first Carrero Blanco and then Arias Navarro – after consultations chose a group of ministers with sufficient ideological and political coherence to function as a team. He then submitted the list to Franco, who, as Head of State, did the actual appointing. It is very probable that these two governments must have been chosen with Franco's opinions and advice very much in mind, to the point that he must have had a *de facto* veto over any candidates for the Council of Ministers. What will happen when the King is on the throne? His opinion is bound to carry some weight too, but how much? It is more than likely that the King's influence will be more noticeable at the earlier stage when the President of the Government is chosen, as once the King has appointed a politician of his liking it is logical to grant him leeway in selecting his own ministers. However, the stable functioning of the bicephalous executive in Spain requires the constant maintenance of a delicate balance through good understanding between Head of State and President of the Government so that the King cannot be totally indifferent to the composition of the Government; and this interpretation is reinforced by the constitutional power of the King to induce a political crisis to bring down the Government.

Except for Spanish nationality there are no formal requirements for a minister.[13] The reasons why a politician enters the Council of Ministers or is excluded from it are basically political and ideological, and fall outside the limits of the constitution. Membership of the Cortes is not even necessary, though appointment to ministerial office automatically means a seat on the 'blue bench' at the Palace of the Cortes.[14] Ministers are subject to incompatibilities whose primary object is to avoid the intermingling and conflict of their public duties as ministers and their private interests as citizens. This system of incompatibilities was established by Franco in 1955 by means of a decree-law[15] based on article 13 of the Law on the Cortes which allows urgent Government legislation to by-pass the Cortes, urgency being determined arbitrarily by the Head of State.

Ministers head their respective departments, they form part of the Comisiones Delegadas de Gobierno or Ministerial Committees, and together with the President constitute the Council of Ministers. Inside his own department a minister enjoys considerable power and independence. He has the overall direction of his ministry. With the help of his subordinates he drafts bills (*anteproyectos*) for submission to the Council of Ministers, and issues executive orders and regulations to apply and supplement the laws passed by the Cortes. With some exceptions he is the final judge in any administrative appeal inside his department.

The constant increase in the political and administrative tasks of the Government has made it necessary to set up committees which bring together the ministers concerned with certain specialized problems, facilitate and speed up debate, and lessen the business arriving at the already overloaded table of the Council of Ministers. There are seven such Comisiones Delegadas de Gobierno at the present moment. The first, the Committee for National Defence, was created soon after the end of the Civil War in 1939. In López Rodó's administrative reform of 1957 four more committees were instituted: Foreign Affairs, Transport and Communications, Cultural Activities, and Health and Social Problems. More recently, in 1963, another was set up to deal with Scientific Policy, and finally, as a reflection of the universal concern with ecology, a Committee for the Environment was formed in 1972.

The work of all these committees is limited to studying and discussing problems, since the power to take decisions rests with the Council of Ministers; its meetings, under normal circumstances, used to be fortnightly, on Fridays, with Franco in the chair, and took place at his official residence of the Pardo Palace. Later, after the appointment of a separate Head of Government in the summer of 1973, meetings were weekly, usually on Thursdays. Their venue alternated between the Pardo Palace, where Franco presided over them, and the residence of the President of the Government without Franco. This system will probably continue, in the same or very similar form, in the post-Franco years. The meetings held without the Head of State differ from those over which he presides, the latter being the real decision-taking meetings or *consejos decisorios*, a system resembling the Conseil de Cabinet and the Conseil des Ministres of the Third and Fourth Republics in France; although the French Conseil de Cabinet chaired by the Prime Minister, without the President of the Republic in attendance, fell into disuse after 1958.

The Council of Ministers determines national policy, ensures the application of the laws, has the power to make regulations, and permanently assists the Head of State in political and administrative matters. This is no more than a legal enumeration[16] with very vague outlines; a more detailed, and even prolix, enumeration can be found in the Law on the Administration of the State of 1957.[17] But it hardly seems worth while to dwell on the legal delimitation of the executive power when this power has in practice accepted few restraints.

The danger is not in the dictatorial discretion Franco held, since this is now part of the past; rather it is that the Government has found a comfortable nest in the shelter of Franco's discretionary powers, it has got used to taking arbitrary measures, to abusing authority, to invading the private spheres of other powers – both the legislative and the judicial – and to disregarding the basic principle of the rule of law. Cases to exemplify all this can easily be encountered in the few historical studies of the Franco regime available or in the foreign press, particularly the French. We shall briefly point out here those areas of most flagrant abuse.

In the legislative sphere, as will be seen later, the subordination of the Cortes to the Government, in their composition and in their functioning, is such that they have done little more than rubber-stamp Government projects. Besides the Government is empowered to legislate by decree in cases of urgency,[18] so that it can bypass the Cortes whenever the Head of State judges it expedient or necessary; this form of legislation – 'decree-laws' – has been fairly frequently used.[19] Another and more subtle way in which the Spanish Government has interfered with and abused legislative power consists of submitting to the Cortes Bills intentionally drafted in an imprecise manner so the Government gives itself a wide margin to interpret them. The Press Law of 1966 or the Syndical Law of 1971 are two obvious examples of this nature.

The activities of the Government infringe also, and this is even more serious, the sacred grounds of the judiciary power. Except for special cases, neither the Government nor its subordinates in a state where the rule of law applies, is entitled to impose sanctions of any kind, this being the monopoly of the courts of justice. In Spain the administration, at all levels, is empowered to impose different sanctions ranging from fines to imprisonment of the individual.[20] We are not talking here about a legal residue from the exceptional post-Civil War years. The powers of the Government to fine and imprison are basically contained in the Public Order Law which was promulgated in the summer of 1959, and some of its most offensive provisions were considerably hardened much more recently. (In the chapter dealing with individual rights and freedoms we shall have more to say about the Public Order Law.) The possibility of appeal against sanctions imposed by the executive before special courts (the *tribunales contencioso-administrativos*) is very often of little relevance. The sanctions are immediately enforceable, and not even an appeal will stop their application; by the time the appeal court passes sentence the harm is done, the Government has achieved its aim, and the person or institution affected by the sanction is left only with the 'satisfaction' of winning the case, if they do. This has repeatedly occurred, for instance, with the confiscation and suspension of newspapers and magazines by the Ministry of Information and Tourism under the provisions of the 1966 Press Law. Once an issue of a daily newspaper or a weekly magazine has been withdrawn and the publication suspended for a time the damage to the publishing firm – in loss of revenue, readers, etc. – is irreparable, whatever the final decision of the courts.

Finally, as if to round off arbitrariness and discretion, the Government as a final tool can declare a state of emergency, acquire extraordinary powers, and suspend constitutional guarantees. Once more this can and has been done without any regard to other spheres of power; the decision to declare an emergency is taken unilaterally by the Government with the only condition that the Cortes be informed.

The danger for the future lies in the hardening of arbitrariness. More than thirty years of government activity with little or no control have tacitly set a pattern not easy to renounce by those who enjoy it, or alter by those who suffer it. Who will bring the Government, so used to an unrestrained *modus operandi*, to book? Without Franco, without his charisma and without his exceptional powers, to whom and how will the Government be politically responsible?

The Political Responsibility of the Executive

The political responsibility of the executive is fundamental for the future democratization of Spain. The executive power must be made accountable for the success or failure of its policies and actions to other institutions rooted in popular sovereignty. There must exist all the time the possibility of dismissing from office the members of the executive either in an exceptional way by means of a crisis or a vote of no confidence, or through the normal channel of periodic elections.

This broad concept of political responsibility is the keystone of the whole system of control and restraint of executive power, for without political responsibility control is weakened and devoid of democratic guarantees. In any event, there are always certain forms of control. Not even in the moments of most inflamed francoist fervour was there a total lack of control over the executive, if by control we signify the ability to exercise influence, either persuading or dissuading. It is impossible to be precise because the activities of Franco and his government have always been enveloped in secrecy, with a public image made up of official communiqués and ministerial speeches. But all the same this control characterizes dictatorial and authoritarian regimes. Its operation is circumscribed to the political oligarchy, in an intra-regime system whose working levers are only within the reach of a few figures heading different social groups, which are in the dictatorial orbit and which control and are controlled by the dictator.

In spite of the secrecy throughout the years of francoism there are examples of these controls. Franco, as a dictator, has not been beyond the controlling influence of figures like Serrano Suñer, Carrero Blanco or Esteban Bilbao; of political groups such as falangists or, in more recent time, the *Opus Dei* 'third force'; and of political and non-political institutions, the Council of the Realm, the army or the ecclesiastical hierarchy. Time and the institutionalization of the regime have made these restraints and pressures more overt and at the same time possibly stronger. During the last few years of the more liberal climate generated by the Organic Law of the State of 1967, the political groups vegetating inside the regime have acquired greater independence from each other, and from the dictator too, and have started to deliver mutual and more aggressive criticisms and attacks; in this way they exercise some reciprocal controls, which became even more apparent after the formation of the first government without Franco as President.

One could look for more remote forms of control – no dictator can afford to ignore totally the aspirations and demands of the people he rules. Public opinion as expressed primarily through the press – and always bearing very much in mind the pattern of newspaper ownership in Spain – has had some influence on the executive. Something similar has happened with certain illegal activities by the people either in the form of industrial unrest, like the wave of strikes in the spring of 1962 that partly caused a change of government in summer 1962; or the student protests which midway through the sixties brought about first the downfall of the state-controlled student union, SEU, and soon after a change at the head of the Ministry of Education, followed by educational reform.

A feature common to all these forms of control is that they are not institutionalized either by the constitution or by common law. They are there, they have been recurring more and more often, their manifestation can be pinpointed in individual cases, but they are not regularized and it is always difficult to quantify their efficacy. Moreover, the definitive evidence of democratic control, that is to say, holding the executive power politically responsible, does not exist. The forms of control institutionalized in liberal democracies are nowhere to be seen: there are no political parties – the groups referred to earlier on are nothing more than pressure or interest groups, and at most they could only be rated as embryo parties; there is no legally organized opposition, the elections, when they are held, do not represent a judgement on the government's record, nor do they have any bearing on how that government is formed. Inside the Cortes, or parliament *a la española*, we find the same state of affairs: the quasi-monopoly of the government in the presentation of bills, amendments suggested by members; the lack of independence of many members; the control by the government over the composition of the different committees and the agenda for their meetings; an emasculated and contrived system for questioning the government; and plenary sessions as notable for their rarity as for the enthusiastic way in which they approve everything that is submitted to them.

The situation in Spain, then, is total political irresponsibility on the part of the executive. Franco as the depositary of national sovereignty, dictator for life, and centre of the government was accountable to nobody; he was subject to certain checks and controls, but it was not possible to make him responsible for his political decisions. The ministers who have shared executive functions in successive governments have acted as secretaries to the Head of State and they have had to assume, before Franco, responsibility for the results of failed policies. These are not however genuine instances of political responsibility; they had no independence or discretion. Ministers have always been subordinated to Franco. The dismissal of a minister is an exercise in authority by a superior over an inferior within a hierarchy; in this sense it does not differ from a minister dismissing a subordinate.

Earlier on we talked of the dangers of prolonged political irresponsibility inasmuch as it was leading towards a dead end, comfortable for the government while it could exercise power with keeping the dictator happy, the sole constraint – but with uncertainties which will appear in the post-Franco years. Unless the dictatorial situation is to continue under a new guise, some form of controlling the executive power and making it responsible for its political acts and decisions will have to be found in the constitutional framework; the initiative for such a move must come from the government itself. The probability of this happening, given the nature of the Fundamental Laws and the political mood of Franco's heirs apparent cannot be rated high.

From a purely juridical viewpoint, any constitution in a legal vacuum can be interpreted in many different and even contradictory ways. It is like a glass vessel which can equally well contain a fine Burgundy or a *vin ordinaire*. Playing with words it could be put thus: it is not what it says but what it is said that it says. With this kind of interpretative pragmatism and with large doses of goodwill it is possible to reach the conclusion that the Fundamental Laws, without any alterations in them, could allow the introduction in Spain of the concept and practice of political responsibility of the executive power. However academically rigorous and technically refined this interpretation may be it will always come up against a harsh and disheartening reality which shows that those same Fundamental Laws have until now served as legal justification for an authoritarian regime unwilling to accept any political responsibility. And this political responsibility, such as it was defined at the beginning of this section, cannot be fitted into the existing Fundamental Laws, unless they are modified or interpreted in such a liberal form that the interpretation will become unconstitutional. In either case the number of conditional 'ifs' required is endless: if the King abstains from an active part in political events, if the Cortes is changed to make the legislative chamber the depository of popular sovereignty, if elections become more direct and sincere, if the

Council of the Realm is seen as a branch of the Cortes, if the formation of parties is allowed, if, if . . .

The subject of political responsibility, and above all how it might be fitted into the constitution, has been for some years the concern of Spanish political scientists and of Spanish politicians too. As far back as 1967 one member in Arias Navarro's government, Carro Martínez, Under-Secretary to the President, while analysing the relations between the higher institutions of the state in the light of the new Organic Law of the State, foresaw the possibility of some form of parliamentary system in Spain.[21] The passing of time has not brought that prediction any nearer to reality. The fact that several years later things remain basically the same may be taken as proof of the theory we are sustaining, that a democratic system in which the executive power bears political responsibility cannot be drifted into without basic changes in legal structure and in attitudes.

More recently two very valuable works, touching on the question of political responsibility, have been published[22] and although both limit themselves to a purely juridical study of the theme, the dangerous constitutional ambiguity is stressed by the mutually contradictory conclusions at which they arrive. The only mention of or reference to political responsibility in the Fundamental Laws is to be found in article 20, paragraph I of the Organic Law of the State, which says: 'The President and the other members of the government are jointly responsible for the resolutions passed at their meetings. Each one individually shall be responsible for what he does or authorizes in his own department.' But responsible to whom? Here these two works differ. For one of the authors, M. Herrero, there is no more governmental responsibility than that which can be demanded and operated by the King either dismissing ministers or forcing them to resign.[23] But this is the situation of a superior dismissing an inferior, not an application of the principle of political responsibility. That is why M. Herrero goes on to say that in Spain nobody has to answer for the supreme decisions of authority. Constitutionally the King is the sole depositary of national sovereignty and the centre of all political, administrative and military power but he cannot be held responsible for anything, he is inviolable.[24]

The authors of the other work[25] believe that national sovereignty does not belong to the King alone; it is shared by the Cortes. This interpretation, however, requires a very delicate and a somewhat far-fetched understanding of the letter of the law – and runs counter to more than thirty years of history – but once accepted it takes the authors very far, and they conclude that there could be three ways in which the government might be held politically responsible:[26] first, by the King if he refuses to sign decrees presented by ministers; second, by the Council of the Realm in pursuance of article 15, paragraph (c) of the Organic Law of the State; and third, the most important and radical departure from the present situation, when the Cortes withdraw their support from the Government by rejecting an important Bill.

The divergence between these two positions is not as great as might seem, because the second contains a fair amount of wishful thinking. For it to become a reality a considerable number of factors – what we earlier called the conditional 'ifs' – would have to concur. Until then we can only reiterate the lack of institutionalized political responsibility in Spain. What does exist is a series of controls and restraints inside the political oligarchy, all based on some kind of loyalty to francoism, inasmuch as francoism represents the defence of oligarchic interests. So far the system has achieved a fair degree of authoritarian stability. Its future viability without Franco is dubious, its transformation only possible within a much wider democratizing change.

Franco's men

This seems the most appropriate heading to refer to the ninety ministers who have sat in Franco's governments. They have different professional backgrounds and even show a certain diversity in political ideology, but what they all have in common is their allegiance to the Caudillo.

Ministers themselves very often have not made clear where they stand politically. In fact, exactly the opposite has often been the case, ministers claiming in public to have no political ambitions, or even to be totally a-political. The nebulous atmosphere surrounding politics in Spain has caused this. In his eagerness to present a united front, Franco has never demanded of his ministers any public expression of their political ideas other than loyalty to him and to his regime. As a result, any classification of Franco's ministers has to be based on a rather mixed bag of indicators. Professor Linz, in the early sixties, analysed the background of all the men who had sat in the Council of Ministers between 1938 and 1962, in order to prove that the Spanish regime allowed some degree of pluralism, but had to base his work on very heterogeneous data, comprising categories as diverse as service under a previous dictator, affiliation to a political party, allegiance to one royal cause rather than another, professional status, or membership of a Catholic organization.[27] Ministers as often as not fit into more than one of these categories, whereas, on the other hand, certain groups are difficult to define. It is simple enough to establish who is a military man, but not so easy to determine falangist allegiance – particularly as the Civil War recedes into the past – or the veiled membership of the semi-secret Opus Dei.

The chart on page 81 duly shows those ministers clearly belonging to one group or another. In it one can see that since Franco established his first government in January 1938 he has had seven major ministerial reshuffles – in 1939, 1945, 1951, 1957, 1962, 1965 and 1969 – with smaller changes during the intervening periods. The first of the main changes came soon after the Civil War had ended. Peace, or such peace as there was in 1939, demanded a new team to rebuild the country along the lines of the victorious ideology.

Spain did not take part in the Second World War, but her internal affairs were considerably affected by it, and many of the ministerial changes between 1939 and 1945 were influenced to a greater or lesser degree by the ups and downs of the War. The replacements in eight ministries and the temporary disappearance of another one during the summer of 1945 were carried out under the threat of Allied victory. Six years later Spain was emerging from the isolation of the late forties. The international boycott imposed in 1946 had been lifted, economic help had started to flow in from the USA, and a new ministerial team, set up in July 1951, was to sign the first agreement with the Americans for military bases, and the Concordat with the Vatican. The same team would eventually gain for Spain membership of the United Nations Organization. From then on all the major changes in the Council of Ministers had primarily economic motivations. In 1957 the country was hovering on the brink of bankruptcy. Another government was formed with thirteen new ministers to reverse the autarchic policies which had proved so fatal. The next two reshuffles, in July 1962 and July 1965, were linked to the move towards economic growth and development planning that permeated the sixties.

Finally, the most important and recent upheaval in the government with Franco as President came in October 1969. It affected fourteen ministers, the largest and possibly the most significant change ever made by Franco. Its cause was the *Matesa* affair, a financial scandal involving a considerable amount of public money. The size of the sum embezzled was enormous and several ministers were implicated.[28] Proceedings were initiated against some of them, and the whole government was in danger of collapse under the principle of ministerial solidarity established by article 20 of the Organic Law of the State. The principle was not applied,

TABLE 6. MINISTERS IN FRANCO'S EARLIER GOVERNMENTS

Date of formation of government	31 Jan. 1938	29 Dec. 1938	9 Aug. 1939	27 Jun. 1940	16 Oct. 1940	5 May 1941	19 May 1941	3 Sept. 1942	15 Mar. 1943	10 Sept. 1944	20 Jul. 1945	19 Jul. 1951	15 Feb. 1956	25 Feb. 1957	20 Apr. 1960	10 Jul. 1962	20 Feb. 1964	7 Jul. 1965	21 Sept. 1967	17 Apr. 1968	29 Oct. 1969	14 Apr. 1970
Vice-Presidency											post does not exist					A. Muñoz Grandes[s]					L. Carrero Blanco[a]	
Undersecretary to President				post does not have ministerial rank								L. Carrero Blanco[a]										
Foreign Affairs	F. Gómez Jordana[a]	F. Gómez Jordana[a]	J. Beigbeder[a]	R. Serrano Suñer				F. Gómez Jordana[a]		J.F. Lequerica[a]	A. Martín Artajo[c]			F. M. Castiella[c]							G. López Bravo[o]	
Justice	Conde de Rodezno[f]		E. Bilbao[f]					E. Aunós Pérez[a]			R. F. Cuesta[f]		A. Iturmendi[f]						A.M. de Oriol y Urquijo[c]			
Finance	A. Amado[m]		J. Larraz López[c]		J. Benjumea Burín						F. Gómez de Llano[a]			M. Navarro Rubio[o]					J. J. Espinosa San Martín[o]		A. Monreal Luque[o]	
Labour	P. González Bueno[a]				J. A. Girón de Velasco[f]									F. Sanz Orrio[f]			J. Romeo Gorría[f]				L. de la Fuente[f]	
Education	P. Sainz Rodríguez[m]		J. Ibáñez Martín[c]								J. Ruiz Giménez[c]		J. Rubio[c]			M. Lora Tamayo				J. L. Villar Palasí		
Interior	R.S. Suñer			Gobernación: R. Serrano Suñer		V. Galarza[a]			B. Pérez González												T. Garicano Goñi	
Public Order	S. M. Anido[a]													C. Alonso Vega[s]								
Public Works	A. Peña Boeuf										J.M.F. Ladreda[a]	Conde de Vallellano[a]		J. Vigón Suerodiaz[m,s]				F. Silva Muñoz[c]			G. Fernández de la Mora[m]	
Industry and Trade	J. A. Suances[s]			L. Alarcón[a]	D. Carceller Segura[f]						J.A. Suances[s]	J. Planell Riera[a]	M. Arburúa	A. Ullastres[o]		G. López Bravo[o]			F. García-Moncó[o]		E. Fontana Codina	
Agriculture	R. Fernández Cuesta[f]				J. Benjumea Burín				M. Primo de Rivera[f]		C. Rein[a]	R. Cavestany[a]		C. Cánovas		A. Díaz-Ambrona				T. Allende y García-Baxter		
Information and Tourism											G. Arias Salgado	post does not exist				M. Fraga Iribarne					A. Sánchez Bella	
Housing						post does not exist								J. M. Martínez Sánchez-Arjona[a]							V. Mortes Alfonso[o]	
Defence	F. Dávila Arrondo[s]						post does not exist															
Army	post does not exist	E. Varela Iglesias[s]						C. Asensio Cabanillas[s]			F. Dávila[a]	A. Muñoz Grandes[s]		A. Barroso[a]		R. M. Alonso[a]	C. Menéndez Tolosa[a]				J. Castañón de Mena[a]	
Navy	post does not exist		S. Moreno Fernández[s]								F. Regalado[a]		S. Moreno[a]	F. Abárzuza[a]		P. Nieto Antúnez[s]					A. Baturone Colombo[a]	
Air	post does not exist		J. Yagüe[f,s]			J. Vigón Suerodiaz[m,s]					E. González Gallarza[m,s]			J. R. Díaz de Lecea[a]		J. Lacalle Larraga[a]					J. Díaz-Benjumea[a]	
National Movement	post does not exist		A.M. Grandes[s]	post vacant			J. L. de Arrese[f]				Vacant	R. F. Cuesta[f]	J. L. de Arrese[f]			J. Solís Ruiz[f]					T. Fernández Miranda	
Syndical Relations												post does not exist									E. García-Ramal[f]	
Development Plan												post does not exist				L. López Rodó[o]						
President National Economic Council				post does not exist								P. Gual Villalbí[c]										
Ministers without portfolio		R. Sánchez Mazas[f]																				
		P. Gamero del Castillo[m]																				

● During his period of office the ministry was known as Ministry of Syndical Organization and Action.

Key

[c] Catholic action or similar background   [f] falangist   [m] monarchist   [o] Opus Die   [s] professional soldier   [t] traditionalist

but there was a large ministerial purge, and the affair was closed by a general pardon granted by Franco in October 1971 to commemorate the thirty-fifth anniversary of his accession to power.

Franco's governments have always been coalitions. The Caudillo has tried to balance the different groups supporting his regime, by giving ministerial posts as rewards and in accordance with their influence or usefulness at different times – the dictator being the only permanent figure amid the permutation of political variables. The principal factions bene-fitting from this sort of spoils system have been traditionalists (the group connected with the Carlist cause and the clerical conservatism that op-posed liberal ideas from the 1830s), falangists, and Catholic organizations such as ACN deP (Asociación Católica Nacional de Propagandistas) or, in more recent times, Opus Dei. Each has had its own territorial domain inside the Council. Traditionalists have usually controlled the Ministry of Justice – and the Presidency of the Cortes too. Falangists have domi-nated the Ministry of Labour, the Syndical Organization, and the National Movement. ACN deP have played their main role in the field of foreign affairs and education. And Opus Dei members have monopolized economic portfolios from 1957.

Professional soldiers form, by far, the largest group of ministers, thirty out of a total of ninety. Many of them, like Franco, had their years of service in the colonial battles of the Moroccan war; twenty-two belong to the 'African generation'. The high number of military men is partly explained by the division of responsibility for national defence between three separate ministries. But the influence of the military is, nevertheless, considerable. Ten generals and admirals have occupied ministries other than those in charge of the Army, the Navy and the Air Force. Franco's three Vice-Presidents were all professional soldiers like himself, and had the hand of terrorism not intervened a military man, Admiral Carrero Blanco, would have been his main successor. Generals, too, have filled the important post of Minister of the Interior for long periods.

During the first four years, the leading figure in the Council of Minis-ters was Franco's brother-in-law, Serrano Suñer. He gathered consider-able power in a relatively short time, starting as Minister of the Interior in 1938. A year later, when General Martínez Anido died, his post as Minis-ter of Public Order was taken over by Serrano Suñer, who fused the two ministries into one under the new name of Ministerio de la Gobernación. Later he held simultaneously with it the Ministry of Foreign Affairs. He had started his political career during the Second Republic as a member of the Catholic party CEDA, but after the establishment of FET y de las JONS as the regime's party – a decision for which he was largely responsible – he turned towards official falangism. His identification with fascist movements – he had visited Hitler in Germany and Mussolini in Italy – became an embarrassment as the Second World War progressed. This and his preponderance, which was turning him into a dangerous competitor for Franco, brought his downfall. In the autumn of 1942 he was dismissed, and he vanished from political life as swiftly as he had appeared.

In spite of the predominance of Serrano Suñer in the early years, a balance between groups can clearly be seen. In the first few governments, there were traditionalists, like the Count of Rodezno and Esteban Bilbao; monarchists, like Sainz Rodríguez and General Vigón; politicians with their roots in Catholic movements, like Larraz López, Ibáñez Martín, or Serrano Suñer himself. The falangists probably had the least influence in that initial period. They had not reacted very favourably to the formation of the all-comprising official party, and Franco and Serrano Suñer kept them away from the centre of power. In the 1938 Government there was just one falangist, Fernández Cuesta, and he was given one of the least influential portfolios, Agriculture. Even when the post of Secretary-General of FET y de las JONS was raised to ministerial level, it was not given to an old falangist, but to one of Franco's army colleagues, Muñoz Grandes, and when he left the post, it remained vacant for nearly a year.

Falangists were given a greater share from the middle of 1941. The Ministry of Labour was put in the hands of a young falangist of 29, José Antonio Girón, who was to be one of Franco's longest-serving ministers. Arrese, a well-known falangist theoretician, became Secretary-General of the party. And the elder brother of the founder of Falange, Miguel Primo de Rivera, took over the post of Minister of Agriculture. With the outcome of the Second World War, falangists saw their fortunes turn again. They were deprived of the party's secretariat, and the post was left vacant for six years. True enough, falangists still held three posts in the Government, but a new man without falangist ties entered the Cabinet as Minister of Foreign Affairs. Martín Artajo, with his strong Catholic background and with the support of the official Church,[29] became the leading figure. He was the man that succeeded in having Franco's Spain accepted by the western world. His ascendency allowed him to bring into the government, in the reshuffle of 1951, one of his closest associates, Ruiz-Giménez, as Minister of Education, and later to promote as his successor another of his friends, Castiella.

The new Government of July 1951 had several significant changes. The balance was still maintained. Besides the Catholic faction represented by

Martín Artajo and Ruiz-Giménez, traditionalists were back in the Ministry of Justice with Iturmendi; the Count of Vallellano, Minister of Public Works, and General González Gallarza in the Air Ministry were monarchists hoping for a restoration; the party's secretariat returned to the falangists. Three new ministries were created. Industry and trade became separate administrative units. The Ministry of Information and Tourism was set up to deal with the former rather than with the latter subject in its title, and Arias Salgado was given the job, and with it the task of applying censorship – he was to do it with utmost zeal and efficiency for eleven years. The third new ministry was simply an upgrading. The post of Under-Secretary to the President of the Government was given ministerial status. This change did not attract much attention, and yet it was to prove the most important of them all. Admiral Carrero Blanco had held this post since May 1940. He was a quiet, almost dull politician, who very rarely appeared in the limelight of public life. His speeches and his writings – usually signed with the name of a Spanish *conquistador* as a pseudonym – reveal reactionary views and an authoritarian nature. From 1940 he quietly burrowed his way up: by 1951 he had been made a minister, by 1967 he became Vice-President of the Government, and in 1972 he reached the pinnacle when he was guaranteed the Presidency after Franco's death. In 1973 he was finally appointed President.

The substitution of two ministers early in 1956 merits some comment. Ruiz-Giménez had been trying, from his position as Minister of Education, to open the doors of Spanish universities to let in some liberal ideas and break up the narrow-mindedness generated in academic circles by the University Law of 1943 and by the activities of the falangist student union, SEU.[30] It led to violent clashes at the University of Madrid between rival groups of students, falangists on one side and more liberal students on the other. The aftermath was Franco's dismissal of the two ministers most directly involved, Ruiz-Giménez and Fernández Cuesta. Ruiz-Giménez little by little drifted away from the system he had served for quite a few years, and eventually became the first, and so far the only, minister to reject unequivocally the very principles of the regime.

From 1957 onwards the main feature is the appearance of Opus Dei ministers, and the progressive expansion of their influence throughout the Cabinet. The balance between the different groups was more or less maintained until the big ministerial reshuffle late in 1969. But from that date the scales were tipped in favour of the 'technocrats', the men who are supposed to have little time or interest for political ideologies, and be primarily concerned with efficiency. Opus Dei entered the Cabinet through the economic ministries. Navarro Rubio, as Minister of Finance, and Ullastres, as Minister of Trade, were the first Opus Dei members to gain a seat in Franco's government. They were given the responsibility of finding an answer to the endemic economic problems, with the help of Gual Villalbí, whose position as President of the National Economic Council was temporarily given ministerial rank.

At the same time – February 1957 – Martín Artajo, after twelve years in the Ministry of Foreign Affairs, handed over to somebody in his own political camp, Castiella, who was himself in office for twelve years. The traditionalists kept their representative in the Ministry of Justice, but the old guard of Falange was finally relegated. Arrese had proposed, during 1956, a new constitution that would move the regime closer to falangist ideals and give the party a greater share in power. It was rejected. Arrese was deprived of his political influence as Secretary-General of the party and demoted to a newly-created Ministry of Housing. It was a serious blow to his political ambitions, but it was more in line with his professional qualifications as an architect. The new Secretary-General of FET y de las JONS, Solís Ruiz, though he wore the party's blue shirt and black tie, was not a genuine falangist in the way that Arrese, Girón or Fernández Cuesta were. He had falangist leanings and paid lip-service to its doctrine, the same as many other ministers, and had behind him a varied political career. When he was promoted to the Cabinet, he was already National Syndical Delegate, a position he had been given back in 1951, and he held both posts all the time he was in government. In 1969, when Solís fell, the post of National Syndical Delegate became a separate ministry.

The sixties saw a promising new figure in the Ministry of Information and Tourism. Fraga Iribarne, a Galician with a brilliant academic career, became Minister at the age of thirty-nine. Under his direction, tourism became a major source of revenue for the Spanish treasury, and he was responsible too for the Press Law of 1966. During his years in office he cultivated his public image, and at one time was tipped for the post of President of the Government. However, he was swept away by the tidal wave of Opus Dei expansion. The size and force of this wave were of such enormous proportions that, in spite of the secrecy enveloping the actions and membership of the organization, its effects were evident everywhere.

Since 1957, at least five full members of Opus Dei have been in the government: Navarro Rubio, Ullastres, López Bravo, López Rodó and Mortes Alfonso. The number has sometimes been estimated to be much higher; it certainly is, if one includes ministers such as Lora Tamayo,

Villar Palasí or Fernández de la Mora who although not affiliated to Opus Dei are in full sympathy with it.[31] Whatever the accuracy of the estimates the rising influence of *opusdeistas* inside the Cabinet during the sixties is beyond any doubt. A minister appoints to the highest posts in his department men who share his ideological principles so as to create a compact and homogeneous ministerial team. Applying this principle to the Spanish governments of the last decade, one can see that many ministers, particularly the ones heading economic departments, had previously served in the team of an Opus Dei minister. Thus Espinosa San Martín worked under Navarro Rubio; Villar Palasí, García Moncó and López Bravo under Ullastres; Fernández de la Mora under López Bravo; Monreal Luque, Allende, Mortes Alfonso and López de Letona under López Rodó, etc.

We need not enter into whether this came as a result of a Machiavellian plot on the part of Opus Dei;[32] it is clear that the partnership of López Rodó and Carrero Blanco – who was always reputed to be a sympathizer of Opus Dei – initiated and sustained the trend and managed to have themselves chosen by the dictator as the overseers of post-francoism. In the Government reshuffle of October 1969 they surrounded themselves with like-minded men in the most homogeneous Cabinet in Spain since the War. They were for the most part men renowned for their expertise, and always referred to as technocrats;[33] they were possibly more efficient and less demagogic than many of their predecessors. From them Spain could expect economic growth, but not democracy. The speeches and writings of Carrero Blanco, López Rodó, Fernández de la Mora or Sanchez Bella contained the same authoritarian message as those of early ministers, though the style might have been more technocratic and politically more cohesive and monochrome.

The Government without Franco

There is little solid information upon which to judge the last two cabinets presided over by Admiral Carrero Blanco and then by Carlos Arias Navarro. Visibility, which in Spanish politics is always blurred by a nebulous atmosphere, is further hindered by a lack of perspective: one of the governments was too short-lived for it had been in existence for barely six months when its President was assassinated; and the other is too close to us, having come into office at the beginning of 1974. Nevertheless, availing ourselves of the political biographies of the members of both Governments,[34] of the reactions and comments in the national and foreign press, and of the government programmes and ministerial speeches, together with their record while in office, we shall try to highlight the main characteristics of the men who appear to be the heirs of francoism.

Continuity – *continuismo* is the Spanish term – is an essential feature common to both governments, the idea that francoism should survive beyond its founder. This thought must have been foremost in Franco's mind when choosing Carrero Blanco first, and Arias Navarro later. We find in both of them an unquestioned loyalty to the dictator, based upon personal friendship and commonality of ideas, plus all the essential requirements for either of them to become a kind of Franco's *alter ego* – without the charisma. Like Franco neither Carrero Blanco nor Arias Navarro can be identified with any of the Spanish political 'families', thus finding themselves, with their political detachment, in an ideal position to play Franco's role as the point of equilibrium of all the tensions and pressures of the regime. The political neutrality of Carrero Blanco was less evident than Arias Navarro's; for some years Carrero Blanco had been linked with the Opus Dei group, although he was never a member. However, in his government and possibly at Franco's suggestion, Opus Dei influence was reduced to a minimum to achieve that neutrality with López Rodó in Foreign Affairs as the only Opus Dei representative left in the cabinet.

A second feature common to both governments is support for Prince Juan Carlos as eventual successor to Franco, hence the absence from their ranks of the old-type falangist with his republican proclivities, of monarchist sympathizers of the Count of Barcelona, and of traditionalists who might still harbour hopes for the Carlist pretender. It is now publicly admitted that Carrero Blanco – together with López Rodó – was the main force behind all the plotting and intrigues which led to the appointment of Prince Juan Carlos as successor. As for the present Government, Arias Navarro in his first address to the Cortes, on 12 February 1974, underlined the wisdom of Franco in his choice of successor, concluding that 'don Juan Carlos de Borbón is generously gifted with all the necessary qualities to discharge the highest duties which will fall upon him the day, as sorrowful as it is inevitable, when Franco will no longer be with us'.[35]

The composition of the *terna* submitted to Franco for his choice of premier is secret. In spite of the official silence some indiscreet voice is always heard insinuating the names of unsuccessful contenders. Apparently in the first *terna* were included two ex-ministers, R. Fernández Cuesta and M. Fraga Iribarne,[36] and in the second one J. Solís, for many years head of the official syndicates and Secretary-General of the National

Movement, and J. García Hernández, who would subsequently become
Vice-President in the new government.[37]

Whatever the names included in the *terna*, the appointment of Carrero
Blanco was a foregone conclusion. He had been the undisputed favourite
for many years; he was the ideal man to guarantee the continuity of
francoism. His loyalty to Franco and to everything that Franco stands
for was carried to the point of self-denial: 'I am a man totally identified
with the work of the Caudillo . . . my loyalty to his person and to all he
has done is total, clear, without any sort of condition, without the slightest
trace of reticence' he said on more than one occasion.[38] Carrero Blanco
was to be the iron-fisted man that many believe the Prince will need in
his early years as Head of State. On the other hand Arias Navarro was not
an obvious choice. During the ten days between Carrero Blanco's assassination and the designation of a new president, political experts in the
national and foreign press ventured lists of possible and probable candidates without including the eventual winner, Arias Navarro.[39] With the
wisdom of hindsight, it is not difficult to explain the choice. The main
reasons are mentioned above, and to them one should perhaps add Arias
Navarro's six years' experience as head of the Spanish police, a real asset
in the crisis generated by the assassination of his predecessor.

Another characteristic shared by both governments was the high turn-
over of ministerial posts, twelve under Carrero Blanco, eleven under
Arias Navarro plus two ministers who changed portfolio. The difference
is particularly surprising since Carrero Blanco's team had only been in
office for six months, and the new President was a member of that team.[40]
Obviously Carrero Blanco's government could not have been as homogeneous as some had thought, and Arias Navarro must have tried to
overcome tensions by surrounding himself with like-minded men.

Carrero Blanco's government shows a loss of balance between the old
francoist forces. There are no longer any traditionalists, nor Catholic
ministers connected with the A CN de P. The trend had started during the
late sixties under the influence of Carrero Blanco and López Rodó,
who now reach their zenith, even though at the price of sacrificing – for
the sake of neutrality, so dear to Franco, and to compensate for the loss of
balance – some of the men they themselves had promoted. It was to be a
succession government, unquestionably loyal to Prince Juan Carlos, and
an authoritarian government, bent on the retrogressive path of the late
sixties, away from the pseudo-liberalization of the regime for fear that it
might lead them from the essential dogmas. The National Movement, as a
political organization, was guaranteed continuity and a more influential

role by the raising of its Secretary-General to the post of Vice-President in the government. And neither Carrero Blanco nor his two main theoreticians, Fernández Miranda and Fernández de la Mora, showed any personal inclination or expressed any future intention of offering Spaniards any possibility of setting up political associations. However, since Carrero Blanco's Government was so short-lived all these latent features are no more than a guide to how it would have developed.

Arias Navarro completed the elimination of Opus Dei members with the dismissal of López Rodó. In his government the dismissals and omissions are more significant than the new appointments; the ministerial team is easier to classify by what it leaves out rather than by what is added. Most of the present government are somewhat diffuse political figures, not easily identified with any of the traditional groups. This is bound to continue; as the years go by and the Civil War recedes the ideology of these groups is obsolescent and the emergence of new forces and different interests makes even their existence precarious.[41] A brilliant academic record and membership of some elitist administrative or civil service corps – e.g. university professors or *abogados del estado* – characterize most of the new ministers, as they did many in past governments;[42] but that is all the new men have to offer because the great majority of them were not known as significant political figures before their appointment. Certain connections with the Catholic group centred around *Editorial Católica* and the daily *Ya* have been insinuated, and on several ministers one can detect the bluish hue of falangism in a rather diluted – some would say modern – form, which tries to be *joseantoniana* and *movimientista*, that is to say, it pretends to be faithful to the original ideas of Falange and to the present National Movement organization at one and the same time.

The beginnings of Arias Navarro's government point to a return to the pseudo-democratic path. It came into office with a great display of oratory, so much so that the press has coined the term 'verbocrats' to describe the new ministers, thus contrasting them with the 'technocrats' of previous governments. The first presidential speech, with its promises of political associations, democratization of local government, a new electoral law and a system of incompatibilities for the Cortes, was received with hopeful commentaries. A new democratic door was being opened by what has become known as the '12 February spirit' from the date of Arias Navarro's speech. A more recent presidential speech on 12 June 1974[43] placed a number of dampers on the elated spirit of February; many of the promises had their democratic content watered down considerably.

TABLE 7 – MINISTERS IN FRANCO'S LATER GOVERNMENTS

Date of formation of government	12 June 1973	5 January 1974	30 October 1974	4 March 1975	17 June 1975
President	L. Carrero Blanco	C. Arias Navarro			
Under-Secretary to President	J.M. Gamazo	A. Carro			
Foreign Affairs	L. López Rodó	P. Cortina			
Justice	F. Ruiz Jarabo			J.M. Sánchez Ventura	
Finance	A. Barrera de Irimo (2nd Vice-President)		R. Cabello de Alba		
Labour	L. de la Fuente (3rd Vice-President)			F. Suárez	
Education	J. Rodríguez	C. Martínez Esteruelas			
Interior	C. Arias Navarro	J. García Hernández (1st Vice-President)			
Public Works	G. Fernández de la Mora	A. Valdés			
Industry	J.M. López de Letona	A. Santos		A. Alvarez Miranda	
Trade	A. Cotarruelo	N. Fernández Cuesta		J.L. Cerón	
Agriculture	T. Allende				
Information	F. Liñán	P. Cabanillas	L. Herrera Esteban		
Housing	J. Utrera	L. Rodríguez de Miguel			
Army	F. Coloma				
Navy	G. Pita da Veiga				
Air	J. Salvador	M. Cuadra			
National Movement	T. Fernández Miranda (Vice-President)	J. Utrera		F. Herrero Tejedor	J. Solís
Syndical Relations	E. García-Ramal	A. Fernández Sordo			
Economic Planning	C. Martínez Esteruelas	J. Gutiérrez			

The tenor of the most important bills so far submitted to the Cortes – the one on local government and the one on incompatibilities affecting the post of *procurador* in particular – the handling of certain events like the Añoveros affair,[44] and the dismissal of a minister who had taken too seriously the democratizing spirit of February[45] all repeat a familiar pattern in which promises and realities never meet.

4 ❧ THE SPANISH CORTES

Organic Democracy

In both political theory and practice few terms have undergone greater changes and adulterations than the word democracy. A quick glance through the pages of a work like Jens A. Christophesen's *The Meaning of Democracy*,[1] shows the enormous diversity of meanings, often contradictory, attached to the word over the years. We now live in a period in history dominated by what might be called a democratic fever. All manner of political regimes throughout the world proclaim themselves to be democratic. Franco's regime is no exception. It was born out of the violent reaction of a motley coalition of conservative forces, who felt threatened by a liberal republic which would be incapable of imposing authority from above and of avoiding political polarization at its base. It followed, for a time, the totalitarian model then predominant in Europe. It declared itself opposed to both liberalism and marxism. But nevertheless, from its very beginnings, it waved the democratic banner. In 1937, in the midst of the Civil War, Franco declared to the press: 'The new Spanish State will be an authentic democracy, in which all citizens will participate in the running of the government through their professions and their specific functions.'[2] These words already reveal the kind of democracy Franco had in mind, a democracy of a corporative nature in which Spaniards would exercise their political rights through their other social activities.

The word democracy is used in this chapter with the limited meaning of the election of parliamentary representatives by the people. This was the meaning of Franco in the above quotation, and that was the democracy established with the creation, on 17 July 1942, of a legislative assembly, the Spanish Cortes. Since that date, the Cortes, like all the other institutions of the regime, have changed their form considerably, evolving always along the same democratic path. Official propaganda never failed to point out how extremely democratic the Cortes were at every stage of their development. The words of Franco, once again, epitomize that attitude. In Palencia, in 1962, he said: 'I challenge anyone to mention one single country in the world that can offer a clearer, more stable and more trustworthy form of democracy.'[3]

The democracy of Franco's Spain was called organic democracy. What 'organic' or 'organic democracy' exactly mean remains to be discovered. There is no official definition, and a search through the constitution for a legal explanation contributes little. The choice of the concept might have been made on account of its pragmatic ambiguity. It satisfied the traditionalists inasmuch as it corroborated, in theory at least, one of their basic tenets; it was in line with the opinions which many right-wing politicians had been expressing during the republican years;[4] and it afforded the falangists the opportunity of making a major contribution to the new state. In the words of one of the better known post-Civil War falangists: 'organic representation in its Spanish version, as different from that of other countries, starts from and is founded on José Antonio's doctrinal thesis about the natural units of coexistence, those authentic and vital realities which are Family, Municipality and Syndicate'.[5]

Whatever the intentions behind the adoption of organic democracy, its repercussions were clear. On the one hand, it rejected the liberal democracy of the Second Republic, with its parliamentary representation organized along political party lines. On the other, it brought in, as a substitute, a system of political representation based upon the fascist-like doctrine of Falange. José Antonio Primo de Rivera condensed this transformation in the following words, so often quoted by his supporters: 'Nobody was born a member of a political party; on the other hand, we are all born into a family; we are all resident in a municipality; we all strive hard at a certain job.'[6] Family, municipality and syndicate; 'the three natural units' as José Antonio called them too,[7] were the social channels through which Spaniards would take part in the legislative process. On a closer examination we find that the 'units' are not perhaps as natural as José Antonio thought (certainly not for the purpose he assigned to them), that they have proved insufficient since other forms of representation were opened, and that the Spanish regime did not feel the need to use one of the three – the family – until 1967.

That the family constitutes in our society a basic cell or unit is an undeniable fact. Nor can the existence of a certain community of interests inside the family nucleus and even between different families be denied. Hence the existence of family associations and the protection usually granted by the law – very often at constitutional level – to families.[8] As an important social group, possibly the most important of all, the family plays a major role. But from this one cannot jump to the conclusion that the 'final complement . . . can be active participation of the family in political affairs through the so-called family vote'.[9] Families as such do not, nor should they, become involved in political activities. Nepotism is too great a temptation. When any member of a family joins a certain group engaged in politics, that person is acting not as husband or wife, father or son, but as an individual. Divergence of opinion on political matters within a family is no unusual occurrence. Jiménez de Parga, Professor of the University of Barcelona, has pointed out this failing of José Antonio's theory by underlining that amongst the groups that take an active part in politics (*sujetos políticos* as he calls them) the family is not included.[10]

Furthermore, the concept of the family is excessively broad. As José Antonio himself said, 'we are *all* born into a family'. Thus, by definition, family representatives do not represent any specific interest, as the deputies for a certain province or trade union might do. They find themselves operating in a vacuum, and in practice – as the Spanish experience of the last few years proves – their political activities are geared by interests and goals which have little or nothing to do with the family. One could even recall here the words of Ortega y Gasset – who exercised a tremendous influence on José Antonio Primo de Rivera – when he wrote that the family came later than the state and was a kind of reaction against in politics (*sujetos políticos* as he calls them) the family is not included.[10] to implement the representation of the family in the Cortes, and when in 1967 it did the formula used was anything but organic.

The second 'natural unit' in José Antonio's secular trinity, is the syndicate. A case may possibly be made for it as a channel for political representation in a corporative system, but the attribution to it of 'natural' is highly questionable. Trade unions, in their present form, are an adaptation to the neo-capitalist structure of the organizations which appeared during the nineteenth century to defend the interests of the working classes. Their relations with political elites took different forms over the years and they vary from country to country. In general, however, the major trade unions have tended to form alliances with left-wing political parties and nowadays they rank amongst the most powerful pressure groups in the western World. But these trade unions are not the same thing as José Antonio's syndicates. The 'natural syndicate' of Falange somersaults over the liberalism of the nineteenth century to find its roots in the medieval guilds, in order to justify bringing together, into the same organization, workers and employers. Far from being natural, this syndicate was created and is maintained by force with the aim of controlling the working classes.[12]

The geographical allegiance of the individual citizen to the area in which he lives constitutes the third unit in the organic democracy of the Spanish regime, the municipality. It is the most acceptable of the three. At its best it could be a kind of constituency in the geographical sense of this term. But then, local ties are not peculiar to this third group, they are found in the other groups too, and practice has shown that the members of the Cortes elected through this channel do not represent the people of a constituency, as much as the institutions of local government in that area.

The word Cortes has a long tradition in Spanish history. It was the name applied to the *junta* or body of noblemen that advised the monarch in the medieval kingdoms of Spain. From the beginning of the nineteenth century, starting with the Constitution of Cadiz of 1812 and throughout the constitutional history of the country, the term Cortes has been identified with the legislative chamber, except for a brief period in the 1920s when General Miguel Primo de Rivera first suspended the Cortes and then tried unsuccessfully to replace it with an advisory body under the name of National Assembly. The Cortes, as a legislative assembly, has normally had a two-chamber structure. Only the constitutions of Cadiz and of the Second Republic opted for a single chamber, thus identifying Cortes with a congress of deputies. Franco's regime too set up a one-chamber Cortes, which in its original form of 1942 resembled the Senate more than the Congress, in that most of its members were worthies and notables allocated a seat in the newly-created institution.

The composition of the Cortes has, since its creation in 1942, gone through three major stages (see Table 8). In this evolution, the Cortes has undergone the usual democratizing process, in that it has been transformed from a gathering of appointees into a, broadly speaking, elected assembly[13] – the high-water mark being represented by the introduction of some degree of direct election in 1967. But free elections are not easily associated with an authoritarian regime. What form do elections take? Can one speak of free elections in Spain?

The Electoral System

The elections of the *procuradores* (the members of the Cortes) are of enormous complexity. According to the Law on the Cortes, article 2, there are no fewer than ten different categories of deputies, and the form of election or appointment not only varies from group to group, but it differs considerably even within a single group. One can safely ignore six of those groups and concentrate on the other four: the National Councillors of the Movement, the municipal representatives, the members of the syndicates, and finally the *procuradores familiares*, whose mission is to represent the family in the Cortes. These major groups, with well over a hundred members each, account for more than four-fifths of the total number of *procuradores* in the chamber.

For the sake of clarity, the form of election or appointment of all the *procuradores* has been systematized in six tables (Tables 8–13). The comments which follow apply to the four main groups.

Electors

It is not possible to speak in the Spanish case of universal suffrage, if this we understand to mean one man, one vote. Some people are entitled to vote more than once, whereas others have no vote at all. An example will make this clear. A married, working man in his early twenties can vote in the elections for the family representatives of his province. Since, as a working man, he is a member of a syndicate, he can vote in the syndical elections. If he belongs to the Organization of the National Movement, he is entitled to vote in this group too. And finally he casts his vote, in a long and roundabout way, in the elections of the local government sector. On the other hand, a man of the same age could find himself without any vote, if he is a university student, living with his parents. Since he is not emancipated he cannot vote for the family representatives. He is not employed and does not belong to a syndicate, and therefore has no vote in this sector either. Nor can he go to the polls of the National Movement if he is not a member. Between these two extreme examples, there are several possible combinations with a varying number of votes.

TABLE 8 – COMPOSITION OF THE CORTES

1942	*1946*	*1967*
(a) The Ministers	(a) The Ministers	(a) The Members of the Government
(b) The National Councillors of FET y de las JONS*	(b) The National Councillors†	(b) The National Councillors
(c) The Presidents of The Council of State, The Supreme Court, The Supreme Council of Military Justice	(c) The Presidents of The Council of State, The Supreme Court, The Supreme Council of Military Justice	(c) The Presidents of The Council of State, The Supreme Court, The Supreme Council of Military Justice, The Court of Accounts, The National Economic Council
(d) Representatives of the National Syndicates (their number to be no more than a third of the Cortes)	(d) Representatives of the National Syndicates (their number to be no more than a third of the Cortes)	(d) 150 representatives of the syndical organization
(e) The Mayors of the 50 provincial capitals and those of Ceuta and Melilla 1 representative of the municipalities of each province appointed by the Provincial Council (Diputación)	(e) The Mayors of the 50 provincial capitals and those of Ceuta and Melilla 1 member per province elected by the municipalities	(e) 1 for the municipalities of each province 1 for each municipality with more than 300,000 inhabitants 1 each for Ceuta and Melilla 1 for each provincial council
(f) The rectors of all Spanish universities	1 member for each provincial council (f) The rectors of all Spanish universities	(f) The rectors of all Spanish universities
(g) The President of the Institute of Spain The Presidents of Royal Academies The Chancellors of *Hispanidad*	(g) The President of the Institute of Spain 2 representatives of Royal Academies The President and 2 representatives of CSIC (High Council for Scientific Research)	(g) The President of the Institute of Spain 2 representatives of Royal Academies The President and 2 representatives of CSIC
(h) 7 representatives of professional bodies	(h) 16 representatives of professional bodies	(h) 21 representatives of professional bodies (this group can be increased to a maximum of 30)
(i) 50 members appointed by the Head of State	(i) 50 members appointed by the Head of State	(i) 25 members appointed by the Head of State
		(j) 2 family representatives per province

*All directly or indirectly appointed by the Head of State.

†By a decree of 3 March 1955 the number of councillors was increased by 50, to allow one to be elected for each province. One of the conditions to be elected was to hold or have held a post of authority in the National Movement.

TABLE 9 – COMPOSITION OF THE CORTES: SYNDICAL SECTOR

150 *Procuradores*:

GROUP (A)

Ex-officio members

1 Secretary-General of Syndical Organization

1 Deputy Secretary-General

4 President and Secretary (National Council of Workers, National Council of Employers)

2 National Directors for Administration and Finance, and for Assistance and Promotion

28 Presidents of National Syndicates

1 President of Brotherhood of Farmers and Stockbreeders

1 President of National Federation of Trade

GROUP (B)

84 three elected for each syndicate, one by employers, one by workers, one by technicians

GROUP (C)

12 for the Brotherhood of Farmers and Stockbreeders

2 for the National Federation of Trade

2 for the cooperatives

1 for craftsmen guilds

1 for fishermen associations

1 for the Federation of Press Associations

GROUP (D)

A variable number of *procuradores* elected by the Syndical Congress to complete the total figure of 150

GROUP (B)

Candidates: (1) must be a member of a committee of workers or employers at local, provincial, or national level; (2) must be or have been a *procurador*; or be proposed by 15 presidents of provincial syndicates; or be proposed by 50 members of the syndicate's national committee

Voters: The members of the respective national unions in each syndicate

GROUP (C)

Various complicated systems not very different from the one above are applied in the election of representatives for these groups

GROUP (D)

Candidates: A list is drawn up by the Syndical Congress Executive

Voters: The members of the Standing Committee of Congress

TABLE 10 – COMPOSITION OF THE CORTES: POLITICAL SECTOR
(NATIONAL COUNCIL OF THE MOVEMENT)

112 *Procuradores*:
  GROUP (A) 53 one per province, and one each for Ceuta and Melilla
  GROUP (B) 12 four from each of the other three main sectors (local, syndical and
                family)
  GROUP (C) 40 appointed by the *Caudillo*
  GROUP (D) 6 appointed by the President of the National Council
  GROUP (E) 1 Secretary-General of the National Movement

GROUP (A)
Candidates: (1) must be a member of the National Movement; (2) must be a native of the
  province; or have lived in the province for five years; or be or have been national
  councillor for the province; (3) must be or have been a national councillor; or be
  proposed by five national councillors; or be proposed by ten provincial or local
  councillors of the National Movement
Voters: (1) Delegates of the municipal councils; (2) Delegates of local councils of the
  National Movement; (3) All the provincial councillors; (4) Delegates of the provincial
  councils of the National Movement

GROUP (B)
All twelve are elected from amongst and by the *procuradores* of each of the three sectors

TABLE 11 – COMPOSITION OF THE CORTES: LOCAL SECTOR

111 *Procuradores*:
  GROUP (A) 51 one for the municipalities of each province
  GROUP (B) 7 one for each municipality with more than 300,000 inhabitants[*]
  GROUP (C) 2 one each for Ceuta and Melilla
  GROUP (D) 51 one for each provincial council (*diputación*)

GROUP (A)
Candidates: must be a mayor or a councillor of one of the municipal councils in the
  province
Voters: A delegate of each municipal council in the province (he has as many votes as
  inhabitants in the municipality he represents)

GROUPS (B), (C), (D)
Canditates and voters are the members of the respective corporations

[*]These are Barcelona, Madrid, Valencia, Seville, Saragossa, Bilbao and Málaga

TABLE 12 – COMPOSITION OF THE CORTES: FAMILY SECTOR

104 *Procuradores*:
  102 two elected per province
  2 one each for Ceuta and Melilla

Candidates: (1) must be included in the provincial register of heads of family and married women; or be a native of the province; or have lived in the province for seven years from the age of fourteen; or have interests in the province; (2) must be or have been a *procurador*; or be proposed by five *procuradores*; or be proposed by seven or more than half of the provincial councillors; or be proposed by 1,000 heads of family and married women in the province
Voters: Heads of family and married women

TABLE 13 – COMPOSITION OF THE CORTES: EX-OFFICIO AND APPOINTED MEMBERS

70 *Procuradores*
25 appointed by the Caudillo
20 members of the government
18 university rectors
  1 President of the Institute of Spain
  1 President of the Council of State
  1 President of the High Council for Scientific Research

1 President of the Supreme Court of Justice
1 President of the Court of Accounts
1 President of the National Economic Council
1 President of the Supreme Court of Military Justice
1 President of the Institute of Civil Engineers

TABLE 14 – COMPOSITION OF THE CORTES: PROFESSIONAL SECTOR

26 *Procuradores*, elected by:
2 Royal Academies
2 High Council for Scientific Research
1 Associations of Engineers
2 Bar Associations
2 Colleges of Doctors
1 Colleges of Stockbrokers
1 Colleges of Architects
1 Colleges of Economists
1 Colleges of Pharmacists
1 Colleges of Graduates and Doctors in Arts and Science

1 Colleges of Graduates and Doctors in Physics and Chemistry
1 Colleges of Notaries
1 Colleges of Attorneys
1 Colleges of Property Registrars
1 Colleges of Veterinary Surgeons
1 Colleges of Graduates and Doctors in Political Science
1 Institute of Actuaries
3 Chambers of Commerce
1 Chambers of Urban Property
1 Associations of Tenants

The form of election varies from group to group, but in all cases, candidates and voters have to be members of the respective institution.

The weight of the votes cast varies considerably too. And it does so in two ways. For purely administrative reasons, the geographical areas or constituencies into which the country is divided for the purpose of elections normally correspond with the provinces. Thus, in the election of family representatives, a vote cast in the province of Alava with an electorate of 84,958, or Soria with 65,307 electors, has much more weight than one cast in Barcelona, which has an electorate of 1,805,235 voters.[14] The vote in the family sector, where the elections are direct, is much more important than in the other sectors, which have indirect elections. And in the indirect elections, which go through a number of stages, the polling becomes more relevant and influential as it moves up the ladder.

In order to vote, a number of general conditions have to be met. All voters must, of course, have Spanish nationality. Since all the elections, except those of the family sector, are indirect – with the electorate becoming smaller as the importance of the election increases – only those elected at any one stage have the right to vote at the next.

Let us now turn to the candidates. After all, what matters is the existence of real choice.

Candidates

The general conditions required to stand as a candidate are those of article 3 of the Law on the Cortes, namely, to be a Spanish citizen, to be at least 21 years of age, to enjoy full civil rights and not to be politically disqualified.[15] The first two qualifications require no further explanation. The third one is found in the electoral laws of other countries. It is logical that a criminal who is serving a prison sentence should not be a candidate for election to the Cortes. But the fourth condition of eligibility is more dubious. No definition of it is given.[16] It appears to preclude political opponents of the regime or those who are against the Principles of the National Movement. We are here confronted with what M. Duverger calls '*indignité politique*',[17] a qualification open to all kinds of abuses.

In liberal democracies candidates are normally selected through the political parties, with all the limitation of choice that this imposes on the voter. Nevertheless, a variety of political possibilities is still offered to the electorate and candidates are not usually excluded on account of their views on social, political or economic issues. As there are no political parties in Spain, the selection of candidates is conducted through the channels of organic democracy, with a number of requirements and conditions to achieve a certain type of candidate: people standing for election must be, for the most part, inserted in the official framework of municipal or provincial councils, of the Syndical Organization, or of the National Movement; they must adhere to official ideology; and they must be part of or supported by the political elite. Political elitism is not, of course, a feature exclusive to the Spanish regime. Political power is in any country in the hands of a minority. It is a question of determining whether the minority can be changed, and what is the degree of accessibility to that minority. And it can be said that, whereas the political elite in the liberal democracies is pluralistic and fairly open, the Spanish political elite is monistic and restrictive. The aim of the rules is to create a kind of net which allows through only politically acceptable candidates. Thus, in order to stand for the Cortes, one has to have been a member before, or be supported by a certain number of members of the Cortes, or by a greater number of provincial deputies or local councillors. Since 1967 it has been possible to enter the electoral arena without any official support, but this only affects the *procuradores* who represent the family, which will be considered separately later.

The Mechanics of Elections

In a way, all elections which involve a large electorate are indirect, as there is normally a prior selection of candidates by the political parties. However, in general terms, one can speak of direct elections, when the people vote for those who will sit in the legislative chamber and of indirect elections, when the elections go through a number of stages with an ever-diminishing number of electors.[18]

All elections in Spain, except in the family sector, are indirect. This raises the question of how representative are the Spanish *procuradores*. Whatever Spanish official propaganda may say, the narrower the gap between electors and elected, the greater is the degree of representativeness.[19] And in the syndical sector we find no fewer than five electoral steps between the man on the factory floor and the *procurador* who represents him in the Cortes (group (B) in Table 9). The process begins when the workers of large firms elect their representatives or shop stewards; these together with the employees of small firms elect local committees; the local committees elect the provincial committees; the provincial committees elect national or central committees and finally, at this fifth stage, the national committees elect the *procuradores*. In the local government sector and in the National Movement sector, it is totally impossible to ascertain the degree of indirectness. The elections at national level are entwined with those at municipal and provincial levels, creating a confused tangle of electors and candidates.

The voting is done by means of ballot papers which are put into a glass box. Each elector votes for as many candidates as there are posts to be filled – usually one or two. The normal procedure is for all the papers balloted at any one stage in the elections to be counted as equal. The elections in the local sector are an exception in this respect. The votes of the deputies from the different municipal councils are weighted in accordance with the population of the municipalities they represent. The simple plurality system or 'first-past-the-post-system'[20] is normally applied to the counting of votes.[21] The votes are counted publicly by the electoral board of each polling station, and the candidate who obtains the highest number of votes is elected. There is no question of proportional representation. The aim is to secure representation for minority groups, but political groups or even electoral alliances are forbidden by law. The Spanish *procuradores* are not supposed to represent any particular group or faction; their representation extends to the whole nation.[22] If the counting of votes should create a tie between two candidates, different solutions are applied: the older candidate is preferred in the National Council elections, the less senior one in the local sector. In the family sector, it is decided by the highest number of children, hence the curiosity – at least to the foreign eye – that nearly all candidates in that sector mention in their electoral manifestos the number of children they have.

Other aspects of the mechanics of election, such as the composition of the electoral boards or the systems of appeal, have also been the target of much criticism.[23] Nevertheless, what has been said will suffice as an overall picture of the system.

There is no reason to believe that any large-scale illegal practices take place in elections. They are not necessary. The regime has made sure that the dice are loaded in its favour. The complex electoral legislation allows them enough room to achieve the desired results without overstepping the boundaries of legality. Four major objections could be levelled at the system in this respect:

1. The executive enjoys a great many discretionary powers. A considerable number of the electoral rules are laid down by governmental decree or by ministerial regulations and can be altered in the same way.
2. The electorate is divided and subdivided into innumerable sections and categories, making it difficult for individual electors to see what they are voting for, and creating an unjust allocation of the suffrage.
3. The candidates are subjected to all kinds of political controls and

checks and they, in their turn, are allowed few and limited forms of redress.
4. The bodies entrusted with the running of elections (Mesas Electorales and Juntas del Censo) cannot, by their composition, act independently and objectively in resolving any case which involves interests of the regime.

All these general objections can be seen in the election of representatives for the family sector. This type of representative did not appear in the Cortes until 1967. Its appearance completed the idea of organic democracy and introduced, for the first time, direct elections to the Cortes. This final point seemed to represent a bold step; at long last some Spaniards would be able to elect *procuradores* directly, without any intermediary. But was this change as radical as it appeared?

The 'Procuradores' of the Family Sector

This group of *procuradores*, though one of the major groups in the Cortes, still represents less than one-fifth of the whole chamber: only 104 of a possible 562 or about 18.5 per cent of the total Cortes are directly elected. It was a small change, but a decisive one, or so it appeared when the family sector was introduced at the beginning of 1967 by the Organic Law of the State. A law was passed soon after to implement the change;[24] and two general elections have since been held, one in autumn 1967 and the other in autumn 1971. The life of the ninth Cortes spanned the two elections, and the tenth Cortes is now well advanced, so we have several years' experience on which to assess how the Cortes are affected by the presence of a directly elected minority. It is not yet possible to determine the long-term effects particularly after Franco's disappearance, but there is already enough information to see how things are likely to develop. The rules established for the election of the family representatives, the two elections so far held, the kind of *procuradores* elected via this channel, and their activities and influence inside the Cortes should provide sufficient indicators.

The universal right to vote is not granted in this sector. Only heads of families and married women are entitled to vote. And although the concept of head of family has been broadened to cover not only heads of households but also those people who, without being married, live independently, the concession of the vote is still highly restrictive.

As for the candidates, the two essential conditions mentioned earlier still apply. Two connections are necessary; a geographical link with the province one wishes to represent, and an affinity with the political elite. The latter can be replaced by the support of 1,000 members of the electorate in the province. This undoubtedly offers people who are not part of, or connected with, the political elite a chance to enter the Cortes. In practice, however, gathering 1,000 authenticated signatures of voters is not easy. The prospective candidate must act alone, without the support of any political group or party. Not surprisingly, a majority of the candidates do not use this system. In 1967 64 per cent of the 328 candidates[25] availed themselves of one of the other forms of support.

The electoral campaign is subject to detailed and strict rules, apparently to give all candidates a fair and equal chance. In practice, however, the well-known candidates, those who have already been *procuradores* and those who hold or have held public office, have a great advantage. Their names are, usually, more familiar to the electorate. The campaign only lasts fifteen days. All candidates can have their programme or manifesto publicized, free of charge, by the provincial press and radio. But it must be limited to 500 words[26] and censored before publication.[27] Censorship is applied to all the other propaganda used by the candidates, and holding electoral meetings requires official approval too. The candidates have to finance their own campaigns since raising of funds through subscriptions, collections, fairs or any other form of public appeal is forbidden, and any candidate who made use of them would be disqualified. In general a candidate, in order to carry out a competitive electoral campaign and have a reasonable chance of success, needs some measure of official support or private means to cover the costs.[28]

Against this oppressive background it is no wonder the 1967 and 1971 elections have yielded such disappointing results, both in terms of electoral participation and in the type of *procurador* elected.

The 1967 and 1971 Elections

It is customary to focus analysis of electoral results on two major aspects: the participation of the electorate, and the failure or success of the different political parties. Only the first is relevant in the Spanish situation. We can, however, look into other problems, such as the regional distribution of votes, and the socio-political status of the successful candidates, which will allow us to draw conclusions from the results.

The electoral register for the family sector was, in 1967, 16,415,139. In 1971, it had gone up to 17,231,172 voters, an increase of 816,033 or 4.9 per cent. This electorate is very unequally distributed over the country. For a number of reasons – geographical, climatological, economic, etc. – the population of Spain is very unevenly spread. The problem is not new, but it has been considerably worsened during the last decade by the massive movements of people from the less developed agricultural areas into the industrialized provinces. The fact that each province returns two *procuradores* creates, as pointed out earlier, an extremely unjust situation, as can be seen in the following table.

TABLE 15 – UNEQUAL DISTRIBUTION OF THE ELECTORATE:
LARGE AND SMALL EXTREMES

Province	Electorate	
	1967	*1971*
Barcelona	1,805,235	1,956,426
Madrid	1,565,777	1,709,086
Valencia	889,818	958,670
Segovia	92,828	89,673
Alava	84,958	91,573
Soria	65,307	71,771

The gap between the extremes of Barcelona and Soria is enormous and it is getting greater. In Segovia the electorate decreased between 1967 and 1971, and the same happened in other provinces, mostly in central Spain, such as Zamora, Teruel, Palencia, Cuenca.

A vote in Soria carries more weight than a vote in Madrid or Barcelona. Soria is over-represented, whereas Madrid and Barcelona are under-represented. The negative effects are also felt by the candidates. It is more costly to run an electoral campaign in a province with a large electorate. In the 1971 elections the two successful candidates in Barcelona polled together 644,770 votes. The two in Soria obtained only 51,817, so to become a *procurador* in Barcelona it was necessary to poll twelve times as many votes as in Soria. And this calculation is made without taking into consideration the much heavier polling in Soria.

The Spain that is over-represented is the conservative Spain of the Castilian plateau, the Spain that at the elections during the Second Republic sent right-wing deputies to the Cortes, the Spain with less demographical weight and populated by the traditional *clases medias*. The other Spain, more developed, more populated, more politically aware and, in general, more troublesome for the regime, is denied fair representation. It is not possible to give any other interpretation to such an unjust distribution. Even if the province is a convenient and ready-made constituency, why is no use made of some method of proportional representation which would take into account the demographical variations? The Second Republic[29] used the provinces as constituencies too, but the number of deputies was calculated on the basis of one for every 50,000 inhabitants.[30]

In 1967, when direct elections were a novelty and a ray of hope for the future, the number of candidates for the 108 seats was 328. In 1971 this figure came down by 24 per cent to 250, and it was further reduced during the electoral campaign by the withdrawal of 17 candidates. In five provinces – Toledo, Avila, Guadalajara, Teruel and Las Palmas – only two candidates stood for elections in 1971, and voters in those constituencies were offered no choice. Less than 50 per cent (48 out of 104)[31] of the 1967 family representatives stood for re-election in 1971. One is left with the impression that between the two elections frustration led to disillusion and finally to a lack of interest, reflected in fewer participants and the retreat of many who might have seen in the family sector a chance to change the system from inside. The purely impressionistic nature of these comments must, however, be underlined. It will be necessary to wait another decade or so to see whether this disappointing trend is confirmed by future elections.

A major concern of the regime has been to secure a high poll in the elections for the family sector. The greater the number of votes, the larger the support for the system of organic democracy. The publicity surrounding the elections and the facilities given to voters, in the form of free paid time to cast their vote, failed to achieve that goal. On 30 September 1971 one of the headlines on the front page of the syndicalist paper *Pueblo* read: '*Gran Participación*' ('Great Participation'). It referred to the elections held the day before. The results printed on the inside pages told a different story. The national average poll was 50 per cent approximately; lower than that of 1967, which had already shown a poor turnout for a general election.[32]

In 1967, 58 per cent of the electorate went to the polls, but the voters were very unevenly distributed, with the more densely populated and more developed provinces showing the lowest interest, and the more traditional and less populated the highest. The two extremes were represented by Soria, in central Spain, where 90 per cent of the electorate voted, and Guipúzcoa, in the Basque country, with 36.8 per cent. The pattern was repeated in 1971, with the general level of participation considerably lower. The map shows quite clearly the contrast in the

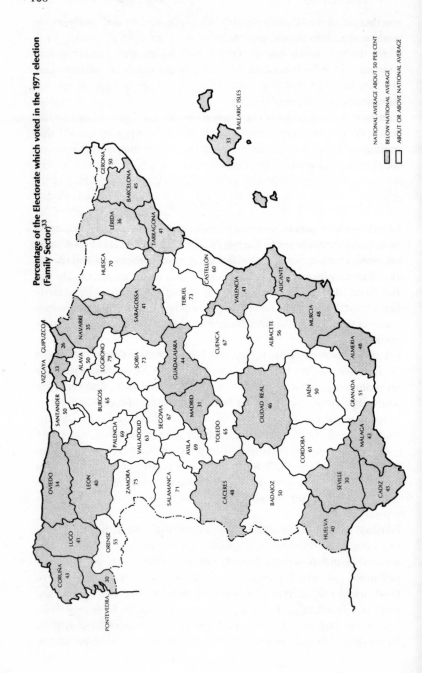

Percentage of the Electorate which voted in the 1971 election (Family Sector)[33]

CORUÑA 43
LUGO 41
PONTEVEDRA 30
ORENSE 55
OVIEDO 34
LEON 40
ZAMORA 75
SALAMANCA 71
VALLADOLID 63
PALENCIA 69
SANTANDER 50
VIZCAYA 33
GUIPUZCOA 26
ALAVA 50
NAVARRE 35
LOGROÑO 79
BURGOS 65
SORIA 73
SEGOVIA 67
AVILA 69
MADRID 31
GUADALAJARA 44
HUESCA 70
SARAGOSSA 41
LÉRIDA 36
GERONA 50
BARCELONA 45
TARRAGONA 41
TERUEL 73
CASTELLON 60
VALENCIA 41
ALICANTE 49
CUENCA 67
ALBACETE 56
MURCIA 48
ALMERIA 48
GRANADA 51
JAEN 50
CIUDAD REAL 46
TOLEDO 65
CACERES 48
BADAJOZ 50
CORDOBA 61
SEVILLE 30
MALAGA 43
CADIZ 45
HUELVA 40
BALEARIC ISLES 33

NATIONAL AVERAGE ABOUT 50 PER CENT

☐ BELOW NATIONAL AVERAGE

☐ ABOUT OR ABOVE NATIONAL AVERAGE

number of votes between central and peripheral Spain, and between developed and traditional provinces.

All the big industrialized centres, such as the two coastal Basque provinces, Oviedo, Barcelona, Madrid, Seville, Valencia, are well below the national average. Local explanations would account for the deviant behaviour of certain provinces. Thus, Guadalajara, for instance, in New Castile, had a low poll, but this may be partly explained by there being only two candidates for the two places.[34] By contrast, three other provinces, Toledo, Ávila and Teruel, in which only two candidates stood for election, had an incredibly high poll.

The 'Procuradores' Political Background

Direct elections in the family sector have had a very small effect on the composition and life of the Cortes. If anything, they have allowed us to see more clearly the limited plurality in the system. The tensions between the right-wing groups behind the regime have come nearer the surface. But that is all. The *procuradores*, and the majority of candidates too, in the family sector are more often than not linked to the regime by two umbilical cords: an ideological one, in that they share the basic principles upon which the regime is founded; and an administrative link with the executive by virtue of their holding posts in the National Movement organization, in the syndicates, in the central administration or in local government, posts to which they have been freely appointed and from which they can be dismissed in the same way. The lack of independence of many of the family representatives *vis-à-vis* the executive is only too evident.

Sixty-two per cent of the candidates[35] who stood for election were in that way dependent on the executive. And they were the most successful, for, of the 104 members of the Cortes who were elected to form the family sector, 71, that is 68 per cent, came from this group.[36] These figures represent a conservative estimate. Only provincial councillors of the National Movement, people holding syndical posts at either national or provincial level, high-ranking officials in the administration – such as Under-Secretaries or Director-Generals – and mayors, presidents of provincial councils, and civil governors,[37] or recent holders of any of these new posts have been included. In the 1967 elections results were very similar, 68 out of the 108 family representatives belonged to one or more of the categories mentioned.[38] The existence in the elections to the family sector of candidates with "official" backing is openly accepted and frequently mentioned in the press, and when the unexpected happens and these candidates fail to win, it causes quite a stir.[39]

In spite of all these limitations, the family representatives enjoy greater independence than any other *procuradores*. Most have close connections with the executive, but, at least, they do not lose their seat in the Cortes if those connections are severed, as do many of their colleagues, such as the *procuradores* in the local sector who were originally all appointed. No democratic claim was made in respect of their position. All the mayors of provincial capitals and all the presidents of provincial councils were nominated by the executive and guaranteed a seat in the Cortes. Now, although mayors and presidents of provincial councils are still appointed, the *procuradores* of the Local Sector are elected (see Table 8, p. 94, and Table 11, p. 96). This apparently democratic change has proved totally irrelevant. The mayors and the presidents of provincial councils, by some strange coincidence, are in all cases elected as *procuradores* of the local sector. In the 1971 elections all but one of the 111 posts were filled in this way.[40] The exception was the province of Albacete, where a municipal councillor was elected, but the mayor of the provincial capital became a *procurador* a few days later when he was re-elected to the National Council of the Movement.

The consequences of this situation are far-reaching. The *procuradores* are totally deprived of freedom. They cannot take a critical stance without the risk of dismissal from their posts as mayors or presidents of provincial councils, which, in turn, would mean losing their seats in the Cortes. The *procuradores* themselves realize their precarious situation. 'Very often mayors and presidents of provincial councils have confided in me their worries saying: how am I going to vote freely if I know that a decision I take in the Cortes may bring about my dismissal?'[41] These are the words of Juan Manuel Fanjul, one of the family representatives for Madrid in the last Cortes. And they are not without foundation. In September 1970, the President of the Provincial Council of Asturias, Sr López Muñiz, was dismissed, against his will, by the Minister of the Interior, with the result that he automatically ceased to be a *procurador* and, what was much more serious, he also lost his post as member of the Council of the Realm. Sr López Muñiz expressed publicly his disagreement with the decision of his superiors and denounced the inherent dangers for the Cortes and the Council of the Realm.[42] The official justification for the dismissal was that Sr López Muñiz had been head of the Provincial Council of Asturias for too long and that the time to change had come.

The situation is very much the same in the other groups of *procuradores*. The whole assembly with its 562 members[43] does not give an encouraging impression. Some 259 members suffer from the same insecurity of tenure as mayors and presidents of provincial councils. Any of them can at any time to replaced by the executive. A big reshuffle in the Government is followed by a large number of changes in the Cortes.[44] The post of *procurador* is not subject to strict conditions of incompatibility.[45] Many of the *procuradores* who cannot be freely dismissed have political or even economic ties with the regime, curtailing considerably their freedom and independence. Should they, however, wish to ignore the weakness and basic insecurity of their position, what are their chances of success?

The Cortes at Work

Strictly speaking, the Cortes is not the legislative power. At the present moment the supreme power to legislate rests with Franco.[46] The Cortes is an organic assembly that partakes in the legislative process and serves as a forum where the viewpoints and plans of the Government are aired and mildly discussed. Constitutionally, it represents the highest share offered to Spaniards in the running of the State, and it is entrusted with the elaboration and approval of the laws.[47] But, once again, its day-to-day running is severely restricted and even dominated by the executive power, and, in its turn, it has few means of control over the latter.

The Cortes met for the first time, after the Civil War, on 16 March 1943. At first the life of a Cortes was three years; after 1967 it was increased to four. The present Cortes is the tenth legislative assembly of Franco's rule. The changes in its composition over the years were mentioned earlier in this chapter. Parallel to those structural changes, the Cortes underwent alterations of functions and procedures, aimed at vivifying its meetings and giving some force to its resolutions and decisions. The effect was partially achieved. The interventions of members in the different committees of the Cortes resemble, if vaguely, a proper debate; the number of amendments to government Bills, put forward by members of the Cortes, has increased considerably in the last few years; the greater attention paid by the press to the chamber has brought into the news the activities of *procuradores*, and has turned some of them into public figures. All this and much more may justify some authors in saying that the Cortes 'will, if they act sensibly, become one of the centres in the political future of Spain'.[48] The double use of future – the tense and the noun – in this quotation is very telling. In the future the Cortes may become more representative, and may enjoy greater autonomy and even become a centre of power, but at present this is far from being the case.

The procedures for the running of the Cortes are contained in a rather lengthy set of Standing Orders, known in Spanish as *Reglamento de las Cortes Españolas*. They were issued by law on 26 December 1957, had some slight alterations in July 1967, and underwent a major overhaul in November 1971, just before the present Cortes came into existence. Prior to 1957, there was a provisional Reglamento, dated 5 January 1943, which was slightly modified too in July 1946. Notwithstanding all these modifications in the set of procedures the basic principles have remained practically unaltered since the 1943 Reglamento.[49] The established rules do not grant much autonomy to the Cortes; in all its proceedings and functions the legislative chamber is put under direct or indirect executive control.

The Cortes are overshadowed by the powerful figure of their President. 'They belong to the kind of assemblies with a strong President', as Fraga Iribarne admits.[50] The President used to be appointed by decree of the Head of State, but in 1967 the procedure was altered. The Council of the Realm is now involved in the appointment, by the system of *ternas*; he selects three names for the post, from which the Head of State chooses the President of the Cortes. So far, the Cortes have had three different Presidents. The first and longest-serving, Esteban de Bilbao y Eguía, held office from 1943 to 1965; he was a traditionalist by conviction and one of the major 'legislative brains' of the regime. He was succeeded by another traditionalist, Antonio Iturmendi Bañales, who, in November 1969, resigned to be replaced by a falangist, Alejandro Rodríguez de Valcárcel. The first two were directly designated by Franco, while the third appointment was made by the new method, with the Council of the Realm in its intermediary role.

Time limits were also imposed on the office of President. It will no longer be possible to chair the meetings of the Cortes for twenty-two years, without interruption, as Esteban Bilbao did. The office of President of the Cortes is held for a period of six years. It does not coincide with the life of the Cortes, which only lasts four years, and it is longer too than the five-year period of the Head of Government. Normally, the President will serve his six years, at the end of which, in view of the silence of the law on this matter, it must be assumed that he could be reappointed. On the other hand, he may not serve his full term, because he resigns – as Sr Iturmendi did – or becomes incapacitated or is dismissed by the Head of State. (The agreement of the Council of the Realm is necessary for his dismissal.)

Together with the President, two Vice-Presidents and four Secretaries – all six elected by the *procuradores* – form the board presiding over the

Cortes. But the real authority inside the chamber is in the hands of the President. His powers are really enormous. He is the supreme arbiter, maintaining discipline in the Cortes, making sure that normal procedures are adhered to, and interpreting and supplementing the Standing Orders when necessary. He convenes all the meetings of the Cortes – both those of the different committees and the plenary sessions. He appoints the chairman and deputy chairman of all the committees. In fact, he himself can chair any committee if he wishes. He appoints, too, at the proposal of the Standing Committee and with the agreement of the government, members of all committees, except where the composition of a committee is determined by law.[51] Conjointly with the government he determines the agenda of any meeting. Indeed, it is an impressive array of powers,[52] which extend beyond the precincts of the Cortes as he also presides over the Council of the Realm and the Regency Council.[53]

The figure and attributions of the ordinary Cortes member look small and emasculated by comparison. He is not elected to represent any specific group, not even the sector to which he owes his election. The *procurador* is expected to represent the Spanish nation as a whole and to enter the Cortes unencumbered by mandates of any nature whatsoever. Detachment from group interests and an altruistic attitude centred on national interests are fine theoretical points. In practice, however, the *procurador* finds himself impotent in isolation, and totally dominated by the President of the Cortes. Affinities between different members of the Cortes do exist, but members are not allowed to develop into concrete groups capable of framing policies. In the Chamber members have to take their seats in alphabetical order and even this seems an obstacle to the formation of groups. Not that the desire to unite has been very prevalent in the Cortes, but whenever it has appeared it has immediately been stifled. During the course of 1968, a group of family representatives held meetings in several Spanish cities – Pamplona, Salamanca, Saragossa, Barcelona – but the government, through the Ministry of the Interior, put a sudden end to this. The meeting which these *procuradores* – about seventy of them – had planned to hold in Ceuta at the end of September to discuss the Statutes of the National Movement, the Syndical Law and the Press Law was banned. The President and the Standing Committee of the Cortes backed up the government's decision. They decided that the *procuradores* could only hold meetings, except for exceptional cases, on the premises of the Cortes.[54]

Of the two principal functions usually carried out by parliaments – legislation and control over the executive – the Cortes partakes in the former and has only a very marginal share in the latter. The initiative in matters of legislation has always been the government's.[55] In theory, any member of the Cortes can put forward a legislative proposal if he can obtain the signatures of fifteen members – if they all belong to the same legislative committee – or of fifty from any part of the chamber. (This is not an easy task when one considers that members always have to act in an individual capacity, without backing and group organization.) Besides, the chances of a private member's Bill being included in the agenda – let alone becoming law – are very remote. In all cases, the agreement of the Government has to be sought, and an unwanted Bill can be postponed from the agenda *sine die* – a device which the government never has to use, for the Cortes has proved itself to be even more conservative than the Government. The Standing Committee of the Cortes has always tended to reject, on the basis of some technicality or other, any forward-looking Bills proposed by *procuradores*.[56]

Once a Bill is fed into the legislative machinery of the Cortes, the procedure is as follows. It is first passed to the appropriate committee and its text published in the Cortes Official Bulletin. Members have twenty days – more in some exceptional cases – to suggest amendments. A *ponencia* – a small group of *procuradores*, members of the committee dealing with the Bill – will then, in view of the amendments submitted, draft a new Bill. This draft is debated by the full committee, and is sent in its final form to the plenary session of the Cortes for approval. The *ponencia* works as a specialized and carefully selected team. The Cortes, in its full meetings, performs a solemn and, at times, enthusiastic rubber-stamping act. Only at committee level does anything approaching a parliamentary debate take place. Debates inside the committee, however, lack vitality. They are conducted within the narrow limits set by the Standing Orders and applied by the chairman, who, as said earlier, is appointed by the President of the Cortes, and the meetings are usually very badly attended.

The number of suggested amendments to Government Bills has increased noticeably in the last few years. The Syndical Bill in 1969 and the Education Reform Bill in 1970 were each followed by more than one thousand papers suggesting amendments. If a Bill is substantially changed under the weight of so many amendments, the government can always withdraw it at any stage; a measure which is never taken since the alterations introduced in the transit from Bill to law, as a result of the amendments suggested by *procuradores*, are rather insignificant as a whole.

The dedication shown and the energy spent in the preparation of so many amendments by the *procuradores* create a false impression of the Cortes as a real hive of legislative activity, when the truth is that indifference and apathy pervade its everyday life. More often than not *procuradores* are not present in the chamber to defend the amendments they have suggested, even when the bill under discussion is of primary importance.[57] The attendance at committee meetings is so low that frequently they are held without the required quorum. The special committee that dealt with the Bill containing the new Standing Orders for the Cortes conducted its proceedings without reaching the necessary quorum at most of its meetings. The article that establishes that more than half of the members of a committee must attend for its decisions to be valid was passed without quorum![58]

The government does not appear to want greater participation, nor is more participation physically possible in many instances. Membership of the Cortes is not a full-time job. All the *procuradores* have other interests to which they will always pay more attention, for it is from them that they earn their livelihood. A Cortes member receives a ridiculously small payment of 10,000 pesetas (£83 approximately) a month, plus travelling and subsistence expenses to attend meetings in Madrid.[59] In consequence, the rooms of the Palace of the Cortes, in the centre of Madrid, are usually frequented by an assiduous minority of *procuradores* dedicated to the monotonous routine of the day-to-day work of the different committees, while the rest reserve their appearance for the more ceremonial gatherings of the full Cortes.

The Cortes has to meet in plenary session at least four times a year. Until 1971 these meetings were even more infrequent; three was the number required. There are, too, extraordinary meetings like the one called in July 1969 for Franco to announce to the Cortes his decision to nominate Prince Juan Carlos as his successor. The plenary sessions deal with all the most important Bills, those which are required by law to be approved at that level.[60] There is no debate at these meetings. The Bill is approved or rejected as a whole. There are no votes on separate aspects or individual items of the Bill.[61] Debate takes the form of a monologue by a minister or a well-known *procurador*.

After the preliminary formalities, the meeting gets under way with the reading to the *procuradores* of the text of the Bill drafted in committee. Then, *procuradores* whose amendments have not been incorporated into the Bill by the committee may put their case to the Cortes, if they wish and if the amendment had at least ten supporting votes at the committee stage. Very rarely does a *procurador* take advantage of this opening, because if he failed to convince the committee, he is much less likely to succeed in the plenary session. The Bill is then defended by a leading member of the committee; he is followed on the rostrum – all the speeches to the Cortes are delivered from a special platform situated in the centre – by the minister concerned; and, finally, a vote is taken, with a result between unanimity and, occasionally a half dozen noes or abstentions.[62]

The course of a Bill through the Cortes is fairly long and procedurally complex, but, for the most part, the share given to the *procuradores* is irrelevant and innocuous. Nevertheless, this legislative function is the most important one of the Cortes. Outside the legislative sphere, the Cortes cannot exercise any control over the executive. The opinion expressed by the government on this question leaves no room for doubt. When the present Standing Orders of the Cortes were at the Bill stage, the Government included a paragraph which read: 'Under no circumstances shall the Cortes have the right to express political opinions or assessments on the actions of the government.' These words were eventually deleted, but they illustrate quite well the government's view of the Cortes's role.

The ministers are not subject to any pressure in the Cortes. The *procuradores* cannot ask spontaneous questions, nor do the ministers take part in debates. There are no searching interrogations or embarrassing confrontations. The *procuradores* can raise questions and requests in writing to the government through the office of the President of the Cortes. The government is not, however, compelled to answer. It may decline to do so for 'reasons of national interest'. Questions on general policy put to the government or to a certain ministry (when they are answered) have to be answered orally. But here too spontaneity is avoided. The questioner is given up to thirty minutes to make his point, to which the minister then responds with his prepared answer.[63] No vote, of course, is taken on the subject. This type of question on general policy is so rare that years go by without a single one being tabled. More common, and of late more frequent, are questions requesting information or clarification on some specific point. These have to be answered in writing within thirty days, but the government seems to hold them in such contempt that in a majority of cases its reply is given well after the thirty days limit.[64] In contrast with the few opportunities the *procuradores* have to address the government, the ministers can speak to the Cortes whenever they judge it necessary.

The Francoist Cortes are now more than thirty years old: thirty years of ministerial monologue delivered to a carefully selected audience. Organic democracy would be more acceptable, even for those who disagree with it in principle, if it were allowed to operate more freely. Freedom is lacking both in the composition and in the functioning of the Spanish Cortes. The Government seems to fear the opposition that might be generated in a more open and flexible situation. And the Cortes remains 'a chamber of applause, amen and silence'.

5 ❧ THE NATIONAL MOVEMENT

To speak of the Movement is to speak of the very essence of the Spanish regime. It is impossible to understand the latter without entering the labyrinthine structure of the former. After Franco, who has always been the major axis of the system, the Movement is its most vital part. We can detect between the two the kind of relationship that connects an artist to the work of his life. Franco was the artist, the creator; the Movement is his work, his creation. Its creation was not the logical outcome of a decision taken with a clear aim and carefully developed. On the contrary, the Movement had a highly pragmatic genesis and evolution, and its structural alterations and changes in direction over the years appear the result more of expediency than of rational planning. They were largely brought about by the desire to survive at moments of crisis, when the regime was threatened by forced changes or even, on one or two occasions, by total overthrow. Consequently, the National Movement is at present almost impossible to define, because Franco has used it as the arena of compromise, as the point of equilibrium for all the rivalries and tensions amongst the political forces inside the regime. The National Movement has become a shapeless, controversial, politically promiscuous institution – the one that offers the best insight into the regime created by Franco.

What is the National Movement?[1] It is much easier to formulate the question than to answer it. There is certainly no short and clear-cut definition of the National Movement. Official sources in Spain claim that it is neither a political ideology nor a political party, though, as we shall see, it has a great deal in common with both. Perhaps it will help our understanding of the Movement to concentrate on the longer but more fruitful task of looking at the National Movement from different angles.

Franco on one occasion gave five different meanings to the expression National Movement.[2] Rodríguez de Valcárcel, President of the Cortes, found four different ways of interpreting it.[3] José Antonio Primo de Rivera had always liked to refer to Falange as a movement rather than a party.[4] It is not unusual to see the label National Movement applied to the combination of military forces and right-wing groups that rose against the government of the Second Republic in July 1936, as well as to the war that followed.[5] In this sense, National Movement is the equivalent of Crusade of Liberation; however, this use of the expression is not common nowadays. National Movement has also been used as a synonym of FET y de las JONS, the political party founded by Franco during the course of the Civil War;[6] and even, at times, its significance has been broadened to the point of considering it as the very basis of the constitutional order and, therefore, of the State.[7]

The legal definition given by article 5 of the Organic Law of the State in 1967 cannot be said to throw much light upon the confused situation. From the semantic maze that confronts us when looking at the National Movement, three main meanings can be discerned at the present moment:

1. A political doctrine, or set of principles contained in one of the Fundamental Laws;
2. A political consensus, or, as it is officially called, a 'communion'; the theoretical sharing of all Spaniards in those principles;
3. A political organization, which has absorbed and diluted the original FET y de las JONS within a larger frame.

All three meanings are closely interrelated and appear deeply rooted in the ideology and structure of FET y de las JONS. Whatever other meanings the expression National Movement may have acquired over the years, whatever transformation, broadening or dilution it may have undergone, it must be viewed as a continuation of FET y de las JONS. Therefore, it seems appropriate to delineate some of the features of the latter before considering in turn the three main meanings listed above.

The Fascist Origins of the National Movement

One of the adjectives most frequently applied to the Spanish regime as a whole, and in particular to the National Movement, is that of fascist. This term has degenerated through overuse, and it would only be applicable to the present-day Spanish situation if it were stretched to cover any right-wing authoritarian regime. But the term was at one time more fitting. In the origins of the Spanish regime, and more so in the origins of the National Movement, one finds most of the features common to the different fascisms prevalent in the Europe of the thirties.

The origin of the National Movement is to be found in the Decree of Unification of 19 April 1937. With that decree Franco forced a kind of political unity amongst the different groups that were fighting under his supreme command in the Civil War. Out of the forces united by the decree two groups stood out for their political commitment: the FET y de las JONS and the Carlists or *Requetés*. In fact, they were the only groups mentioned in the text of the decree.[8] We can safely ignore the Carlists now. They provided a few ministers to Franco's cabinets, but most Carlists, in the words of Dionisio Ridruejo,[9] 'returned to their Navarrese mountains' at the end of the Civil War and have remained there ever since, except for the occasional sally in support of the Carlist pretender to the Spanish throne.

It was left to the Falange to provide the political ideology of the regime, and this ideology was clearly a fascist one. It is true that the main theorists of Spanish fascism often denied that the political organizations they created were simply reproductions of the Italian and the German models. The following passage exemplifies this attitude: 'FET y de las JONS is not a fascist movement; it coincides with fascism is some essential matters of universal value, but it is progressively acquiring individual features and it is along this path that it will find its most rewarding development.'[10] This kind of denial must, however, be put into perspective. What José Antonio Primo de Rivera was rejecting was not the features that his movement obviously shared with other fascist movements, but rather the existence of fascism as a supranational movement. Whereas communism has always had an international aim, fascism never had any serious desire to create a supranational community. Fascism, in one form or another, spread to a great many countries during the thirties, but it was always founded upon certain national values: racial, historical, cultural, traditional, etc. which varied from country to country. Once again, this was overtly stated by J. A. Primo de Rivera: 'We are told that we are but imitators because our movement, our returning to the genuine Spain, is a movement which has already occurred in other places. Italy and Germany have turned inwards, despairing, from myths which were threatening to render them sterile. But just because Italy and Germany have turned inwards and found their real selves, are we to say that Spain is imitating them when searching for her own self? These countries turned toward their own reality and when we do the same, what we shall find is our own reality; it will not be Italy's or Germany's, and, therefore, when we reproduce what the Italians or the Germans have done we shall be more Spanish than ever before.'[11]

R. Ledesma Ramos, the other major theoretician of Spanish fascism, expressed similar thought in a more abbreviated form: 'It is obvious that whenever we use the word 'fascism' we do so as a concession to its world-wide use, but without much faith in its accuracy, since we are inclined to deny that fascism as such has universal characteristics.'[12]

The fascist nature of FE and the JONS, both before and after their fusion, is so clear that it is already accepted in official circles in Spain.[13] All the major features of fascism are found in the falangist doctrine. Falange is fascist, not only in external aspect – uniform, salute, para-military organization, etc. – but in its real essence. Irrationality, violence as a legitimate means to an end, the idea of a ruling elite, the totalitarian concept of the state, its corporative nature, are all characteristics clear in the falangist doctrine. That it was never able to put that doctrine into practice is a different matter.

Falange, José Antonio's Falange, disappeared with the Decree of Unification in April 1937. Before the war it was a small party. Stanley Payne says that 'by no method of computation could the party's immediate following [in February 1936] have been fixed at more than 25,000'.[14] It was a minute party compared to anarchists or socialists, whose membership reached the hundreds of thousands. The number of early falangists killed during the war was considerable. Payne believes that as many as 60 per cent of the *camisas viejas* – as the original members came to be called – might have been killed during the conflict.[15] On top of this, the Decree of Unification not only threw together Falangists and *Requetés*, but, by turning FET y de las JONS into the one and only political party officially accepted, opened the flood-gates of membership to a considerable number of people, who joined the party either compulsorily – as in the case of Army officers – or because they were hoping that the official uniform of blue shirt and red beret would bring them some gain. The real falangists were drowned by this sudden flood of new arrivals. José

Antonio's movement or party had reached the end of its short and not very brilliant history.

What happened afterwards to the *camisas viejas* constitutes a rather sad story. Some rejected the falangist ideals as an impossible dream, a youthful mistake generated in the politically explosive atmosphere of the thirties.[16] Some fell into nostalgia; they could not bring themselves to accept the change forced by the Decree of Unification, and longed for a return to the purity of José Antonio's ideas. Many adopted a chameleon-like attitude, adapting themselves to the changes imposed by Franco and explaining them in the light of the falangist doctrine.

Ideologically the party created by Franco was based upon the Falange of José Antonio. FET y de las JONS took as its official ideology the twenty-six points of Falange, which were drafted by Ledesma Ramos, founder of the JONS, and José Antonio in 1934, as a kind of programme for Falange. Originally there were twenty-seven points, but the final one had to be left out by Franco, since it opposed any kind of political alliance unless Falange was given control of it. This choice of political doctrine was understandable. It was the reverse of the system of the Second Republic, against which Franco's troops and followers were fighting. It rejected all political parties, thus providing a justification for imposing doctrinal unity – a very valuable tool in a war. It favoured the idea of a single and omnipotent *jefe*, which Franco must have found appealing. And behind all the trumpeting of a national–syndicalist revolution, it recognized private property and private enterprise to appease those who were in favour of a capitalist economy. The falangist doctrine may not have entirely satisfied anybody on the nationalist side, but it was a ready-made solution, an ideal compromise that Franco was quick to accept and impose.

Did the acceptance of the falangist creed as the official doctrine turn Franco's Spain into a totalitarian state of the fascist type? The answer must be negative. The totalitarian idea never quite crystallized in Spain, although all the necessary ingredients were available, for a number of reasons, both external and internal. Internationally, the Second World War had a considerable influence on Spanish politics, although Spain did not become directly involved. There can be no doubt that if the Axis powers had fared more successfully, Franco would have embraced openly the political principles of Germany and Italy at the time. The argument sometimes used that totalitarianism did not fit in with Franco's own ideas about society and politics[17] is difficult to accept; he has revealed tremendous ideological fickleness over the years in order to maintain his own position at the top. At home, a number of reasons could be found. It might have been, as Professor Weiss has pointed out, that Spain at the end of the thirties had not reached that stage of socio-economic development in which fascist ideas easily prosper.[18] The strange collusion of forces behind Franco, the influence of the clerical element, the predominance of the military in a war situation all influenced non-totalitarian development. The major one, however – and at the same time cause and effect – was the fact that the party FET y de las JONS was never allowed or able to gain overall control of the State. The party was no more than a tool in the hands of the dictator. FET y de las JONS did not have the vitality or influence of the Nazi party in Germany, or even of the fascist party in Italy. It shared, nevertheless, many of their features and it was a *partido único.*

It has often been denied that the FET y de las JONS was a political party and the Spanish regime a single party system. 'Our Falange is not a party, it is a Movement for all Spaniards', said Franco in 1945,[19] this idea frequently recurs in his speeches, and avoids the use of 'political party', a term abhorrent to the regime, since political parties were blamed for all the evils the nation had suffered from the beginning of the nineteenth century. However, in the Decree of Unification, the legislator, possibly inadvertently, accepted, by implication, that FET y de las JONS was a political party. In the first of its three articles, after establishing the creation of the new political entity, the decree went on to say: '*All other* political organizations and parties are hereby dissolved' (emphasis added). Were this indirect reference not clear enough, one could summon the conclusive evidence of a most important witness. Serrano Suñer,[20] brother-in-law of Franco, and, according to many historians, the masterbrain behind the political move of the Unification, wrote: 'The action undertaken [the Decree of Unification] had the significance of an historical and political proposal from which the regime was to emerge. A regime with a single leader and a single party . . .'[21]

What was the real nature of this political party? If what has been said about its fascist origins is correct, then we can expect to find in it features of the totalitarian parties of the thirties. Maurice Duverger[22] has grouped those features according to the opinions expressed by the supporters and by the opponents of the single-party system. Supporters see the following advantages in the single party: (a) it serves to select a ruling elite; (b) it does not govern, but it inspects the activities of the government to avoid deviations from the basic doctrine; (c) it serves as a channel of communication between the government and the people, both in an upward and in a downward direction. Those against the single party consider its characteristics to be: (a) the creation of a privileged class; (b) loyalty to the dictator brings to the party members certain gains in the form of well-rewarded posts; (c) it serves as a channel of communication between the government and the people, but only downwards, by means of its propaganda machinery.

FET y de las JONS, in its early days, had all three features. An attempt was made at creating a privileged political class by setting limitations to membership and granting the authorities discretion to dismiss any unwanted member,[23] though the controls were not as strict as in other totalitarian parties at that time and, in the Spanish case, the balance inside the party leaned heavily in favour of the army. Loyalty to Franco and to the system offered members all kinds of openings, from a ministerial post or the office of provincial governor at the top, to thousands of jobs in the massive structure of the official syndicates or inside the party itself. The party was unequivocally entrusted with the function of communicating between rulers and people by its Statutes: 'FET y de las JONS is the disciplinary channel through which the people, united and in an orderly manner, ascend to the State, and the State instils into the people the virtues of service, brotherhood and hierarchy.'[24]

We have, then, to begin with, a party, a movement, or a political organization – the identifying label is, at this point, of little relevance – which has sufficient elements to justify our calling it fascist. With this premise clarified, we can consider how it has evolved to become what it now is.

The Principles of the National Movement

The Law on the Principles of the National Movement is a kind of ideological compendium; a résumé abstracted, in 1958, from all the Fundamental Laws issued up to that date, the quintessence of the regime's doctrine. Not that the official ideology can be said to be contained in this legal text only, but what it does contain has been granted a superior legal status and has been formally placed beyond any possibility of change.

Up to 1958 the official doctrine, in theory at least, had been represented by the twenty-six points of Falange. The Principles of the National Movement replaced and implicitly abrogated those twenty-six points, though there is no mention in them of such replacement or abrogation. The Law containing the Principles of the National Movement comprises a short introduction in the form of a grandiose promulgating formula –

'I, Francisco Franco Bahamonde, Caudillo of Spain, conscious of my responsibility before God and History . . .' – twelve principles, and three articles. It is, after the Law on the Referendum, the shortest of all the Fundamental Laws of the country, but it is the most important of them all.

Two major characteristics emerge from the text of the Law. It is drafted at a very high level of abstraction in a style which fluctuates between vacuous generalities and downright obscurity. It is imbued with a most conservative and paternalistic spirit. Twenty-four years separate these principles from the original twenty-six-point doctrine of Falange. A comparison between the two texts is most illuminating. There has been a certain transfer of content accompanied by a very thorough linguistic purge. Words and phrases like 'separatism' (point 2), 'empire' (point 3), 'totalitarian' (point 6), 'national-syndicalist state' (point 7), 'revolution' (point 26) are all gone. Their fascist tone and style, officially fostered after the Civil War, was no longer acceptable in 1958. Gone too are the radical expressions which seemed to promise a socio-economic revolution. 'Nationalization of banks' (point 14), 'expropriation of land without compensation' (point 21) were useful propaganda slogans at one time, but they had lost their value for a regime openly pursuing a rather crude capitalist development. However, much of the content was decanted from one text into the other. The Principles of the National Movement still owe more to falangism than to any other political ideology or movement, even though the non-falangist elements became more evident. A certain correlation could be established between many of the Principles and the twenty-six points. The content of Principle number one corresponds to point number two; three to three; four to two and four; five to seven; six and eight to six; and so on. The Principles now called 'of the National Movement' are still – the fact must be reiterated – falangist. They are not perhaps purely falangist, nor are they entirely falangist, but essentially falangist nevertheless.

The term 'Principle' may create some misunderstanding. In the law they are numbered in Roman figures from I to XII, but several of these twelve sections comprise more than one basic principle. Thus, for instance, number XII entrusts the State with no fewer than six different tasks; and in number X are lumped together the importance of labour, the recognition of private ownership and the idea of a mixed economy. The abstract nature of the Principles and the wordiness of their style makes it difficult to group them systematically. C. Ollero, Professor at the University of Madrid, suggests a tripartite classification: dogmatic principles, in which the political creed of the system is formulated; organic principles, which outline the institutional structure; and finally those principles which could be said to lay down the guidelines of a political programme or manifesto.[25] For the sake of simplicity, one might follow a more abbreviated classification, dividing the twelve principles into two groups. The first eight principles are basically of a political kind, whereas the last four have a socio-economic content. This classification is in accordance with the suggestions made by the propaganda office of the National Movement.[26] Let us now consider the actual content of the Principles, limiting our analysis to those aspects of a controversial nature.

The idea of a united Spain could be singled out as the main theme running throughout the Principles. In one form or another, a united Spain appears in no fewer than five of those Principles. The formula used varies. Sometimes it is referred to as the 'Spanish nation', the 'national conscience' or the 'national community'; other times it is more precisely defined: 'the unity of the peoples and the lands of Spain is intangible'; 'the Nation, which comprises all generations past, present and future'; 'the Spanish people . . . constitute the National State'. We are here confronted not only with a clear rejection of regional separatism, or even autonomy, but with the remnants of what had been a fascist interpretation of the State. It is well known that nationalism, the idea of a national community, transcending the individual and based upon some vague general values shared by all, was a feature of fascism.[27] It was prevalent in the twenty-six-point programme of Falange: 'We believe in the supreme reality of Spain. The strengthening, raising and exalting of this reality is the urgent collective task of all Spaniards. Individual, group, and class interests must of necessity give way in order to achieve this goal', proclaimed point one. And point two: 'Spain constitutes a unit with a universal mission. Any conspiracy against this unity is repulsive. Any kind of separatism is a crime which we shall not forgive.' The spirit of these points was transferred to the Principles of the National Movement. The poetical definition of José Antonio – 'Spain constitutes a unit with a universal mission' – was also saved. The rest had to be changed in 1958.

The Principles of the National Movement are 'a synthesis of those inspiring all the other Fundamental Laws'.[28] From article 6 of the Charter of the Spanish People they inherited the idea of Roman Catholicism as the official religion of the State, and from the Law on the Succession the monarchist principle. Both were alien to the falangist doctrine, one in degree, the other in substance.

Falangists had felt that Catholicism should form part of their national revolution, giving to it inspiration and meaning, since Spanish history and tradition were steeped in Catholicism. They were, on the other hand, in favour of the separation of Church and State.[29] But Franco's regime, from the beginning of the Civil War, had had the backing of the Catholic Church; the exaltation of Roman Catholicism, to the point of proclaiming it, constitutionally, 'the only true faith, inseparable from the national conscience', was the price paid for that support, as well as a kind of expiation for the extreme anticlericalism of the Second Republic. Principle II of the National Movement was the natural outcome of close understanding and mutual support between the regime and the Catholic Church. The high-water mark of that period is represented by the Concordat signed in August 1953.

In recent years a profound shake-up has affected the Church of Rome. The second Vatican Council opened the door to 'the wind of change' and a mild desire to evolve became, in some sectors of the Church at least, a fairly radical movement. The Spanish Church, which through the younger clergy had already started to show some measure of dissent, was encouraged by the Vatican Council to adopt a more critical stance and a considerable gap now separates them. In view of that attitude of the Spanish Church and the changes brought about by the second Vatican Council, it could be said that both the Concordat of 1953 and Principle II of the National Movement have become outdated. The Concordat will probably disappear or be replaced by something more in accordance with the present situation. Principle II will remain because, like all the other Principles of the National Movement, it is permanent and unalterable.

Restoring the monarchy was never part of the falangist doctrine either. José Antonio, who often expressed admiration and even nostalgia for the victorious days of the Spanish empire and the Spanish monarchy of the sixteenth century, considered this institution 'gloriously dead'.[30] The monarchist principle originated elsewhere. The republican solution was officially discredited; the regime had built its legitimacy upon the destruction of the Second Republic. There were other forces behind Franco – amongst them the Carlists and supporters of the Count of Barcelona – advocating the return of the monarchy. And their aspirations were satisfied – at least formally – with the Law on the Succession in 1947.[31] Principle VII of the National Movement was an echo of that Law.

Principles VI and VIII confirm the organic view of society. Family, municipality and syndicate are the natural organs of social life and political representation must flow through them. Accepting other organic units is left to the discretion of the law, but political parties are openly rejected and declared illegal. One has to assume that the rejection is based on their 'inorganic nature'. In this Principle any kind of genuine political development is most likely to flounder. Political plurality cannot be achieved within the framework inherited from Falange. The efforts made to break up that framework have so far failed. Finally, in the last four Principles – those which deal with socio-economic matters – we are confronted with a few general ideals of unquestionable virtue but many of them still far from reality. In Principle X the capitalist option is taken. Principle XI gives a definition of *empresa* based on the falangist concept of the communal interest of employer and employee. And Principle XII seems to point vaguely in the direction of the welfare state.

The Principles of the National Movement are the political dogma of the regime. The law in which they are contained is above all other laws, including the Fundamental ones, which can be altered by referendum. The Principles are beyond any possibility of change, they are immutable;[32] they have a kind of supra-legal status. All other laws, whatever their rank, all decisions and measures must conform with them. And every Spaniard is supposed to share those ideals. This is implied in the conception of the National Movement as a communion. The term communion, with its Catholic and Carlist flavour, hides the intention to create an enforced consensus. Some measure of commonly held beliefs seems necessary for the stability of any political system. In a system that allows plurality, the 'common ground' constitutes the political consensus upon which that plurality is built. In a monolithic system, by various means – propaganda and repression primarily – a façade of general acceptance is created. Everything is made to look as though the *status quo*, the principles upheld by those in power, enjoy the support of every citizen or at least of the vast majority of them. Franco's regime appears to be shifting from one system to the other, a move which became more apparent after the Organic Law of the State of January 1967. The Principles of the National Movement had been, until then, the ideological façade of an enforced unity. But from 1967 a tendency to transform the Principles of the National Movement into a broader constitutional order can be detected. The Principles would be the minimum political consensus for an orderly and peaceful diversity of opinions. But a consensus which is narrowly based, one-sided and imposed from above cannot be a consensus. Furthermore, the survival of the National Movement organization made the foundation of any other independent political group, even within the narrow base of the official consensus, impossible. The unborn political associations are there – or are not there – as proof of failure.

The National Movement Organization

When is a political party not a political party? When it is a National Movement. If the National Movement organization is not a political party, what is it?

There is no agreement among political scientists as to where the line separating parties and movements lies. A movement is broader and closer to a set of ideals than a party, which, at its simplest, could be defined as a political organization seeking power. It is not unusual for parties to be born out of movements or to be supported by them. On the other hand, the vaguer and more idealistic concept of a movement has often disguised a single-party system. The Spanish case provides a good example of this.

The National Movement organization is perhaps the clearest example of the general theory of this work that the Spanish regime has been left with remnants from its early days that hinder genuine development towards a more democratic situation. The National Movement is the continuation of the single party created in April 1937 under the provisional name of FET y de las JONS. It may seem an oversimplification to say that, since FET y de las JONS was a single political party, the National Movement organization is a single political party also. But if this deduction is rejected, we have the impossible task of finding an alternative category into which the National Movement organization could be fitted. FET y de las JONS, as suggested earlier in this chapter, was to be the political party of a totalitarian state that never crystallized. It was not strong enough to gain control of the State. Over the years it became weaker, it was bureaucratized, and its ideology watered down. The end-product of this process is the National Movement organization in its present form: still a political party, still the only legal political organization in Spain, still unable and unwilling to open the doors to real plurality.

The major steps in the history of the National Movement organization are the following. In the Decree of Unification of 18 April 1937 Franco created FET y de las JONS. The Statutes of the newly founded FET y de las JONS were approved by decree of 4 August 1937, and subsequently reformed, also by decree, on 31 July 1939. A decree of 3 March 1955 altered the composition of the National Council of the Movement, including for the first time elected members – one per province. In 1957 two decrees affected the National Movement organization. On 25 February Franco carried out a major reshuffle of his Cabinet and the posts of Secretary-General of the Movement and National Delegate in charge of the Syndicates were united in the same person.[33] Later that year, on

26 July, a further decree restructured the General Secretariat of the Movement and created a new Delegation of Associations. The composition of the National Council of the Movement was changed once more by a decree dated 22 April 1964. The change this time meant an enlargement: twenty-five new members, representing the syndicates, the municipal councils and the family were included.

Such was the situation when the Organic Law of the State was issued in January 1967. A most striking feature of the National Movement organization to this point is that its legal development never reached a higher status than decree level[34] – a relevant fact which perhaps reflects a desire to stop the party from acquiring too much importance but one which can be over-stressed.[35] It could be argued that the status of the National Movement organization had been raised to constitutional level when in 1942 all the members of its National Council were declared *ex-officio* members of the Cortes.[36] The events which followed the Organic Law of the State in 1967 clarified this point, whilst at the same time giving a new slant to the problem.

In the Organic Law of the State, the National Movement is never mentioned as an organization. The other meanings of the expressions – a set of principles, and a 'communion' – are given priority. However, the organization is implied on a number of occasions.[37] A National Leader, a Secretary-General and a National Council seem to require some kind of organization to justify their existence. It would be a contradiction in terms to have all three and not a National Movement organization.[38] The ambiguity was finally dispelled by the Organic Law of the Movement and of its National Council[39] and the Statutes of the Movement,[40] both of which lay down general lines of structure.

The National Movement organization comprises a National Leader, a National Council, a General Secretariat, and Provincial and Local Councils. Basically this structure is the same as the one set up by the Statutes of FET y de las JONS of 1939, though changes in terminology have been introduced, and there has been a certain redistribution of functions and some readjustment in the allocation of power. There has also been a widening of the door to membership of the National Movement. The only condition now required of members is acceptance of and loyalty to the Principles of the National Movement and other Fundamental Laws of the country. Under this broad definition of membership all Spaniards – and there are more than 34 million of them – would be included, since the rejecting of the Principles of the National Movement would be tantamount to illegality. However, this wide view is valid only for the Movement as a 'communion', not as an organization. The National Movement organization must perforce have a more restrictive interpretation. It is very difficult to assess with any accuracy the size of that membership. There are a number of categories, male and female sections, a youth movement, plus some other groups such as the Vieja Guardia, the Guardia de Franco, etc. The official numbers of male members since the war are given in Table 16.

TABLE 16[41]– OFFICIAL NATIONAL MOVEMENT MEMBERSHIP (MALE MEMBERS ONLY)

1936	35,630	1945	908,000	1954	951,000
1937	240,000	1946	934,000	1955	950,000
1938	362,000	1947	933,000	1956	928,257
1939	650,000	1948	941,000	1957	923,305
1940	725,000	1949	940,000	1958	926,514
1941	890,000	1950	938,000	1959	914,057
1942	932,000	1951	944,000	1960	918,950
1943	925,000	1952	946,000	1961	925,729
1944	922,000	1953	952,000	1962	931,802

More recent official sources have given a more up-to-date figure of 980,054 men in the organization. According to Fernández Miranda, until quite recently Secretary-General of the National Movement, the total figure is more than two million members of all types.[42] The figures show that the membership, after the upsurge which followed the Civil War, has remained fairly stable. What is not possible to establish at the moment is the degree of militancy of that nearly one million militant members. In many cases the connection between party and member could very well be purely functional, bureaucratic, or even opportunist.[43]

The National Movement organization has a double structure. There is an infrastructure which pretends to be democratic by means of a number of councils – local, provincial and national – with a majority of their members elected through a rather complex system. Imposed upon it there is a hierarchical superstructure made up of *Jefaturas* and *Delegaciones* – local, provincial and national too – whose main posts are filled by appointment from above. Real power within the National Movement organization is in their hands, and all of them are in the final instance controlled by the government.

When considering the post of National Chief of the Movement it is, as ever, essential to distinguish what has been with Franco from what will be without. The leadership of the National Movement belongs to the

Caudillo for life.[44] After the succession has been completed, the King will be the nominal Head of the National Movement, but the President of the Government will in practice exercise that leadership, either personally or through the Secretary-General of the Movement, who is a member of his government.

At the top of the organization, but below its National Chief, is a National Council. Here we are confronted with another institution that defies definition. In some ways it resembles the second or upper chamber in a two-chamber parliamentary system, and the location of its headquarters in the former Palace of the Senate in Madrid might reinforce this idea. However, all the members of the National Council are automatically members of the Cortes, thus destroying the possibility of two independent chambers. The National Council is a political body, in contrast with the other sectors of the Cortes which have more of an organic, or even corporative nature, as they represent socio-economic components of the nation. The comparison with the Grand Council of Fascism in the Italy of the thirties springs immediately to mind, though one should beware of carrying this comparison too far.

The National Council has undergone the same democratizing process as other institutions of the regime. To begin with, all its members were appointed by the Caudillo and they could be equally dismissed by him. In the post-war period some *ex-officio* members were included[45] and years later, from 1955,[46] fifty councillors were elected – one for each province. The number of elected councillors was increased in 1964;[47] and finally the Organic Law of the State gave the National Council its present form: 112 members, 65 elected and 47 appointed.[48] The elected members fall into two categories. 53 represent the provinces,[49] and 12 are elected by the other three major groups in the Cortes, namely the groups of *procuradores* representing syndicates, families and municipalities. Each of these three groups elects, from amongst its members, four councillors.

In order to be a candidate, it is not sufficient to be connected by birth or residence to the province one wishes to be elected for, and to swear loyalty to the Principles of the National Movement. It is also necessary to have the support of the National Movement organization.[50] The electors are delegates extracted from the Provincial and Local Councils of the Movement, as well as from the Municipal Councils and the *Diputaciones*. The vitality of the election cannot be measured by resorting to percentages of voters. Since the voting is done through delegates, fluctuations in the level of polling do not occur. More significant, however, is the lack of competition between candidates. In the last elections held in October 1971, more than 50 per cent of the new National Councillors representing the provinces gained their seat without election; there was only one candidate in 28 out of the 53 cases.[51] As a result of this system a large number of elected Councillors not only belong to the official political elite, but in many cases hold posts which make them, in a higher or lesser degree, dependent on the government.[52] This pattern becomes more apparent amongst the National Councillors appointed by Franco. They are nominated on account of the services rendered to the regime and consequently all forty of them have very close links with it.[53]

The National Council of the Movement has had a languid existence. Its meetings have provided a suitable atmosphere in which to echo the emotiveness of José Antonio's language without much regard for reality, or concern with any practical application. The falangist myth, the way the members of the Council are selected, and the nature of the functions allocated to it, all account for its wordy inefficiency. It is not that the functions entrusted to the Council are unimportant, but rather that those functions are either too diffuse, or else represent only a transitional stage towards a final decision taken elsewhere. The Council could be considered as the doctrinal filter or conscience of the regime, since its main role appears to be ensuring that political evolution brings in no unwanted elements, and does not deviate from the strict path of original legitimacy. However, given the strange amalgam of its composition, the controls the government exercises over it, and its inability to implement whatever resolutions or decisions it may take or pass, the balance sheet of the Council, in terms of political efficiency, offers a very poor record.

All the members of the National Council are also members of the Cortes and participate in the legislative functions of this chamber. The National Council, too, has a number of functions and attributions as a separate body.[54] They could all be grouped as follows:

1. The primary function of the Council is to act as watchdog over the Principles of the National Movement, to ensure they are not contravened. In this respect, the Council can initiate the *recurso de contrafuero* or appeal against any decision or regulation which appears to infringe any Fundamental Law. However, the National Council can only initiate the appeal of *contrafuero*. It is left to the Council of the Realm, and finally to the Head of State, to decide on the matter.[55]
2. The National Council is also given the rather vague task of making sure that all Spaniards are allowed to exercise the rights and liberties

granted by the constitution. In this task it complements the Courts of Justice, which offer the more formal and slow-moving protection of the judicial machinery. The National Council can supposedly provide a more agile and flexible response to the complaints of the citizen who feels his rights are being trampled on. The Council would be acting as the equivalent of the Ombudsman.[56] How the National Council is going to fulfil this function is difficult to foresee. To carry it to its final conclusion would probably mean, at some stage, confronting the executive power – on which it is totally dependent. This is likely to remain one more subject about which to speechify in the Palace of the Senate, rather than one to act upon.

3. Of all the tasks entrusted to the National Council by the Organic Law of the State, the most promising and challenging by far was that of 'channelling contrasting opinions on political matters'. Its aim, generously interpreted, was clear. The National Council was to direct and control, and in a way encourage, the formation of different political groups or associations within the National Movement. As we shall see in a moment, the National Council is rather unwilling to move in that direction. It might be fairer to say that the National Council – apart from the high-sounding and innocuous speeches of a few dissenting Councillors – has limited itself to reflecting faithfully the cautious procrastination of the Government in these matters; both Government and National Council hope, perhaps, to find the magic formula that will allow them to combine unity with a degree of limited plurality.

4. Finally, the Council advises the Government on constitutional matters. Its opinion has to be heard before any Bill affecting the Fundamental Laws is sent to the Cortes. The National Council can also raise petitions and send reports to the Government.

The overall impression given by the National Council is of an impotent, inefficient institution, totally subservient to the executive. Yet as a corporate body the National Council, and the National Movement it heads, have played valuable supporting roles in the long life of the regime. On a purely doctrinal basis they have served as one of the principal stays for the dictator with their dogmatic acceptance and defence of his unquestioned leadership. At a more practical level, the bureaucratic arms of the National Movement reach, horizontally and vertically, all social and political corners, in local and provincial life and government, and in the huge structure of the syndical organization, which gave them, at least until 1969, a large measure of control over the working class. Since the direct election of some members of the Cortes in 1967 the offices and personnel of the National Movement have been used to support the campaigns – illegal as this is supposed to be – of officially-wanted candidates. The National Movement has proved particularly valuable to the regime in propaganda and political indoctrination. It is not possible at the moment to quantify its impact. A thorough study of its brainwashing effect upon the post-Civil War generations in Spain will have to be done one day. Nearly all the delegations or departments of the organization of the Movement fulfil, together with other functions, some kind of propaganda role: among the female population, youth, university students, in the world of sport, etc. The Delegación de Prensa, Propaganda y Radio plays the major role in this respect. It controls nearly 40 per cent of the Spanish press and a considerable number of radio stations, and through these powerful media pours out, in a continuous flow, all manner of propaganda, ranging from the careful selection of foreign news, to contrasting 'bad' news abroad and 'good' news at home; and from the reproduction in full of the speeches of Franco and his ministers to regular warnings about the dangerous traps Spaniards will fall into, if they should ignore the regime's doctrinal principles in favour of liberal democracy or communism. A quick perusal in any of the National Movement newspapers provides abundant proof for these comments. The situation has changed somewhat in the last few years – particularly after the 1966 Press Law – but the National Movement continues to serve the regime well in this sphere.

The National Movement has been an excellent dissuader as well as a persuader. First as a single political party with totalitarian aspirations and later as a diffused, all-comprising organization incompatible with other political parties, the National Movement has provided the regime, in theory and practice, with an excuse to avoid the danger and challenge which would arise from the setting-up of other political groups. Political plurality has been latent from the early days of the Francoist regime, but the monopoly granted to the National Movement has stopped any ideologically coherent group from acquiring the independence and organization necessary to vie for power. All the interest or pressure groups which have emerged in Spain over the last thirty years have had to accept, willingly or otherwise, the monopoly of the National Movement. Since the need for organized political pluralism was constitutionally recognized in 1967, an essential requirement of any scheme for implementing it has been that any political association must fit into the ideological and organizational framework of the National Movement.

Plurality inside the National Movement

A reason often adduced to account for the failure of the attempts to establish a totalitarian party in Spain is that the National Movement tried to encompass too heterogeneous a mixture of ideological groups and political forces. Earlier in this chapter the point was made that the plurality had only a marginal influence in bringing about that failure. That plurality was to become more important later. As the Civil War receded into the past, as the totalitarian dreams became an impossibility, a number of groups started to detach themselves from the organization FET y de las JONS, and a *de facto* plurality developed. In a way, it was the beginning of the dichotomous National Movement: the Movement as an organization, and the Movement as a political doctrine. It was possible to be faithful to the doctrine, to serve the system, without being a member of the organization of the Movement. And this situation, tacitly accepted, has continued.

However, there have also been attempts at giving legal status to political plurality through the creation of an official system of associations. Their fate in the future appears very uncertain, and their history is practically non-existent. It could not be otherwise. Any initiative of this kind must come up against the insurmountable barrier of the official condemnation of political parties and the constitution's acceptance of the falangist dogma in matters of political representation.

Associations in this context mean political associations, a euphemism coined to avoid the expression political parties, which are totally incompatible with the Spanish regime. But even political associations may represent an unconstitutional step. This question has sometimes been raised.[57] Principle VIII of the National Movement establishes that 'the participation of Spaniards in the legislative process and other functions of general interest shall be effected through the family, the municipality, the syndicate and any other bodies endowed with an organic representation . . .' It is difficult to see how the political associations could be considered 'bodies endowed with an organic representation'. Furthermore, the same Principle VIII says that 'any political organization, whatever its character, outside this representative system, shall be deemed illegal'. And, although article 10 of the Charter of the Spanish People may seem to take a more flexible line, the Principles of the National Movement enjoy a supra-legal status that places them above all the other Fundamental Laws.

There was not to be a constitutional battle. The pressures of plurality, particularly after the Press Law of March 1966, which allowed some measure of free expression, forced the regime to accept the need for legal political groups. A legal structure would offer some means of control and would be preferable to unrestrained plurality which would, sooner or later, degenerate into a system of political parties.

The right of all Spaniards to associate freely for licit purpose and in accordance with the law was recognized by article 16 of the Charter of the Spanish People in July 1945. Putting this right into practice whenever political aims were involved remained, however, impossible for nearly twenty years. And when a law was passed in December 1964 to allow freedom of association, the limits set to legality were so narrow as to make the creation of any political organization unthinkable. The concept of illicit associations was extended to cover not only associations which were against the Principles of the National Movement and other Fundamental Laws, but also those which would endanger the 'social and political unity of Spain'.[58] In July 1957 a National Delegation for Associations had been inserted into the structure of the National Movement, but its effectiveness was bound to be limited since it only aimed at directing the aspirations of the Spanish people, and at encouraging the creation of professional associations and associations of heads of families.

The opening for the creation of political associations was found in a semantic shift of the expression National Movement, a shift from the Movement as an organization to the Movement as a set of principles. The change was initiated in 1958, when, in the preamble to the Principles of the National Movement, the Movement defined as a 'communion' or sharing of all Spaniards in the ideals that gave birth to the Crusade. The Organic Law of January 1967 completed the transfer of meaning. The organization of the Movement, as we have already seen, would not disappear, but its importance was diminished and the concept of the Movement as a set of basic principles established. The Organic Law of the State not only completed the semantic shift; it also accepted, for the first time in thirty years of Franco's rule, the possibility of divergent political opinions. The formula used to express the idea was once more euphemistic: *concurrencia de criterios*[59] and *contraste de pareceres*[60] are the expressions conveying the idea and both could be translated as 'contrast or diversity of opinions'.

The change seemed to give the National Movement a different perspective. Its political ideology had to be accepted by all who wished to take part in politics. It had become the minimum degree of communal ideas, the basis of the constitutional order, the political consensus within which, and only within which, divergent criteria would be allowed. Of all the changes introduced by the Organic Law of the State, this seemed to be the most adventurous and promising; if, in spite of all its limitations, it had been interpreted and implemented with a progressive mind, it would have changed profoundly the political structure of the country. However, too many stood to lose too much by a change of that nature – and political suicide is not common in societies dominated by reactionary forces. The associations took a very long time to get off the ground, and even today, nine years later, they remain in their infancy and their chances of developing into a viable reality are as tenuous as ever.

The continued survival of the organization of the Movement was perhaps the major cause of this frustrated development. Although all Spaniards supposedly share the principles of the National Movement and can build their political associations upon those principles, it was left to the National Council, at the head of the organization of the Movement, to lay down the conditions for the creation of such associations and to exercise control over them once created. The National Council could not allow any association, even when acting within the limits of the official doctrine, to develop into a threat to the organization of the Movement. The associations were totally subservient to the National Council and to the lower echelons of the organization of the Movement. If to this we add the fears of those who see in political association the kernel that will grow into a political party, the scepticism that has been bred amongst many sectors of Spanish society with regard to any democratic advance, and the professed opposition to association by members of the government, we shall understand the fate of political associations in Spain.

When a new set of Statutes of the National Movement were issued by decree in December 1968,[61] to replace the outmoded Statute of 1939, a section was included implementing a system of associations. An editorial of *Cuadernos para el Diálogo* commented at the time: 'Such statutes are overtly restrictive and it is to be feared that the situation will worsen, since it is left to the Secretary-General of the Movement to draft the law of associations.'[62] This was an accurate forecast. The National Council approved almost unanimously – only two votes were cast against it – on 3 July 1969 the plan put to them by the then Secretary-General of the Movement, José Solís.[63] As the laws went into greater detail, the restrictive nature of the system became more apparent. Nevertheless, and within the terms of that system of associations, several groups expressed the desire to set up organizations of this kind.[64] The plan put by Solís was approved by the National Council, but never received the signature of Franco which would put it into practice.

In October 1969 Franco carried out a major reshuffle in his Council of Ministers. Solís had to step down and a new Secretary-General was appointed. It was Torcuato Fernández Miranda, a Professor at the University of Madrid; in his hands the associations would become an even more remote possibility. In December 1969 Fernández Miranda announced to the National Council[65] certain structural changes in the organization of the Movement. The National Delegation for Associations would disappear and its functions would be divided up. He created, to take up some of these functions, a National Delegation for Political Action and Participation. Solís's plan was sentenced to death and the creation of associations was postponed even further. The changes met with some opposition inside the National Council. Fraga Iribarne, ex-Minister of Information and Tourism, ousted in the ministerial upheaval two months before, and a few other councillors, attacked the proposals with unprecedented determination. They accused Fernández Miranda of attempting to elude a problem basic to the future of the nation: that of political associations. In spite of this, and as if to demonstrate its total subservience to the executive power personified this time by the Secretary-General of the Movement, the National Council that had approved almost unanimously Solís's bill on associations, passed now the new proposal with only twelve votes against.

Five months later, Fernández Miranda released to the press his new plan for political associations.[66] But that was the end of his contribution. The draft bill on associations remained dormant for the rest of his period in office, and no official explanation for the delay was ever given. Could it still be the fear of creating something that would vaguely resemble political parties? Looking at Fernández Miranda's bill such a development seems impossible. Let us consider it more closely.

The original bill, prepared when Solís was Secretary-General of the Movement, dealt with all kinds of associations: professional, historical, cultural, etc., and 'public opinion associations', the name used to avoid the adjective political. Fernández Miranda's bill represented some progress in this direction. It dealt only with political associations, which were re-christened 'associations for political action'. But apart from this improvement, and without now entering into the legal technicalities which differentiate the two bills, it could be said that Fernández Miranda's plan set limits as narrow, and controls as oppressive, as Solís's.[67] Three main features characterized the associations planned by Fernández Miranda: they all had to be based upon a common ideology, the ideology contained in the Principles of the National Movement and other Fundamental Laws; the associations had very limited control over their members; the National Council of the Movement had total control over the associations.

The first feature became almost obsessive in the text of the bill. The need for the associations to support the official ideology and to act in accordance with it was openly stated eleven times[68] in the sixty-two article text. If the indirect references to the same question were taken into account, the number would be considerably higher. Possibly this fear of the associations moving away from ideological unity held up the whole process. During his term in office – he ceased to be a minister in January 1974 – Fernández Miranda was interviewed by the press a number of times. Three of these interviews were widely reported for their particular significance.[69] On all three occasions, the Secretary-General of the Movement made it abundantly clear that no departure or split from the ideology of the National Movement would be allowed, since this would amount to the creation of political parties. There is, in his opinion, a clear difference between 'ideological plurality' and what he calls *pluriformismo*, which means the acceptance of 'several forms of understanding and faithfully serving the Fundamental Principles'.[70] And this is what he expected of the associations.

Secondly, the associations were given little or no control over their members. This could be defended as a protection for the rights of the individual. However, there was a sharp contrast between the freedom granted to Spaniards to join and act inside the associations and the total dependence in which those same associations were to find themselves in relation to the National Council of the Movement. The associations would not be able to control membership since accepting any applicant who met the minimum requirements was obligatory. In fact, it was to be made possible to join as many associations as one wished. Nor could the associations establish any kind of internal discipline, unless it was to denounce any member who acted against the Principles of the National Movement. If they did not denounce such behaviour, the association would become responsible for it. These restrictions could only lead to very loosely organized associations incapable of any coherent action or forceful pursuit. Nevertheless, the National Council of the Movement still considered it necessary to exert all manner of controls over them. In their foundation, in their development and in their dissolution, they were at the mercy of the National Council. It was the National Council that decided whether an association met official requirements, the National Council that decided whether an association deviated from its stated aims or whether it acted against the Principles of the National Movement. And against the decisions of the National Council there would be no recourse or appeal. In view of all that has been said, even the definition of associations for political action given in a Spanish magazine may appear too generous: 'The associations are the political parties of the establishment.'[71]

Fernández Miranda's bill never became law. The bill was a legal hoax to quieten the demand for political associations which was particularly strong in the late sixties and early seventies. The will to put it into the statute book and implement it did not exist. As time went on the attitude of Fernández Miranda and many of his colleagues in the government, became increasingly hostile to the formation of any political associations. Their hostility was candidly expressed by Fernández Miranda when answering questions from members of the Cortes on 6 November 1972: his main concern was, as he said, to search for a formula that would allow the creation of associations which did not, sooner or later, degenerate into political parties. This was, and still is, the crux of the matter.

Arias Navarro's Government issued a new decree on political associations in December 1974.[72] It introduces certain improvements, the major one being to allow associations to put forward candidates in elections. But in matters of ideology and organization the associations are still enclosed within the high walls of the National Movement, and carefully supervised and disciplined by its National Council. Hence all the moves to set up associations under the new statutes have come, so far, from those already inside the system. All the opposition groups, even the most moderate ones, have refused to participate.

The legal aspects are only the external manifestations of a deeper problem: the lack of any flexibility in the Spanish regime which could accommodate different political parties, and the unwillingness of those who could perhaps produce that flexibility to do so. So far nobody has come up with a satisfactory solution for a politically plural Spain. Associations – like those proposed by Solís or Fernández Miranda, and more recently by Arias Navarro – within the boundaries of the National Movement organization and controlled by its National Council would not represent an improvement of substance; they would be nothing more than a further pseudo-democratic ornament on the façade of an authoritarian regime. Real political associations, enjoying autonomy and competing for power, are constitutionally ruled out since they would in fact be political parties. Their creation would amount to the disappearance of the National Movement as an organization or, at least, its downgrading to the level of one party amongst many.

6 ❧ THE SYNDICAL ORGANIZATION[1]

The National-Syndicalist Doctrine

In the syndical sphere, like in any other, Franco's Spain presents a
deceptive appearance. Words and intentions do not coincide, projects and
plans differ widely from the paths followed and from the goals achieved.
This dichotomy in Spanish socio-political evolution over the last thirty-
five years is particularly clear in the field of syndicalism; it can be best
seen in the present structure of the Spanish syndical organization through
the doctrinal lens of falangist National Syndicalism. We shall bring
together elements belonging to different historical stages, for this is
simply a matter of perspective, of getting the right angle of vision, in
order to see how things have changed, if they have changed, and what
links still exist between the present and the past.

The whole of post-Civil-War Spain has been built to a model exactly
opposite to the previous historical period. The victor's will was imposed
upon the vanquished. The Second Republic in Spain was largely supported, if not governed, by the majority of the working class. The two
major trade unions, the socialist UGT (Unión General de Trabajadores),
and the anarchist CNT (Confederación Nacional del Trabajo) fought the
Civil War on the republican side, and when defeat came, many of the

workers affiliated to them went into exile or into nationalist prisons. The submission of the working class went to the extreme of banning its name. The expression 'working class' (*clase obrera*) was tacitly forbidden for a number of years, and even today it is not very common in official terminology. One of Franco's first decisions was to deprive the workers of the organizations which had given them coherence, leadership and strength. A decree of 13 September 1936 outlawed all parties, and political and social groups belonging to the Popular Front, as well as other organizations which had opposed the military uprising. A few months later, on 10 January 1937, the UGT and CNT were expressly included in the ban.

To replace the old trade unions there appeared, as part of the State and under the direct control of the government, a new organization inspired by the national-syndicalist principles of Falange, which served as a basis, as a starting-point, although the falangist doctrine was not accepted in its entirety, nor faithfully followed over the years. This is an opinion which has been expressed by many falangists. In December 1968, a short-lived Spanish daily, SP, carried out a survey to find out what national-syndicalism was, and whether its ideals had materialized in Spain. One of the interviewees, José Antonio Girón, an old falangist and Minister of Labour for nearly sixteen years, declared: 'Historically, Spain has not known the social and economic conditions which are required to have a syndicalist state. Out of all the social forces that achieved victory in the Civil War, only a fraction would have been willing to serve a state in which the two elements of production – labour and capital – are equal.'[2]

National-syndicalism is not only a way of understanding the productive process and its inherent labour problems. It is much more. It attempts a global interpretation of society and state. It has a great deal in common with German national-socialism and Italian fascism, though it also presents certain indigenous features. Falangists as a whole praise and admire the German and Italian movements and accept their similarities with Falange, but nevertheless stress the national side of their own movement – not just as a result of the Axis defeat in the Second World War, for all three movements, and in fact, all those which are called fascist, like to proclaim their individuality.[3] Only the labour and trade union side of the whole doctrine need concern us now, as we look first at the doctrine through the eyes of its theoreticians, and later see how far it has been accepted by Franco's regime, and how it has been implemented.[4]

National-syndicalism has, as a final goal, the disappearance of liberal capitalism – or capitalist liberalism – and of socialism in its most materialistic form, communism. The class struggle is something of the past, and through the national-syndicalist system it is possible to bring together in a common task all elements which intervene in the process of production, namely: labour, technique and capital. The advent of the machine meant the disappearance of the 'working family' and of the guild. Industrialization pushed man into a subsidiary role in the production process. The individual, working by the side of other individuals on the factory floor, became a number, a mere instrument, a spare part. The friendly, family atmosphere between master and apprentice ended and the worker did not even know the person he was working for. Labour relations were dehumanized. The cold statistics of production gained precedence over individual problems. The capitalist became obsessed with the increase of his own wealth regardless of means. Thus appeared what national-syndicalists call the social problem, the class struggle.

Liberalism and marxism were the formulae the nineteenth century found to solve the social problem. Needless to say, both failed in the eyes of national–syndicalists. Liberals thought in making bombastic declarations that they were creating realities. They believed that, by proclaiming equality, all men became equal and that if freedom was granted to all, everybody would benefit from it. This was the great fallacy of nineteenth-century liberalism. Under the famous *laissez faire*, it was the rich and powerful who did *faire*. Thus liberalism meant greater freedom for the stronger members of society; the weaker ones found their position further weakened in a world of free enterprise. As J. A. Primo de Rivera put it, '. . . the liberal state creates a deeper inequality. With the worker and the capitalist theoretically side by side in a free labour market, the worker will end up as the slave of the capitalist.'[5] To check the growth of capitalism enslaving the working classes there appeared the marxist theory. But from its very inception marxism suffered from the same evil: its aim was to give control of society to a section of it; proletarian rule as against plutocratic rule. Both theories were class conscious, both tried to subject society to the dictatorship of a certain class. This was the great failing of marxism. Its aim was not the welfare of the *Patria*, only the welfare of the proletariat. The falangists condemned marxism also for being too materialistic, with its interpretation of history in purely economic terms, and its rejection of all spiritual heritage as unnecessary, and even noxious. Capitalism and marxism divided up society into watertight compartments. They brought into collision worker and employer, when neither stood to gain from such confrontation.

Falangist theoreticians seem obsessed with the need to avoid the class struggle; according to them it is totally unnecessary and only leads to the destruction of society. This view was expressed in a clear and concise way in the first issue of FE:[6] 'The class struggle ignores the unity of the fatherland because it destroys the idea of national production as a whole. In the struggle the employer tries to earn more. The worker does the same. And they enslave each other in turn. Neither worker nor employer are aware of the fact that they are both cooperating in the joint task that is national production. When, instead of having in mind national production, they consider the interest or ambition of their own class, both employer and worker end up destroying and ruining themselves.'

In the thirties, when José Antonio Primo de Rivera wrote the above lines, capitalism, according to him, was dying; liberalism was totally discredited through the infamous behaviour of political parties, and there was no longer any justification for the class struggle. Falangist ideas were the new panacea to cure all the evils Spain had suffered since the Napoleonic invasion. The national-syndicalist doctrine would solve the social problem. In the new state he envisaged – a national-syndicalist state – there would be no need for independent workers' organizations, as their interests, as well as the employers', would be absorbed into the higher interest of the nation. This goal would be achieved by vertical syndicates. In the past, workers' unions and employers' organizations had always been horizontally formed along class lines. Verticalism represented, in his view, a completely different concept. Men, whatever their rank in the social scale, should be grouped according to their trade or profession. All those who contributed to a certain branch of production, from the unskilled labourer to the provider of capital, formed a natural unit, a vertical syndicate. The vertical syndicate, then, would go from the shop-floor to the very top of the state, including in its ascent all social classes. All the vertical syndicates would be integrated into the national-syndicalist State, which was to be the source of all authority, and would guarantee just and peaceful development of the productive process and a fair distribution of wealth.

Thus run falangist theories. Their socio-economic principles show, on the whole, an almost childish naïvete,[7] and they are presented under a linguistic disguise which, though at times poetic, is more often demagogic. Their emotiveness rather than their rationality appealed to a small section of young Spaniards; their hierarchical verticalism offered the victorious side in the Civil War an ideal means for controlling the working class. National-syndicalism wanted a revolution from above. Aping the fascist theories fashionable in the thirties, it advocated an omnipotent state that, as the chivalrous knight-errant, would right all wrongs in the social structure until perfect harmony was reached. The two major aspects of national-syndicalism were, then, an authoritarian state, with a considerable totalitarian bent in it, and a social revolution which vaguely promised a better tomorrow. This was the ideal solution for the nationalist forces at the time of the Civil War, and what happened afterwards seems now, in retrospect, only too logical. Authoritarianism prevailed, though some of its sharper corners have since been smoothed down; the social revolution, with all its slogans and promises, became an ideal propaganda banner to be waved at more and more infrequent intervals.

It is impossible to establish whether the result – the rejection of one part of the doctrine and the acceptance of the other – was intended at the beginning, when national-syndicalism was first adopted, though Girón's words, quoted earlier, seem to suggest that it was. Whatever the intentions, the results are clear: the national–syndicalist revolution was never carried out, nor even attempted. There is some risk of misunderstanding here. We are not suggesting that Spain needed the falangist solution nor even that it was a viable proposition. We are simply underlining an historical fact, that national–syndicalism gave the conglomerate of right-wing forces behind Franco a ready-made solution. On the one hand they had a suitable propaganda tool in the 'social revolution', particularly useful in the post-War years; and on the other, the authoritarian theory and vertical syndicalism explained and justified a state-controlled trade union system.

The Authoritarian Trend in Early Syndical Legislation

The national-syndicalist ideals were first given legal form in the Labour Charter of 9 March 1938. Between this and the latest major Syndical Law promulgated in February 1971, there has been a process of evolution and change that can perhaps be best illustrated by the two different versions of declaration XIII of the Charter. Originally its first paragraph read: 'The National-Syndicalist Organization of the State shall be inspired by the principles of Unity, Totality, and Hierarchy.' In 1967 it was altered to: 'Spaniards, insofar as they work and contribute to production, constitute the Syndical Organization.' The new definition is far from satisfactory. It is too broadly based, all-comprising, almost totalitarian. Nevertheless the contrast between the two texts suggests a considerable change of direction. The original national-syndicalist label disappears, and so do its principles. But since reality, as so often happens, in Franco's Spain, is very different from the legal texts, the evolution is largely semantic.

Some official publications maintain that the Labour Charter lay down the foundations for an authentic 'social democracy',[8] to be followed by democratization in other sectors. However, the actual text of the Charter does not point in that direction. History shows that in a capitalist economy workers find strength in unity, achieved by means of trade unions, which, to defend workers' interests effectively, must fulfil at least two conditions: they must be free and independent from any other organization or institution; and they must be representative at all levels, that is to say, all posts with executive power within the union must be filled through democratic elections and be answerable to the members. This type of union or syndicate becomes a major – some would say the major – force in a capitalist society; a state that labelled itself totalitarian could not accept such an independent and powerful force in its midst.

The Labour Charter, issued by decree in 1938, comprises a preamble and sixteen declarations. The text is unnecessarily verbose, full of high-sounding sentences and emotive undertones. It echoes falangist oratory in its form, and in its contents includes and stresses the authoritarian side of national-syndicalism. The preamble, in its original 1938 version, clearly illustrates not only the style, but also the spirit which inspired all its declarations. After linking the 'new' Spain with the Imperial Spain of the Golden Age, it goes on to say: '. . . the National State, insofar as it is a totalitarian instrument serving the unity of the fatherland, and a syndicalist one opposing both liberal capitalism and marxist materialism, undertakes the task of carrying out – with a military, constructive and seriously religious attitude – Spain's long-overdue revolution, which will bring back to Spaniards, once and for all, Fatherland, Bread, and Justice.'

The actual text corroborates the totalitarian inclinations of the new state. The state was to establish working conditions.[9] Strikes were not only illegal but a crime against the state.[10] All those holding office in the syndicates had to be members of the party.[11] The syndicates were to be a tool of the state.[12] Unity, totality, and hierarchy were the principles of the Syndical organization.[13]

What was the meaning of these principles? Unity meant that only the official syndicates would be recognized; any other union outside the official framework would be illegal. Totality implied the automatic integration in a single syndicate of all those in any one branch of production, whether employer or employee. And finally the hierarchical principle followed the falangist idea of authority: power flowing from top to bottom, creating a state of subordination, obedience without appeal or objection.

A number of laws implemented the doctrine of the Labour Charter. Two, the most important, appeared in 1940. One established syndical unity;[14] the other laid down the bases of the syndical organization.[15] The former put into practice the monolithic idea implied by the principles mentioned above: 'The Syndical Organization of FET y de las JONS is the only one recognized by the State. The State shall not allow the existence of any other organization with analogous or similar aims . . .'[16] The Basic Law (Ley de Bases) simply confirmed the ideas and principles which had passed from the falangist doctrine to the Labour Charter, and later to the Law on Syndical Unity (Ley de Unidad Sindical). Some of its legalistic prose is most illuminating: 'The law guarantees the subordination of the Syndical Organization to the Party, since only the Party can infuse it with the necessary discipline, unity and spirit . . .'[17] Representative democracy within the syndicates was rejected. All the posts with executive power in the syndical organization were to be filled by appointment.[18] What else could be expected when one of the paragraphs in the preamble of the law began: 'All democratic illusions overcome . . .'

The Evolution of Syndicalism

We have looked at the national-syndicalist doctrine and at its legal implementation during and immediately after the Civil War. There has been a certain reiteration of ideas and examples, and even an attempt to reproduce its style, so as to make the initial intentions quite clear. Since then the syndical organization has undergone a number of changes. The pattern of pseudo-democratic evolution which typifies the regime as a whole is found here. The initial position soon showed its internal limitations, and became totally untenable from the moment autarchic policies were abandoned. The economic take-off, the transition from a sluggish, old-fashioned capitalist economy to the fast cycle of neo-capitalism required some flexibility in labour relations, and consequently in syndical structures. Change came, particularly during the sixties, and with it a basically contradictory situation developed. The gap between syndicalist theory and laws on the one side and daily practice on the other, was considerable, and by 1961 an official publication could say 'a wide chasm has opened between the first legal definitions and the present reality'.[19] Years later this was to become the major argument of official syndicalist theoreticians to underline the need for, and foster the idea of, a new law to update the syndical organization. After all, one of them wrote in 1968, 'the real evolution of synicalism has gone well beyond syndical legislation, which remains anchored to the law of 6 December 1940'.[20]

The evolution of syndicalism in Spain was inevitable rather than intended and its implementation shows quite clearly the direction in which the forces of change have been channelled. Some cracks appeared in the original monolithic façade of the syndical organization, and since they could not be eradicated, they had to be integrated into the system. Integration is, then, the key word in the evolutionary process of the syndical organization, integration in the sense of absorbing the demands for change coming from below by minimal concessions that placate those demands without altering the basis of the system. Authoritarianism is still apparent in spite of the rejection of some of the most reactionary labels, such as vertical, totalitarian or hierarchical. The syndical organization remains under state control, and still forces into the same union or syndicate workers and employers, with all the disadvantages for the worker and advantages for the employer this entails in a capitalist economy.

The most important stages in the syndical evolution have been the following: the introduction of a system of elections; the creation of the post of *enlace sindical* and the setting up of *jurados de empresa*;[21] the acceptance of collective bargaining; and the promising reform of the Labour Charter in 1967, and its sequel, the new syndical law approved in February 1971. All of them represented changes but not necessarily towards democracy. A detailed study of all those changes is not possible here; only the major aspects and characteristics will be outlined, beginning with the *jurados de empresa*.

The *jurados de empresa* are really committees, whose aim, as legally defined, is 'to secure peaceful coexistence inside the firm, the increase of production, and the development of the economy'.[22] These were first created by decree in 1947, but since they represented liberalization in the form of marginal worker participation, they took six years to materialize, not coming into existence until 1953. The main functions of the *jurados de empresa* are the following: to propose to management forms of improving production; to put workers' complaints to management; to see that the firm adheres to and applies labour and safety regulations; to obtain information about the financial state of the firm; to represent workers in collective bargaining.

The listed functions make these committees relatively important, and their relevance is increased by the fact that their members are directly elected by the workers every four years.[23] The creation of the *jurados* was undoubtedly a move forward that workers were to exploit in later years. But its real value must not be exaggerated. In practice all kind of obstacles have stopped the *jurados*, and the workers through them, from becoming too active and independent *vis-à-vis* both management and the official syndicates. *Jurados* are always chaired by a management representative. Their functions are largely consultative or advisory, since they have no official power to force management to accept a deal. To do this, they would need the backing of a free workers' union, and the present syndicates can hardly be said to do that. Whenever shop stewards or members of *jurados de empresa* have shown initiative and determination to the point of leading the workers into collision with the firm, bypassing protracted syndical procedures, they themselves have become the victims of the labour conflict, suffering in many cases dismissal. In a period of three years – 1964, 1965, 1966 – something like 1,800 shop stewards were dismissed by Spanish firms.[24] The system of guarantees introduced in 1966, and updated in 1971,[25] to protect *enlaces* and members of *jurados* has not altered the situation much, since although they are elected by the workers, their continuity as shop stewards is dependent on decisions from above.[26] In other words, the position and effectiveness of shop stewards must always be viewed against the corporative and authoritarian image of the syndical system. Nevertheless, only at factory level are workers' demands and aspirations likely to be openly expressed. The *enlaces* and members of *jurados* have at times risked their positions and jobs to defend the interests of fellow workers, but these actions have very often been channelled through and supported by illegal workers' organizations such as the exiled UGT and CNT, and particularly the Workers' Commissions.

Collective Bargaining

In one form or another collective bargaining is used in the capitalist countries of the western world to establish working conditions which can cover anything from the recognition of a certain union, to matters of hygiene, wages or participation of workers in the running of the firm. Collective bargaining requires the existence of two independent sides which, by discussion, give-and-take talks, aim at a temporary equilibrium between their often-conflicting interests. This kind of collective bargaining was rejected at the outset by Franco's regime. It was incompatible with the national-syndicalist doctrine, which maintained that the interests of employers and employees do not clash leaving no conflicts to be solved through bargaining. A substitute had to be found to replace the free collective bargaining system. This substitute was the State. 'The State shall set the bases for the regulation of labour and the relations between firms and workers shall be established in accordance with them. The said labour relations shall comprise not only work and wages, but also a reciprocal duty of loyalty, assistance and protection on the part of the employers, and of fidelity and subordination on the part of the workers.'[27] This extremist attitude became untenable once the post-War euphoria subsided. Implementing the general principle was carried out through the Reglamentaciones of 1942 which set employment conditions. With time the compulsory standards set by the government were transformed into the minimum acceptable level; the conditions of work and wages had to meet at least that level.[28] From then on the evolution was not intentional since it contradicted the basic principle of communal interest between workers and employers. It was forced on the regime by a number of events. Industrial development, the need to 'democratize', the end of autarchic policies, and workers' unrest finally brought about a reluctant acceptance of collective bargaining and agreements in 1958. It is worth noticing that the stress was put on agreement rather than bargaining, and on the syndical nature of such agreements by issuing the new regulations under the heading Ley de Convenios Colectivos Sindicales (Law on Syndical Collective Agreements).[29]

The mere acceptance of collective bargaining amounts to a tacit recognition of labour disagreements and conflicts, and to a rejection of the common interest of management and workers so dear to national-syndicalism. A compromise was attempted, collective bargaining within official syndicates. Dealings prior to an agreement must be conducted by the syndical representatives of both workers and employers inside the syndicate to which they all compulsorily belong. In a way, the syndicate is bargaining and reaching an agreement with itself. To the argument that each syndicate has two parts, one social section and one economic, representing workers and employers respectively, the following question can be put: if the need to organize employers and workers separately is accepted, why force them into a single syndicate? This interrogation does not beg an answer; the answer is self-evident. It is the simplest way for the regime, and the economic interests it represents, to keep under control the force that free trade unions would represent. Thus the introduction of collective bargaining in 1958 was thwarted by the lack of one inescapable premise: authentic trade unions.

Since 1958 the number of collective agreements has steadily increased and the syndical organization has widely advertised this fact to prove with statistics their efficiency. This is undeniable, as it is true also that the

workers, often concerned with short-term results, have tried and succeeded in using the system to obtain some improvement or financial gain.
However, these must be considered as concessions from above, or else as
gains in the face of opposition, rather than agreements freely made
between equals. The major concern in any negotiation is to prove the
effectiveness of the syndical machinery, and avoid conflict. Thus, when
syndical representatives are not able to solve a labour dispute, the
Ministry of Labour will intervene, either giving a compulsory ruling, or
handing the matter over to the labour courts for the magistrates to decide.
The latest law on collective bargaining has largely transferred the task of
arbitration from the Ministry of Labour to the syndical organization, a
purely formal change since the latter is as much government-controlled
as the former.

In these circumstances collective bargaining could not be very ad-
vantageous for the workers. During the sixties it was in the industries
where the workers were more militant and less willing to accept state
control that syndical collective bargaining was least effective. In the
steel industry, for example, in 1966 78.58 per cent of workers had their
working conditions fixed not by collective agreement, but by the compulsory ruling of the Ministry of Labour.[30] The system of collective
bargaining has been used as a more subtle way of control than the blunt
measures operated prior to 1958. Overall it has had an integrative effect in
partially defusing working-class opposition without conceding too
much. The statistical evidence of collective agreements shows that the
system has done very little to redistribute wealth, that increases in wages
have been tied to rises in productivity levels, and that it has even kept
down the number of stoppages and other forms of protest.[31]

Syndical Elections

Syndical elections were started as early as 1943 so that workers and employers could select within their syndicate the persons who would represent them and defend their interests. Representativeness had to be made
compatible with the national-syndicalist principle of hierarchy. After all,
the syndical organization had been made subordinate to the party in
1940,[32] and prior to that the Labour Charter had required all those in a
syndicated hierarchy to be members of FET. As a result Spanish syndicalism is characterized by two vertical lines, the representative line which
goes from the factory floor to the top of each individual syndicate, and the

hierarchical line which comes down from the minister in charge to the provincial and local levels. The latter is usually referred to as the 'political line' or 'line of command'.[33]

In 1941 the Spanish government[34] divided up and classified all workers and employers into syndicates applying a triple criteria: firstly, branches of industrial production (e.g. textiles); secondly, basic products (e.g. sugar); thirdly, services rendered (e.g. insurance). On this basis twenty-four syndicates were originally set up. Their number has now been increased to twenty-eight.[35] Inside these twenty-eight syndicates the representative line is chosen by means of elections. The electoral system is of enormous length and complexity. It goes through a series of stages, beginning at factory level with the election of shop stewards (*enlaces sindicales* and *jurados de empresa*) and moving up inside each syndicate to local, provincial and national levels. The general feature at all stages is that the electorate becomes smaller and less representative as the posts to be filled increase in importance. This type of election generates an atmosphere of mistrust and doubt as to the authenticity and independence of the elected representatives. An ILO team that visited Spain in 1969 to examine the labour and trade union situation became aware of these feelings amongst Spanish workers. 'There are many Spaniards', they wrote in their report, 'who consider that the authenticity of the representative line decreases as it ascends from the factory, through the local, provincial and national levels.'[36] Furthermore, the political line is a kind of insurmountable barrier that surrounds and oppresses the representative line, quashing down any unwanted initiative. The people elected can offer advice, prepare reports, formulate proposals, raise petitions, but have no real share in decision-making. Effective control of the syndical organization is with the people integrating the political line, all of them designated. Glancing down the hierarchical ranks quickly we see first the minister in charge, or Minister of Syndical Relations as he is now called. Below him there is a secretary-general, a deputy secretary-general, and a bureaucratic machinery structured into four major departments or secretariats, dealing with workers' affairs, employers' affairs, administration and finance, and assistance and promotion. In the provinces the same pattern is repeated at a lower level, in the so-called Syndical Centres, with their appointed provincial delegate and provincial secretary.

This political hierarchy has remained basically the same since the forties in spite of changes of official titles, principles, and definitions, and in their authoritarian structures have foundered all evolutionary attempts. To the ones already mentioned others could be added, such as the creation of a Syndical Congress in 1961, or the setting up three years later of separate councils of workers and employers. The latter change could have had a great impact, had it been sincere. It meant organizations based not on the branch of production, but on the condition as employer or worker of the person affiliated to a syndicate. The ILO report saw in the creation of these councils of workers and employers 'a step in the trend toward a state of affairs in which workers and employers, within the syndical organization, would become more independent from each other and from the State'.[37] However, this gain must be set in perspective. To begin with these councils have no executive power, all they can do is to study, to advise, to inform, to propose . . . Then, some kind of separation between workers and employers had become unavoidable by the mid sixties. The inevitable led to the paradoxical. Accepting such councils implies rejecting – though this has never been officially admitted – one of the basic aspects of national-syndicalism, and also exemplifies the inner contradictions of a regime determined to save authoritarian unity, but forced to allow some plurality. A very similar situation in another sphere is the tension between the unitary structure of the National Movement and the creation of political associations within it. Paradoxically enough, the councils of workers and employers have made the Spanish syndical organization look even more like the corporative system of fascist Italy, where workers and employers were in separate unions, but over and above them there was an all-comprising and powerful body, the corporation. It is one more contradiction in a syndical system whose only constant feature has been the protection by the regime, through an enforced order, of the class interests it represents, so as to perpetuate the ascendency of that hegemony over the wider strata lower down the social pyramid. The rest, as far as the evolution of the syndical organization is concerned, has been no more than a confused set of measures, half window dressing, half adjustment to a changing reality. The Syndical Law of 1971 partakes of both.

The New Syndical Law

A new syndical law was announced as early as June 1966 by the minister in charge of the syndical organization.[38] Some other rumblings were also heard that year from less authoritative sources, but it was not until January 1967 that the door was opened for reform. The Organic Law of the State, issued at that time, purged the Labour Charter of many of its outmoded and obsolete elements. Its preamble and five of its sixteen declarations were altered.[39] The new form given to declaration XIII was the death sentence for all the syndical legislation of the early forties. Something different, something better, something more democratic was to replace those anachronistic legal texts. But that 'something' proved extremely evasive and difficult to define. It took four years to find a formula. Never before had there been so much public controversy – within the confined limits that freedom of expression is granted in Spain, of course – over one single issue. The politicians and the syndical authorities kept asking for patience from the people, and suggested at regular intervals that the new law was proving difficult, but would be worth waiting for. The most active among the workers kept demanding a say in the shaping of the new syndicates. The Spanish bishops felt it necessary to express, as a corporate body and individually, the view of the Church in such matters. The ILO was invited by the Spanish government to investigate the labour and trade union situation in the country during this period too. And at the end of this long and painful gestation, the birth of the new law was an anticlimax, or, to use a very befitting Spanish expression, a real *parto de los montes*.

The whole process started with consultation in the form of a question-naire, put not to the workers on the shop floor, but to the syndical repre-sentatives both at provincial and national levels. The results of this survey were largely irrelevant, since 'the key decisions were to be taken at other levels'.[40] The results, well advertised by the national press, were dis-cussed at a special meeting of the Syndical Congress held in Tarragona in May 1968. The conclusions adopted by Congress were to serve as the basis for the new law. These conclusions did not go very far; and if they were to bring legislation into line with the real changes which had occur-red since the Civil War, those changes must have been very small. The proposals contained in the Tarragona conclusions did not alter any basic aspects of Spanish syndicalism, though this was never the intention, as the minister in charge of the syndicates at the time implied when he addressed Congress: 'Let us be quite clear about this. The old laws are out of date; not so, however, the syndical movement itself. Therefore, what we shall change in substance is not syndicalism, though we do want to improve it. What we want to change is the legislation.'[41]

The Catholic Church in Spain, affected by the Second Vatican Council, felt it her duty to make clear the views of the Church, and in July 1968 the Episcopal Conference made public a document outlining its principles on trade union matters.[42] This document, although very moderate and even conservative in its views,[43] became a source of embarrassment for a regime that proclaims its legislation to be inspired by the principles of the Catholic Church.[44] The chasm between the Tarragona conclusions and the opinion of the Church was considerable, greater in the spirit than in the actual wording. Though both documents talked of autonomy, of representativeness, of independent associations, the meaning attached to such words was very different as the final text of the syndical law eventually was to show. Nevertheless, the official newspaper of the syndical organization, *Pueblo*, was quick to point out, through the cunning pen of its editor, that there was no gap 'between the syndicalism founded, installed and developed inside the present political system and the views of the bishops in syndical matters'.[45] The gap would become apparent when moving from the abstract level of basic principles to actually giving institutional form to those principles.[46]

The Bill was first drafted within the syndical organization and sent to the government in October 1968. The government took a whole year to redraft the text before passing it on to the Cortes. They even went to the extreme of placing the subject for a whole month – from 4 September to 3 October 1969 – beyond public comment and criticism under the special shelter provided by the Official Secrets Act. The passage through the Cortes was equally long, complex and ineffective.[47] The Bill went through a number of stages and committees and was finally approved on 16 February 1971. In the end very little had changed. Or perhaps everything had been changed so that everything could remain the same. Throughout this chapter we have been talking of the 'new syndical law', and in so doing we have been misusing the adjective 'new'. There is very little new about the law. The 'major change' is the replacement of politically loaded terms by others of a more technical nature. The essence of the original syndical organization has come through unscathed.

The report of the ILO team was published in August 1969, when the Bill was still in the hands of the government. Therefore, the ILO representatives were not able to express any views on the actual text of the law. They did, however, come to the conclusion that the new law would have to fulfil five conditions:

1. All posts of authority in the syndical movement, including the highest, should be filled by election.
2. The law should ensure the complete autonomy and effective practical equality of unions of workers and unions of employers.

3. The law should ensure that all appointed officials of the syndical organization are subject to the authority of, and receive their instructions from, the elected officers.
4. The syndical organization, while subject to the law of the State, should not be subject to direction or control by any political movement; any relations which it may have with a political movement should be freely determined by its members.
5. The law should guarantee freedom of expression and assembly to allow all types of syndical opinion to enjoy liberty within a freely accepted unity.[48]

The new syndical law does not meet any of these five requirements. All the posts wielding authority are still filled by appointment. The political line is no longer called this, but it still controls the whole syndical organization. The syndical organization is still headed by a minister in the government who, as all other ministers, is appointed by the Head of State.[49] In fact, here the government took a regressive step from the original draft of the Bill, in which the minister in charge of the syndical organization was to be selected by the Head of State from a *terna*, a list of three names submitted to him by the Syndical Congress. Nominated too are the secretary-general, the deputy secretary-general, and all the provincial delegates. Together they make up, under new disguises, the old political line, and exert their will over the elected members of the syndicates, who are still indirectly elected. Employers and employees are forced to belong to the same syndicate as they were before, and all syndicates are brought together under the watchful eye of the state-controlled syndical organization.

The experience over the last few years since the 1971 syndical law ratifies this interpretation that nothing has altered. The law had appeared with the birth-mark of all Francoist legislation: an excessive generality or lack of definition, leaving the government a free hand to implement it arbitrarily by decree. Many decrees have been issued since 1971. Their content and the day-to-day running of the syndicates confirm that everything remains the same. Two were thought to be great steps forward from the 1971 syndical law. One was a clear separation between representative syndicates, with all their officials elected from below, and the syndical organization as a channel of communication between the state and those syndicates. A second was to allow workers to set up, within their own syndicate, unions or associations to defend their class interests *vis-à-vis* the employers. Looking beyond the political propaganda and demagoguery of such changes it is easy to see their irrelevance. To quote but one clear example, the progress that the election – as against the previous system of appointment from above – of the president of each syndicate might have represented, is more than compensated for by the electoral system, which has sufficient checks for the syndical bureaucrats to secure the result they want. As a further control, the elected president can be, at any time, freely dismissed by the Minister of Syndical Relations. The workers' unions, when and if they are formed, will find themselves caught up in a complex of syndical bodies, and deprived of significant autonomy, as in their creation and functioning they are at the mercy of political and syndical authorities. Here too, the discretionary powers of the Minister of Syndical Relations to dissolve any union are practically unlimited. The old laws of the forties were as reactionary as they were sincere. They did not try to hide their nature. They openly proclaimed their unifying, totalitarian and hierarchical aims. The present law does not seem to aim very differently, but technical subtlety and disguise make it appear more liberal. The principles on which it is officially based are unity, generality, representativeness, autonomy, association, participation and freedom.[50] And what about the hierarchical principle? It has been omitted. A strange omission, for the whole law seems to rest upon that principle.

7 ❧ THE JUDICIARY

Introduction

In a country with a long history like Spain most political institutions find their roots in a past far beyond the present regime. The regime has adapted this institutional legacy to its specific needs and aims. The administration of justice is no exception in this respect. The Spanish legal system, and the judicial structure and practices within it, belong to what has sometimes been called the 'Romano-Germanic family',[1] and other times the 'civil law tradition'.[2] J. Merryman, who uses the latter, defines a legal tradition as 'a set of deeply rooted, historically conditioned attitudes about the nature of law, about the role of law in society and the polity, about the proper organization and operation of a legal system, and about the way law is or should be made, applied, studied, perfected, and taught'.[3] Specifically the civil law tradition comprises a considerable variety of elements and features from which the following could be singled out as more important: Roman law and canon law constitute the original sources; the laws are seen as almost perfect, providing clarity in their definition and certainty in their interpretation and application (hence statutes and regulations tend to be gathered in codes, the Napoleonic model being the most influential); considerable importance is allocated to the doctrinal and scientific work of scholars – Germanic in particular – in establishing the basic legal principles. This systematic approach generates juridical variety: specialized jurisdictions, professional fragmentation and scholarly divisions. The principle of the separation of powers brings about the rejection of the doctrine of *stare decisis*, and turns the judge into a civil servant, whose function must not surpass the automatic application of the statutes passed by the legislative power.

The above constitutes, in a very abbreviated form and excluding the idiosyncratic features of different countries, the heritage of legal traditions which Franco's regime found on coming to power. That the Organic Law on the Judiciary of 1870[4] is still in force confirms this beyond any need of proof. However, it is not so much the traditional infra-structure that one should notice, but the use to which it has been put, and the deformations it has suffered when compressed by an anti-liberal ideology and by openly autocratic objectives.

The most noticeable result is the rejection of any separation of powers. This principle, which originated with Locke, and through Montesquieu was incorporated into nineteenth-century liberalism, could not be accepted by the Spanish regime. It was totally incompatible with the more extreme dictatorship of the early days, and was later bypassed when the regime, in its search for institutions that would provide stability and continuity, opted to follow a road other than the liberal-democratic one. There was to be no separation of powers; instead a new principle would be applied – or rather two principles since the law speaks in the plural: 'unity of power and coordination of functions'.[5] What does this mean? The expression is ambiguous even for those who might not disagree with its ultimate purpose.[6] There is neither legal definition nor official clarification of its exact significance. The principle amounts to much more than mere coordination. What one can see is mutual institutional penetration as the main political bodies – Government, Cortes, Council of the Realm, National Council of the Movement, etc.– overlap each other in composition and functions. This allows the executive to invade and control the other powers, thus achieving coordination through submission. The judicial power – and 'power' is never used in official terminology to avoid any misunderstanding, the more generic label 'justice' being preferred[7] – is no exception, though the controls to which it is subjected are not as oppressive as those imposed on the Cortes, for instance, and they are exercised in a more indirect and subtle way. Even so, the opinion of some Spanish magistrates and judges is, in this respect, uncompromisingly condemnatory: 'the power of the judge is a purely nominal power *vis-à-vis* the effective power wielded by economic and political interests'; or even more explicitly expressed: 'magistrates enjoy only the degree of independence graciously granted to them by the government'.[8]

The Fundamental Laws, with their slow and staggered promulgation, took a long time to include any significant reference to the judiciary. Until the Organic Law of the State was issued in 1967 the only mention was in the Law on the Principles of the National Movement, recognizing the right of all citizens to free and independent courts of justice. The initial omission and the long delay which followed are rather surprising – the more surprising because the Organic Law of the State did no more than to proclaim general and elementary principles – and this delay can hardly be accounted for by the most popular of all official justifications; the need to build the constitutional framework with great care so as to avoid errors and contradictions cannot apply to the basic principles contained in Section V of the Organic Law of the State. Besides, since this law appeared no real progressive change has occurred. All lesser legislation referring to the judiciary and all judicial procedures are essentially the same as they were nearly a decade ago. The new Ley Orgánica de la Justicia – to which we shall refer later in the chapter – is taking as long, or even longer, than the ones on syndicalism, local government, or political associations – all three famous in their day for their incredibly slow elaboration.

As in so many other administrative, juridical, or political aspects of Spanish life, the organization of the judiciary follows the French model. Within a hierarchical structure, the judiciary is organized and divided, in accordance with the intrinsic nature of the cases judged, into three major groups of courts – civil, penal, and administrative. At the head of the judiciary is the Supreme Court of Justice, divided too into sections (*salas* – court-rooms – in Spanish) by areas of speciality, of which there are at present six, usually identified by an ordinal number. The first section is entrusted with civil jurisdiction; the second with penal offences; the third, fourth and fifth with administrative cases; and the sixth with labour problems, or as they are frequently referred to in Spanish, with social matters. Another section, the Governing Body (Sala de Gobierno), prepares reports on any aspect of the administration of justice at the request of the government or the president of the Supreme Court of Justice, allocates business to the various sections, and applies, in certain cases, disciplinary measures. Each of the six sections of the Supreme Court has a judge as its president and below him a certain number of magistrates. The Governing Body is made up of the president of the Supreme Court, the presidents of the various sections, and the Supreme Court's public prosecutor.

The Supreme Court of Justice is primarily a court of appeal. Its judgement represents the final stage in the process of justice, beyond which only the Head of State has the prerogative of pardon. The Supreme Court deals too with matters of jurisdiction between lower courts, and with cases in which high Church dignitaries or important public officials are implicated. Below the Supreme Court the administration of justice is in the hands of the *audiencias territoriales* and the *audiencias provinciales*, courts whose jurisdiction covers a certain geographical area. Finally, there are *juzgados* to handle cases in the first instance. These do not operate as corporate bodies, but through the office of a single judge. The fifteen[9] *audiencias territoriales* act as courts of appeal. The *audiencias provinciales*, one in each provincial capital, hear cases within their province, and serve also as courts of appeal against sentences passed by the *juzgados*. Both types of *audiencias* are organized, at a lower level, in very much the same way as the Supreme Court. Their judges, magistrates, and public prosecutors are grouped into sections to deal with different kinds of cases, and they all have their own governing body as well. All these courts are composed of professional men. They are university-trained lawyers, who later become specialists in any of the branches of the administration of justice. Trial by jury, which had been used during the years of the Second Republic, was stopped by the present regime, and this change has now become permanent, for article 31 of the Organic Law of the State says that the jurisdictional function rests exclusively with courts and judges.

There exists too, as part of the Supreme Court, a Judicial Council, first created in 1952.[10] Its main function is to help select and appoint judges for certain posts, by recommendation or by the submission of a list of three names – the *ternas* system. The president of the Supreme Court is also president of the Judicial Council; other members of this council are the section presidents of the Supreme Court, and a magistrate elected by each of the six sections of the latter. Since 1945 there has been a system for the inspection of courts, although it was not properly established until 1952–3.[11] The inspectors who work this service are also under the control of the powerful figure of the Supreme Court president.[12] Finally, a Minister of Justice is a member of the government. He is an executive figure not unknown in other countries, but his existence always casts certain doubts over the independence of the judiciary.

Against the above description, factual and schematic,[13] of judges and courts, we shall now deal with problems of political significance. Methodological reasons and limitations of space force out of the text other themes within the administration of justice, such as the position of the defending attorney, the role of the public prosecutor, or the procedural system; and even fundamental ones like the juridical control – or lack of it – of the executive. However, reduction and selection are partly facilitated by the specialization and fragmentation typical of legal systems within the 'civil law tradition', and without detriment to our general purpose the study can be limited to two specific aspects of the judiciary: the degree of independence enjoyed by judges, and the role played by special courts.

The Independence of the Judiciary

A good starting-point is offered by the learned and far from suspect opinion of Castán Tobeñas, who was for many years president of the Supreme Court of Justice: 'The independence of the judge's function,' he wrote, 'is imperative in any kind of legal system. Furthermore, it could be said that the principle of independent justice is essential in any civilized society, whatever its political form.'[14] How Castán Tobeñas was able to make this viewpoint compatible with his duties as head of a judiciary deprived of basic guarantees of independence is not easy to understand. But official and legal declarations are plentiful. 'The judiciary shall enjoy complete independence' proclaims article 29 in the Organic Law of the State. Behind the glitter of those resounding words lies a rather different reality, 'for the secret of judicial independence depends to a large degree not on the establishing of abstract constitutional principles but on their implementation'.[15] And along the road which stretches from high-sounding constitutional declarations to the daily administration of justice the freedom and independence of the courts are eroded and curtailed. Here one could recall the words popularly attributed to a Spanish politician: 'you make the laws and leave their implementation to me'.

The lack of judicial independence, although expected in an authoritarian system, is nevertheless extremely serious for the ordinary citizen, deprived of the barrier which should serve as the final and safest protection of individual rights. When magistrates and judges are enmeshed in complex legal and extra-legal controls imposed by the executive the principle of the rule of law becomes untenable. And when we talk here of independence we are thinking not of an ideal, a pure and absolute aspiration unattainable within a political structure with degrees of inter-relation between the different powers of the state, nor even of the less ambitious and much-talked-about idea of a self-governing judiciary. No, the lack of independence suffered by the judiciary in Spain is much more basic, and in both fundamental facets of the concept, the organic and the functional, the static and the dynamic.[16] This means that in both organization – appointments, promotions, dismissals, etc. – and in operation, the courts are constantly subject to executive interference – or at least the possibility of interference is present all the time. The organizational aspects seem the more important, as they predetermine the functional ones.

The independence of the judiciary in Spain was discussed in a report published by the International Commission of Jurists in 1962.[17] At that time the Commission, housed in Geneva, thought it opportune to denounce the way in which judges were selected, appointed and dismissed, without the guarantees necessary to safeguard their independence. The Spanish regime reacted in a somewhat aggressive way, entrusting the compilation of a reply to a group of loyal experts from the official Institute of Political Studies. Their reply,[18] as was to be expected, denounced the accusations and counter-attacked by pointing out errors in the International Commission of Jurists' report, and proclaiming that Spain was a nation under the rule of law, where judges and magistrates enjoyed total independence. Since that time, well over a decade ago, legislation on this matter has been partially changed, and, what is even more important, the political climate has altered. New rules have been laid down, and some of the accusations made by the Commission may have lost some validity. But is it possible to maintain that the judiciary is now free from political interference?

The answer to the question has, perforce, to be negative. The independence of the judiciary requires that it be regulated by laws passed by the legislature, and not as is the case in Spain, by norms established by governmental decree.[19] The mere fact that the government can discretionally determine and control wide areas of the organization and administration of justice reduces the freedom of the courts to a minimum. A much more recent report, compiled and written by Spanish jurists, who know and live through the reality of the administration of justice in Spain day by day, has denounced the situation once again, and condemned the system even more categorically and with greater wealth of evidence than the International Commission of Jurists did back in 1962. The report is a pamphlet under the title *Justicia y Política, España* 1972,[20] written and published anonymously by 'a group of magistrates, judges, public prose-cutors, and court secretaries united by democratic beliefs'.[21] Using this publication[22] and the relevant legal texts as a basis, we shall now outline the most flagrant instances of governmental interference in the organic independence of the judiciary. This approach may appear excessively legalistic in its details, but it seems better than to accept the proclamations of the Fundamental Laws,[23] and, certainly, far more acceptable than the doctrinal distortions and justifications pervading the speeches and declara-tions of the Minister of Justice or the President of the Supreme Court.

The president of the Supreme Court of Justice, who is the highest authority in the judicial hierarchy and whose powers are enormous, is appointed by the Head of State by the system of *ternas* from a list of three names put to him by the Council of the Realm. The appointment is for six years, though he can be dismissed at any time by an agreement between those who appointed him, the Head of State and the Council of the Realm.[24] The political nature of the appointment and of the post itself is quite clear, and the following accusation is totally irrefutable: 'The president of the Supreme Court of Justice cannot act with independence, on the contrary, he will submit to the will of the Head of State and of the minis-ters surrounding him, for if he does not he will run the risk of being dis-missed from office.'[25] The regime will always choose for such a post men of proven loyalty. The political biographies of all those who have held the post include not only a brilliant judicial career, but also ample proof of ideological conservatism along official lines, and in most cases an outstanding record of political services to the regime. The same can be said of the office of public prosecutor in the Supreme Court, who is appointed by the government at the proposal of the Minister of Justice, even though this post is in a different category.

The powers enjoyed by the government in the appointment of judges is not limited to the highest posts of the hierarchy. In the Supreme Court it also appoints, at the proposal of the Minister of Justice, the presidents of all six sections. At a lower level, the government selects the presidents of *audiencias territoriales* and *audiencias provinciales*. The only limit set to government discretion is that they must be selected from a certain cate-gory of magistrates, and, in some instances, the government has to listen to the advice of the Judicial Council. Neither requirement is very restrictive. The government has always sufficient choice to exclude any unwanted man, and the Judicial Council's advice cannot be very pressing when a majority of its members are government appointees. Again, the Minister of Justice may, at the proposal of the Supreme Court's Governing Body – whose members are all appointed by the government – decree the transfer of magistrates from one section to another 'when the requirements of service make it advisable to do so'. And what is even more startling, since there is no shadow of control over it, the government may freely remove or change the president of any *audiencia*.[26]

There are no grounds for the belief that nowadays, with the Civil War over three decades behind, judges and magistrates are subjected to any kind of political purge. Nor are the existing controls a condemnation of the people who fill the professional ranks of the judicial career, many of whom would very much welcome the abrogation of all the rules which reduce their independence and degrade their functions. All the same, while discharging their duties, they are forced to bear in mind the fact that their promotion, their professional future, is dependent on the executive. Political deviation could have painful consequences for them, since the government has the power to dismiss by decree any judge or magistrate, under legally defined conditions which are as vague as they are threatening, such as cases of incapacity, committing serious faults which even though they do not constitute an offence are deemed to endanger the dignity of the profession; or when loose living, dishonest behaviour, or repeated negligence render them unfit to discharge their duties. The procedure for dismissal includes certain guarantees. A report has to be compiled by the Courts Inspection Office, and the government is obliged to listen to the opinion of the Supreme Court's Governing Body before taking any decision. These safeguards are largely devoid of efficacy since the courts inspectors are appointed by decree and a majority of the members in the Supreme Court's Governing Body are named by the executive too.

The document *Justicia y Política, España 1972* sums up the conclusions to be drawn from all this in the words already quoted: 'magistrates and judges enjoy only the degree of independence graciously granted to them by the government'. Yet the authoritative pen of a well-known Spanish jurist wrote recently: 'the Spanish system allows any judge to be independent if he so wishes'.[27] The rules, as they are at present, leave very little room to exercise independence. The implication that within the rules, or perhaps more aptly in spite of them, a judge can and must fight for his independence shifts the attention from the organic aspects of the system to the people inside it, and this takes us on to the functional or dynamic problems in the independence of the judiciary.

Although the organization of the courts predetermines their functioning, there is very little, if any, executive interference in the day-to-day administration of justice. Wide areas of judicial activity – civil, penal, administrative – have little or no direct political relevance. But when a case has political repercussions, affecting the essence or the prestige of the regime, there is, if necessary, a tightening up of controls to secure the wanted sentence, or even take away the case from the jurisdiction of the courts – the Matesa financial scandal is a recent example of this nature. Spanish judges and law men in general are profoundly conservative, a feature shared with judges and law men in any country. It has been said that 'whoever administers it [the law], in whatever position, is, in that capacity, chained to the *status quo* of social and political conditions. A certain conservatism is therefore not idiosyncracy, much less personal default, on the part of the lawyers, but a necessary attribute of their role in society.'[28] This comment was applied to West German lawyers, but is equally valid for the Spanish situation, with the additional social and political ingredients that typify Spain. The body of Spanish magistrates and judges is made up of civil servants who monopolize the jurisdictional function, since jury trials were abandoned after the Civil War, and these magistrates and judges are to a large degree a force for continuity rather than change. It is not only the intrinsically conservative nature of their profession; the socio-economic background of judges,[29] their political experience as servants of the regime, their training, their own awareness of the precarious situation they are in, all help turn the judiciary into a pliable, reactionary force, whose contribution to political change in Spain has so far been minimal. Hence the functioning of courts and tribunals, at least at the higher levels, has tended to be conservative, legalistic, a permanent and at-all-costs justification of the regime. The jurisprudence of the Supreme Court, over the last few years, on cases of strikes is a good illustration.

Special Courts

The existence of special courts is clearly related to the independence of the judiciary. The special courts provide the method – at once subtle and brutal – used by the regime to gain greater control over the politically sensitive areas of operation of the courts. They deny the ordinary courts jurisdiction over a wide number of cases, more often than not involving individuals or groups of individuals exercising their political rights. No other theme has been more hotly debated than this in connection with the long-delayed project to reform the laws applying to the judiciary, to the point that, very often, discussions or works on this subject seem to hinge solely on to the reasons for and against the existence of special courts[30] – a position which, although one-sided, is understandable, given the politically loaded nature of such courts, and the obstinate refusal of those in power to accept any compromise that will reduce their control.

When a court is a special court rather than an ordinary one is not always clear. We mean those courts whose magistrates and judges, whose jurisdiction, and whose functioning are outside the normal structure of the judiciary as described in previous sections. The special or extra-ordinary courts should not be allowed to hide behind the specialization in a legal system of the 'civil law tradition' which divides the courts and apportions cases to them according to their juridical nature. Insofar as the special courts reduce the powers of the ordinary courts or judiciary, their existence – except in very few cases – represents a flagrant attack on the independence of the judiciary, and the greater their number and the wider their jurisdiction the less independent the judiciary becomes. Hence the proliferation of special courts is common in authoritarian regimes. A recent study on the subject has shown how Franco's Spain has reached a new high-water mark in the proliferation of special courts, unequalled since the beginning of the nineteenth century.[31]

Most constitutional texts include some article or declaration comprising the principle of a unified jurisdictional structure, and the Spanish Fundamental Laws are no exception, although a clearer wording would have avoided any possible misinterpretation.[32] The highest officers in the Ministry of Justice often pay lip service to the ideal of a united judiciary, and yet their own official publications admit the existence of a considerable number of special courts – no fewer than twenty-one,[33] excluding some others as politically significant as the Public Order Court. This profound fragmentation of the administration of justice is accounted for in a rather casual way by saying that 'it is a situation that develops in any country during periods of crisis, war or revolution, and whose duration is usually limited to the life of those circumstances, though it often survives due to inertia, to the natural preservation instinct of any established body, and to the need to undertake a reform affecting wider areas of civil and penal legislation'.[34] The explanation is partially valid but in some important instances clashes with the evidence of dates, as some of the special courts were set up in the fifties and sixties, when the exceptional circumstances of the Civil War were far behind. Military tribunals and the Public Order Court cannot be explained away with that generic justification: military tribunals have in the last few years been increasing their non-military functions; the Public Order Court was created as late as 1963.

The splitting up of the administration of justice, and reduction of judicial authority and independence has often been denounced as un-democratic by many members of the Spanish Bar, especially younger lawyers. The Madrid Bar Association – the largest, the most active, and the most politically-involved in the country – in January 1969 passed by 439 votes to 197 a resolution requesting the suppression of all special courts, the Public Order Court included.[35] The National Congress of Lawyers held in León in 1970, and recently described 'as the most important gathering of Spanish lawyers since the end of the Civil War'[36] – these gatherings are not very common, the previous one had taken place in 1953 – unanimously approved a resolution requesting from the authorities the suppression of special jurisdictions.[37] In the last few years, particularly after the first draft of a new Bill on the organization of the judiciary was sent to the Cortes, similar opinions have been expressed by political figures and lawyers in the daily press and specialized publications. Faced with this mounting criticism the regime has adopted the pseudo-democratic and pseudo-evolutionary formula so often applied to other institutions; principles are recognized and proclaimed, re-adjustments are made, institutions are updated, new legal texts are issued . . . but the special courts, possibly under new names, remain. Nor is their disappearance likely in the foreseeable future. The regime continues to feel the need of special courts to try its political opponents.

There are special courts in all fields: economic, academic, military, commercial, administrative, canonical, labour relations, etc. Their existence is not only an attempt at curtailing the freedom of the judiciary – this point must be reiterated – but it also makes citizens unequal before the law, it deprives the accused of his rightful judge, and destroys one of the basic principles of democracy.

A detailed study of all special courts is neither possible nor necessary. It will suffice to refer to those with greater relevance here, namely, labour courts, ecclesiastical courts, military courts and the Public Order Court. Labour courts had been foreseen in 1938 by the Labour Charter[38] and came into existence in 1940 soon after the War had finished. The organization of these courts has at its base the *magistraturas del trabajo*, which hear cases arising from disagreements and conflicts between workers and employers. At the other end of the scale the Central Labour Court is a corporate body of appeal, it is headed by a Director-General appointed by the Minister of Labour, upon whom – not on the Minister of Justice – these courts are dependent. In the final instance, it is possible in some cases to appeal to the Supreme Court. Even though during the last few years and for a number of reasons – pressure from the shop-floor being the main one – some of the sentences passed by these labour courts have gone against what might be called 'official interests', the objections raised to their existence remain valid. Not only do they come under the control of the Ministry of Labour, thus opening an obvious and unnecessary – since there already is a Ministry of Justice – gap for government interference, but they deal with cases arising out of an unequal contest between private industry on the one side, and on the other workers handicapped by their obligatory integration in a government-controlled vertical syndicate. As a result not infrequently the labour courts try to protect the official syndical line. The syndicates must be made to appear to work as a negotiating and conciliatory instrument. To this effect the procedural rules are loaded against any deviation from the normal syndical path; thus any worker who steps out of line – to quote but one flagrant example – who becomes too active or belligerent, who affiliates to any organization outside the official syndicate, may find himself dismissed by the firm, and even if the labour courts should declare the dismissal unfounded, the firm can still refuse to readmit him by simply paying a compensation.

The ecclesiastical courts, whose existence is logical and admissible in matters relating solely to the internal affairs of the Church, have given rise to a number of problems of a political nature. Both the courts themselves and their political dimension were born out of the special bond uniting Church and State in Spain. The Concordat of 1953 grants the Catholic Church special rights to set up its own courts to deal with cases covered exclusively by ecclesiastical regulations. Furthermore, under the provisions of the Concordat members of the clergy cannot be detained or tried by lay courts without the consent of the Church authorities; when proceedings are allowed they take place in secret, and if a term of detention is imposed it is served in a special prison. In the climate which has followed the Second Vatican Council, charged with ever-increasing tension between the regime and the *avant-garde* sectors of the Church, these privileges have become a constant point of friction and embarrassment. The protests and denunciations by a high number of priests, expressed verbally from the pulpit and even, at times, through direct involvement in the workers' demands or in the struggle of the Basques to reassert their regional traits, have made the *status quo* untenable. Frequently the clergy implicated in such activities have refused the privileges and protection granted by the Concordat, as was the case in the famous Burgos trial of 1970. In other instances bishops have refused to acquiesce to the detention or trial of priests in their diocese, and, contrariwise, the authorities have sometimes ignored the provisions of the Concordat and acted with total disregard for the accorded privileges. All this highlights the pressing need for a separation of Church and State, through the revision or abrogation of the Concordat, thus bringing to an end the collusion between both institutions, reducing the possibilities of collision, and putting the clergy on a level with all other citizens, to act freely, and accept fully responsibility for their actions.

Finally, two other types of special courts, the military tribunals and the Public Order Court, have political functions which are essentially a form of legalized repression, totally inadmissible, and incompatible with the claims made by a regime that prides itself in having guaranteed freedom, social justice, and peace for its subjects. The existence of courts with military jurisdiction requires no justification: it is a feature common to all countries regardless of their political structure. But the activities of these courts, in peacetime, normally extend only to military personnel, and in cases such as espionage, attempts on military installations, mutiny, etc. The outrage occurs when courts martial are held to deal with offences that have nothing to do with the military, and even, in some cases, to pass judgment on acts which should not constitute an offence at all. Military courts in Spain show three main characteristics. Firstly, they are less independent than the civil courts. All members of the Supreme Council, the highest corporate authority in the scale of military justice, are appointed by decree. Courts martial are set up *ad hoc* to hear specific cases; they are appointed by and function under the authority of the Captain-General of the military region where they are held. Secondly, the procedures at courts martial take a rather swift and abbreviated form, denying the accused many of the safeguards of the civil courts. Thirdly, by comparison with other courts, punishments imposed tend to be much more severe, the grounds for appeal much more limited, and the execution of the sentence, in the case of death penalty, carried out much sooner.[39]

One cannot help being scandalized at such a situation. Measures taken in the exceptional atmosphere of the Civil War and its aftermath are still in existence. The decree on military rebellion, banditry and terrorism promulgated in 1960 and still in force is a faithful reproduction of a law of 1943 and a decree of 1947. These latter were themselves based on dispositions made during the Civil War, and appeared when the regime was trying to rid itself of the groups of guerrillas still at large. And although since 1971 these courts no longer deal with political crimes – their criminal nature being artificially created, as most are forms of behaviour arising from the exercise of basic human rights – the broad label of terrorism and rebellion still brings under the summary procedures of military justice many people who have nothing to do with the armed forces, and whose only reason to be court-martialled is to represent or have represented a serious peril to the stability of the regime. In the last few years the activities of these courts have concentrated almost entirely on the trial of Basque separatists[40] and other similar groups.

In 1963 a Public Order Court was set up to deal with any activities aiming at 'undermining the foundations of the State, altering public order, or creating anxiety for the national conscience'.[41] The total lack of definition in these words shields the attempt to legalize the punishment of any activity which falls outside the narrow limits imposed on individual and collective rights in Spain. As this subject is treated extensively in another chapter there is no need to be more explicit here on how the Public Order Court carries out its repressive measures in matters such as press freedom, or the right of political and syndical association. The examples in the daily press are so frequent as to make it all look normal and acceptable. Besides the artificial nature of the offences which come before the Public Order Court, the independence of this tribunal, which operates only from Madrid, is considerably less than that of the rest of the judiciary. Its judge and magistrates are appointed by the government, after hearing the advice of the Judicial Council, which is not binding, and they can be freely dismissed and replaced at any time.

The Reform of the Judiciary

Repression in the name of justice is particularly unpalatable. The final bastion in the defence of human rights affords the Spanish citizen little or no protection. The judicial defences are perforated by the constant meddling of the executive, which reduces the judiciary's independence and parcels up its jurisdiction to facilitate its emasculation. Criticism in this chapter has tried to reflect the many voices of protest raised in anger inside and outside Spain, to which the official reply has usually been the promise of reform in judicial organization. A long-standing promise, its origins can be traced back to the beginning of the fifties when the falangist Raimundo Fernández Cuesta was Minister of Justice. Since then every single minister in charge of that department has reiterated the promise, announcing the more or less imminent promulgation of new basic norms. The inclusion of a section on the judiciary in the Organic Law of the State in 1967 gave renewed impetus to the reformist trend, but the road to any kind of political change is, in Spain, a long one. By 1970 the reason given for a legalistic reform of the judiciary was coloured by senti-mentality: reform should coincide with the centenary of the previous basic law on the judiciary, dated 1870. It was not to be. It took three more years before the first draft of a new Bill was published in the *Boletín oficial de las Cortes*.[42]

When an authentic reformist spirit does not exist reform can only be superficial and technical, limited to readjustments that improve and bring up to date the judicial machinery without affecting its essential parts. Even a restrictive legal system can be infused with flexibility in its application when the desire to do so exists. This desire is totally lacking in the Spanish case. Were it there the authorities would have abrogated long ago most of the restrictive and repressive laws and decrees, some of them still remnants from the Civil War; the judiciary would have been granted some measure of self-government; courts martial would have been restricted to specifically military cases; lawyers would have been allowed to organize and control their own associations free from govern-mental interference; the executive would have renounced its penal powers; the Public Order Court would have been absorbed into a unified juris-dictional system. And yet exactly the opposite has been happening. During all these years when official spokesmen were repeatedly announc-ing the reform of the judiciary, all sorts of legal and executive measures were being taken in flagrant contradiction with the professed reformist spirit; the real ingredient for reform – the desire to carry it out – had never been present.

A partial reform is unlikely to change much. It is not sufficient, not even possible in our way of seeing things, to alter the norms relating to the law courts without undertaking many other institutional changes all the way up to the top of the constitution. Other previous 'reforms', in education, syndicalism, or political associations, carried out by the regime during the last few years, suffered from this same defect, and their pitiful results are there for all to see. The *Bases para la Ley Orgánica de la Justicia* are very much in this predicament. They are bases for con-tinuation rather than change, as the official reasons for the law make abundantly clear. We are told in the introduction that the reform is motivated primarily by the profound change in social and economic conditions, so different, both quantitatively and qualitatively, from those of a century ago, when the last basic law on the judiciary was promulgated. The growing technical nature and complexity of the administration of justice is added as a further cause. All are purely functional reasons; no reference, however vague or indirect, is made to the need, or the desire, to democratize or grant the judiciary greater independence. Following the directives of the Organic Law of the State, judicial independence is mentioned as a principle, and so too is a unified judiciary, with military and ecclesiastical courts as the only exceptions to the rule; but these are not respected in the text of the law, which can be easily faulted and criticized all the way from its elaboration, through its contents, to its final aims.

The first draft of the Bill arrived at the Cortes, after a very long process of political and bureaucratic elaboration in the Ministry of Justice. Wide sectors of the legal profession – the Bar Associations in particular – had little or no say in the formulation of its contents. The many liberalizing demands and dissident opinions expressed in the press were ignored. A general form was preferred to preciseness and detail, with the result that the Cortes have been presented with a set of general principles or legal bases which, once approved, leave the government totally free to implement them as they consider appropriate. 'The Bill,' we are told in the introduction, 'has tried to maintain the many useful aspects of the *status quo* while at the same time adapting them to new circumstances, present and future', which means that in the fundamental questions the new situation contemplated in the contents of the law will be little different from the present one. The selection and appointment of judges and magistrates remains exactly the same. Special jurisdictions continue to exist, though we are told the opposite. There will still be special labour courts. The Public Order Court simply changes its name to become the Central Penal Court (Tribunal Central de lo Penal), entrusted with '. . . offences which, given their nature, seriousness, or significance, are damaging to the general interests of the nation, or to its economy, or they endanger social peace, public order, or the security of the state . . .',[43] or in non-legalistic parlance political repression which will extend, as it does at present, from the suspension of publications to the imprisonment of political opponents. The Bill is not very explicit about the role of military courts, but a very recent government decree on the repression of terrorism[44] seems to have strengthened, for the time being at least, their non-military functions. Reform has thus left things very much as they were. The administration of justice as conceived in the new Bill is not likely to turn the judiciary into an independent judicial power, and the words of Pablo Castellano, a Spanish lawyer, written in 1969 when legal reform was no more than a possibility, are equally valid today, when that reform is under way: 'The Ley Orgánica de la Justicia represents, within our country's legal system, a partial and theoretical reform, totally unrelated to the present-day problems of the administration of justice. To use a graphic image, it is like installing an air-conditioning system in an old building whose foundations and general state of repair are ruinous.'[45]

8 ❧ SPANIARDS AND THEIR RIGHTS

Introduction

No better vantage point could be found from which to gain a clear view of a regime than the respect for individual freedom, the protection of personal rights, or the lack of this respect and protection. These problems have universal dimensions. It is not necessary to cast one's eyes far in order to see abuses of all kinds against freedom and individual rights. People suffer discrimination and injustice for a host of political, religious, racial, or cultural reasons. No country as yet has found the political formula to achieve a perfect balance between the authority of the state and the independence and equality of its citizens. Tyranny threatens from one end, chaos and disintegration from the other. Political regimes place themselves between the two extremes in accordance with their ideology. Some are inclined to grant citizens as much freedom as is compatible with the communal interests of the society to which they belong; others, like the Spanish one, lean heavily towards authoritarian solutions, curtailing that freedom while denying that they do so.

The basic rights and duties of Spaniards as citizens of the national state are contained in the Charter of the Spanish People. It is a lengthy legal document in the form of a declaration of rights, following the formula set up more than a century and a half before by the American Declaration of Independence written by Thomas Jefferson in 1776, and the *Les Droits de l'homme et du citoyen*, approved by the French National Assembly in 1789. Since those early days of the liberal era, declarations of rights have become more complex documents. The nineteenth century saw the lower classes fighting to achieve the extension of political rights to all citizens, and the recognition of some basic social rights. Above all, it became obvious that declarations by themselves were not enough, they had to be implemented, they had to become a tangible reality for each and every individual.

The Universal Declaration of Human Rights, approved by the General Assembly of the United Nations on 10 December 1948, is a fundamental document. The Charter of the Spanish People preceded this declaration by nearly three and a half years, a fact often proclaimed in official circles in Spain, and underlined as important by certain authors.[1] What they usually forget to mention is that by the middle of 1945, when the Charter of the Spanish People was promulgated, the Axis powers had lost the war, and the Spanish regime was forced to put on a democratic mask in order to survive.

Reading the United Nations' Declaration today, one is struck by its naïve idealism. More than a quarter of a century after its proclamation, many of its tenets are as far as ever from reality. The United Nations lacks the authority and power to implement them as the most recent history has shown

The Charter of the Spanish People must be carefully read. Its thirty-six articles compare badly with the thirty comprised in the United Nations Declaration. They are inspired by a less generous spirit towards the individual, they display the hallmark of the more authoritarian days when they were drafted, and they clearly show the influence of the Church of Rome prior to the Second Vatican Council. The declaration in itself is important, but far more important is the way in which it is put into practice. Here the Spanish regime has the power the United Nations lacks. It can give full and liberal implementation to the rights included in the Charter of the Spanish People, but it has only made use of that power to curtail them.

It is necessary to set legal limits to individual rights. The words of Montesquieu still hold their validity: 'Freedom is the right to do what is allowed by the laws. If a citizen were to do what is forbidden he would no longer enjoy freedom; since all other citizens would be able to do likewise.'[3] Certain rules are necessary to guarantee the fair interplay of rights between individuals, groups, and society as a whole. It could be said that freedom must flow through legal channels. As a result, one has to accept some limitations to freedom, and rights and duties are indivisible. But the rules set must serve this purpose, not the wishes and aims of a ruling minority bent upon the maintenance of the *status quo*. When laws and decrees protect the authorities rather than the citizens, when decisions are arbitrary and leave little room for redress, when even the existence of the rule of law and of juridical guarantees is doubtful, a declaration of rights turns into an empty and meaningless document.

The Charter of the Spanish People, together with the Labour Charter, comprises an impressive number of rights and basic freedoms. Civil rights concerning the person as an individual: freedom of residence, freedom of movement, secrecy of mail, privacy of the home, etc. Civil rights concerning the person as a member of the community: freedom of expression, freedom of association, religious freedom, etc. Political rights, limited practically to the franchise and the right to raise petitions to the authorities. And finally the so-called social or labour rights: right to work, right to a basic wage, right to receive an education, social security rights, etc. All these rights and their ancillary duties, such as loyalty to the Head of State, obedience to the laws, compulsory military service and the obligation to pay taxes, are grouped in the Charter in four sections which cover the exercise of rights, the rights concerning labour and ownership, the rights of the family, and a section comprising all other rights.

There seems no need to analyse these rights in detail. It will suffice to look at a few with some special relevance here, as good indicators of the general attitude of the Spanish regime towards individual rights. They are freedom of association, and its corollary, the right to free assembly; freedom of expression; religious freedom; and the right to strike, which, though not included in the Charter of the Spanish People, is indirectly referred to in other laws and is, of course, of primary importance.

Freedom of Association

Article 12 of the Charter of the Spanish People says in its first paragraph: 'Spaniards may meet and associate freely for lawful purposes and in accordance with the Law.' As a declaration it cannot be faulted. It bears comparison with its parallel in the Universal Declaration of Human Rights (Article 20) which reads: 'Everyone has the right to freedom of peaceful assembly and association. No-one may be compelled to belong to an association'; and with similar articles in any constitution of the Western World. Thus, for instance, article 9 of the Basic Law of the German Federal Republic establishes that: 'All Germans have the right to form associations and societies. Any association whose objectives and activities break penal laws, or go against the constitutional order or international harmony shall be banned.' The likeness at this level is considerable. In spite of their different wording, article 16 of the Spanish Charter and article 9 of West Germany's Basic Law resemble each other like two drops of water. One has to let them fall into their respective realities to appreciate the difference separating the two countries in this respect. A Spanish philosopher, Ortega y Gasset, gave a warning against errors of appreciation of this kind: 'We must always bear in mind that the perspective is decisive in the understanding of social reality . . . What happens in one nation happens more or less in the others. When one points out a case as specific to the Spanish situation, there is always some shrewd person who mentions a similar case in France, in England, in Germany, without realizing that what is being pointed out is not the case itself but its weight and prominence in the national anatomy.'[4]

When, following Ortega's advice, one adopts the right perspective, article 16 of the Spanish Charter loses most of its significance. There are three kinds of associations which may challenge an authoritarian regime: namely, students unions, trade unions and political parties. None of them enjoy a legal and free existence in Spain. Political parties are illegal and they are considered incompatible with the regime. The creation of trade unions outside the corporative structure of the official syndicates is forbidden, and even inside the syndicates the limitations and controls to set up associations are so numerous that one cannot properly speak of the existence of the right to associate. Until 1965 all university students were compulsorily enlisted in the ranks of the SEU (Sindicato Español Universitario), a falangist union founded in the thirties, and adopted by the present regime as a means of control and indoctrination. Under pressure from mounting protest by students the authorities dismantled the SEU in 1965, and have since made several attempts at replacing it by some other type of students' union which will look more democratic but still be under the control of the Ministry of Education. The future of these unions, like the future of the universities as a whole, appears extremely confused in the turbulent upheavals of an educational reform imposed from above, with little regard for the opinion of either students or teaching staff.[5]

Associations in general are subject to a special law[6] to implement the general principle contained in the declaration of the Charter of the Spanish People. The Law on Associations is so restrictive that even its constitutionality can be put into question, a technique repeatedly found in all the other laws issued to implement the rights and freedoms proclaimed by the Charter. Legality is set very vague boundaries, while the government is given wide and discretionary powers of control.

Spaniards may associate freely provided their purposes are lawful and that they act in accordance with the law. What are unlawful purposes? Those which go against the Principles of the National Movement and other Fundamental Laws; those which break some penal law; those that threaten morals or public order; and *any other which may represent a danger for the social and political unity of Spain*[7] (emphasis added). These are the ambiguous boundaries separating legality from illegality, and it is left to the Minister of the Interior, or his appointee, the Provincial Governor, to decide whether an association is on the right or the wrong side of that tenuous dividing line. Equally, even after an association has been given official approval it may be heavily fined or suspended for up to three months by the same authorities, if it should fall into any of the legal traps mentioned above. These decisions of the executive are immediately applicable, though there is the possibility of appeal through the appropriate courts. And the regime's attitude in these matters is not changing as demonstrated by the frustrated history of political associations during the last few years (discussed in Chapter 5), and even more recently by the law regulating associations of lawyers, doctors, economists and other liberal professions – passed by the Cortes on 12 February 1974 – which has turned all these bodies into little more than adjuncts of the State.

Only the Catholic Church could be said to enjoy more freedom of association under the provisions of the 1953 Concordat. The Church is free to create associations with purely religious aims, and this has led to frequent frictions with the regime, particularly through the activities of some branches of Spanish Catholic Action. The HOAC (Hermandades Obreras de Acción Católica) and the JOC (Juventud Obrera Católica), lay associations created to carry out a pastoral activity amongst the workers, have often gone beyond purely religious functions to support workers involved in labour struggles over pay and conditions. Their backing of the Asturian miners during a wave of strikes in 1962 is possibly the best-known case,[8] but there have been many others which could serve as proof of the basic incompatibility of the regime with any form of free association.

The right to free assembly is inseparable from that of free association, for it is difficult to conceive of the latter without the former. Both appear in the Charter of the Spanish People, and both are subject to similar restrictions. Freedom of assembly is still regulated by ministerial decrees issued immediately after the end of the Civil War.[9] Any public gathering of more than twenty people, whatever its nature, must be previously approved by the Ministry of the Interior. The prior approval extends not only to the meeting itself, but also to the speakers who are to address the meeting, and the subjects discussed.[10] And, of course, a meeting held without official permission is considered as an attempt against public order and all those taking part, as well as the organizers, are liable to heavy penalties.

Freedom of Expression

Freedom of expression, taken in a broad sense, implies freedom of opinion and the right to be properly informed. People should be free to communicate their own ideas and feelings to others by whatever means are available to them, and they should also be able to receive information and news in a variety of ways so as to be able to form their own opinions. In this wide context the right to free expression acquires its full significance. The influence of the mass media in the formation of public opinion is obvious, and any government wishing to restrict or suppress freedom of expression only has to set tight controls to the media in order to achieve its aims.

The official policy of the Spanish regime in these matters is clearly divided into two periods, with the Press Law of 1966 acting as the dividing line. Before that date – 18 March 1966 – Spaniards did not enjoy freedom of expression, and after that date they have only been allowed to exercise it with very severe limitations.

For a very long time, from 1938 to 1966, the Spanish press played an instrumental role at the service of the state. In the totalitarian fever of the Civil War, the press was conceived as a 'national institution', submissive to the objectives of the state. The press Law of 1938[11] was promulgated as a provisional measure,[12] and some grounds could be found in the exceptional circumstances of the time to justify the toughness of its contents. However, the 'temporary' 1938 regulations lasted twenty-eight years! During that time all printed material in Spain was subject to censorship before publication, exercised first by the Ministry of Education, and from 1951 by the Ministry of Information and Tourism. The activities of the censor took a variety of forms. The material written by the editorial staff of any publication was carefully scanned and any unwanted article, phrase or reference duly deleted by the red pencil of the censor. Directives (*consignas de prensa*) were issued to editors as to what could or could not be included in the newspaper, the style and form of presentation of a certain topic, the importance to be allocated to a specific news item, the names of people who could not be mentioned, etc.[13] Newspapers also had to print in full the speeches of the Head of State, and any material sent to them by the Ministry of Information for obligatory publication. All national news was selected and distributed by the official news agency, *Efe*, which had the monopoly in these matters.

Censorship was not enough. All manner of controls were imposed on the firms which issued periodicals, and journalists were constrained by strict disciplinarian measures and by the threat of sanctions. The government published, through FET y de las JONS, approximately 40 per cent of all dailies and controlled all others by such devious means as fixing of newspaper prices, establishing the space that could be taken up by advertisements, and regulating the vital supply of newsprint. The government too, appointed the editor of every newspaper, who became an official agent rather than the employee of the publishing firm paying his salary. In fact, editors of provincial newspapers were entrusted with the task of censoring their own papers, since a centralized system of censor-ship was too cumbersome to keep pace with daily publications. An attempt was made to create a new breed of journalists, whose ideas would be in accordance with the spirit of the 1938 Press Law. A school of journalism was founded in 1941, and there was an official register of journalists in which one had to be included in order to belong to the staff of any news-paper or magazine. Any faults committed by journalists, any deviations from the official guidelines were followed by severe penalties: fines, dis-missal of the editor, withdrawal or definite cancellation of publications, or the striking of a journalist' name from the official register.

This was the degree of freedom enjoyed by the Spanish press for almost thirty years. The same could be said about radio, television – when it came – books, theatre and cinema. All of them were subjected to a crude and remorseless censorship, making a mockery of article 12 of the Charter of the Spanish People that had proclaimed since 1945: 'all Spaniards may express their ideas freely, provided they do not endanger the fundamental principles of the State'.

The Spanish regime could not ignore the discrepancy between the general principle proclaimed and the reality of its censorship and oppressive controls. Arias Salgado, Minister of Information and Tourism from 1951 to 1962, found a way of reconciling the two extremes in his own interpretation of truth, freedom and censorship. According to him there is an absolute truth, which must be proclaimed by the press. He even insinuates that absolute truth is on the side of the authorities: 'It is the duty of the Press to reveal the truth, and when it is the public authorities and not public opinion that are on the side of truth the Press must recognize it.'[14] Only the expression of that truth is entitled to freedom, mistakes and half-truths cannot be allowed to spread: 'Freedom of expression for all that is good and true, no freedom for error and evil.'[15] Censorship follows naturally from his way of understanding truth and freedom. The State must ensure that the press does in fact serve the common good of the people by publishing the truth, and it may censor the work of any journalist or newspaper when it is not in accordance with 'the truth, the doctrine of the Church, or the authentic interests of the community'.[16]

Nineteen sixty-six was the year when there was a change of direction in the freedom of the press. Arias Salgado left the Ministry of Information and Tourism in 1962. His substitute, Manuel Fraga Iribarne, came into office with the announcement of a new law for the press, and with the promise of a more liberal attitude. Four years elapsed before Fraga's law was passed by the Spanish Cortes,[17] and during those years censorship and directives were still very much in evidence.[18]

The law came at last, and censorship disappeared. But, how great was the change? The new system introduced by Fraga Iribarne, taken as a whole, undoubtedly represents an important step forward. However, it still falls far short of authentic freedom of expression, and in some aspects is almost regressive.

It claims to put into practice article 12 of the Charter of the Spanish People, but then, using the well-known technique of ambiguous definition, sets as limits to the right to free expression the following: respect for truth and morals; loyalty to the Principles of the National Movement and other Fundamental Laws; the demands of national defence, the State's security, and the maintenance of public order at home and peace abroad; proper respect for institutions and for people when assessing political and administrative actions; the independence of the Courts; and the safeguarding of privacy, and of the honour of the individual and his family.[19] The authorities, as can be seen, allow themselves plenty of room to initiate proceedings against any newspaper or publication that should become too critical about the activities of the government or the regime as a whole. The vagueness of article 2 has created permanent uncertainty in the press, and it has made all the disciplinary decisions of the authorities look rather arbitrary, as they impose heavy penalties for very small offences – if they can be called offences[20] – and at other times allow dissenting articles in much stronger terms.

There is no longer any compulsion to submit material to the censor.[21] Fraga's law has introduced instead a kind of self-imposed censorship, which operates in two ways: first, through a system of voluntary consultation; second, through fear. To avoid running risks publishers may submit material to the approval of the Ministry of Information. It is a kind of insurance policy. Material passed by the authorities cannot be the object of subsequent prosecution. The second method has more wide-reaching effects, since it encompasses all journalists, and any other writer whose work is published. They are in constant danger of overstepping the obscure limits of article 2, mentioned above. And the penalties for any infringement are heavy and may endanger their professional career. Editors, now appointed by the owner and not by the government, are held responsible for the material published in their newspapers, and any editor whose newspaper commits three serious infringements during the course of one year shall be deprived of the post for life. The sanctions of the authorities are immediately applicable, even if the sanctioned person or firm lodges an appeal before the courts. Even if the courts do not appreciate the existence of any offence, the authorities may still impose administrative sanctions.

In spite of all its controlling devices, the Press Law was not considered a sufficiently strong deterrent, and some other limitations were soon imposed. A year later, in April 1967, the transgressions of its ambiguous article 2 were included in the Penal Code as a crime that can lead to imprisonment.[22] A new and very serious restriction, a real gag when applied, was imposed by the Official Secrets Act in April 1968.[23] Under this regulation the authorities may declare secret – 'reserved or classified material' in the legal terminology – any document, piece of information, business or object which, if spread, might endanger the security of the State, or the fundamental interests of the nation in matters of national defence, external peace or constitutional order.[24] Here, too, the authorities are given total discretion to stop the press, and public opinion in general. The list of items which have been classified as secret is fairly long and very telling indeed. It includes the conference on the independence of Spanish Guinea held in Madrid in May 1968, the Bill on Students' associations in the autumn of the same year, the Bill on the organization of the syndicates in September 1969, the documents and information used by a special Cortes committee which discussed the financial scandal of Matesa in May 1970, and the subjects discussed at several meetings of the National Council of the Movement.

The legal threat to any person who puts pen to paper in Spain is a most effective form of self-imposed censorship. The professional writer has the Press Law suspended over his head like Damocles' sword. And many journalists' heads have rolled during the years the law has been in existence. The magazine *Destino* was suspended for two months in 1967. Two successive suspensions, amounting to a total of four months, were imposed on the daily *Madrid* during the course of 1968. In 1969 a new paper *Nivel* had its first and final issue, for the firm publishing it had its permit cancelled by the authorities. *Sábado gráfico*, a Madrid weekly, was under suspension for eight months. And 1971 witnessed the definitive suppression of the newspaper *Madrid*. These are some of the outstanding cases of a very long list[25] of prosecutions, fines, suspensions, withdrawals, affecting newspapers and magazines ideologically as diverse as ABC and *El Alcázar*, *El Noticiero universal* and *El Pensamiento navarro*, *Cuadernos para el diálogo* and *SP*, *Triunfo* and *Ya*. Except for a brief period of relaxation during the first half of 1974, which finally cost the Minister of Information, Pío Cabanillas, his post, this repressive trend has continued to the present day with an interminable list of fines, suspensions, and prosecutions.

Books too have been the target of official prohibition. The buyer of *Informe sociológico sobre la situación social de España, 1970* will find that the fifth chapter of this voluminous and scholarly work, prepared by a team of sociologists, is missing. Its sixty-one pages have been replaced by a brief note that reads: 'Chapter 5 has been suppressed by the authorities'. The subject of this chapter was, of course, politics. It simply showed and analysed the attitudes of Spaniards to politics in the light of a survey the authors had undertaken. Fernández Areal's book on the freedom of the press in Spain, mentioned earlier, was ready for publication in 1968, but it had to wait in cold store three years before being finally allowed to appear in 1971.

Bleak as the situation is, it would be an error to think that nothing was changed by the law of 1966. A comparison of newspapers before and after the law soon shows a considerable difference in the quantity and quality of the news reported.[26] Particularly noticeable is the greater weight given to national politics, and the reporting on subjects which were previously taboo, such as strikes, students' demonstrations, political parties, etc.[27] However, the change must always be viewed in comparison with the previous period in Spain and not in relation to other countries where freedom of expression is not affected by the same kind of State interference.

The regime is very aware that all the Spanish daily press is either official or in the hands of right-wing groups, which are unlikely to take more than a mildly critical stance.[28] Besides, Spaniards do not read many papers. Only three dailies, *Pueblo* and *ABC* from Madrid and *La Vanguardia* from Barcelona, have a circulation of more than 200,000. The newspapers, then, can only have a limited effect on public opinion. Television is little by little becoming the medium that sends the message to Spanish homes. With economic development a forest of TV aerials is now the most prominent feature in the skyline of any Spanish town. The two channels of Spanish television are under the direct control of the Ministry of Information and Tourism, and they are fully exploited to make Spaniards believe that their country is a paradise where nothing unpleasant ever happens. It is not that television is used as a vehicle for indoctrination. The desire to indoctrinate was abandoned a few years after the Civil War together with the totalitarian aspirations. Passive acceptance of the *status quo* and deviation of the public interest away from major issues are the goals. The whole programming suffers from a high dose of conservatism with the expected ingredients: fostering of alienating consumption, exaltation of traditional and authoritarian values, deviation away from the why and how and towards the acceptance of official solutions, total lack of any form of political criticism, dogmatic presentation of ministerial speeches and views, etc. No discordant voice is ever heard, no social or political conflict ever reported. A curious discrepancy thus exists between what the papers say and what appears on the television screen. With all the limitations under which they labour newspapers at least do mention strikes and student demonstrations, and their editorial articles show a contrast of opinions – rather timid and narrow but all the same a contrast – on some, if not all, the political issues facing the country. Television entertains and 'informs' as if those problems and conflicts did not exist. The contrast that does appear in television is between the peace enjoyed in Spain and the upheavals suffered abroad. The situation has a comic side to it. The *telediarios* (news bulletins) have become a source of humour for the most alert cartoonists. One can only react humorously to a television that after full coverage of strikes, political crises, electoral problems or student unrest abroad, gives as home news that a minister has opened a trade fair, that the Development Plan is a real success, or that the Head of State has received at El Pardo Palace some foreign dignitary.[29]

To sum up, the situation as far as freedom of expression is concerned is thus. Information is regulated to steer public opinion in the wanted direction. Conformism is fostered to the highest possible degree. Official propaganda and control on the one side, and a few dissenting voices, heard inasmuch as they are allowed, on the other. It is a sad picture for any Spaniard who may take seriously his right to free speech and thought.

Religious Freedom

The attitude of Spaniards to this question is deeply rooted in history. To understand it, one would probably have to go as far back as Isabella I, the Castilian queen who achieved the political unification of Spain at the end of the fifteenth century, and then saw in the expulsion of Jews and Muslims the way to achieving spiritual unity. From that moment, one would have to follow the reformist movement initiated by Luther, the zealous efforts of Philip II to preserve Roman orthodoxy throughout his European domains, the reality and the legend of the Inquisition, the seesaw of clericalism and anti-clericalism . . .

Much closer to the present and with a direct bearing on it, special consideration has to be given to the years of the Second Republic. The importance of the religious question during those years was outlined and stressed in the Introduction. The Civil War took on the appearance of a holy war. The Church of Rome sided openly with the eventual winners and religious freedom has since suffered from the effects of the alliance. The identification of the Spanish Catholic Church and Franco's regime was total in the post-War years. The regime found in religious unity one more way of exercising control over the country. The Church hierarchy was a pliant and useful tool in the hands of the dictator. In return, the Church was offered the monopoly in spiritual matters, as well as the reversal of all the anti-clerical legislation passed by the Second Republic. They gladly accepted the deal at the time and got down to repairing the Catholic body of the nation, and restoring the spiritual unity the Republic was supposed to have damaged.

Unity was the word of the forties. No dissident opinion or action was allowed. A dogmatic attitude pervaded everything from politics to religion. All Spaniards were Catholics. Those were the years when someone wrote: 'For Spaniards there is no difference between fatherland and religion. To serve God is to serve Spain, to serve Spain is to serve God',[30] an echo of the nineteenth-century orthodoxy of Menéndez y Pelayo: 'nothing that is not Catholic is Spanish'. It is no hyperbole to say that during the forties Spain experienced a kind of counter-reformation. Non-Catholics were identified with the enemies of Spain; Catholics were herded along narrow paths of strict morality, a morality imposed on the individual from outside. The mass media were censored on religious as well as on political grounds. Religion became a compulsory subject at all levels of education. Teaching in all subjects had to be in accordance with the views of the Catholic Church, and text books had to receive the ecclesiastical censor's *nihil obstat* before being published. Religious freedom did not exist, nor was it officially wanted. Church and regime were determined to maintain unity at any cost.

But that unity was never a reality. This was the great fallacy behind the argument, so frequently used in Spain, that the problem of religious freedom did not really arise since all Spaniards were Catholics. Such an argument disregarded the small pockets of Protestants and non-Christian groups scattered all over the country, and it ignored the fact that large numbers of Spaniards were only Catholics by name. Their contacts with the Church, if they had any, were limited to birth, marriage and death.

Sociological research in recent years was to uncover the true situation.[31] After the artificial inflation of the forties, religious fervour and practice have steadily declined all over the country, reaching, in some areas, and in certain social groups, dramatically low levels. Thus, for instance, in a survey carried out amongst workers in 1958, 89.8 per cent said they were anti-clerical, 41.3 per cent anti-religious, and 54.7 per cent indifferent to religion.[32] Attendance at mass on Sundays and days of obligation – possibly the best indicator on account of its regularity – can be put somewhere in the region of 40 per cent for the whole country,[33] but it descends to 2.5 per cent in the slums of big cities like Barcelona.[34] Other indicators, such as the number of vocations to the priesthood or the proportion of people who receive the last sacraments, show equally low percentages.

Religious freedom in Spain has, then, a very profound significance. It is not just a matter of improving the status of non-Catholic minorities, important though this is. It affects the whole community. All Spaniards, whatever their creed, are directly involved, and only by taking this fact into account can a solution be found. But such a solution is impossible without some basic changes in the relationship of the official Church and the regime. Although the post-war honeymoon came to an end, the matrimonial bond between the two, in true Catholic fashion, has remained indissoluble to this day. The Concordat of 1953 is still in force. Its first article precludes the possibility of genuine religious freedom: 'The

Roman Catholic and Apostolic Religion continues to be the only religion of the Spanish Nation and it shall enjoy the rights and prerogatives it is entitled to in accordance with divine and canon Law.'

Similar references can be found in the Fundamental Laws.[35] If Roman Catholicism is the only religion of the Spanish nation, the only true doctrine, and inseparable from the national conscience, there is not much room left for religious freedom. That is why the Charter of the Spanish People had interpreted religious freedom, in its article 6, in a very restrictive way: 'The profession and practice of the Catholic religion, which is that of the Spanish State, shall enjoy official protection. Nobody shall be troubled because of his religious beliefs or the private exercise of his creed. No external ceremonies or manifestations, other than those of the Catholic religion, shall be allowed.' Rather than religious freedom, this article proclaimed freedom of conscience in religious matters. It denied non-Catholics the right to worship in public, an essential part of religious freedom. 'Freedom of worship consists of the right of each person to practise outwardly the religion of his choice, performing its rites and conducting its ceremonies. This right postulates the opportunity of *public* worship, since private worship does not answer to all the exigencies of a true freedom.'[36]

The reality was no better than the laws. The intolerance of the forties was softened as Spain opened her doors to the world, but the privileged position of Catholicism was maintained, while dissident minorities suffered a great deal both spiritually and materially.[37] The responsibility of the Church in these matters was even greater than that of the regime. As spiritual leaders, they cannot justify their intransigence and their collusion with temporal powers, with purely pragmatic reasons, in the way the regime so often does.

The change came in the sixties. It is only fair, however, to acknowledge that Fernando M. Castiella, from the moment he became Foreign Minister in February 1957, initiated a movement to introduce statutes that would protect religious minorities in Spain. Although there was no question of granting religious freedom, Castiella's efforts encountered bitter opposition from those who adhered tenaciously to the traditional image of a totally unified and Catholic Spain.[38] And nothing was achieved until the Church of Rome took the initiative under Pope John XXIII.

The Second Vatican Council tried to put the Catholic Church in line with new developments and with the change of mentality in a modern world that questions most traditional values. Amongst the decisions of the Council, the most important is possibly the one contained in the

Declaration *Dignitatis Humanae* recognizing the inalienable right of all human beings to religious freedom: 'This Vatican Council declares that all human beings have the right to religious freedom.'[39] Consequently, the Roman bishops asked all governments to protect and promote this basic right, even in countries like Spain where, for special reasons, a certain religious community may enjoy special recognition.

The Vatican Council's declaration on religious freedom had a great impact on Spain. The regime had to do something since its legislation, according to the Principles of the National Movement, is inspired by the Catholic doctrine. The initial step was to alter the wording of article 6 of the Charter of the Spanish People in January 1967, not to proclaim unambiguously the right of all Spaniards to enjoy religious freedom, but to restate the official nature of Catholicism in Spain, and to add that 'the State shall undertake to defend religious freedom'. This constitutional amendment was followed, six months later, by a law regulating the civil right to religious freedom.[40]

The new situation falls short of the Vatican declaration. The regime has not gone as far as the Church of Rome suggested. The open and generous approach found in *Dignitatis Humanae* has not been taken up by Spanish legislators. Confronted with an established Church and an official faith on the one hand, and on the other by the need to recognize the right of all Spaniards to religious freedom, they opted in favour of the former to the detriment of the latter; in consequence the 1967 law is not so much concerned with the recognition of religious freedom, as with giving non-Catholic minorities certain protections, which very often have a restrictive effect.

A second and very important objection from a democratic viewpoint which could be raised against the new law on religious freedom is that those most directly affected by it, namely the thirty thousand Spanish Protestants[41] had neither say in nor influence on the making of that law.

As long as the present ties between Church and State continue the chances of authentic religious freedom are considerably diminished. The mere fact that the Concordat considers Catholicism as the only religion of the Spanish nation implies that those following other faiths are not true Spaniards. And the oath of loyalty to the Fundamental Laws, which is required of those who take public office,[42] forces non-Catholics to go against their conscience, since it involves them in swearing, amongst other things, that Catholicism is the only true faith.

However, was the new law the best possible under the circumstances? The answer must be a forthright no, and this assertion is supported by

some distinguished Catholic groups in Spain.[43] Not only does it insist on
the fallacious idea that Catholicism is the religion of the Spanish nation –
even though it is true that it is the religion of the majority – but it says that
the exercise of religious freedom is subject to compatibility with the
privileged position of Catholicism as the official religion of the State. The
rest of the law combines concessions and restrictions resulting from the
position taken *ab initio*. The limits set to religious freedom are as ill-
defined as those concerning other basic rights. The intention to control
non-Catholic churches and the discrimination against them is only too
evident. The administrative shackles are numerous. Other churches have
to apply for official recognition to acquire legal existence and thus be able
to exercise their rights. They have to be entered in a special register at the
Ministry of Justice, specifying everything from their official address to
their assets and property. They must keep a register of members and
accounts, which shall be yearly inspected by the authorities. Local
branches, places of worship, schools, and centres for the training of
ministers can only be set up with an authorization from the Ministry of
Justice. The ministers of non-Catholic religions are not exempted from
military service . . . These are some of the most blatant restrictions
imposed. There are many others,[44] all springing from a desire to enforce
unity at all costs.

We cannot conclude the study of the problems of religious freedom in
Spain without referring, even if only briefly, to the inhuman treatment
meted out to the conscientious objectors, not less inhuman because until
now it has only affected a handful of people. The law on religious freedom
makes no reference to them, and no other regulation seemed directly
applicable. So the legal vacuum was filled by the Code of Military
Justice, whose harsh measures have been repeatedly applied to those
Spaniards – Jehovah's Witnesses for the most part – who refuse to do
compulsory military service on grounds of conscience; and this has been
done on a 'chain system', that is to say, if a conscientious objector after
serving a sentence for his refusal was still adhering steadfastly to his
principles he would be court-martialled once more, with the extra charge
of being recidivist. As a result, up until 1973 there have been cases of
conscientious objectors who have been in prison for more than fifteen
years.[45]

The Spanish government made two half-hearted attempts at a legal
solution and witnessed impassively how the National Defence Committee
of the Cortes thwarted both, rejecting the first Bill and altering the second
so profoundly that the government was forced to withdraw it.[46] A very

serious human problem was left pending and the government did not make use of its powers to legislate by decree when, in fact, 'few times there has been more pressing reason to resort to the decree-law'.[47]

All this was happening in May 1970 (the first Bill) and July 1971 (the second Bill). At long last, at the third attempt, the Spanish Cortes, in their plenary session of 18 December 1973, passed a law concerning those who refuse to do their military service. There is no recognition of any right to refuse, there is no possibility of any alternative non-military service, there is not even mention of conscientious objectors. All the law does is to put an end to the system of repeated sentences, replacing it by a single term of imprisonment of between three and eight years together with the deprivation for life of all political and some civil rights.[48]

The law on religious freedom was not received very favourably by the Protestant churches in Spain.[49] It represented a considerable improvement, but it came as a gift or concession, not as recognition of a basic right. True religious freedom is nearer now than it was before 1967, although not yet near enough. Will the law on religious freedom lead to it? Possibly, but only if the established Church renounces her privileges, comes down to the level of others, and makes the regime accept the inevitable. The following words, written by a Spanish priest, contain a great deal of encouragement and hope for the future: "It will be necessary to break down many prejudices. We shall have to get to know each other better. There are millions of Spaniards who have never spoken with a Protestant. We shall have to know much better the Bible, our common book of prayer and life. We shall have to pray together more often... But, above all, we shall have to share more intensely our communal struggle for freedom, justice, truth and love.'[50]

The Right to Strike

Huelga is the Spanish word meaning strike, or withdrawal of labour by employed workers. In all countries with a capitalist economy, strikes have become frequent, and in many of those countries, the right to strike has been recognized and granted legal protection. In some cases, as in France or Italy, it has been included in the constitution, in others, as in the United States of America, although not proclaimed by the constitution, the right to strike has been given tacit recognition and regulated by ordinary laws. But in Spain Franco's regime has given the word *huelga* a different meaning.

Words and expressions like *huelga, clase obrera, partido político*, are not very familiar to Spaniards who grew up after the Civil War or, if they are, must always bring to mind forbidden and subversive connotations. *Huelga* was a word very rarely used in the early years of the regime. To go on strike was a serious offence against the nation. The Labour Charter, in its original version of 1938, made no bones about it: 'Any individual or collective action which endangers or disturbs, in any way, normal production, shall be considered a crime against the country.'[51] The Penal Code included the strike as a criminal offence of a seditious nature.[52] The Charter of the Spanish People totally ignored the matter, and strikers continued to be regarded as criminals for many years.

Some softening in the official attitude was brought about by the demands of economic development. During the forties and early fifties workers in a poor country like Spain had to be content with having a job, any job, and had to concentrate all their efforts on earning enough to keep their families and themselves alive. Social injustices at a general level are not easily perceived by those who have to consume their energies at a very elementary level of existence.[53] But the boom that came with the sixties had a double effect. Workers acquired an awareness of their situation as a class. Economic growth required that some of the controls imposed on labour relations were removed, so as to facilitate a smoother path towards neo-capitalism.

As a prelude of things to come, in 1958 a rather crude system of collective bargaining – which ignored labour conflicts – was established.[54] But a year later the Spanish Cortes were still passing penal legislation on strikes. A law of 1959 declared that all actions that disturbed the normal functioning of public services or the regularity of supply and prices, and all collective stoppages and lock-outs were offences against public order.[55] And in 1960 politically motivated strikes, or strikes that represented a serious threat to public order, were classed by a government decree as acts of military rebellion subject to the jurisdiction of military courts.[56]

In 1962, a more sophisticated set of rules to deal with labour conflicts was produced by the government.[57] Solutions were sought through the mediation and arbitration of the special Labour Courts (Magistraturas del Trabajo), and of the offices of the Ministry of Labour and the syndical organization. These regular channels applied only to labour conflicts affecting the parties involved in negotiating an agreement. Outside those regular channels, any labour conflict became illegal.

There is no direct reference to strikes in the 1962 decree, but the course of subsequent developments in this field can already be made out. The refusal to legalize the strike is clear, and by its side the intention to reduce the area of illegality of the strike can also be detected. Given the inevitability of conflicts the decree was an attempt to minimize their repercussions and to integrate them into the existing system. It is from about this time that the debate on the question of how to differentiate labour strikes from political strikes starts in Spain. In 1965 the Penal Code was amended. Previously all strikers were guilty of sedition; now only stoppages affecting public or essential services, or those which are directed against the security of the State or have a serious effect on national production are seditious.[58] The Labour Charter was amended too along the same lines in 1967, as can be seen in its declaration XI, 2.

The Second Development Plan in 1969 announced new regulations to deal with collective labour conflicts, including the stoppages which might occur as a result of them.[59] This announcement was followed in 1970 by a short decree[60] which made practically no new contribution to legalizing strikes, and by updating, in 1973, of the system of collective bargaining introduced fifteen years previously. The updating, if anything, has brought collective bargaining even more under the control of the official syndicates, thus predetermining perforce the nature of any future legislation on strikes.[61] The most recent item in this long legal dossier on strikes has been a new decree – it is worth noticing how the most controversial questions are still being settled by decree – issued in April 1975, legalizing certain types of labour conflicts. It adds very little that is new. There is no recognition of the strike as a worker's right. The new legality of strikes is narrow and strictly limited to matters arising out of the renewal or interpretation of a collective agreement. One could speak of a bureaucratization of strikes. The procedure to legalize a conflict is long and complex, and totally controlled by the official syndicates. The bureaucratic barrier is carefully placed as a dissuasive factor. All other stoppages continue to be illegal, either on grounds of motivation – solidarity, political objectives – or for procedural reasons, and the strikers involved in them are threatened by dismissal and by the sanctions of the Public Order Court. Which, in practice, means that the majority of strikes will still be illegal.

Legal prohibitions and the threat of dismissal, fines or imprisonment have not stopped strikes, which have become a part of industrial life in Spain, and the authorities, much as they may regret their occurrence, have had to face up to reality and recognize their *de facto* existence.

Up until 1962, the number of strikes in Spain was fairly low – though some important ones did occur during the previous decade – but the new economic and political orientation of the sixties put into practice the collective bargaining system of 1958 and brought about a proliferation of labour conflicts, and, amongst them, many total or partial strikes. The information available on this subject is not always reliable. All the same, several studies[62] have been carried out on the basis of that information and their results are rather revealing. The number of labour conflicts has fluctuated during the last decade in accordance with the political and economic temperature of the country – years of economic recession (e.g. 1966) show fewer strikes, and years with a politically explosive climate (e.g. 1970) are characterized by a great upsurge of labour conflicts. However, the general trend was until the end of 1973 upwards, in the overall number of conflicts and even more in the number of working hours lost, as the conflicts become larger and more embittered. The proportion of conflicts ending up in a partial or total stoppage has increased dramatically as can be seen on the following table.

TABLE 17 – ACTION OF WORKERS IN LABOUR CONFLICTS (PERCENTAGES)[63]

Action	1963	1964	1965	1966	1967	1968	1969	1970
Total stoppage	22	24	28	36	42	57	51	77.3
Partial stoppage	—	—	34	20	48	31	37	16.3
Work to rule	13	14	19	20	3	4	7	2.2
Other forms	65	62	19	24	7	8	5	3

The figures for the period 1971–3 continue exactly the same pattern.

Another important factor is the motivation of the conflict. It is difficult to establish, when, as so often happens, a conflict is due to a number of causes. The problem is further complicated in the Spanish case by the illegality of certain types of conflict, which may force workers to disguise their real motivation. All the same, and on the basis of the statistics provided by the Ministry of Labour, it can be seen that the percentage of conflicts motivated by socio-political reasons has been increasing steadily. By 1970 more than 40 per cent of the conflicts had some socio-political motivations behind them.[64] And in 1971, 'almost 50 per cent of the total conflicts were motivated by socio-political causes or by solidarity'.[65]

What conclusions can, then, be drawn from the divorce between the legal texts of the regime and the actual behaviour of Spanish workers?

Strikes in most cases are not legal in Spain. The right to strike is not protected by law, and in many cases to go on strike constitutes a crime. The ambiguities of the decree of 1962 on collective labour conflicts and the changes introduced in the Penal Code and the Labour Charter had given grounds for thinking that non-political strikes would become legal, but the Supreme Court of Justice settled the question and destroyed all hopes by declaring that under Spanish law all strikes were illegal,[66] a position which bluntly collided with the advice of the Catholic Church on this matter: '. . . in the present position, the strike may still be a necessary, but last resort for the workers to defend their rights, and to achieve their just aspirations'.[67] This is a clear anomaly, since the Spanish regime proclaims that its legislation is inspired by the doctrine of the Catholic Church. Essentially this situation has not been altered by the latest legislation on labour conflicts.

Strikes take place regardless of their illegality, very often unchecked by the authorities, who have to show a certain tolerance towards the inevitable. Nevertheless, the regime has at its disposal the means of repression, which it can legally justify, and it will use them whenever it feels threatened.[68]

The need to recognize the right to strike is widely felt in Spain. According to the ILO report, workers, employers and even government officials are in favour of recognition.[69] Why does the regime oppose it, when strikes keep recurring and even the needs of the capitalist system seem to require it? The answer is simple. There is no possible symbiosis between the authoritarian nature of the regime and the right to strike. To begin with, the syndical organization would collapse. If the workers were granted freedom to strike, they would need to organize independently to exercise that freedom. This, in turn, would require freedom of association, and the whole process would escalate to the point of questioning the very essence of the regime.

In a way, this is already happening with strikes in Spain. Even if their causes and their objectives are simply related to wages or conditions of work, they often 'degenerate' into political struggles out of the frustration felt by workers, who find that they have neither union to support their struggle, nor freedom to put their case, and that the official syndicates are more concerned with bringing conflicts to an end than with the defence of the workers' interests. The *politización* of strikes is thus inevitable. And the regime avails itself of that excuse not to legalize the right to strike. Spanish workers are fighting a battle their counterparts in Western Europe won long ago, not so much for higher wages or better conditions as for their fundamental rights.

The Suspension of Rights

It is much easier for an authoritarian regime to proclaim rights in abstract, than to define generous limits to the exercise of those rights. Specific examples in the Spanish case show how the general declaration of freedom is usually accompanied by a number of vague and, in practice, restrictive limitations. In fact, this applies to all the rights contained in the Charter of the Spanish People. Their exercise must not endanger 'the spiritual, national and social unity of Spain'.[70] And when these undefined and indefinable boundaries are overstepped, the government is entitled to suspend, totally or partially, some of the rights contained in the Charter for as long as they judge it necessary.[71] The suspension of rights is an eventuality foreseen in most constitutions. What characterizes the Spanish system in this respect is, first, that the government is given discretionary powers to decide when the situation warrants a state of emergency; and secondly, that no time limits are imposed on the government. It can maintain the emergency for as long as it likes. The constitution of the Second Republic, far from a model in this respect, compares very favourably with the present situation. The republican governments could only impose a state of emergency with the backing of the Cortes, and the maximum period of suspension of rights was only thirty days.[72] By contrast, all that the Spanish government must do now is inform the Cortes of the decision taken and set its own limits of time.

It could be said that the Spanish regime has not resorted very often to such exceptional powers. This argument is not infrequent in official circles. It was used by Carrero Blanco, then Vice-President of the government, when informing the Cortes of the declaration of the state of emergency at the beginning of 1969: 'Most of you will remember the numerous and almost permanent suspensions of constitutional guarantees during the republican quinquennium. It was only when our regime came in that the state of emergency (*estado de excepción*) became really exceptional.'[73]

The first state of emergency declared in Spain after the promulgation of the Charter of the Spanish People was in February 1956. It came as a result of student demonstrations, clashes, and general unrest at the University of Madrid. In 1958, in answer to a wave of miners' strikes in the Asturian coalfields, the government put the whole province under a state of emergency, suspending for a period of four months articles 14 (freedom of residence), 15 (privacy of the home), and 18 (*habeas corpus*). The later suspension of article 14, for a period of two years from June

1962, had great resonance abroad. Eighty Spaniards, belonging to different opposition groups, together with some Spanish exiles, attended the Congress of the European Movement held at Munich. They passed unanimously a resolution calling on the Spanish government to set up democratic institutions, and to recognize and guarantee human rights. There was no further demand in the resolution. It was worded in very clear but far from extremist terms. However, the participants were branded as traitors by the Spanish press, and on their return home were detained by the police and given the choice of exile or confinement to the small island of Fuerteventura in the Canaries.

For a period of three years starting in April 1967, the two coastal provinces of the Basque country, Vizcaya and Guipúzcoa, were repeatedly under emergency measures. Workers' unrest and the terrorist activities of the separatist group ETA were the reasons for such harsh treatment. Articles 14, 15 and 18 were suspended for three months, by decree of 21 April 1967, in the whole of the province of Vizcaya. Guipúzcoa suffered the same fate by a decision of the Council of Ministers taken on 26 July 1968. Before this suspension had come to an end, it was considered necessary to lengthen it for a further three months 'to facilitate some police investigations which are already very advanced', as the government's decree put it. Guipúzcoa came under emergency powers once again on 5 December 1970, after ETA members had kidnapped the German consul in San Sebastián.

On three other recent occasions the government assumed emergency powers. On 24 January 1969, articles 12 (freedom of expression), 14, 15, 16 (freedom of assembly and association) and 18 of the Spanish Charter were suspended for three months throughout the country (in the event the suspension only lasted two months). This was the strictest emergency ever applied by the present regime. It was intended simply to put an end to the activities of subversive minorities in the universities, because 'socially and politically the country enjoyed excellent health', according to Fraga Iribarne, Minister of Information and Tourism at the time.[74] At the end of the two months the Ministry of the Interior released a note to the press giving details of the police activities during the state of emergency. The maximum number of people detained at any one time had been 338 (76 students and 262 others); legal proceedings had been initiated against 175 people, and 180 had been brought before the military courts; 74 students and 169 other people were in prison when the emergency was lifted.[75] By 22 April the government could inform the Cortes that the police had broken up several communist and anarchist groups, and that university life was back to normal.[76] Eight months later the state of emergency was back, first, in the province of Guipúzcoa, and a few days later, from 15 December 1970, article 18 was suspended for six months in the whole of Spain. This time the reason was the tense atmosphere generated, both at home and abroad, by the court-martialling of some members of ETA at Burgos. Finally, in April 1975, terrorist activities, involving the killing of several policemen in the Basque country, were given as the reason for declaring, once again, the state of emergency in the provinces of Guipúzcoa and Vizcaya.

The overall number of times the regime had to make use of its extraordinary powers is fairly high. It seems to contradict the official claim of Spain's peaceful life under Franco's rule. But much more serious than the number of times Spain has been under a state of emergency is the fact that these states of emergency only represent a hardening of an already hard situation. By comparison with most countries in the western world, Spain has been under a permanent state of emergency for the last three decades.

In 1962 the International Commission of Jurists denounced the lack of respect for and the constant breaching of the principles of the rule of law in Spain. More than a decade has gone by, and the changes introduced by the regime affecting basic rights and freedoms have done little to counter that serious accusation.

The expression of dissenting opinions, participation in demonstrations or strikes, attendance at non-authorized meetings, attempts to set up free trade unions or political parties all actions which may, and very often do, give rise to heavy fines and terms of imprisonment, under the Penal Code and the Public Order Law of 1959. The latter is a kind of 'penal law enforced by the administration'.[77] A number of amendments in several articles have strengthened the powers of the executive, and made penalties much heavier.[78] Under the new provisions of the Public Order Law the executive may arrest, without trial, for a period of up to three months, any person who, having been fined, is unable to pay the fine immediately or at least to put down a third of it in order to be allowed to appeal. This the law euphemistically calls 'subsidiary personal responsibility'.[79] The authorities have not been slow to avail themselves of the wide powers the Public Order Law gives them. In fact, this law 'has been applied so profusely – only last academic year [1970–71] hundreds of students were fined for *disturbios estudiantiles* – that it has become a permanent substitute for other emergency measures'.[80]

Such behaviour, which – it must be repeatedly underlined – in other countries is accepted as normal and legal in the expression of individual freedom, can in Spain lead to imprisonment under the regulations of the Penal Code, the Code of Military Justice, the Decree on Banditry and Terrorism of 1960, and even the Law for the Repression of Freemasonry and Communism of 1940, which is still in force. It is not possible here to give even a summary of the numerous regulations in the above laws which represent a curtailment of freedom or stand as a constant threat to it. The following two will serve as an illustration.

Actions or opinions which go against the Principles of the National Movement, or which encourage the repeal or amendment of the Fundamental Laws, outside the legal channels, can be punished with up to six years' imprisonment, and a 100,000 pesetas (£830) fine.[81] And article 2 of the Decree on Banditry and Terrorism, referred to above when discussing the question of strikes, considers as guilty of military rebellion:

'1. Any person who spreads false or tendentious news with a view to disturbing law and order, to causing international conflicts or to damaging the prestige of the State, its institutions, its army or its public authorities.

'2. Any person who by whatsoever means conspires or takes part in meetings, conferences or demonstrations having as their object one of those mentioned in the preceding paragraph.

'. . . strikes, sabotage, and any other similar act, if they are inspired by political motives or seriously disturb law and order, may also be considered as acts of military rebellion.'

This is the general tenor of all the laws claiming to regulate the rights of Spaniards. They are not concerned so much with guaranteeing individual freedom as with protecting not just the State but the regime. These laws are interpreted and applied by the special court, the Public Order Court, created expressly for that purpose in December 1963, and in the more serious cases, foreseen in the Decree on Banditry and Terrorism of 1960, by military courts. The repressive nature of much of the legislation, and the frequency and harshness of the sentences imposed on many a dissenting voice or action, makes one doubt the real validity of the Charter of the Spanish People. Echoing a rhetorical question of Jorge Manrique, the fifteenth-century Spanish poet, in his most famous work,[82] one might ask: freedom of expression, freedom of association, freedom of assembly, religious freedom . . . *qué se hicieron?* (what happened to them?).

The official answer may very well be summed up with the words of a member of the Cortes who, during the debate on the amendments to the Public Order Law in June 1971 said: '. . . the freedoms most Spaniards want are not the constitutional ones, but the freedom to go to work, to send their children to school, and to go to the pictures at night.'[83]

9 POLITICAL FORCES, PRESSURE GROUPS AND OPPOSITION

Introduction

Throughout their modern history, going back to the early days of liberalism in the nineteenth century, Spaniards have shown a great weakness when it comes to organizing themselves into units or groups that will together form a stable social pattern capable of withstanding the tensions and struggles normally generated within the boundaries of any nation. The reasons for this have long been the focus of attention of many eminent Spaniards. Whether the reasons are to be found in the historical development of Spain, attributed to the proverbial individualism of Spaniards, or inevitably contained in the texture of an underdeveloped society, need not concern us now. It is sufficient to point out that the problem is not new. It had existed long before Franco came into power. In politics it meant that Spain never had a stable party system. Political life had always suffered from excessive plurality and continuous mutation. 'Not in vain,' wrote Madariaga a few years back, '*la gauche* and *la droite*, on crossing the Pyrenees, become *las izquierdas* and *las derechas*.'[1] The present regime was quick to exploit this national weakness to justify imposing an authoritarian system. Spaniards were repeatedly told that the country needed enforced unity to progress and develop, for the feuds and divisiveness of political parties were at the root of the nation's problems. Opposition to organized political plurality has been constant in the Franco regime. But more than thirty years of this policy have not brought a discernible solution any nearer. All the studies on the subject published in Spain and abroad, coincide on one point: after the long dictatorial period, political forces in Spain, both inside and outside the established system, are fragmented beyond any coherent and identifiable structure, so that they are either reduced to a purely elitist level – small groups orbiting around some well-known public figure – or else sunk into the obscure world of illegality and subversion – as are the communist party or ETA – where it is always difficult to separate fact from fiction, reality from propaganda.

Thus the 'unifying' policies of francoism have come home to roost. Political forces are more disorganized than ever before. Instead of unity and consensus all that can be discerned inside the system is a host of *heredípetas*[2] anxious to secure some form of political continuity beyond Franco, that will guarantee their positions or, if possible, their advancement. On the outside is an equally divided opposition, varying in its degree of detachment from the regime, and beyond them all, silent and with unknown political views, is the mass of the Spanish people.

The organizational vacuum has as its corollary an extremely confused ideological set-up. It is difficult to see very often what views political figures represent, who stands for what and who stands next to whom, confusion which stems from a number of factors, from the progressive reduction and dilution of dogmatic areas in official ideology, to the lack of channels for expressing political viewpoints; and ideological promiscuity has affected many Spanish politicians over the last decade, for they stand, as Professor Aranguren has sharply indicated,[3] with one foot in power and the other in opposition: while in office they exercise and defend the authoritarian ways of the regime, only to proclaim their love for democracy when displaced from power.

Confronted with this confused and confusing picture, shapeless in both composition and ideas, we have opted for the most elementary classification of political forces: we divide all the public figures and groups that operate inside the established system, lending their support, in different ways, to the Franco regime, from those whose primary aim is replacing the regime by a different one, either by progressive reform or by sudden reversal. Within this simple scheme[4] recognizable groups and relevant political figures have been fitted, without circumventing the use of proper names. The list cannot by any means be taken as exhaustive. It is only indicative, for the political game in Spain is highly personalized, and has become even more so in the climate of the last few years – a reflection perhaps of the extreme personalization represented by the life-long investiture of national sovereignty in one man. Names, such as Fraga, López Rodó, Girón, Silva Muñoz seem to have greater echo and significance than generic terms like socialists, Christian-democrats or conservatives. Rather telling is the fact that of late in Spain one hears and reads references not to political forces, groups or parties, but to *familias políticas*. All this is valid for the politics of the establishment, and it could be possibly applied too to those who fill the ranks of the allowed opposition; beyond that line subversion leads to anonymity.

The Political Forces inside the Regime

Inside the regime itself is a number of groups, as we saw when discussing the composition of successive governments. They form the political establishment, and in spite of their varied background, have shown a coherent and united front. Tensions exist between these groups and rivalries separate their leaders. All the same, they have kept together because they have enough ideology and interests in common. Over the years, they have all had a considerable share in power, they have pursued their objectives under official protection, they have monopolized the best posts, they have enjoyed a large measure of influence, and they have become the recipients of wealth in the capitalist development of the economy. These groups are not political parties; some, like the army or the Church, are not parties, and others, like falangists or monarchists, even though they could have the makings of a party, have not been allowed to organize themselves as one outside the official framework of the National Movement.

Spain has been labelled 'a *latifundio* of pressure groups'.[5] With political parties banned and the confused nature and role of the National Movement, a variegated host of pressure groups, interest groups, military, religious and economic forces has climbed on to the political stage and taken over the running of the play. These groups are made up principally of monarchists, falangists and Catholic politicians; and behind them or next to them three other forces: the army, which is the force *par excellence*; the Church, incarnating the moral force; and the economic forces represented by industrial, financial and agrarian capital.

Amongst them an understanding has been reached. They have compromised and tacitly accepted an *entente cordiale* based upon the following principles:

1. Militarism: the armed forces have been given a place, either by law or in practice, on all the major bodies – Council of the Realm, Regency Council, Government, Cortes – and they have been made the guarantors of the political *status quo*.[6]
2. Catholicism: seats at the top have also been reserved for the Church hierarchy; the Catholic faith has been declared as the only true faith and as such inseparable from the national conscience; Spanish legislation must be in accordance with the principles laid down by the Church of Rome;[7] Church and regime have their respective interests carefully protected by a concordat.
3. Falangism: the general lines of the institutional structure of the regime have been drawn following the falangist doctrine.
4. Capitalism: in economic matters private ownership of the means of production, accumulation of wealth by a few and monopolistic tendencies have been the predominant features.
5. Monarchism: since 1947 Spain has been an uncrowned monarchy and a Prince is already waiting to sit on the throne the day Franco dies.

A sixth characteristic that sums up the previous five and could well serve as a general heading for them all is francoism. All the groups and forces inside the regime have shown a permanent and undiminished loyalty to the dictator, lending him their support, contributing with their constant praise to the maintenance of his charismatic image,[8] and reaping rewards in return.

Monarchists constitute a fair section of the francoist establishment.[9] They are divided by their backing one or other of the pretenders to the Spanish throne. The main division separates the supporters of the Bourbon dynasty in the line of descent of the Spanish king, Alfonso XIII, from the followers of carlism, a Bourbon splinter party whose descendants have claimed since the 1830s to be the legitimate heirs to the Spanish throne. Both groups have been further subdivided by personalities and events. A majority of the Bourbon group had for long favoured a monarchy with don Juan, Count of Barcelona, son and rightful heir to Alfonso XIII, as King. Their ranks included, at least until summer 1969, an assorted bag of very well-known figures such as the writer José María Pemán; Rafael Calvo Serer, member of Opus Dei and master-brain behind the now defunct evening newspaper *Madrid*; Gonzalo Fernández de la Mora, conservative writer and thinker and until the end of 1973

Minister of Public Works (his allegiance to don Juan was possibly with-drawn well before 1969); Jose María de Areilza, Count of Motrico, at one time Spanish ambassador in Paris and Washington, and now better known as an advocate of liberal democracy; and the Luca de Tena family, whose newspaper *ABC* has been the loudest hailer in don Juan's case. Legitimism did not prevail in spite of this distinguished backing. Another monarchist faction, smaller but closer to the Caudillo, eventually won the day. The supporters of Prince Juan Carlos, don Juan's son,[10] succeeded in by-passing his father's right to the throne, and the Prince was chosen as successor to Franco. The consternation of legitimists when confronted with Prince Juan Carlos's appointment in July 1969 was reflected in the dismal reaction of the monarchist press. Nevertheless, it is more than likely that the gap between the two factions will be bridged by time, and that the *juanistas*, as don Juan's supporters are sometimes called, will change their allegiance the day Prince Juan Carlos becomes King, with Calvo Serer in exile in Paris one of the few exceptions.[11]

The carlists are also split, though in a different way. Their direct line of descent was halted in 1936 by the lack of an heir. The present pretender, Carlos Hugo of Bourbon-Parma, has no direct blood ties with his carlist predecessors. This, of course, has weakened considerably the carlist claim. Hopeless as their cause is, especially after the expulsion of Prince Carlos Hugo from Spanish soil in December 1968 and the subsequent appointment of his rival Prince Juan Carlos, carlism still survives. Geographically, it only extends over the province of Navarre and some adjacent areas. The political influence of these carlists is very limited. They have a handful of *procuradores* in the Cortes, and a few other minor political figures. They come onto the scene once a year when they gather in Montejurra – where they won a military victory in 1873 – to pray and demonstrate their unfailing support for the carlist pretender.

But the most influential carlists in Franco's regime have not been real carlists. Men like Esteban Bilbao or Antonio Iturmendi are always referred to as traditionalists, because although followers of the carlist doctrine known as traditionalist communion, condensed in the motto 'God, Fatherland and King', they have not openly supported the claims of carlist pretenders. The contribution of these traditionalists to the regime has been important. Their ambivalent attitude has been of great value to Franco. They have helped to shape the future monarchy along traditionalist lines, without contributing any embarrassing support for the carlist cause. Here, as in the other monarchist camps, time may very well diffuse the differences, obliterating the dynastic side of carlism and leaving it as a purely traditionalist movement, defender, for the most part, of reactionary and outmoded values.[12]

It is rather ironic that the falangists should now find themselves split up into factions, when one of the founding principles of Falange was to overcome the eternal division of 'right' and 'left', to create a unitary political organization that would comprise the whole nation. The division in the falangist ranks springs from the eventful history of the party over the last forty years. As a party they were diluted and taken over by the National Movement organization. The political side of their doctrine was largely accepted if not very faithfully implemented, but their so-called social revolution was never carried out. The acceptance or rejection of this historical fate separates falangists into two groups. To the 'right' of the dividing line are the collaborationists, the falangists who have adapted themselves to all the changes imposed by Franco, without any noticeable signs of objection. Many early falangists, men who belonged to Falange before the war, are in this category. Raimundo Fernández Cuesta, who was Secretary-General of Falange and three times a minister in Franco's government, could be taken as the prototype, and next to him other well-known falangists such as Sancho Dávila, Agustín Aznar, Pilar Primo de Rivera, Fermín Sanz Orrio, and even José Luis de Arrese.

To the 'left' of the dividing line mentioned above, stand the purists, or falangists who object to the adulterations introduced in José Antonio's doctrine. They want to put the clock back and return to the early days of the party: blue shirt and black tie, para-military organization and the writings of José Antonio Primo de Rivera as their political bible. They consider themselves very left wing and claim that their plans for a social revolution go even further than marxist communism, but with the great advantage that they intend to save the traditional values of Spain.[13] Their stronghold is found in the Círculos doctrinales José Antonio, and their opinions expressed in publications such as the weekly magazine SP. The figure of José Antonio Girón, Minister of Labour for nearly sixteen years, has frequently been associated with this section of the falangist camp. After leaving office in 1957 he disappeared from the political scene, but then re-emerged with a forceful political speech delivered in Valladolid on 4 May 1972,[14] and more recently published, in *Arriba*,[15] a thundering article, full of ominous overtones, denouncing, in a style reminiscent of the thirties and forties, the dangers the government would run if it were to follow a deviationist democratizing path. The popular support for this outmoded idea cannot be very large nowadays. Nevertheless, the falangist groups, with their various shades of neo-fascism, should not be ignored.[16] Not far from them, more often than not in collusion with them, stand some elements representative of an ultra-right form of conservatism, whose reactionary views do not exclude the resort to violence; amongst them Blas Piñar and his weekly publication *Fuerza Nueva* are possibly the most prominent, but one could also mention at a lower level the commando-like group known as 'The Guerrillas of Christ the King', or some of the units operating in the university world, such as FIES or FUNS.[17]

Another falangist group is made up largely by former members of Falange's Youth Front (Frente de Juventudes). They too think that falangism has been exploited by reactionary forces in Spain, and yearn for a purification of José Antonio's ideas. Their attitude is not, however, as dogmatic and intolerant, and it can be viewed as an attempt to update the ideas of the founder of Falange. Their most representative figure is Manuel Cantarero del Castillo, President of the Association of Former Members of the Youth Front, and leader of one of the newly formed political associations.[18] He claims that the ideologies of falangism and socialism are converging to constitute what he calls syndicalist socialism or socialist syndicalism.[19] His group is part of the falangist 'left', and their revolution, he says,[20] can be carried out by taking a reformist stance within the present constitutional structure without resorting to subversion.

Finally, syndicalists may also be classified as a falangist breed. The massive framework of the official syndicates has given shelter to an equally massive body of bureaucrats, a majority of them falangists either by conviction or convenience – at one time it was necessary to be a member of FET y de las JONS to hold a post of authority in the syndical organization. But the syndical bureaucrats have shown more concern for survival than for falangist principles. The history of the Spanish syndical organization is an excellent example of bureaucracy based upon expediency. Syndicalists do not constitute a coherent political body, but the size and weight of their organization turn them into a very powerful pressure group indeed.

The Catholic camp is rather heterogeneous too, but for the sake of simplicity, can be reduced to two groups, whose fortunes have marched in opposite directions. One of them is set around Editorial Católica, a publishing firm, and the Asociación Católica Nacional de Propagandistas. Their roots are in two parties of the republican years: Acción Popular and CEDA. Their promoter was, until his death in 1968, Cardinal Herrera Oria. They reached their moment of greatest influence during the fifties when they had two of their leading figures, Alberto Martín Artajo and

Joaquín Ruiz-Giménez, in key posts in the Government. Since those days, however, their importance has declined. Their last representative in the government, Federico Silva Muñoz, was relieved of his post as Minister of Public Works in April 1970. Many of their members have drifted away to take up positions of opposition to the regime. Nevertheless, they are still a force that cannot be ignored, with a powerful voice in their national daily *Ya*, and with some degree of influence in Arias Navarro's government.

The newest, the most secretive and the one considered until quite recently as the most powerful of all the groups behind Franco is Opus Dei. What exactly is Opus Dei? A straightforward question to which nobody has as yet been able to give an equally straightforward answer. Its defenders see Opus Dei as nothing more than a religious organization whose aim is to foster among its members – laymen for the most part – the search for spiritual values and the identification with Christ in the events of their daily lives and in their work, whatever this may be.[21] Its detractors see it very differently. For them, Opus Dei is based upon a very crude and egocentric philosophy, and they accuse it of pursuing material objectives and worldly power under the cover of spirituality.[22]

Anyone who takes a close look at Opus Dei – or as close as the secrecy of the organization allows – cannot but notice the rapidity of its development. It was founded in 1928 by an Aragonese priest, Jose María Escrivá de Balaguer. Until 1939 it remained a very small and unknown organization. Its real growth started in the atmosphere of Catholic zeal which invaded Spain in the forties. In 1947 the Vatican recognized Opus Dei as the first secular institute in the Catholic Church, and from then it has grown and grown to become a world-wide organization, though it is still much stronger in Spain than in any other country.

The exact size of its membership is not known. There are different categories of members in accordance with their commitment to the Opus Dei cause. A majority are laymen: there is also a feminine branch and a section made up of priests. Their actions and behaviour are guided by a little manual written by Mgr Escrivá de Balaguer and published in 1939 under the simple title *Camino (The Way)*.[23] Its contents are just 999 aphorisms or maxims advising and encouraging members to succeed in their respective professions. Unsystematic and bizarre are two befitting adjectives for *Camino*.[24] Escrivá de Balaguer places a spiritual value on success and personal advancement to the detriment of Christian virtues such as humility and charity.[25] His followers have not let him down.

Opus Dei members can be found in all walks of life in Spain: in the academic sphere, in the world of finance, in high administrative posts, in publishing, in industry, etc. The fundamental question here is to what extent Opus Dei members are coordinated and directed by the organization. The existence of control from above in temporal matters is denied by Opus Dei and by its members. One of the most distinguished and politically important figures of Opus Dei, López Rodó, wrote: 'The fact that I am a member of the Catholic association Opus Dei does not in any way imply that I have to accept directives in those fields [he is referring to his post, at the time, as Minister in charge of Economic Development], or, indeed, of any other kind.'[26]

The opposite opinion is widely spread and in recent times openly expressed in Spain.[27] The information that has oozed out of the confined secrecy of the Opus Dei and the massive compilation of accusatory evidence in some recently published works[28] may be distorted and in some instances even untrue. This conceded, one is still left with too many indications that Opus Dei has become one of the predominant pressure groups in Spain.

It is common knowledge that Opus Dei – or its members – has its own university in Pamplona (Navarre), that it controls the Banco Popular (one of the big banks in Spain), that it controls publishing firms too, like Rialp, and newspapers and magazines, like *Actualidad Económica* or *Actualidad Española*. Known also is the fact that more and more of its members have, during the last fifteen years, appeared in positions of authority within Spanish society. Can all this be pure coincidence and the result of Escrivá de Balaguer's aphoristic advice in *Camino*? The hierarchical nature of Opus Dei and what appears to be its coordinated action in public life clearly suggest the existence of overall directives – directives that may be purely spiritual but which render surprisingly profitable dividends for its members.

Now and then some signs of what happens backstage come out into the open. During the discussion of the budget in March 1968 it was discovered that the Opus Dei University of Navarre, supposedly a private institution, was receiving government subsidies amounting to 100 million pesetas (£830,000). The Matesa scandal in 1969 implicated Opus Dei members, some at ministerial level, but the affair was very skilfully interred by the government. The disappearance of the newspaper *Madrid* in November 1971, although attributed to administrative irregularities, had other reasons. *Madrid* was an Opus Dei newspaper. Tensions between rival factions to gain control of the paper led Rafael Calvo Serer – a 'black sheep' in the Opus Dei flock – to publish an article in which he made it unmistakably clear that the offices of the Banco Popular and the backing of Luis Valls-Taberner, its Vice-Chairman, and a prominent figure in the Opus Dei organization, were a safe road to a high post in public administration.[29]

These examples look very much like the tip of an iceberg, the size of which remains a mystery. All the official disclaimers regularly put out by Opus Dei denying any connection between the organization and the temporal activities of its members are insufficient to counteract the accusations. Unless Opus Dei lifts the veil surrounding all its business, one has to conclude on the evidence available, that it has become one of the most powerful individual groups in Spanish life, and that although in the ministerial reshuffle of January 1974 the last of its members in the government, López Rodó, was dismissed, Opus Dei – or at least the politically active faction of its membership – remains a force to be reckoned with.

Militarism as a feature of the regime in general and of the army in particular was previously mentioned. Without the backing of the armed forces, Franco's regime could not have survived all these years, and it is doubtful whether it would be able to maintain its present authoritarian trend without that backing. The affinity between regime and army stems from the Civil War. The leading military figures on the nationalist side, known as the African generation[30] because most of them 'learned their trade' in the Moroccan war earlier this century, together with the body of officers improvised during the course of the Civil War (the *alféreces provisionales*) now appear at the top of the armed forces hierarchy. Their mentality is imbued with the 'crusading spirit' of the War. Like most professional soldiers, they hold order and discipline in great esteem, but uppermost in their priorities too are nationalism and anti-liberalism. Only the maintenance of the *status quo* can be expected from them.

Time, however, is having some effect on the armed forces. The economic development of the country is noticeable in the modernization of military equipment and in the more rational and technical training of new officers. The social background of these future generations of generals is changing too.[31] By 1980 the old guard of Civil War officers will have gone into retirement.[32] The political presence of the army is becoming less evident. One even hears from some of the most enlightened generals that the army must be subservient to civil power and that its role must be totally apolitical.[33] The indicators, then, for the future point towards a different and possibly more liberal military. Signs of discontent have already appeared amongst lower ranking officers, unhappy with the regime as a whole, and particularly worried by support it receives from the armed forces. But for the time being the army continues to be a mainstay of the regime, and it is unlikely that it will allow any radical liberalization that brings about unrest or division in the country, or that imperils constitutional order. The declaration of the state of emergency in January 1969 was said to have come about as a result of the pressure applied on the government by some hard-liners amongst the generals.[34] Many of these, on account of their age, are fast disappearing from active service, but the not infrequent speeches and declarations of some – García Rebull, Pérez Viñeta, Iniesta Cano, etc. – make it abundantly clear that 'if it were necessary the army would initiate another crusade',[35] to make sure 'that francoism continues after Franco, that francoism lasts for centuries'.[36]

The Catholic Church in Spain has had an evolution in some ways opposite to the army's. Whereas the political role of the army is declining or at least remaining static, the Church is becoming increasingly involved in politics. Some sections of it are today deeply politicized, committed to opposing the francoist establishment on social, on economic and even on political issues, and finding grounds for their opposition in a less dogmatic interpretation of the Christian doctrine.

The closeness of catholicism and marxism, fostered at an intellectual level by the works of men like Jose L. Aranguren, ex-Professor of the University of Madrid, and Jose M. González Ruiz, an Andalusian priest,[37] and by the direct involvement of some priests in the plight and struggle of the working classes, has had a considerable impact. It reversed the policy of the official Church since the end of the Civil War. The outright condemnation of marxism, communism, socialism and any other leftist –ism under the common denominator of enemies of Spain and of catholicism was put in question.

At an institutional level, the Church has not taken such a radical attitude. The Vatican moves at the slow pace of any large conservative body. By its own standards, however, the conclusions of the Second Vatican Council have meant a great step forward. Its specific effects were discussed in previous chapters. In general terms, a large gap now separates the doctrine of the Church and the ideology of the regime. The collusion between the two, sealed by the Concordat of 1953, cannot be sustained much longer, even though the material interests of both parts would suffer by ending it. The regime would have to renounce its right to intervene in the nomination of bishops, while the Church would have to give up most of the privileges and financial help it now enjoys. Up to this moment neither side has made a unilateral move to put an end to the Concordat,[38] but the end of this stalemate cannot be far distant.

While the official peace is maintained, the tension between Church and regime keeps building up. Priests and bishops denounce abuses and injustices both individually and collectively. The voices of many Church dignitaries – Mgr Cirarda, now Bishop of Cordova but at one time in charge of the delicate diocese of Bilbao; Mgr Añoveros, first in Cadiz and now in Bilbao; Mgr Tarancón, Archbishop of Madrid; Mgr Díaz Merchán, Archbishop of Oviedo; to mention but a few relevant figures – have been heard from the pulpit and outspoken pastoral letters, condemning police activities, requesting greater freedom and understanding for the diverse cultures and peoples of Spain, or denouncing the plight of miners in the north or farm labourers on the large estates of southern Spain. A special prison in the province of Zamora houses a number of priests who also raised a voice of protest from the pulpit, or became involved in the ETA movement or in some other illegal activity. The Episcopal Conference, the corporate body of Spanish bishops, has passed on several occasions resolutions criticizing the regime's line on specific issues. Their document on trade union problems, published to show the contrast between the teaching of the Church on such matters and the Syndical Law of 1971, is a well-known example, as is the more general document that came out of their meetings in November–December 1972, under the title *The Church and the Political Community*. At a joint assembly of bishops and priests gathered in Madrid in September 1971, some of the papers read were extremely critical of the social and political situation in Spain.[39]

All the examples given, which could be easily multiplied, convey the idea of a Church that is becoming increasingly dissatisfied with the regime and is expressing that dissatisfaction. Amongst the eighty-nine Spanish bishops[40] criticism still takes, for the most part, a rather carefully worded form. Many of them, and the older priests, are the same men who in the 1940s lived the 'crusading spirit' of the Spanish Church, and this mental ballast is not easy to shake off. It is amongst the younger clergy, the under-forties, where criticism takes a more radical form. In a survey carried out amongst some 15,500 clergymen in Spain during the 1969–70, more than 40 per cent of those below the age of forty chose socialism as the political ideology they favour, and more than 80 per cent confessed to dissatisfaction with the official position of the Spanish Church in social and political matters.[41]

The situation worries the regime. It realizes it is losing the moral legitimacy provided by Church backing. In the past they were happy to allow the Church to voice its favourable opinion on political issues; now that the Church raises objections they demand that the Church refrain from passing judgement on temporal matters.[42]

The chasm between the two is getting wider and deeper, with the Church becoming bolder and bolder in its denunciations, and the regime answering back by showing a mixture of fear and contempt towards the institution and the faith that for many years they had claimed to have saved from destruction in Spain. The Catholic Church cannot be considered as a political force *per se*, but it is a most powerful interest group, and it has a still-considerable moral influence amongst large sections of the population. Its role in political development over the next decade is bound to be very important, for, even if no Camilo Torres springs out of the ranks of the Spanish clergy, a total withdrawal of support by the Church could have a profound effect. Whether this complete severance is likely is very much open to question in view of the very strong financial links between Church and State in Spain.

The obvious must now and then be stated if only to avoid it being taken for granted. In a capitalist society, the most powerful groups have their hands on the levers that control the economy, or vice versa, the controllers of the economy constitute the dominant pressure groups. Franco's victory in the Civil War was, too, the victory of the financial oligarchy, of the big landowners and of the great industrial concerns. They all abetted or sided with the military uprising of 1936 for fear of losing their privileges before the left-wing tidal wave of the Popular Front. They could not accept a strengthening of the trades unions; an agrarian reform more radical than the hesitant attempts of 1932 was anathema to them; and they opposed in principle any democratic alteration whether political, economic or social. As expert economists they backed the winning side and have since been counting their increasing profits.

Capitalism in the Spain of the forties had, like the country itself, all the traces of underdevelopment. Now in the developed seventies, it is acquiring some of the features – though not always the most dynamic ones – of neo-capitalism. Both the old and the new capitalist forces have been and are wholeheartedly behind the regime and their support is not likely to waver.

The concentration of economic power in Spain, already of alarming proportions, is on the increase. A few banks and a few dozen families – 100 families has been the symbolic number sometimes given[43] – monopolize economic and financial resources. Overwhelming evidence to prove the reality of this situation is available in the publications of some

Spanish economists.[44] And economic planning directed by the government through a specially created ministry – Comisaría del Plan de Desarrollo – is only serving to bolster this state of affairs.[45]

This oligarchy, small, exclusive, and self-perpetuating through the laws of inheritance, and endogamy, overlaps with some of the other groups mentioned. Links with Opus Dei are considered to be particularly strong,[46] as are the ideological affinities with certain sectors of the army and of the Church hierarchy. Monarchists abound at this level, and so do noblemen.[47] There exist, too, close connections with foreign capital – American above all – profitably invested in Spain.[48] The stakes all these economic oligarchs have in the present regime are very high indeed. They only stand to lose by any change in the situation. Their future behaviour is fairly predictable.

The Opposition

Dominant forces and groups within society generate their own kind of political regime and this, in turn, fosters, either by attraction or rejection, a certain type or types of opposition. To speak of a dominant group necessarily implies the existence of dominated groups. If the latter are allowed to vie for power, to compete for the control of political institutions, by means of a legally established game, the opposition offered by these dominated groups, or at any rate by some of them, is attracted into the system, it becomes part of it. This is the case in liberal democracies, where political opposition has been institutionalized. By contrast, Franco's regime has always rejected overt opposition. With all power concentrated in the hands of the dictator, and the supporting groups, and with a unified vision of Spanish society – no class struggle, no divisive parties, no regional autonomy – political opposition was ousted from the legal framework. Rejection brought about, as it usually does, an illegal, subversive and at times violent opposition. The many thousands of politically active Spaniards who were first displaced by the Civil War, and later excluded by Franco's system, were confronted with the daunting alternative of giving up their political ideals or following the dangerous path of subversive opposition. Those who opted for the latter – and there were many of them – have struggled unsuccessfully to this day to bring down the regime. As years went by, younger Spaniards, men and women who did not take part in the Civil War, but who also felt unable to identify with the official system, have joined the illegal opposition. They do not accept much of the political ideology of the republican generation; they are not impelled by the resentment of defeat; all they share with their elder colleagues in opposition is the desire to overthrow the present regime.

But Franco's regime has generated a milder form of opposition too. It might be called, for lack of a better word, amoebic opposition or opposition created by detachment from the official cell. These groups formed around public figures who, at some time in the past, were part of or close to the regime, but have, little by little, drifted away from it. Now they stand in opposition to the groups still inside, hoping that the after-Franco years will bring some liberalization and offer them the chance of power. The more idealistic and extreme amongst them aspire to alter the basic principles of the regime, to put democracy where now there is authoritarianism, but their goal must be achieved by peaceful means. Their objectives overlap to some extent with those of the more moderate groups in the rejected or illegal opposition.

Politics in Spain are becoming more and more strange. An authoritarian regime pretending that it is playing a democratic game can provide unexpected and at times bizarre results. A certain amount of dissent is allowed, the areas it can touch have been extended, and its forms of expression have gained subtlety in the wake of the regime's pseudo-democratic evolution. But there is a limit to the dissent the regime is able to absorb before running into danger. What has happened – to apply to the Spanish case a general idea of R. Aron – has been 'a progressive reduction in the monopoly of ideology, so that certain areas are being freed as years go on. But there is a limit beyond which the reduction of the extension of ideology cannot go. The limit was reached at that point which touched those ideas or principles which were absolutely necessary in order to justify the existence of a single party.'[49] (Perhaps one ought to say regime rather than single party in the Spanish context). Caught within this shifting zone of permitted dissent is the amoebic opposition. It is not its existence that is peculiar, but the way in which it is forced to act. As it is allowed to exist but not to manifest itself too openly lest it should gather any mass following, it has taken recourse to all kinds of roundabout and imaginative forms of expression.

Members of this opposition have developed a highly intellectualized style of writing, partly because many of them have an academic background, but more because they try to say in abstract terms or by means of imagery what they cannot say clearly without risk. This reduces their audience to the small public able to communicate at that same level. Under these circumstances, all their actions, intentionally or unintentionally, acquire oppositionist significance. A candidature in the election of a certain professional body like the Bar Association, a collection of interviews published in book form,[50] a note of protest denouncing police behaviour, even a piece of research or a survey are often taken as manifestations of opposition to the regime. Nothing but confusion emerges from it all. It is difficult to see where these opposition figures stand in relation to each other. There is no mass following for them, so they stand in isolation or form small groups around certain well-known personalities, expressing their affinities by their contribution to this or that magazine or publication.

The fact that they form an elite opposition must be stressed. If allowed to operate and organize more freely they might muster a considerable support, but for the time being their support is only potential, not real. The regime permits their existence as long as they remain inside their individual ivory towers.

As has so often been the case with opposition movements in Spanish history, a majority of them are part of the intelligentsia, either academics or writers. Their list of intellectual figures is really impressive: Joaquín Ruiz-Giménez, professor of natural law; J. L. Aranguren, philosopher; Manuel Jiménez de Parga, professor of politics; J. M. de Areilza, writer; Mariano Aguilar Navarro, professor of international law; Pedro Laín Entralgo, ex-Rector of the University of Madrid; and so many others. The biographies of some of these men show a sharp reversal in their political ideology. At some time in the more or less distant past they supported the regime. Many of them lent their intellectual powers to the formulation and defence of the political philosophy of Franco's 'new' Spain. The early writings of Aranguren, Laín Entralgo, Areilza, or the recently deceased Ridruejo, are unashamedly favourable to the dictator. From a different camp, Calvo Serer has experienced a similar development, as exemplified by the gulf separating his well-known work *España, sin problema*, from his later writings, like *España ante la libertad, la democracia y el progreso* (1968), or those published since his exile in 1971. In some instances, collaboration with the regime took the form of actual participation in power. Dionisio Ridruejo and Antonio Tovar were in charge of the party's propaganda machinery in the early days of the regime. Ruiz-Giménez was Minister of Education during the fifties. Jose María de Areilza, Count of Montrico, mentioned earlier amongst the monarchists – he too has of late taken up an oppositionist stance – was for seventeen years a Spanish ambassador.

One can only guess at the motivations for this change of opinion and attitude: an honest alteration in their scale of social and political values; disappointment with the regime's adherence to its authoritarian principles; frustration at inability to alter the situation from within in the case of those who had themselves been in power; even injured pride as a result of displacement by other groups. One or more of these reasons, and possibly some others too, must have been behind the change of political camp by many of these men. Whatever their motivations, and even though in politics steadfast adherence to a certain position may be the exception rather than the rule, the scars left by their past weaken their position, and badly tarnish the public image of those who may aspire to be party leaders in a future democratic situation. Most of these men are unlikely to reach a preponderant position in Spanish politics over the next few years, unless circumstances change radically. The regime will not let them. Besides their past and their age also play against them. However, insofar as they propound the establishment of democracy in Spain, they create discomfort and uneasiness for the regime, which cannot afford to ignore their existence altogether, and they are bringing up a new generation of like-minded intellectuals who share their democratic aspirations but do not drag behind the dead weight of an undemocratic past. From amongst these young men, most of them between 35 and 40 – 'the democratic generation of 1936'[51] – some of the political leaders of a future democratic Spain may emerge.

The political ideology of these opposition groups fluctuates for the most part within the area of Christian democracy, with some elements leaning towards mild forms of democratic socialism. The existence of groups with various degrees of commitment to the opposition cause and their different programmes do not eradicate the features they have in common. They are all reformist. They want a transformation of the political structure of the country to bring it into line with western Europe, but this must be achieved by peaceful means. One fairly recent statement, a document submitted to Franco as head of the Spanish government on 23 December 1970, with the backing of 131 signatures, may be taken as a summary of their communal democratic expectations and demands in the short term. These are the following: (a) freedom for workers and employers to organize their own unions and associations without the interference of the Government; (b) the recognition of the right to associate for political purposes; (c) amnesty for all Spaniards imprisoned for social or political 'crimes'; (d) a more democratic elaboration of the plans for social and economic development; (e) a revision of the 1953 Concordat to achieve the separation of Church and State; (f) freedom of expression so that the mass media may reflect the different currents of opinion in the country. The signatories of the document finally tell Franco that these democratic steps can only mean greater stability and progress since the signatories do not believe that Spaniards and democracy are incompatible – one of Franco's favourite bogeys.[52]

These demands are so basic that they could well attract the support of the whole spread of opposition. More extreme groups, like communists or socialists, not officially included in the petition, would also welcome such changes.[53] These groups have a clandestine existence, operating very often from headquarters abroad. They too find themselves divided into innumerable factions, a tendency of all opposition movements when their access to power is barred for too long.

In very broad terms, the clandestine opposition still resembles the republican forces that went into exile at the end of the Civil War. The communist party, the socialist party (PSOE, Partido Socialista Obrero Español), and workers' unions like the anarchist CNT (Confederación Nacional del Trabajo), and the socialist UGT (Unión General de Traba-jadores) still exist, and a host of other groups have sprung up over the last three decades. Farcical, but also a wonderful example of loyalty to an ideal: there still exists a republican government in exile.

Many of these left-wing movements, possibly since their old leaders have been in exile for far too long, lost touch with the reality of Spain. Attitudes, policies, and programmes are hopelessly anachronistic. This may be unfair to the direct struggle of groups of young socialists, com-munists and anarchists inside Spain, but it certainly applies to their elders in exile, many of whom have not been capable of adapting themselves to the changes which have occurred, and still act as if the Civil War were not yet part of history – in this they parallel the regime's view of the war as a crusade.

The PSOE, having lost some of its socialist zeal and unable to exercise influence on the spheres of power, has led, since the end of the Civil War, a very precarious existence, even though its ramifications – either directly, or indirectly through the socialist trades union UGT – do appear now and then in the industrial areas of Spain such as Madrid, Barcelona, or the Basque country. However, socialist ideology has been formulated and developed for quite a few years now by some prominent intellectuals – amongst them, Professor Tierno Galván possibly the most outstanding and next to him younger figures such as Raúl Morodo, Ramón Tamames or Pablo Castellano. There is an ideological revival manifesting itself in the translation, analysis, and publication of the writings of the outstanding socialist and marxist thinkers; through historiographical works on the most relevant events and figures of Spanish socialism; and also by applying socialist formulae to the study of the social, political and economic reality of present-day Spain – although the fruits yielded by this third outlet are fewer and less apprehensible than those of the other two. Spanish socialism is confronted by this internal dilemma: it is disjointed and weak in its organization and praxis, divided into two major groups, the PSOE and the PSP, undecided very often in practical reactions to the political situation, but endowed with considerable ideological vigour, which – and this, in many ways, is promising – has a wide appeal in certain sectors of the new generations, amongst the younger clergy and university students.[54] However, inherent in this situation, lies a danger of creating an intellectualized socialism devoid of practicality, socialism 'for' the working class 'without' the working class, an almost bourgeois (in Spanish one would probably use the more pejorative term *aburguesado*) socialism.[55]

The position of the anarchists is, if anything, more precarious. They appear to be fractionized into total disarray. Since the beginning of the fifties when guerrilla activities – the aftermath of the Civil War – came to an end, anarchist activism in Spain has declined steadily, and during the last few years only the new blood of FIJL (Federación Ibérica de Juventudes Libertarias) has occasionally rekindled the fading light of Spanish anarchism. The eternal contradiction of anarchism, torn between the need to organize for action and the beautiful utopia of libertarian aspirations, continues to cause constant feuds and divisions inside the movement. Rather than organize action directly, Spanish anarchism of late has supported workers in protests, demonstrations and strikes, and attempted to set up trade union structures outside the official syndicates. But in this field too, the weakness of present-day anarchism is apparent; sometimes they act independently through their own CNT; sometimes they join forces with the socialists, as they did when they agreed to form part of the ASE (Alianza Sindical Española), and the ASO (Alianza Sindical Obrera);[56] and even at one point, in April 1965, they entered into secret short-lived negotiations with representatives of the official syndicates.[57]

The communist movement is possibly the strongest and most influential, certainly the best-organized force of the illegal opposition, both inside Spain and amongst the exiles. At the centre of it is the PCE (Partido Comunista de España), presided over by the matriarchal figure of Dolores Ibarruri, '*La Pasionaria*', and directed by its Secretary-General, Santiago Carrillo. The PCE's short-term programme is far from revolutionary. Their major aspiration is to overthrow the present regime and

establish in Spain what they call 'a system of political freedoms', which is
nothing more than a liberal democracy in the western European style.
Their minimum requirements would be: amnesty for political prisoners
and exiles; recognition of the right to strike; independent trade unions;
freedom of expression, association and conscience; and universal suffrage.[58] These demands are identical to those of the democratic opposition
mentioned above. To achieve this initial goal the PCE is willing to cooperate
with other democratic forces, and has occasionally entered into program-
matic alliances with them.[59] Santiago Carrillo and his followers would be
quite happy to gain for the PCE a situation similar to the one enjoyed at
present by the French and Italian communist parties. At a later stage the
change from capitalism to socialism would be achieved also by peaceful
means, and by the cooperation of various forces – no monopoly is granted
to the proletariat – 'since the building up of socialism, in the world of
today, is not the exclusive task of the working classes, but falls to other
social groups too'.[60]

   This lack of radicalism in official PCE policy and its willingness to ally
with bourgeois forces on the road to socialism, has been the object of much
criticism[61] and the cause of a number of splits in the communist movement. This, together with occasional disagreements between the PCE
and Moscow's official policies– e.g. over the invasion of Czechoslovakia
in 1968 – have brought factionalism to the communist camp too. During
the last decade more than ten different communist organizations have
been formed in opposition to the PCE,[62] most of them from the left wing
of the movement.

Workers, Students and Separatists

Socialists, anarchists, communists, and the more advanced Christian
democrats, constitute, with their ideologies and organizations, the main
inspiration behind the activities and protests of workers, students and
separatists. It is not possible to establish in individual events where
inspiration originates since political fragmentation is undergoing constant
change: organizations appear and disappear with bewildering rapidity,
their membership fluctuates with alliances and splits. Assessing individual
weight and influence outside the general trend of events would be foolhardy, given the lack of reliable information in most cases, and the tremendous proliferation of organizations – it has been estimated that more
than 150 clandestine organizations were set up in Spain during the period
1948–68.[63]

The working-class movement, with its strikes and attempts at setting up independent unions; university students, with their demonstrations, sit-ins, and parallel struggle for free unions; and the regionalists, with their ambivalent tendencies between autonomy and separatism, although they are not *per se* political forces – except perhaps for the nationalists – are high politicized, since the solutions of their problems are, in the final instance, political solutions. The nature of this political permeation is double. For a long time workers, students and Catalans or Basques have realized that achieving their goals presupposes profound political change, and so the academic, regionalist or social class content of their aspirations has turned political. Of course, transmutations of this kind are not exclusive to the Spanish situation; they occur in similar social movements in other countries, but in Spain they have, in their clandestine existence, a more direct, a more elementary – and therefore more acute – nature. Opposition groups have found this politicized climate an ideal medium, inspiring, supporting, and directing a great number of the protests which take place, and helping to further politicize the issues by encouraging the drift from the social, geographical or cultural skirmishes to the wider political front.

The problems of syndicalism are discussed elsewhere (Chapter 6); here we shall only refer to a certain movement which, since the beginning of the sixties, has had a considerable influence in the working-class world and has attracted much interest amongst the opposition groups – the workers' commissions (*comisiones obreras*).

The organization of the working class, both as a protest against and as an alternative to official corporativism, did not gain momentum until the late fifties and early sixties. By that time new generations of workers, without any direct memory of the Civil War, were entering the factories; in 1958, the regime, incapable of maintaining official control over working conditions and wages, had introduced a timid system of collective bargaining; the economy was suffering the pains of a stabilization plan to moderate the imbalances of development; the country as a whole was becoming urbanized and industrialized, with big pockets of workers forming in strategic areas. All these factors produced the ideal conditions for the take-off of an illegal working-class movement. Amidst a confusing proliferation of acronyms representing various tendencies and groups (AS, ASO, USO, STV, FOC, etc.) there appeared, from working-class roots and in an almost spontaneous manner the workers' commissions, which remain to this day the most serious attempt at creating a syndicalism outside the state-run system.

The emergence of the workers' commissions occurred towards the middle of 1962, during a wave of strikes that affected many parts of the country, particularly the coal-mining industry in Asturias, where an almost general strike lasted the whole summer. Initially the workers' commissions adopted lightning tactics, that is, they were set up in a certain area or factory for a specific purpose; once the objective was achieved they dispersed. They also proclaimed their working-class roots and underlined their independence from any political group or ideology.[64] Their achievements have been considerable. At an illegal level, they have been behind most of the increasingly numerous strikes and protests in Spain. Extra-officially, and with the connivance of some sectors of management who have seen in the workers' commission a more genuine representation of working-class interests than in the bureaucratic syndicates, they have negotiated labour agreements. At times they have even made use of official channels; for example in 1966 they entered candidates for the syndical elections, successfully in many instances, particularly in the Madrid area. However, these tactics of attempted reform from inside have been largely abandoned following the repressive measures taken against many of those elected, and in later elections the number of members of the workers' commissions standing as candidates has decreased considerably.

The impact of the workers' commissions has been profound and their successes continue to this day. They have made progress in the face of repression, and, above all, they have spread amongst large sections of the workers a class consciousness and an awareness of their situation. On the other hand, the workers' commissions are by no means free from internal problems affecting both organization and objectives. They have lost many of their leaders through repression; and during the last few years – some would say almost from their beginning – they have been losing their working-class pedigree and their political neutrality as they are penetrated by many of the political groups mentioned earlier. The Spanish communist party has been since the mid sixties the most influential force, but political fragmentation is now rife in the workers' commissions. This political permeation has brought internal clashes between the autonomous tendencies with which the workers' commissions were born, and attempts by some groups – the communist party in particular – to impose a national structure, with its corollaries of bureaucratization and accepting a political vanguard. There is a similar ambivalence of aims between the concrete objectives in certain industries or firms, and the requirements of a national strategy, and the no less frequent collision between what some consider a class struggle against capitalism and others a slow reform with compromise inevitable on the way.

The situation in the universities is in many ways the same; there are striking parallels behind the obvious differences – students do not see themselves as an exploited social class since an overwhelming majority of them belong to the middle and upper strata, their numerical weight and distribution over the country are much more limited, their student status is temporary, etc.

Protest and dissent were also slow to appear in the universities. The earliest manifestations took place about 1956, but the protest movement did not gather momentum until the beginning of the sixties. Before that date the universities, stunted and feeble – with few students, little equipment, no research, and many of the best teachers gone with the War – had suffered clumsy attempts at pervading it with fascist ideology and the imposition of an obligatory party-controlled students' union, as well as an atmosphere of traditional Catholic values within which members of the then little-known Opus Dei were trying to monopolize professorial posts.

New generations of students, without any personal experience or memory of the Civil War, set the ball of dissent rolling. Their first target was the destruction of the official students' union, SEU. It took some time and effort, but by 1965 the regime had to give way to mounting protest and the growing strength of some illegal organizations – the left-wing FUDE (Federación Universitaria Democrática Española), and the Christian-democrat UED (Unión de Estudiantes Democráticos) were perhaps those with the widest support at the time – and the SEU was scrapped. Since then the regime has produced a number of schemes for students' unions, all unsatisfactory, unworkable, and undemocratic; neither teaching staff nor, of course, students were consulted, or intervened in any way in the process of elaboration.[65] The students' basic demand for an independent union, free from State interference, was not satisfied and protests in the universities have continued to this day: clandestine unions, like the SDE (Sindicato Democrático de Estudiantes) in Madrid and Barcelona, sit-ins, illegal assemblies, and demonstrations of various kinds have been a feature of academic life during the last few years. The regime has only been able to answer with half-hearted reforms – the 1970 Education Act – or with repressive measures – the declaration of the state of emergency at the beginning of 1969 or the permanent posting of police in university campuses.

In the students' movement we find, as in the working-class movement, together with the proliferation of clandestine organizations, a certain ambivalence in aims. Protest in the universities is often directed at specifically academic and professional targets: deficient teaching, overcrowding, insufficient facilities for research, absenteeism of professors, lack of employment for graduates, etc., deficiencies which have become much more acute over the last ten years with the demographic explosion in student numbers – the official figure has gone up from 92,983 in 1965–6 to 150,094 in 1969–70.[66] But students have come to realize that their goal is a higher one, that academic changes and the right to organize free unions cannot be achieved without serious political repercussions, for, in the words of Professor Tierno Galván, 'liberty is indivisible, and to demand or obtain freedom for one sector of society is bound to have an impact in other, unfree sectors'.[67] Thus, large sectors of the students' movement see now the need for radical change in the political nature of the regime.

Finally, the difference separating the international from the national ingredients in the students' protest movement must be stressed. The regime has often tried to explain away unrest in Spanish universities by presenting it solely as part of a malaise affecting universities all over the western world. The links are obvious, but it is equally clear that the major component in the protest of Spanish students is specifically Spanish. Their primary objectives are freedom to express dissent, the right to set up and control their own unions, and an overall updating and democratizing of education.

The Spanish Civil War represented a defeat for the working classes, for a large section of the intelligentsia, and for the movements for regional autonomy. The regional movements have a very long and complex history in Spain, their ups and downs and their motivations varying from region to region, and from period to period. That history, relevant as it is, cannot be even touched on here.[68] After the Civil War any outward sign of regional conscience or personality was suppressed. The official view of national unity was totally uncompromising. Not only were separatist tendencies and movements legally forbidden and mercilessly put down, but any expression of local culture, language, or folklore was banned whether it originated in Catalonia, the Basque Country, Galicia, or Valencia.

The regime's pseudo-democratization brought about the re-emergence of many regional traits, which had never died but had hibernated in the confines of private homes or in the remote areas of the provinces. Even their recent and often timid revival is not always easily separated from workers' or students' movements; it is not infrequently encouraged by the most advanced sections of the Church, and expressed for the most part through cultural manifestations such as lectures, popular music, publications, or conferences. This has certainly been the case with Catalan nationalism. After a dormant or, at the most, defensive attitude during the years of post-War repression catalanism has reappeared. It has been impelled primarily by a bourgeoisie which does not strive after a secessionist solution since its class interests are well protected under the *status quo* but which nevertheless likes to reaffirm the distinctiveness of its native region by encouraging the publication of magazines and books in the vernacular[69] – although they have no Catalan daily paper yet – through new music with a social or a political message – *la nova cançó* – or even by identifying with their leading football teams. Catalanism does not seem to manifest itself overtly in the lower strata of society: if it does exist it is latent. The working class has nationalism lower down in its priorities; the Catalan ingredient is considerably diluted in the enormous pool of immigrant labour, which produces problems of a diverse nature.

Basque nationalism has taken on quite a different aspect, largely obliterating its regionalist values, or at least relegating cultural, racial, or linguistic goals in favour of social or political ones – the class struggle, the overthrow of the regime – without which they have come to consider the realization of their nationalist aspirations an impossibility. ETA (Euskadi Ta Askatasuna), with its mixture of terrorist tactics and left-wing idealism, is the spearhead of the Basque movement. The level of popular support ETA enjoys is unknown, though it would not be too hazardous to assume that support cannot be very wide, given ETA's radicalism and extremist activities. ETA was born towards the end of the fifties as a splinter group which detached itself from the old PNV (Partido Nacionalista Vasco) to replace legalistic and religious tactics by a policy of direct action. Its history over the last fifteen years has followed a fast-escalating curve of terrorist activities, while internally it has been suffering from ideological factionalism; by 1970 three different tendencies within the movement divided as to whether their battle should be fought on a separatist or a social class front, and as to whether it should have national or international dimensions.[70]

The Catalan and the Basque movements, on account of their long history, the high level of development of the two regions, their demographic weight, and the strength of their language and culture, constitute the two best-known cases of a wider problem all round the country's periphery, from the Balearics to Andalusia, and from Galicia to the Canary Islands. The threat to the cohesion of the national state, of any national state, is considerable, even more so in Spain due to the high rate of regional diversity and to the specific weight it has acquired in some cases. No democratic country has yet found a satisfactory way to accommodate nationalist-minded minorities within the unitary structure of the national state. One thing, however, is clear; that solution cannot be found in the repressive policies the Franco regime has for long imposed on the regions.

10   PERSONAL CONCLUSION

Having reached this final stage, the author can take off the formal mask covering his statements and opinions. The plural 'we', in which presumably the reader is included, and the impersonal forms of the verb now give way to an 'I', which not only provides more intimate tone, but also means assuming personal responsibility for all that is said.

As a Spaniard I cannot help feeling uneasy when I think of the political future of my country, and this uneasiness is turning to fear as time passes. No other attitude, no other feelings seem possible when the horizon appears so bleak. The pages of this book are a witness to the fact that my fears are, unfortunately, well founded. Nevertheless, there are optimists around. Some believe that the solution will be found in the EEC. Once Franco dies – Franco who is a living symbol of dictatorial Spain – the doors of the EEC will open to receive a Spain which really will be different. It has repeatedly been said, with surprising naïvety, by a number of Spanish ministers that there is no incompatibility between the political reality of Spain and that of the EEC! But the reality behind such expressions of wishful thinking and political propaganda is quite different. If the EEC is more than a huge market of consumers established to satisfy the constantly accelerating process of production; if the plans for a future united Europe do not remain for ever as mere lucubrations in the minds of one or two visionaries; if a directly elected parliament and a European government ever bring together all the member countries of the Community under one political umbrella . . . how can one even imagine that the Spain of the present time, and the future Spain promised by the regime or deduced from the constitution, could fit into a political union of western Europe? The political union of Europe can only be achieved on the basis of liberal democratic principles since all the Community countries run on these principles. To believe in any other solution is to close one's eyes to reality. To think that Spain, as she is now, can enter a Community of clear liberal and democratic values is to dream of false solutions or to indulge in crude propaganda.

And if the future is not to be Europe, what is it to be? I must be sincere and confess that I do not know. This uncertainty, the impossibility on my part to answer such a fundamental question, reveals in very dramatic terms the greatest failure of francoism. Spain has been a dictatorship since 1936, for nearly four decades, and now that the moment has arrived to collect the inheritance, she finds a legacy of dubious quality and fraught with dangers. Here lies, I repeat, the greatest political failure of francoism. Franco has not wished or has not been able to use his powers to put Spain on the way towards democratic goals. Franco is leaving behind him a coun'ry which in many aspects is very different from the one in which he seized power during the Civil War, but which politically has evolved very little within very narrow margins. Perhaps his greatest triumph is to have given Spain more than thirty years of tranquillity, although in exchange Spaniards have had to renounce many of their freedoms. In this atmosphere of tranquillity – not peace, for peace only flourishes in the midst of liberty – many Spaniards have begun to enjoy the pleasures of the affluent society. Tranquillity and prosperity, both as a tangible reality and a propaganda tool, have aroused a feeling of gratitude in large sectors of the Spanish population, and on that gratitude, at least in part, the Franco regime has come to rest. The Spaniard who has witnessed the economic development of his country over the last few decades cannot but be grateful to those in power, even if his gratitude is rather servile. It has not occurred to him that perhaps he would have been able to progress within a political system in which he, the average Spaniard, was not a mere spectator but took an active role.

Here one comes up against another element on which the regime has rested in the past and which could be one of its greatest weaknesses in the future: the political alienation of the majority of Spaniards. It is difficult to reach an exact measurement of this, but nearly all the surveys carried out by Spanish sociologists during the last few years reveal an alarming ignorance of all things political, and a lack of interest, bordering on scorn, in public matters. Not for nothing was it said after the assassination of Carrero Blanco that the reaction of the Spanish people (in fact there was no reaction at all) was not so much proof of their political maturity, as official spokesmen repeatedly said, as of their indifference to what had happened.[1] And neither gratitude for favours received nor tranquillity based on submission and indifference can be solid bases for a stable future.

The great task, still to be undertaken, is to make Spaniards masters of their own lives, of their own country, of their own destiny. How is this to be achieved? It is not my intention, and certainly beyond my capabilities, to offer my countrymen a blueprint for success. It is up to them to find a solution. However, that solution requires besides radical social and economic changes, a profound political transformation. It is imperative to reject the 'spirit of 18 July' – the date of the outbreak of the Civil War – and to accept the consequences which would follow. The Civil War must now be relegated to the history books. Trying to justify that war and using it as a means of justifying all things done since then has survived for too long. The time to rectify is well overdue. The political evolution which has taken place under the Civil War spirit has led Spain into an ideological and institutional cul-de-sac from which she will find it difficult to escape, for the exit though clear is painful.

I am not suggesting a return to zero, as if the Civil War and the last three and a half decades had not existed. No, that attitude would be as erroneous as it is impossible. The history of Franco's Spain, with its long political, social, economic, and cultural legacy is there, whether one likes it or not, and must be the starting-point. However, accepting this should not be allowed to degenerate into political immobility, which has happened until now. The established system has managed to absorb reformers into itself, thus proving right the dictum that even the bitterest form of opposition, once it is legalized and plays the game according to the official rules, reinforces the *status quo*. Therefore accepting the present situation as the starting-point must have with it a clear intention to alter the rules of the game, and to alter them basically, so as to achieve a complete change in the direction of political evolution.

One of the first consequences of such a move would be the recognition of 'the other Spain' as an integral part of the body politic, the Spain that was defeated in the Civil War, the one that lives in exile abroad, and the one that, though living at home, feels spiritually exiled. There is no better way of leaving behind the memories of 18 July 1936 than by uniting the two Spains. The present regime has done little or nothing to heal the deep wound opened by the War. The idea of the two Spains originated well before 1936, but the Civil War finally drove them asunder, and from that time the only interpretation of Spain permitted has been that of the victorious side. Since the division is fundamentally ideological the cure must be ideological too. Thus a second requirement would be an ideological widening that would legalize ways of understanding society and political theories different from the official ones. It is imperative to renounce the right-wing dogmatism that accepts no view of Spain other than what it sees through its own ultra-conservative lens.

The new generations of Spaniards who did not experience the Civil War – and I count myself amongst them – are looking ahead in search of new roads to freedom and peaceful co-existence, and along the way lies the third essential requirement for change – change which, I insist, must be sincere in its intention and profound in its effect. I would call this third requirement popular legitimacy. The expression is somewhat ambiguous and needs clarification. It amounts to the completion of the change. Its principal objective is to replace all the spurious formulae the regime has manipulated to create a legitimate image with which to hide or justify its authoritarianism, from the original legitimacy extracted out of the transformation of the Civil War into a 'crusade', to the legitimacy based on the maintenance of public order as the highest priority and on the complacent use of the statistics of economic growth.

Popular legitimacy cannot be imposed by the force of arms nor by the charismatic power of a dictator. If it is to be authentic it must originate amongst the people and flow in an upward direction. Rigged plebiscites and mass demonstrations of support orchestrated by the authorities have no legitimizing value, and are anything but popular. The process of legitimation must start from the basis that national sovereignty rests with the Spanish people. At the present moment this conclusion could only be reached by stretching the interpretation of the Fundamental Laws to almost unconstitutional limits, and in reality the people are totally absent from politics. A corollary to popular sovereignty would be the freedom and the capacity to participate, both individually and through groups and associations, in public life; and I use the verb 'participate' in the widest possible sense.

Although these suggestions do not provide a political programme – they are little more than self-evident conclusions – I might still be drifting into those areas where mythical goals are so attractive as to hide their unachievable nature. Be that as it may, I still believe that a simple move in the direction indicated, towards popular legitimacy, towards the rejection of the 18 July spirit, towards ideological plurality, would eventually lead to the disappearance of the Franco regime, or at least of some of its most important institutions. Without pretending to be exhaustive I could mention a few examples.

The organic Cortes are the body most in need of renovation, both in composition and in function. Adherence to an entirely organic structure would have to be abandoned to make it compatible with political parties. This would mean dismantling the National Movement as an organization and its supposedly permanent ideological principles. These changes would demand, for the sake of institutional harmony, other parallel changes in the Council of the Realm, the Government, the local and provincial councils, etc. In the socio-economic sphere the syndicates would have to be turned into proper trade unions, independent from the state, self-governed, and geared towards the class interests of their members.

All the above changes, and many more which easily come to mind, would prove irrefutably that the 18 July had been left behind, that ideological diversity had been recognized, and that the system was willing to seek the legitimate backing of a free people. But does the will to do all this exist? I write these final lines towards the end of 1974 and I see no evidence that it does. And it is naïve to expect Franco's death to work a miracle, for as an editorial in *Le Monde* put it: '*le charisme ne s'hérite pas, les méthodes autoritaires, si*'.[2] It is sad to have to finish on such a sombre note. To end on any other would amount to a falsification of the truth on the face of overwhelming evidence. In the political future of Spain I see a great deal of darkness and hardly any light; my forecast must be pessimistic, although never did a forecaster wish to be proved wrong more sincerely than I.

⁊ POSTSCRIPT

This book deals fundamentally with the political transition from Franco-ism to post-Francoism in Spain. It hinges on that historical event, Franco's death. Yet, the original idea of the book, the subsequent research carried out, and the actual writing of it, all took place before that moment. It seems appropriate to me now to add a few *a posteriori* comments, to enlarge the personal conclusion at the end of the book with the hindsight of several months of post-Francoism.

It will soon be the first anniversary of Franco's death. He died in the early hours of 20 November 1975. The day on which, thirty-nine years earlier, J. A. Primo de Rivera, founder of Falange, had been executed by the republicans in Alicante prison. Pure coincidence had made history, bringing together the two most important right-wing symbols in the recent life of the country. Franco's demise lifted off the lid of the future, a future which has to be shaped as something different. The struggle for the future had been simmering for some years past, but from 20 November 1975 it burst out into the open. Everybody, except for the extreme right, accepts that the political physiognomy of the country will have to change now that Franco is gone. But how much and in which way is the bone of contention.

Franco's dictatorship was highly personalized. Much more so, I believe, than Salazar's in Portugal, for instance. Franco's adherence to power till the very last moment of his life was in line with his belief that the country wanted and needed him. It was, too, the final expression of his naked love of power. But above all it was the regime he had created that needed his survival for as long as possible. The regime has lost its main-stay. The institutional structure, carefully erected over a period of three decades, is sinking as if its foundations were resting on quicksands. Is it worth propping up, will it collapse, or is it better to pull it down to the ground?

The *heredípetas* – discussed in chapter nine – are desperately trying to save as much as possible, whilst at the same time making provisions to safeguard their own interests in the event of a total collapse. On the one hand they now publicly confess their democratic proclivities – sincerely held for a long time, they say, but for many years compatible with their support for the dictator – and on the other, they are attempting to preserve as much as possible of Francoism, for they know that this is their only chance of political survival. Caught up in that contradictory situation and badgered by an opposition which has erupted onto the scene through the narrow door of tolerance, Franco's heirs are pinning their hopes on slow reform.

But during these last months Spain has been experiencing unrest on a scale not seen in the country since the days of the Civil War. Political meetings held in public places, marches and rallies demanding regional autonomy or political amnesty, clashes between demonstrators and police, strikes, left-wing propaganda openly distributed, even the more or less erotic publications now freely available at any news-stall could be taken as indicators of a change in the political climate. Below this surface agitation, at the root of it all, there lies the basic problem facing Spain: a crisis of legitimacy.

Until his death Franco was the only source of political legitimacy. He had originally been given the irrational power to create and legitimize a new regime. He had done so, holding all the time on to that power and having it ratified occasionally by means of rigged plebiscites or pre-arranged public demonstrations of support. To transfer that irrational, charismatic legitimacy to the institutions – the monarchy included – left behind by Franco, is an impossible task. That type of legitimacy without the dictator offers little credibility – nobody believes in it – nor is it now possible to create the pretence of general acceptance. Nevertheless, Franco's heirs remain adamant in their belief that whatever new form of legitimacy is introduced, it must always be a continuation of the previous one. This is in essence what the political reformists want: change within continuity. The first attempt at reform – Fraga's blueprint in the last Arias Navarro's government – foundered without even being put to the test. A second attempt is now being made by the new prime minister, Adolfo Suárez, but his plans are not yet known. Francoism without Franco is neither viable nor reformable. The only alternative open to francoists is between a move back in search of a new dictatorial legitimacy, or the continuation of the pseudo-democratic process already initiated during Franco's life. The former is undoubtedly a threatening possibility, the latter is the one so far tried.

In order to gain support for the policies of change within continuity King Juan Carlos's government has adopted a much more flexible and tolerant attitude than Franco's ever did. The bait was too obvious to make the opposition forces fall into the trap. Instead the opposition has taken advantage of this relaxation to denounce the official plans for reform as unviable. Such plans can never create a broadly-based consensus and a new legitimacy, they say. In fact, in the eyes of the opposition, they are little more than a clumsy attempt to secure power for those who have held it for the last forty years. On the more positive side the opposition is demanding a break with the francoist past which will allow the establishment of a new democratic form of legitimacy based upon the will of the people expressed through the ballot box. They want a provisional coalition government, comprising all the major political forces in the country. This government would build the bridge towards a freely-elected constituent assembly, which would be the initial point of the new legitimacy. The regime does not appear willing to accept this solution, nor does the opposition accept the official proposals.

The liberalization which has taken place since Franco's death deserves some comment. New, less restrictive legislation has been passed concerning political associations or the right of assembly, for instance. Greater tolerance is shown these days towards Spanish citizens in the exercise of their individual and collective rights. A welcome change, if not an entirely satisfactory one. It smacks of paternalism. It is one more adornment on the pseudo-democratic façade of the regime. The relaxing of repression is no more than a concession, which can be, and often is, withdrawn. It is being offered as a sign of goodwill on the part of the government, not as a recognition of the inalienable rights of the governed. The issue of an amnesty for political prisoners offers an excellent example. The King and his government wasted an ideal opportunity to prove their good intentions by offering a generous amnesty to all those Spaniards who had been imprisoned or exiled by Franco for political reasons. Instead, all they were willing to grant was a partial pardon in instalments, and even that, only under duress from public demand.

Whatever the intention the greater freedom now allowed is considered by all as the most positive change since Franco's death. The spreading of news and information has received a real boost. Freedom of expression in the press has reached limits not even imagined during Franco's life. Many old political taboos are now openly discussed on the pages of newspapers and magazines. (In contrast the government-controlled television has not altered at all.) There is even in circulation a daily in Catalan, *Avui*. The opposition is using this freedom to make itself known and publicize its viewpoints and programmes. Information about the opposition is much more easily available than ten or twelve months ago. Many of the leaders of that opposition have jumped from a clandestine and anonymous status to become well known public figures. The opposition can now be seen, though it may not be any nearer to power than it was.

Fragmentation continues to be a malaise affecting the ranks of the opposition, and, in fact, of all political forces in Spain. The official daily *Arriba*, in its issue of 2 May 1976, listed no fewer than 236 political organizations in Spain. Undoubtedly, many of them are no more than minor groupings without the strength to survive the electoral test. Otherwise, the overall picture of political forces in Spain, now that it can be seen more clearly, does not differ greatly from the one described in chapter nine. The socialists may be proving a more vigorous force than their performance during the Franco years suggested; the Carlist faction of Prince Carlos Hugo seems to have definitely rejected its most conservative roots; and, above all, regionalist organizations, Catalan in particular, have emerged forcefully into the open.

Over and above the fragmentation of its ranks the opposition is united on the question of how to establish in Spain a democratic legitimacy. *Coordinación Democrática* is a loosely formed organization, encompassing all the major groups of the opposition, from the conservative wing of the Christian-democrats to the Spanish communist party. Its only aim is to find a peaceful way to break with the francoist past. The way is barred, as has already been said, by the refusal of the King's government and the host of *heredípetas* supporting them, to have anything other than a simple reform. Beyond them, the extreme right of the regime, the so called *Bunker*, strategically placed in the Cortes, the Council of the Realm, the National Council, and other major institutions, observes the struggle, ready to intervene the moment they detect any adulteration in the essence of Francoism, which for them is the essence of Spain.

The struggle for a new legitimacy or for the continuation of the old one in a different guise is drawing to a stalemate position. The role of the King could be decisive, but also fatal for him. The monarchy itself could be in danger in this struggle. The final decision may be in the hands of the Armed Forces, which in their highest ranks appear to favour continuity, or, at most, slow reform.

Towards the end of his days Franco used to say that he was leaving everything *atado y bien atado*, which could be translated as 'safely tied up'. In view of what is happening in Spain, it would be more appropriate to say that Franco's political legacy has left everything tied up in knots.

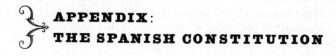

APPENDIX:
THE SPANISH CONSTITUTION

Principles of the National Movement (15 May 1958)

I, Francisco Franco Bahamonde, Caudillo of Spain
Conscious of my responsibility before God and History and in the presence of the
Cortes of the Kingdom, do promulgate as Principles of the National Movement,
which is to be understood as the sharing by all Spaniards in the ideals that gave
birth to the Crusade, the following:

I

Spain is a unity with a universal mission. It is the sacred duty and collective task
of all Spaniards to contribute to the unity, greatness and freedom of the country.

II

The Spanish Nation consider it an honour to obey the Law of God according to
the doctrine of the Holy Catholic Apostolic and Roman Church, which is the only
true doctrine. This faith is inseparable from the national conscience and shall
inspire her legislation.

III

Spain, founder of a great family of peoples, with whom she feels indissolubly
united by fraternal bonds, aspires to the achievement of justice and peace among
nations.

IV

The unity of the peoples and the lands of Spain is intangible. The integrity and independence of the country are the essential requirements of the national community. The Armed Forces of Spain, being the guarantee of her security and the expression of the heroic virtues of our people, must possess the strength necessary to render the country their best service.

V

The national community is founded upon man, as the depositary of eternal values, and upon the family, as the basis of social life; but individual and collective interests must always be subordinated to the common good of the Nation, which comprises all generations past, present and future. All Spaniards are equal before the law.

VI

The family, the municipality and the syndicate are the natural units of social life, and the basic elements of the national community. All other institutions and corporations which meet social needs generally felt must be protected, so that they may effectively participate in the pursuit of the national community's purposes.

VII

The Spanish people, united under a legally constituted order, inspired by the postulates of authority, liberty and service, constitute the national State. Its political form within the framework of the immutable principles of the National Movement and those defined in the Law on the Succession and the other Fundamental Laws is that of a traditional, Catholic, social and representative Monarchy.

VIII

The representative nature of the political system is the basic principle of our public institutions. The participation of the people in the legislative process and other functions of general interest shall be effected through the family, the municipality, the syndicate and any other organizations endowed with an inherently representative nature and recognized for that purpose by the law. Any political organization, whatever its character, outside this representative system, shall be deemed illegal.

Public appointments and offices are open to all Spaniards according to their merits and capabilities.

IX

Every Spaniard has the right to: an independent Judiciary, the access to which shall be free to those who lack financial resources; a general and professional training, which no one will be deprived of for lack of material means; the benefits of social assistance and security; an equitable distribution of the national income and taxation. The Christian ideal of social justice found in the Labour Charter shall inspire politics and laws.

X

Work is regarded as the basis of hierarchy and as a duty and an honour for all Spaniards; and private property, in all its forms, is regarded as a right, the exercise of which is conditioned by its social function. Private enterprise, which is the basis of economic activity, must be stimulated, directed and, where necessary, supplemented by State action.

XI

The *Empresa*, which is an association of men and means for the purpose of production, constitutes a community of interests and a unity of aims. Relations between the constituent elements must be based on justice and mutual loyalty, and economic values shall be subordinate to human and social values.

XII

The State shall endeavour by all the means at its disposal to improve the physical and moral health of Spaniards, and to provide them with worthy conditions of work; to encourage the economic progress of the nation by improving agriculture, extending irrigation works and reforming the social structure of rural areas; to direct public funds towards the best possible use and distribution; to safeguard and promote the prospecting and development of mining resources; to intensify the process of industrialization; to support scientific research and to promote maritime activities as befits the number of our seafaring people and our naval tradition.

I hereby resolve:

Article 1 – The principles contained in the present law, which are a synthesis of those inspiring all the other Fundamental Laws approved by the Nation on 6 July 1947, are, by their very nature, permanent and immutable.

Article 2 – All bodies and authorities shall be required to adhere strictly to these principles. The oath required from all persons to be invested with public office shall refer to the present text of the Fundamental Principles.

Article 3 – Any law or disposition of whatever nature which violates or impeaches the principles proclaimed in the present Fundamental Law of the Kingdom shall be null and void.

Charter of the Spanish People (17 July 1945, modified 10 January 1967)

Whereas the Spanish Cortes, as the supreme body for the participation of the people in the affairs of the State, have, in accordance with their founding law, drawn up the Charter of the Spanish People, a fundamental text which defines and protects the rights and duties of Spaniards; bearing in mind that, as in the case of the Labour Charter, basically it serves as proof of the permanent value of its ideals, and that a great many of its declarations and rules are a faithful interpretation of Catholic social doctrine, recently updated by the Second Vatican Council; and, finally, in view of the amendments introduced in its article 6 by the Organic Law of the State – approved subsequent to a national referendum – for the purpose of adapting the text of the said article to the declaration of the Council on religious freedom – dated 1 December 1965 – which requires the explicit recognition of this right, and in accordance with the second Principle of the National Movement, which establishes that the doctrine of the Church shall inspire our legislation.

I, Francisco Franco Bahamonde, Caudillo of Spain, Head of State and Commander-in-Chief of the Armed Forces of the Nation, hereby resolve the following:

The Charter of the Spanish People, the text of which appears hereinafter, is approved as a Fundamental Law regulating the rights and duties of Spaniards.

Preliminary Title

Article 1 – The Spanish State proclaims respect for the dignity, integrity and freedom of human beings to be the guiding principle of its acts, recognizing that man, as depositary of eternal values and member of a national community, has duties and rights, the exercise of which it guarantees for the common good.

Title I   Duties and Rights of the Spanish People

Chapter I

Article 2 – Spaniards owe faithful service to their country, loyalty to the Head of State and obedience to its laws.

Article 3 – All Spaniards are equal before the law, without preference in respect of classes or favour in respect of persons.

Article 4 – Respect for their personal and their family honour is a right of all Spaniards. He who should offend it, whatever his status, shall bear the responsibility.

Article 5 – All Spaniards have a right to be educated and trained and the duty to do so, either in the family circle or in private or public centres of their own free choice. The State shall see that no talent is wasted for lack of economic means.

Article 6 – The profession and practice of the Catholic Religion, which is that of the Spanish State, shall enjoy official protection.

The State shall undertake to defend religious freedom, which shall be protected by effective laws; these laws shall, at the same time, safeguard morals and public order.

Article 7 – It is an honour for Spaniards to serve in the Armed Forces of their country.

This service is obligatory for all Spaniards when they are called to it according to law.

Article 8 – On a statutory basis, and always with a general character, those personal services that the interest of the nation and public welfare require shall be made obligatory.

Article 9 – Spaniards shall contribute to public expenditure according to their economic means. Nobody shall be obliged to pay taxes which have not been established by a law voted by the Cortes.

Article 10 – All Spaniards have the right to participate in public life, through the family, the municipality and the syndicate, without this barring other channels of representation that the laws may establish.

Article 11 – All Spaniards shall be eligible for public office according to their merits and capacity.

Article 12 – All Spaniards may express their ideas freely, provided they do not go against the fundamental principles of the State.

Article 13 – Within the national territory the State guarantees the freedom and secrecy of correspondence.

Article 14 – Spaniards are at liberty to fix their residence within the national territory.

Article 15 – Nobody may enter or make a search in the home of a Spaniard without his consent, unless it be with a warrant from the competent authority and in the cases and manner established by law.

Article 16 – Spaniards may assemble and associate freely for lawful purposes and in accordance with the law. The State may create and maintain such institutions as are deemed necessary for the achievement of its aims. The basic statutes, which shall become law, shall coordinate the exercise of this right with that recognized in the preceding paragraph.

Article 17 – Spaniards have a right to legal security. All State bodies shall act according to a hierarchically-ordered and pre-established set of norms, which may not be interpreted or altered arbitrarily.

Article 18 – No Spaniard may be arrested except in the cases and in the manner prescribed by law.
Within a period of seventy-two hours, any arrested person shall be set free or turned over to the judicial authorities.

Article 19 – Nobody may be condemned except under a law issued prior to the offence, and when sentenced by the competent court of justice, and after the hearing and defence of the interested party.

Article 20 – No Spaniard may be deprived of his nationality except for committing treason, as defined in the penal laws, or for joining the Armed Forces or assuming public office in a foreign country against the express wish of the Head of State.

Article 21 – Spaniards may address individual petitions to the Head of State, to the Cortes and to the authorities.

Corporations, public officials and members of the Armed Forces may only exercise this right according to the laws by which they are ruled.

Chapter II

Article 22 – The State recognizes and protects the family as a natural institution and as the basis of society, with rights and duties before and above any human positive law.

Marriage shall be indissoluble.

The State shall grant special protection to large families.

Article 23 – Parents are obliged to provide for, educate and instruct their children. The State shall suspend the rights of parents or deprive them of such rights when they do not exercise them properly, and the custody and education of minors shall be transferred to those who are legally entitled to it.

Chapter III

Article 24 – All Spaniards have the right to work and the duty to engage in some socially useful activity.

Article 25 – Labour, because of its essentially human nature, cannot be brought down to the material level of merchandise, nor be the object of any deal incompatible with the personal dignity of the worker. Labour is in itself an honour and gives the right to demand protection and assistance from the State.

Article 26 – The State considers the *Empresa* as a community to which technical skill, labour, and capital in their various forms all contribute and, therefore, it proclaims the right of these elements to share the profits.

The State shall ensure that relations between them are maintained in the strictest equity, and within a hierarchical order, in which economic values are subordinate to human values, to the interest of the Nation and to the demands of the common good.

Article 27 – The State shall protect the right of all workers to a fair wage, sufficient, at least, to provide them and their families with the means to lead a moral and dignified life.

Article 28 – The State guarantees workers protection in times of misfortune, and recognizes their right to assistance in cases of old age, death, sickness, maternity, labour accidents, disability, unemployment, and any other risk which may be the object of social security.

Article 29 – The State shall maintain social welfare institutions and shall protect and foster those set up by the Church, by corporations and by private enterprise.

Article 30 – Private property, as a natural means for the fulfilment of individual, family, or social aims, is recognized and protected by the State.

All property of whatever kind is subordinate to the needs of the Nation and to the common good.

Wealth cannot remain unproductive, be unduly destroyed or be applied to illicit ends.

Article 31 – The State shall make available to all Spaniards the means of access to those forms of property most intimately connected with the person: home, land, and instruments and tools for daily use.

Article 32 – In no case shall the penalty of confiscation of property be imposed. Nobody may be expropriated except for reasons of public interest or general welfare, and subject to the payment of appropriate indemnities, and in accordance with the provisions of the law.

Title II On the Exercise and Guarantee of Rights

Article 33 – The exercise of the rights recognized in this Charter may not go against the spiritual, national and social unity of Spain.

Article 34 – The Cortes shall pass the laws needed to exercise the rights recognized in this Charter.

Article 35 – Articles 12, 13, 14, 15, 16 and 18, in part or in whole, may be temporarily suspended by the Government by means of a decree which must state clearly the scope and duration of such a measure.

Article 36 – Any violation of any of the rights proclaimed in this Charter shall be penalized by laws which shall establish the actions that can be taken in each case before the competent authorities for the defence and guarantee of such rights.

Labour Charter (9 March 1938, modified 10 January 1967)

Following the Catholic tradition of social justice and the lofty human values that inspired the laws of our glorious past, the State undertakes to secure for all Spaniards *la Patria, el Pan y la Justicia*.

To attain this aim – and strengthening at the same time the unity, the liberty and the greatness of Spain – the State confronts the social question intent upon placing the wealth of the nation at the service of the Spanish people, subordinating the economy to the dignity of human beings, taking full account of their material needs and of the demands of their intellectual, moral, spiritual and religious life.

Basing itself upon the idea of Spain as a unit with a common destiny, it hereby declares as its aim that national production – in the fellowship of all its components – be also a unit to strengthen the country and serve the common good of all Spaniards.

These declarations shall inspire social and economic policies, and they are set forth by the Spanish State to achieve justice, and to satisfy the wishes and demands of all those who, having worked for their country, constitute, on account of their honour, their courage and their labour, the leading aristocracy in the nation at this time. Before the Spanish people, irrevocably united in sacrifice and hope, we declare:

I

1 – Work is man's voluntary participation in production through the use of his intellectual and manual aptitudes, in accordance with his personal vocation, so that he may lead an honourable and comfortable life and best contribute to the development of the national economy.

2 – Work, being essentially personal and human, cannot be brought down to the merely material level of merchandise, nor be the object of any transaction incompatible with the dignity of the worker.

3 – The right to work derives from the duty imposed on man by God, for the fulfilment of his individual ends and for the prosperity and greatness of his country.

4 – The State values and exalts work, fruitful expression of man's creative spirit, and, as such, will grant to it the full protection of the law, holding it in the greatest esteem and making it compatible with all other individual, family and social ends.

5 – Work, being a social duty, shall be demanded, in one form or another, of all able-bodied Spaniards as a compulsory contribution to the national wealth.

6 – Work is one of the noblest attributes of hierarchy and honour, and it is sufficient in itself to demand the assistance and protection of the State.

7 – Service is work undertaken with heroism, generosity, or self-sacrifice, and with the intention of contributing to the supreme good that Spain represents.

8 – Every Spaniard has the right to work. The fulfilment of this right is one of the major concerns of the State.

II

1 – The State undertakes to defend constantly and effectively the worker – both his private life and his work. It shall set proper time limits to the working day and shall grant labour all manner of protective and humanitarian guarantees. It shall, in particular, forbid the night work of women and children, regulate the work done at home, and liberate married women from the workshop and the factory.

2 – The State shall ensure that the keeping of Sunday as a day of rest is a sacred condition of work.

3 – The law shall make it obligatory to keep, without loss of pay and bearing in mind the technical requirements of different firms, all the dates officially declared as religious festivities or public holidays.

4 – The 18th of July, already a national holiday as the anniversary of the Glorious Uprising, shall be celebrated too as Labour Day.

5 – Every worker shall be entitled to annual paid holidays so that he may enjoy a well-deserved rest. Institutions shall be set up to implement this provision in the best possible way.

6 – All the necessary institutions shall be created so that, in their leisure time,

workers may have access to all means of culture, entertainment, military training, health and sport.

III

1 – Wages shall, as a minimum, enable the worker and his family to lead an honest and dignified life.
2 – A system of family allowances shall be established through the appropriate agencies.
3 – The standard of living of workers shall be raised gradually and inexorably, insofar as it is allowed by the higher interest of the Nation.
4 – The State shall lay down the minimum standards for work, and relations between workers and firms shall be established in accordance with such provisions. These relations shall comprise work and its remuneration, as well as the organization of the firm upon the bases of justice, mutual loyalty and the subordination of economic values to human and social values.
5 – The State, through the Syndicate, shall watch that economic and other conditions of work are in keeping with the just deserts of the worker.
6 – The State shall watch over the safety and continuity of work.
7 – Firms shall keep their employees informed of the progress of production, insofar as it is necessary to strengthen their sense of responsibility, and in the terms laid down by the law.

IV

All kinds of handicrafts – as the inheritors of a glorious past – shall be encouraged and protected, for they allow the full expression of the human being through his work, and they represent a form of production divorced from both capitalist monopoly and communist massification.

V

1 – The standards of work in farming shall be adapted to the special characteristics of this sector and to the seasonal variations imposed by nature.
2 – The State shall pay special attention to the training of the agricultural producer, thus enabling him to undertake all the tasks demanded by different types of farms.
3 – The prices of all main produce shall be controlled and re-assessed, in order to guarantee the farmer a minimum profit under normal conditions, and, consequently, to demand from him wages which will allow workers to raise their living standards.
4 – Efforts shall be made to give each peasant family a small-holding or allotment, which will allow them to cover their basic needs and which will provide them with some occupation in time of unemployment.

5 – Rural life shall be enhanced by improving peasants' dwellings and the sanitary conditions of the villages and farms of Spain.

6 – The State shall guarantee tenant farmers some security of tenure through long-term contracts, which will safeguard them against unjust evictions and allow them to pay back any debt they may have incurred to improve the farm. It is the aim of the State to find ways and means for the transfer of the property of land, on equitable terms, to those who work it.

VI

The State shall pay special attention to those who work at sea, providing them with adequate institutions to prevent the depreciation of their merchandise, and to allow them to own all the equipment necessary to carry on their trade.

VII

A new Labour Court shall be created, based upon the principle that this judicial function pertains to the State.

VIII

1 – Capital is instrumental to production.

2 – Any firm, as a unit of production, shall arrange all its elements in a hierarchical order, subordinating instrumental factors to human values, and all of them to the common good.

3 – The management of any firm shall be responsible for its contribution to the common interest of the national economy.

4 – The profits of any firm, after allowing a fair interest on the capital, shall be primarily applied to building up strong reserves, to improving production and to raising the living and working standards of workers.

IX

1 – Credit shall be so arranged that, apart from fulfilling its role in the development of national wealth, it contributes to the creation and maintenance of small agricultural, fishing, industrial and commercial concerns.

2 – Integrity and the trust resulting from competence and work shall be considered as effective guarantees for the granting of credit.

3 – The State shall suppress relentlessly all forms of usury.

X

1 – The social welfare system shall offer the worker the security of its services when in misfortune.

2 – Social security benefits for old age, disablement, maternity, accidents at work, occupational diseases, tuberculosis and unemployment shall be increased, the ultimate aim being to establish a comprehensive insurance system. A first priority shall be to give old workers an adequate pension.

XI

1 – National production constitutes an economic unit at the service of the country. It is the duty of every Spaniard to defend, improve and increase it. All factors involved in production are subordinate to the supreme interest of the Nation.
2 – Any illegal act, whether individual or collective, that seriously interferes with production or goes against it shall be punishable by law.
3 – The fraudulent decrease in work output shall be subject to the appropriate penalties.
4 – In general, the State shall engage in business only when private enterprise is lacking, or when the higher interest of the Nation demands it.
5 – Either directly or through the Syndicates, the State shall prevent all unfair competition in the field of production, as well as those activities that hinder the normal development of the national economy, encouraging, on the other hand, any initiative to improve it.
6 – The State regards private enterprise as a perennial source in the economic life of the Nation.

XII

1 – The State recognizes and protects private property as a natural means to fulfil individual, family and social functions. All forms of ownership are subordinate to the supreme interest of the Nation as interpreted by the State.
2 – The State undertakes to multiply and make accessible to all Spaniards those forms of ownership vitally linked to the person: home, land, and instruments and tools for daily use.
3 – The State considers the family as the natural nucleus and the basis of society; it considers it too as a moral institution endowed with inalienable rights, and superior to all positive law. As a further guarantee of its continuity, there shall be a family inheritance exempt from attachment.

XIII

1 – Spaniards, by virtue of their participation in work and production, constitute the Syndical Organization.
2 – The Syndical Organization comprises a number of industrial, agrarian and service syndicates, organized according to their activities on a regional or national level, and covering all sectors of production.
3 – Syndicates shall have the status of public corporations with a representative

nature, enjoying legal capacity and full rights to operate within their respective spheres. Within each syndicate, and in the manner legally established, associations of employers, technicians and workers shall be set up and organized to defend their respective interests, and as a free and representative means of partaking in syndical activities and, through the syndicates, in the communal tasks of political, social and economic life.

4 – The syndicates channel professional and economic interests to achieve the objectives of the national community, and they represent those interests.

5 – The syndicates shall collaborate in the study of production problems; they may put forward solutions and may take part in the regulation, inspection and implementation of working conditions.

6 – The syndicates may create and maintain bodies for research; for moral, cultural and professional training; for welfare and relief, and for other social purposes affecting the persons engaged in production.

7 – Labour exchange offices shall be established to find employment for workers in accordance with their aptitude and merit.

8 – It is the function of the syndicates to supply the State with the data necessary to prepare the statistics on production.

9 – The Syndical Law shall determine the way in which existing economic and professional associations will be incorporated into the new organization.

XIV

The State shall issue the appropriate measures for the protection of labour in our country and, through labour treaties with other nations, shall seek to protect the position of Spanish workers resident abroad.

XV

At the time of issue of this Charter, Spain is engaged in a heroic military undertaking to save spiritual values and world culture at the cost of sacrificing a large part of her own wealth.

National production in its entirety must respond unselfishly to the generosity shown by young Spaniards on the battlefield, and by Spain herself.

That is why in this Charter of rights and duties, the most urgent and peremptory consideration is that all those engaged in production should make a fair and determined contribution to the rebuilding of Spain and her powers.

XVI

The State undertakes to give all its fighting young soldiers the employment, honour and authority that they are entitled to as Spaniards, and that they have won as heroes.

The Organic Law of the State (10 January 1967)

During the last thirty years, the State which came into existence on 18 July 1936 has carried out a profound reconstruction over the whole of national life. Our fundamental legislation has kept pace with the needs of the country, bringing about, thanks to its gradual introduction, the firm establishment of institutions, and avoiding at the same time misleading rectifications which would have been the inevitable outcome of premature decisions.

The laws so far issued deal with the greater part of the institutional structure. The Law on the Principles of the National Movement contains the directives which govern Spanish policy and will serve as a permanent guide and unchangeable basis for all legislative and governmental action. The Charter of the Spanish People and the Labour Charter define and protect the duties and rights of all Spaniards. The Law on the Referendum submits to the consideration and direct decision of the people Bills of particular relevance or those in which the public interest is involved. The Law on the Cortes establishes the composition and power of the supreme body for the participation of the Spanish people in the affairs of the State. Finally, the Law on the Succession proclaims Spain, as a political unit, to be a Kingdom, and creates the Council of the Realm, which shall assist the Head of State in all important matters and resolutions pertaining to his office.

Nevertheless, the legal vitality and political vigour of the regime, its adaptability to present-day needs and the perspective gained with its vast experience, have made it possible and advisable to complete and improve the fundamental legislation. The time has come to round off the institutional process of the National State; to define the normal powers of the Head of State as they will be after the succession; to determine the composition of the Government, the procedure for the appointment and dismissal of Ministers, the responsibilities and incompatibilities of their office; to establish the organization and functions of the National Council; to raise to the level of fundamental law the general principles concerning the Judiciary, the Armed Forces and Public Administration; to regulate the relations between the Head of State, the Cortes, the Government and the Council of the Realm; to determine the procedure for the appointment and dismissal, and the term of office of the President of the Cortes and the Presidents of the highest Courts and Consultative Bodies; and to open legal channels to halt any action of the legislative or the executive which may go against our system of Fundamental Laws.

These are the aims of the present Law. It will improve and bring harmony into the institutional system of the regime and it will effectively guarantee for the future the loyalty of the highest institutions of the State to the Principles of the National Movement.

In virtue whereof, on the basis of the legislative powers conferred upon me by the laws of 30 January 1938, and 8 August 1939, pursuant to the agreement of the Spanish Cortes adopted in the plenary session of 22 November 1966, and with the authentic and direct consent of the Spanish people expressed by the approval of

85.5 per cent of the electorate, which represents 95.8 per cent of those who voted, in the national Referendum held on 14 December 1966, I hereby resolve:

Title I   The National State

Article 1

I – The Spanish State, constituted as a Kingdom, is the supreme institution of the national community.

II – The State exercises sovereignty through the institutions set up to that end.

Article 2

I – National sovereignty is one and indivisible and it can neither be delegated nor transferred.

II – The institutional system of the Spanish State is based upon the principles of unity of power and co-ordination of functions.

Article 3

The fundamental aims of the State are: to defend the unity among the different peoples and regions of Spain; to maintain the integrity, independence and security of the Nation; to safeguard the material and spiritual heritage of the Spanish people; to protect the rights of the individual, of the family and of society; and to advance a just social order in which private interests be subordinate to the common good. All these aims shall be inspired by, and absolutely faithful to the Principles of the National Movement – issued by the Fundamental Law of 17 May 1958 – which are by their very nature permanent and immutable.

Article 4

The National Movement, the sharing of all Spaniards in the Principles referred to in the preceding article, permeates the political system, which is open to all Spaniards; and, in order to serve the best interest of the country, it promotes an orderly concurrence of criteria in political life.

Article 5

The national flag is made up of three horizontal stripes: red, yellow and red; the yellow stripe being twice the width of each red one.

Title II   The Head of State

Article 6

The Head of State is the highest representative of the Nation; he personifies national sovereignty; he exercises supreme political and administrative power; he is the National Leader of the Movement; he sees to it that the Principles and other Fundamental Laws of the Kingdom are strictly observed and watches over the continuity of the State and of the National Movement; he guarantees and safeguards the normal functioning of, and the proper coordination between the main institutions of the State; he sanctions and promulgates laws and sees that they are implemented; he exercises the supreme command of the Army, Navy and Air Force; he ensures the maintenance of public order at home, and the security of the State abroad; justice is administered in his name; he exercises the prerogative of pardon; he confers public appointments and honours; he accredits and receives diplomatic representatives; and he undertakes whatever other tasks pertain to his office according to the Fundamental Laws of the Kingdom.

Article 7

It is the Head of State's special responsibility:
(a) – To summon the Cortes in accordance with the law, to preside over the opening session of each Cortes, and to deliver, in agreement with the Government, the inaugural address and other speeches.
(b) – To extend for as long as it is necessary, at the request of the Cortes or the Government, and with the agreement of the Council of the Realm, the life of a Cortes when there is some serious impediment for the normal replacement of deputies.
(c) – To put to a national referendum the bills referred to in article 10, paragraph 2 of the Law on the Succession, and Article 1 of the Law on the Referendum.
(d) – To appoint and relieve of their functions the President of the Government, the President of the Cortes, and other high officials in the manner prescribed by law.
(e) – To call the meetings of the Council of Ministers and of the National Defence Junta and to preside over them when in attendance.
(f) – To preside, should he judge it advisable, over the debates of the Council of the Realm and of the National Council, provided that those of the former do not refer to him personally or to the heirs to the throne. In no case shall voting take place in the presence of the Head of State.
(g) – To seek the advice and guidance of the Council of the Realm.
(h) – To request reports from the National Council.

Article 8

I – The person of the Head of State is inviolable. All Spaniards shall show him respect and obedience.

II – All the decisions taken by the Head of State in the exercise of his authority shall be countersigned, as the case may be, by the President of the Government or the Minister concerned, by the President of the Cortes or by the President of the Council of the Realm, any disposition which does not comply with this formality being invalid.

III – The responsibility for the acts of the Head of State shall rest with the persons who countersign them.

Article 9

The Head of State shall require a law, or, where applicable, the agreement or authorization of the Cortes, in the following cases:

(a) – To ratify international treaties and agreements affecting national sovereignty or the integrity of Spanish territory.

(b) – To declare war and agree to peace.

(c) – To put into effect all the acts referred to in article 12 of the Law on the Succession, and any other that may be equally defined elsewhere in the Fundamental Laws of the Kingdom.

Article 10

The Head of State shall be assisted by the Council of the Realm:

(a) – To propose to the Cortes those decisions which, according to the provisions of the preceding article, require a law or their approval or authorization.

(b) – To return to the Cortes for further consideration a law they have passed.

(c) – To extend the life of the Cortes for as long as it is necessary when there are serious reasons.

(d) – To take exceptional measures when the external security, the independence of the Nation, the integrity of her territory or the institutional system of the Kingdom are seriously and imminently threatened. The Cortes shall be given a documented account of such measures.

(e) – To put to a national referendum major bills, when such a referendum is not mandatory.

(f) – To take any other decision for which, according to one of the Fundamental Laws, the assistance of the Council of the Realm is required.

Article 11

Should the Head of State be absent from the national territory or in ill health, his duties shall be discharged by the heir to the throne, if there is one and he is over thirty, or otherwise by the Regency Council. In any event, the President of the Government shall inform the Cortes.

Article 12

The guardianship of minors of royal blood in the line of succession, or of the incapacitated King, shall have to be proposed by the Council of the Realm and approved by the Cortes. The designated person must be a Spaniard and a Catholic and the post is incompatible with that of Regent, President of the Government or President of the Cortes.

Title III   The Government of the Nation

Article 13

I – The Head of State directs the running of the Kingdom through the Council of Ministers.

II – The Council of Ministers, consisting of the President of the Government, the Vice-President or Vice-Presidents, if there are any, and the Ministers, is the body that determines national policy, ensures the application of the laws, has the power to make regulations, and permanently assists the Head of State in political and administrative matters.

III – The resolutions of the Government shall always be countersigned by its President or by the Minister concerned.

Article 14

I – The President of the Government shall be Spanish, and shall be appointed by the Head of State from a list of three candidates proposed by the Council of the Realm.

II – His term of office shall last five years. Fifteen days before his term expires, the Council of the Realm shall submit the proposal referred to in the preceding paragraph.

III – The post of President of the Government shall be subject to the incompatibilities determined by law.

IV – It is incumbent upon the President to represent the Government of the Nation, to direct general policy and to ensure the coordination of all the institutions of government and administration.

V – The President of the Government exercises, on behalf of the Head of State, the National Leadership of the Movement, assisted by the National Council and the Secretary-General.

Article 15

The President of the Government shall relinquish his post:

(a) – When his term of office expires.

(b) – At his own request, once the Head of State has accepted his resignation after consulting the Council of the Realm.

(c) – By the decision of the Head of State, in agreement with the Council of the Realm.

(d) – Upon the proposal made by the Council of the Realm because of incapacity recognized by two-thirds of its members.

Article 16

I – In the event of the death of the President of the Government, or in any of the events foreseen in paragraphs (b), (c) and (d) in the preceding article, his functions shall be temporarily assumed by the Vice-President or Vice-Presidents, in the order established, or, should there be no Vice-President, by the Minister appointed by the Head of State.

II – A new President shall be nominated in the manner established in article 14 within ten days.

Article 17

I – The other members of the Government shall be Spanish and their appointment and dismissal shall be effected by the Head of State at the proposal of the President of the Government.

II – Their posts shall be subject to the incompatibilities determined by law.

Article 18

The members of the Government shall relinquish their posts:

(a) – When the President of the Government changes.

(b) – At the instance of the President of the Government, with the approval of the Head of State.

(c) – At their own request, once the resignation has been accepted by the Head of State at the proposal of the President of the Government.

Article 19

Before taking office, the President and the other members of the Government shall, in the presence of the Head of State, swear allegiance to him, to the Principles of the National Movement and to the other Fundamental Laws of the Kingdom; and they shall undertake to keep their deliberations secret.

Article 20

I – The President and the other members of the Government are jointly responsible for the resolutions passed at their meetings. Each one individually shall be responsible for what he does or authorizes in his own Department.

II – The penal liability of the President of the Government and of the other members of the Government, and the civil liability they may incur in the exercise of their function, shall be judged by the Supreme Court of Justice in plenary session.

Title IV   The National Council

Article 21

The National Council, as the corporate representative of the Movement, has the following functions:

(a) – To strengthen the unity among the peoples and regions of Spain.

(b) – To defend the integrity of the Principles of the National Movement, and to ensure that the transformation and development of the economic, social and cultural structures meet the requirements of social justice.

(c) – To watch over the development and exercise of all the rights and liberties recognized by the Fundamental Laws and to encourage a real and effective participation of the natural entities and of public opinion in political affairs.

(d) – To contribute to the spreading of loyalty to the Principles of the National Movement amongst young Spaniards, and to make the new generations participate in the collective enterprise.

(e) – To channel, within the Principles of the Movement, contrasting opinions on political matters.

(f) – To safeguard the continuity and improvement of the National Movement.

Article 22

The National Council shall be composed of the following members:

(a) – One Councillor elected for each province, in the manner established by the appropriate organic law.

(b) – Forty Councillors nominated by the Caudillo from among persons who have rendered valuable service. After the succession these forty Councillors shall remain in office up to the age of seventy-five, and such vacancies as may arise subsequently shall be filled by election from a list of three candidates proposed by this group of Councillors to the Council's Plenary Session.

(c) – Twelve Councillors who will represent the basic structures of the national community:

Four elected from among themselves by the Deputies representing the family in the Cortes;

Four elected from among themselves by the Deputies representing the local Corporations in the Cortes;

Four elected from among themselves by the Deputies representing the Syndical Organization in the Cortes.

(d) – Six Councillors nominated by the President of the Council from among persons rendering services relevant to the functions enumerated in the preceding article.

(e) – The Secretary-General, who shall exercise the functions of Vice-President.

Article 23

In order to carry out the functions mentioned in article 21, the National Council shall be able:

(a) – To promote the compliance of laws and general regulations with the Principles of the National Movement and other Fundamental Laws of the Kingdom, enjoying for this purpose the right of appeal foreseen under Title X of the present Law.

(b) – To recommend to the Government whatever measures it may consider appropriate to increase the effectiveness of the Principles of the Movement and other Fundamental Laws of the Kingdom, and, in any case, to study and to report on any new Fundamental Law or amendment to an existing one, before it is sent to the Cortes.

(c) – To submit to the Government such reports and memoranda as it may consider appropriate, and to express an opinion on any matter put to it by the Government, having the power, in such cases, to request any information it may consider necessary.

Article 24

The National Council shall operate by means of plenary sessions and through the Standing Committee, in accordance with the provisions of its organic law.

Article 25

The President of the Government, in his capacity as National Leader of the Movement by delegation of the Head of State, shall act as President of the National Council and of its Standing Committee, assisted by the Secretary-General, to whom he may delegate such functions as he sees fit.

Article 26

The Secretary-General shall be appointed by the Head of State, at the proposal of the President of the Government. The post of Secretary-General shall be subject to the incompatibilities determined by law.

Article 27

I – The President of the National Council shall relinquish his post when he ceases to be President of the Government.

II – The Secretary-General shall relinquish his post:
  (a) When the President of the Government changes.
  (b) At the instance of the President of the Government, with the approval of the Head of State.
  (c) At his own request, once the resignation has been accepted by the Head of State at the proposal of the President of the Government.

III – The National Councillors shall relinquish their posts:
  (a) At the end of their term of office those of groups (a) and (c); on reaching the age of seventy-five those of group (b); and by the decision of the President of the Council those of group (d).
  (b) At their own request, once their resignation has been accepted by the Head of State at the proposal of the President of the Government.
  (c) For reasons of incapacity, recognized by the Council.
  (d) For any other reason which may cause their retirement as Deputies of the Cortes.

Article 28

An organic law shall establish the norms governing the National Council.

Title V   The Judiciary

Article 29

The Judiciary shall enjoy complete independence. Justice shall be administered in the name of the Head of State, in accordance with the laws, by Judges and Magistrates, who shall be independent, immovable and responsible, as prescribed by the Law.

Article 30

Every Spaniard shall have free access to the Courts of Justice. Their services shall be free for those lacking economic means.

Article 31

The juridical function, both in passing sentence and in ensuring the execution of that sentence, in civil, penal, administrative, labour or any other cases determined by law, rests exclusively with the Courts and Tribunals defined in the Organic Law of the Judiciary, according to their various terms of reference.

Article 32

I – Military jurisdiction shall be governed by its own and exclusive laws and regulations.

II – Ecclesiastical jurisdiction shall extend to those areas determined by the Concordat with the Holy See.

Article 33

The superintendence of the Judiciary is incumbent on the President of the Supreme Court, who shall be appointed from among Spanish jurists of high repute.

Article 34

Judges and Magistrates may not be dismissed, suspended, transferred or pensioned off except for reasons and with the guarantee prescribed by law.

Article 35

I – The Office of the Public Prosecutor, which serves as a link between the Government and the Courts, is entrusted with the task of promoting the action of the Judiciary to defend the public interests protected by law, and of procuring before the Courts and Tribunals the maintenance of juridical order and the satisfaction of social interests.

II – The functions entrusted to the Office of the Public Prosecutor shall be exercised through its various bodies and agencies, organized in accordance with the principles of unity and hierarchical dependence.

Article 36

Public authorities and bodies, as well as private people, are obliged to give the Courts and Tribunals the help necessary for the exercise of the juridical function.

Title VI   The Armed Forces

Article 37

The Armed Forces of the Nation, consisting of the Army, the Navy, the Air Force and the Police, guarantee the unity and independence of the country, the integrity of her territory, national security and the defence of the institutional system.

Article 38

A National Defence Junta, composed of the President of the Government, the Ministers of the Military Departments, the Chief of the Supreme Staff and the Chiefs of Staff of the Army, the Navy and the Air Force, shall propose to the Government the general lines to be followed in matters of security and national defence. Any Minister or high-ranking official may be included in the National Defence Junta when his attendance is advisable on account of the business under consideration.

Article 39

A Supreme Staff, dependent on the President of the Government, shall be the technical centre of National Defence, having the mission of coordinating the activities of the Staffs of the Army, the Navy and the Air Force.

Title VII   The Administration of the State

Article 40

I – The Administration, with its hierarchically organized bodies, undertakes to fulfil the aims of the State so as to achieve a prompt and effective satisfaction of the general interest.

II – The higher bodies of the Administration, their respective authority, and the basic rules applying to civil servants shall be determined by law.

III – The Administration shall be advised by the consultative bodies established by law.

IV – The Council of State is the supreme consultative body of the Administration; its authority and functioning shall be determined by law.

V – The National Economic Council is the consultative, advisory and technical body concerned with all important matters affecting the national economy.

Article 41

I – The Administration may not issue dispositions contrary to the laws, nor regulate, save by express authorization of a law, those matters pertaining exclusively to the Cortes.

II – Any administrative disposition contravening what is laid down in the preceding paragraph shall be null and void.

Article 42

I – The resolutions and decisions taken by the Administration shall follow the rules governing administrative procedure.

II – It shall be possible to bring before the competent court whatever actions and appeals are appropriate, in accordance with the law, once administrative channels have been exhausted.

III – The responsibility of the Administration, its authorities, civil servants and agents may be demanded for the reasons and in the manner determined by law.

Article 43

All public authorities and civil servants owe allegiance to the Principles of the National Movement and other Fundamental Laws of the Kingdom and shall take, prior to assuming office, the appropriate oath.

Article 44

It is the task of the Court of Accounts to audit and verify, with complete independence, the accounts stating the operations undertaken in the implementation of the budgetary and fiscal laws, as well as the accounts of all official bodies receiving aids or subsidies out of the General Budget of the State and of its autonomous bodies, and to carry out all the other functions allocated to the Court by its organic Law.

Title VIII   Local Government

Article 45

I – The Municipalities are natural entities and constitute the basic elements of the national community. They are grouped territorially into provinces.

II – The Province is an area determined by the grouping of Municipalities as well as a territorial division of the State Administration. Territorial divisions other than the Province may also be established.

Article 46

I – The Municipalities and the Provinces enjoy legal status and are fully capable of carrying out their particular functions in the manner established by law, without prejudice to their cooperative functions in the service of the State.

II – The municipal and provincial Corporations, which are the representative and administrative bodies of the Municipality and the Province, respectively, shall be elected by vote through the representative channels specified in article 10 of the Charter of the Spanish People.

Article 47

The State promotes the betterment of municipal and provincial life, it protects and encourages the development of the resources of local Corporations, and it guarantees them the economic means necessary for the fulfilment of their aims.

Article 48

The system of Local Government and of its Corporations, in accordance with the provisions of the preceding articles and the guarantees demanded by the common good in this respect, shall be determined by law.

Title IX   Relations between the Highest Institutions of the State

Article 49

The appointment of a new Government and the replacement of any of its members shall be immediately reported to the Spanish Cortes.

Article 50

Apart from its participation in the legislative process, it is the responsibility of the Cortes in relation to the Head of State:

(a) – To receive from the Head of State, and from the heir to the Throne, when the latter reaches the age of thirty, an oath of allegiance to the Principles of the National Movement and other Fundamental Laws of the Kingdom.

(b) – To solve, in accordance with the Law on the Succession, all the questions that may arise in respect of the succession to the Headship of the State.

(c) – To authorize the Head of State to carry out those acts that require, by Fundamental Law, the intervention of the Cortes.

(d) – Any other functions entrusted to them by the Fundamental Laws.

Article 51

The Government, with the express authorization of the Cortes, may submit to the sanction of the Head of State dispositions with the force of law.

Article 52

Except in the event foreseen in the preceding article, and in those included in paragraph (d) of article 10 of this Law, and in article 13 of the Law on the Cortes, the Government may not issue dispositions which, according to articles 10 and 12 of the Law on the Cortes, must take the form of a law.

Article 53

The President of the Government and the Ministers shall inform the Cortes of the activities of the Government and of their respective Departments, and, when appropriate, shall answer requests and questions made according to the standing orders.

Article 54

I – It is the responsibility of the Government to draw up the General Budget of the State and it is the responsibility of the Cortes to pass, amend or reject it. If the Budget is not passed before the beginning of the next financial year, the previous Budget shall automatically remain in force until the new one is passed.

II – Once the General Budget of the State has been passed, only the Government may present Bills that represent an increase in public expenditure or a decrease in revenue; and any private member's Bill, or any amendment to a Government's Bill or a private member's Bill which entails an increase in expenditure or a decrease in revenue, shall require the approval of the Government.

III – The Government shall submit to the Cortes, for their approval, the General Accounts of the State, once they have been audited and verified by the Court of Accounts.

Article 55

In accordance with the law, the Court of Accounts, by reason of its controlling capacity, shall inform the Government and the Cortes, by means of memoranda and reports, of its views on the manner in which the budgetary and fiscal laws have been implemented, and also in all those cases in which, by virtue of their exceptional importance, the Court may deem it necessary to make use of this faculty.

Article 56

Only the Head of State may seek the advice of the Council of the Realm.

Article 57

It is the responsibility of the Head of State to settle, in accordance with the laws, any questions of competence between the Administration and the Judiciary or any ordinary or special Court, and those arising between the Court of Accounts and the Administration, or between the Court of Accounts and the other ordinary and special Courts.

Article 58

I – The Presidents of the Supreme Court of Justice, the Council of State, the Court of Accounts and the National Economic Council shall be appointed, in each case, by the Head of State from a list of three candidates proposed by the Council of the Realm.

II – Their term of office shall last four years, and their posts shall be subject to the incompatibilities determined by the laws.

III – They shall relinquish their posts:

(a) When their term of office expires.

(b) At their own request, once the Head of State has accepted their resignation after consulting the Council of the Realm.

(c) By the decisions of the Head of State, in agreement with the Council of the Realm.

(d) Upon the proposal made by the Council of the Realm, because of incapacity recognized by two-thirds of its members.

Title X　The Appeal of 'Contrafuero'

Article 59

I – *Contrafuero* is any legislative act or any general disposition of the Government which goes against the Principles of the National Movement or the other Fundamental Laws of the Kingdom.

II – As a protection for the principles and norms infringed by *contrafuero* the right of appeal to the Head of State has been established.

Article 60

The appeal of *contrafuero* may be lodged by:

(a) – The National Council, in all cases, by a resolution taken by two-thirds of its Councillors.

(b) – The Standing Committee of the Cortes in the case of general dispositions of the Government, by a resolution taken by two-thirds of its members.

Article 61

I – The appeal of *contrafuero* must be brought before the Council of the Realm within two months of the publication in the *Boletín Oficial del Estado* of the law or general disposition giving rise to it.

II – The President of the Council of the Realm shall notify the Head of State at once of the lodging of an appeal of *contrafuero*, and shall bring it to the attention of the Standing Committee of the Cortes or of the President of the Government, as the case may be, so that they may appoint, if they consider it necessary, a representative to defend before the Council of the Realm the legitimacy of the law or general disposition under appeal.

III – If there are well-founded reasons, the Council of the Realm may propose to the Head of State the suspension, during the proceedings, of the law or general disposition under appeal, or, alternatively, of whatever part of it is affected by the appeal.

Article 62

I – On the question posed by the appeal of *contrafuero*, the Council of the Realm shall request a ruling from a Committee chaired by the President of one of the Sections of the Supreme Court of Justice and composed of: a National Councillor, a Permanent Councillor of State, a Magistrate of the Supreme Court of Justice and a Member of the Cortes, all of them nominated by the Standing Committee of their respective institutions, and, in the case of the Supreme Court of Justice, by its Governing Body. The said ruling shall be passed on to the Council of the Realm, stating the individual votes if any.

II – The Council of the Realm, chaired for this purpose by the President of the Supreme Court of Justice, shall propose to the Head of State the appropriate resolution.

Article 63

In the event of the Standing Committee of the Cortes detecting an infringement of the Principles of the Movement, or of the other Fundamental Laws, in a Government's or a private member's Bill on which a ruling has already been given by the appropriate Committee of the Cortes, it shall raise the matter, in a detailed document, with the President of the Cortes within eight days of the publication of the ruling in the *Boletín Oficial* of the Cortes. The President shall pass it on to the Committee responsible for the ruling, so that it may consider again the Government's or Private Member's Bill in question. In the meantime, the Bill shall not be included amongst the orders of the day in the Cortes, or, if already included, it shall be withdrawn.

Article 64

The resolution which revokes, for reasons of *contrafuero*, the legislative act or general disposition of the Government under appeal, shall require the immediate publication in the *Boletín Oficial del Estado* of the declared nullity, stating the extent of its effects.

Article 65

I – The Head of State, before putting to referendum a Government or Private

Member's Bill which has gone through the Cortes, shall request the National Council to declare, within fifteen days, whether, in their opinion, there are grounds for an appeal of *contrafuero*.

II – If the National Council considers that such grounds exist, it shall proceed to lodge an appeal as foreseen in article 61. If there are no grounds for an appeal, or in the case of the appeal being rejected, the law shall be put to referendum, and once promulgated, it cannot be the object of an appeal of *contrafuero*.

Article 66

A special law shall establish the form, the conditions and terms under which the case arising out of an appeal of *contrafuero* should be brought and substantiated.

Transitory Provisions

First

I – Once the provisions of the Law on the Succession have been fulfilled, the person called upon to become Head of State, as King or Regent, shall assume the functions and duties assigned to that office in the present Law.

II – The powers given to the Head of State by the Laws of 30 January 1938 and 8 August 1939, as well as the prerogatives granted to him by articles 6 and 13 of the Law on the Succession, shall remain in force until the event referred to in the preceding paragraph should take place.

III – Francisco Franco, Caudillo of Spain, is vested for life with the National Leadership of the Movement. Once the provisions for the succession have been fulfilled, this office shall pass to the Head of State and, by his delegation, to the President of the Government.

Final Provisions

First

As from the date this Law comes into force, all dispositions contrary to it are repealed.

Second

The Present Law is a Fundamental Law, as defined in article 10 of the Law on the Succession to the Head of State.

Law on the Cortes (17 July 1942, modified 9 March 1946 and 10 January 1967)

The creation of a juridical system, the organization of the administrative activities of the State, all require a process of elaboration from which, to obtain the highest quality and stability in the country, it is unwise to exclude representation of all sections of the national community. The contrast of opinions – within the unity of the regime – the airing of aspirations, well-founded and responsible criticism, and legislative technique should all contribute to bringing vitality, justice and constant improvement to the Laws of the Revolution and to the new Economy of the Spanish people.

Abnormal events, so evident that it would be idle to explain, have delayed the achievement of this goal. But the time has come to set up a body to undertake those tasks, now that we have left behind that period in the life of the National Movement when it was not possible to do so.

Although the Head of State retains the supreme power to legislate in the terms of the laws of 30 January 1938, and 8 August 1939, the newly created body shall represent a principle of self-limitation for a more systematic institution of authority, as well as an effective instrument of collaboration in that function.

In keeping with the National Movement, the Cortes now being created shall revive glorious Spanish traditions, both in their name and in their composition and functions.

The amendments introduced by the Organic Law of the State and by its additional provisions improve and accentuate the representative nature of political life which is a basic feature of our public institutions. As regards the Cortes, this means: introducing a new group of *Procuradores* as representatives of the family, elected by heads of families and married women in keeping with the principle of equal political rights for women; extending representation to other Professional Bodies, Corporations and Associations, and, at the same time, carefully reducing their total number of *Procuradores* and, in general, securing a more authentic representation and considerably increasing the ratio of elected *Procuradores* in relation to ex-officio members. The election of two Vice-Presidents and four Secretaries by the Cortes, in plenary session, and for each legislative term, is in keeping with this.

In virtue of which, I resolve:

Article 1

The Cortes are the highest body for the participation of the Spanish people in the affairs of the State. The principal task of the Cortes is the elaboration and approval of laws, without prejudice to the sanction pertaining to the Head of State.

Article 2

I – The Cortes are composed of the following groups of *Procuradores*:

(a) The Members of the Government.

(b) The National Councillors.

(c) The Presidents of the Supreme Court of Justice, the Council of State, the Supreme Council of Military Justice, the Court of Accounts and the National Economic Council.

(d) One hundred and fifty representatives of the Syndical Organization.

(e) One representative for the Municipalities of each Province elected by the Town Councils from among their members, and another one for each Municipality with more than 300,000 inhabitants and one each for Ceuta and Melilla, elected by the respective Town Councils from among their members. One representative for each *Diputación Provincial* (Provincial Council) and Canary Islands District, elected by the respective Corporations from among their members, and the representatives of local Corporations from those territories which do not form part of a province, elected in like manner.

(f) Two family representatives for each province elected by those included in the heads of family electoral register and by married women, in the manner established by law.

(g) The University Rectors.

(h) The President of the Institute of Spain and two representatives elected from among the members of the Royal Academies forming part of the said Institute; the President of the Council for Advanced Scientific Research and two representatives of this Council elected by its members.

(i) The President of the Institute of Civil Engineers and one representative of the Association of Engineers forming that Institute, two representatives of the Medical Associations; one representative each for the Associations of: Stockbrokers, Architects, Economists, Pharmacists, Graduates and Doctors in Political Science, Graduates and Doctors in Arts and Science, Doctors in Chemical and Physico-Chemical Sciences, Notaries, Attorneys, Property Registrars, Veterinary Surgeons, and of any other professional body of higher academic status which may be recognized for this purpose in the future. These representatives shall be elected by their respective Associations. Three representatives of the Official Chambers of Commerce; one representative of the Chambers of Urban Property, and another one of the Tenants' Associations, elected by their Boards or representative bodies. All those elected under the provisions of this section must be members of the respective Colleges, Corporations or Associations electing them. The number and distribution of the *Procuradores* included in this section may be altered by law, provided that the total does not exceed thirty.

(j) Those persons who, on account of their ecclesiastical, military or administrative rank or of the service rendered to the country, may be appointed by the Head of State, after consultation with the Council of the Realm, to a maximum of twenty-five.

II – All the *Procuradores* represent the Spanish people, must serve the nation and the common good, and must not be bound by any compulsory mandate.

Article 3

To be *Procurador* it is necessary:
1 – To be Spanish and of age.
2 – To enjoy full civil rights and not to be under any political disqualification.

Article 4

The *Procuradores* shall verify before the President of the Cortes the election, appointment, or office which entitles them to such an investiture. The President of the Cortes shall witness their oath, seat them, and issue the corresponding titles.

Article 5

The *Procuradores* may not be arrested without the previous authorization of the President of the Cortes, except in cases *flagrante delicto*. In such cases, the arrest shall be notified to the President of the Cortes.

Article 6

Ex-officio members of the Cortes shall cease to be *Procuradores* when they relinquish the post that entitled them to the seat. Those nominated by the Head of State shall cease to be *Procuradores* upon the revocation of their appointment by the Head of State. Otherwise, their term of office shall last four years and they may be re-elected, but if, during those four years, a representative of a Provincial Council, a Town Council or a Corporation ceases to be a member of any such body, he shall cease to be a *Procurador* too.

Article 7

I – The President of the Cortes shall be appointed by the Head of State from a list of three names submitted to him by the Council of the Realm within ten days of the post falling vacant. His appointment shall be approved by the acting President of the Council of the Realm.

II – His term of office shall last six years, during which period he shall retain his seat as *Procurador*. The post of President of the Cortes shall be subject to the incompatibilities determined by law.

III – The President of the Cortes shall relinquish his post:
    (a) When his term of office expires.
    (b) At his own request, once his resignation has been accepted by the Head of State, after consideration by the Council of the Realm in a meeting not attended by the President of the Cortes.
    (c) By the decision of the Head of State, and with the agreement of the Council of the Realm granted in a meeting like the one foreseen in the previous paragraph.
    (d) For reasons of incapacity recognized by two-thirds of the members of the Cortes, chaired for the purpose by the first or second Vice-President, as the case may be, after a well-reasoned proposal made by the Standing Committee, under the same Chairman, or by the Government.
IV – Should the post of President of the Cortes fall vacant, it shall be assumed by the first or second Vice-President, as the case may be, until a new President be appointed within ten days.
V – The two Vice-Presidents and the four Secretaries of the Cortes shall be elected, for each four-year term, from among the *Procuradores* by the Cortes in plenary session.

Article 8

The Cortes shall meet in plenary sessions and in committees. The Committees are set up and appointed by the President of the Cortes, at the proposal of the Standing Committee and in agreement with the Government. The President, in agreement with the Government, draws up the agenda for both the Plenary Sessions and the Committee Meetings.

Article 9

The Cortes shall meet in plenary session to consider laws subject to that requirement, and whenever they are called to do so by their President, in agreement with the Government.

Article 10

The Cortes shall examine, in plenary session, all those matters and laws concerned with any of the following subjects:
(a) – The ordinary and extraordinary budgets of the State.
(b) – Major economic and financial operations.
(c) – The establishment or reform of the system of taxation.
(d) – Banking and monetary regulations.
(e) – The economic activity of the Syndicates and any legislative measure which may have a considerable influence on the economy of the Nation.

(f) – Basic laws regulating the acquisition and the loss of Spanish nationality and the duties and rights of Spaniards.

(g) – The juridical organization of the political institutions of the State.

(h) – The fundamental aspects of local government.

(i) – The fundamental aspects of Civil, Commercial, Social, Penal and Procedural Law.

(j) – The fundamental aspects of the Judiciary and of Public Administration.

(k) – The fundamental aspects of agrarian, commercial and industrial organizations.

(l) – National education planning.

(m) – Any other law which the Government, on its own initiative or at the proposal of the appropriate Committee, should decide to submit to the plenary session of the Cortes.

The Government may also submit to the plenary session any matters or resolutions not intended as laws.

Article 11

Bills to be submitted to a plenary session shall first go to the appropriate Committees for their report and proposals.

Article 12

I – The Committees of the Cortes have jurisdiction over all those dispositions not included in article 10, but which must take the form of law, either because it is so established by a later law, or because it is suggested by a Committee composed of the President of the Cortes, a Minister appointed by the Government, a member of the Standing Committee of the National Council, a member of the Cortes with a degree in law, the President of the Council of State, and the President of the Supreme Court of Justice. This Committee shall issue a ruling at the request of the Government or of the Standing Committee of the Cortes.

II – If any of the Cortes Committees should raise, during the reading of a Government bill, a private member's bill, or an independent motion, some question which does not fall within the jurisdiction of the Cortes, the President, on his own initiative or at the Government's request, may ask the Committee mentioned in the previous paragraph to give a ruling. Should the ruling consider the matter to be outside the jurisdiction of the Cortes, it shall be withdrawn from the agenda.

Article 13

The Government may, for reasons of urgency, propose to the Head of State the sanctioning of decrees with the force of law to regulate the matters mentioned in articles 10 and 12. The urgency of the case shall be determined by the Head of State, after consultation with the Committee referred to in the preceding article. Should this Committee detect any form of *contrafuero*, it may bring the matter to the attention of the Standing Committee. The promulgation of a decree with the force of law shall be immediately notified to the Cortes.

Article 14

I – The ratification of international treaties and agreements affecting Spain's sovereignty or territorial integrity shall be the object of a law approved by the Cortes in plenary session.

II – The Cortes, in plenary session or through one of its committees, as the case may be, shall be consulted about the ratification of any other treaty affecting matters which, according to articles 10 and 12, fall within its jurisdiction.

Article 15

I – Besides examining Government bills and passing them on to the Plenary Session, the legislative Committees may submit their own bills to the President of the Cortes, who shall decide, in agreement with the Government, whether to include them in the order of the day.

II – The President of the Cortes may entrust the legislative Committees with other tasks, such as carrying out studies, obtaining information and formulating petitions and proposals. For such a purpose, special Committees, other than the legislative ones, may be set up.

Article 16

The laws passed by the Cortes shall be submitted by its President to the sanction of the Head of State, and they must be promulgated within one month of being received by the Head of State.

Article 17

The Head of State may, by means of an explanatory report and with a concurrent ruling from the Council of the Realm, return a law to the Cortes for further consideration.

Additional Provision

The Cortes, in agreement with the Government, shall draw up their own standing orders.

Law on the Succession to the Head of State
(7 July 1947, modified 10 January 1967)

Whereas the Spanish Cortes, as the highest of the institutions through which the people participate in the affairs of the State, have drawn up the Fundamental Law which, proclaiming Spain to be a Kingdom, creates its Council and establishes the regulations for the Succession of the Head of State; the text of which law put to the referendum of the Nation was approved by 82 per cent of the electorate, representing 93 per cent of the voters.

And whereas The Organic Law of the State amends certain articles of the said Fundamental Law in respect of the composition of the Council of the Realm, establishing that ten of the Councillors, as against four previously, shall be elected, and introduces other amendments to clarify certain points in the system of succession in order to foresee any possible eventuality.

Pursuant to the approval of the Cortes and supported by the true and direct expression of the will of the Nation, I hereby resolve:

Article 1

Spain, as a political unit, is a Catholic, social and representative state, which, in accordance with her traditions, proclaims herself to be a Kingdom.

Article 2

The post of Head of State is held by the Caudillo of Spain and of the Crusade, Generalissimo of the Armed Forces, don Francisco Franco Bahamonde.

Article 3

Should the post of Head of State fall vacant, its powers shall be assumed by a Council of Regency composed of the President of the Cortes, the Prelate, member of the Council of the Realm, with the highest rank and seniority, and the Captain-General, or else the most senior Lieutenant-General, serving in the Army, the Navy or the Air Force, in that order; or their deputies nominated in accordance with the provisions of the next article. The President of the Cortes shall be the President of this Council and for its resolutions to be valid, the presence of at least two of its three members shall be required, including always that of the President, or, in his absence, the Vice-President of the Council of the Realm.

Article 4

I – A Council of the Realm, which shall have precedence over all other consultative bodies in the Nation, shall assist the Head of State in important matters and resolutions pertaining to his office. Its President shall be the President of the Cortes and its members the following:

The Prelate with the highest rank and seniority, amongst those members of the Cortes

The Captain-General, or else the most senior Lieutenant-General, serving in the Army, the Navy, or the Air Force, in that order

The General in charge of the Supreme Staff, or, in his absence, the most senior of the three Generals, Chiefs of Staff in the Army, the Navy and the Air Force

The President of the Supreme Court of Justice

The President of the Council of State

The President of the Institute of Spain

Two Councillors elected by ballot for each of the following groups of members of the Cortes:

(a) National Councillors

(b) Syndical Organization representatives

(c) Local Government representatives

(d) Family representatives

One Councillor elected by ballot for each of the following groups of members of the Cortes:

(a) University Rectors

(b) Professional Associations.

II – Membership of the Council shall be dependent upon the position which motivated nomination or election.

III – The Head of State shall nominate, at the proposal of the Council of the Realm, and from amongst its members, a Vice-President and a deputy for each of the Councillors who are members of the Council of Regency.

IV – When the President is unable to attend, or when the office of President of the Cortes falls vacant, and, in the latter case, until such a time as the post is filled, the Vice-President of the Council of the Realm shall act as his deputy.

V – The resolutions, rulings, and proposals of the Council of the Realm shall be taken by majority vote among the attending Councillors, whose number may not be less than half plus one of the total membership, except in those cases when the Fundamental Laws require a certain majority. In the event of a tie, the President shall have the casting vote.

Article 5

The Head of State shall necessarily be assisted by the Council of the Realm when this, or any other Fundamental Law, should establish such a requirement.

Article 6

At any time the Head of State may propose to the Cortes the person he considers should succeed him, either as King or as Regent, under the conditions required by this Law. He may, likewise, submit to the approval of the Cortes the repeal of any previous proposal, even when the latter has already been accepted by the Cortes.

Article 7

When the post of Head of State falls vacant and the person nominated in accordance with the preceding article is called upon to succeed, the Council of Regency shall assume power on his behalf, and shall call a joint meeting of the Cortes and the Council of the Realm to witness the successor's oath of office as prescribed in the present law, and to proclaim him King or Regent.

Article 8

I – Should the Head of State die or be declared incapacitated, without a successor having been nominated, the Council of Regency shall assume all powers, except that of revoking the appointment of any of its members, who shall, in any event, retain their office; and, within three days, it shall call on the members of the Government and the Council of the Realm to hold an uninterrupted and secret session to decide, by a two-thirds majority of those present, which must represent at least an absolute majority, on the person of royal blood whom, having all the conditions required by the present Law and in consideration of the highest interest of the nation, they should propose to the Cortes as King. Should the proposal not be accepted, the Government and the Council of the Realm may, following the same procedure, propose another person of royal blood who meets the legal requirements too.

II – If, in the opinion of the meeting, there exists no person of royal blood with all the aforementioned conditions, or those proposed should not meet with the approval of the Cortes, they shall propose, following the same procedure, the person who, on the basis of his prestige, capacity and expected support from the Nation, should act as Regent. When putting forward this proposal, the meeting may set a limit and conditions to the duration of the Regency, and the Cortes must decide upon each of these points.

Should the person proposed as Regent not be accepted by the Cortes, the Government and the Council of the Realm must put forward, following the same procedure, new proposals until one meets with the approval of the Cortes.

III – If, in the cases referred to in the preceding paragraphs, a two-thirds majority should not be reached in the first ballot, a second-ballot and, if necessary, a third one shall be held. In the third ballot, a three-fifths majority, which must, at least, be equivalent to the absolute majority, shall be sufficient to give validity to the decision.

IV – A plenary session of the Cortes shall be held within eight days of each proposal, and the Successor, having obtained the approval of the Cortes, in accordance with the stipulations of article 15, shall take the oath required by the present law, by virtue of which the Council of Regency shall immediately transfer all powers to him.

V – Until such time as the provisions of article 11 of the present Law should become applicable, the nomination of the Successor, when the office of Head of State falls vacant, shall be made in accordance with the stipulations of this article.

Article 9

To exercise the office of Head of State, it shall be necessary to be a Spanish male, to have reached the age of thirty, to profess the Catholic religion, to have the qualities needed to undertake such a high mission and to swear allegiance to the Fundamental Laws and to the Principles of the National Movement. This same oath shall be taken by the successor on reaching the age of thirty.

Article 10

The Fundamental Laws of the Nation are: the Charter of the Spanish People, the Labour Charter, the Law on the Cortes, the present Law on the Succession, the Law on the National Referendum and any other which, in the future, be promulgated as fundamental.

To repeal or amend these laws a national referendum shall be necessary, as well as the approval of the Cortes.

Article 11

I – Once the King has been crowned, the regular order of succession shall be based on primogeniture and priority of right, with preference for descendants over ancestors; within the same line the closer over the more distant degree of kinship; in the same degree of kinship the male over the female, who may not reign, but may transmit her rights to her heirs; and, in the same sex, the older over the younger; all this without prejudice to the exceptions and requirements established in the preceding articles.

II – If the heir to the Crown, according to the order established in the preceding paragraph, were not thirty years of age when the throne fell vacant, his public duties shall be undertaken, until he reaches the legal age, by a Regent nominated in accordance with article 8 of the present Law.

III – The same rule shall apply if, having become incapacitated the King, in accordance with article 14 of the present Law, and the heir not having yet reached the age of thirty, the Cortes should decree the installation of the Regency.

IV – In the events referred to in the last two paragraphs, the Regency shall cease when the reasons motivating its existence disappear.

Article 12

Any cession of rights before acceding to the throne, abdications when the successor has been appointed, renunciations of any nature, and royal marriages, as well as the marriages of the immediate successors, shall be considered by the Council of the Realm and approved by the Cortes.

Article 13

The Head of State, after consultation with the Council of the Realm, may propose to the Cortes the exclusion from the line of succession of those persons of royal blood who lack the necessary capacity to rule, or deserve to lose their rights, on account of their clear deviation from the fundamental principles of the State, or because of their behaviour.

Article 14

The incapacity of the Head of State, recognized by a two-thirds majority of the members of the Government, shall be notified to the Council of the Realm in a detailed report. Should this Council recognize it too by the same majority, its President shall submit the matter to the Cortes, which, at a meeting held within eight days, shall adopt the appropriate resolution.

Article 15

I – The validity of the resolutions passed by the Cortes in respect of the present Law shall require the favourable vote of two-thirds of the *Procuradores* present, which must be at least equivalent to the absolute majority.

II – However, should a two-thirds majority not be reached in the first voting, a second and, if necessary, a third vote shall be taken. In the third voting, a three-fifths majority, which must at least be equivalent to the absolute majority, shall be sufficient to validate the resolution.

Law on the Referendum (22 October 1945)

All Spaniards are entitled to collaborate in the affairs of the State through the natural entities – family, municipality and syndicate – and the basic Laws which are to infuse new life and greater spontaneity into these representative bodies within a system of Christian coexistence have already been promulgated. In order to safeguard the Nation now against the deviation shown in recent political history, when in matters of the utmost importance or public interest, the will of the Nation can be supplanted by the subjective judgement of its rulers, the Head of State, invoking the powers conferred upon him by the Laws of 30 January 1938 and 8 August 1939, has considered it advisable to institute a direct consultation of the Nation by public referendum, whenever he should deem such a consultation appropriate, in view of the exceptional nature of the laws or the uncertainty of public opinion.

In virtue of which, I resolve:

Article 1

When the exceptional nature of certain laws should make it advisable, or the public interest should demand it, the Head of State, may, for the better service of the Nation, submit to referendum the Bills drawn up by the Cortes.

Article 2

The referendum shall include all nationals, men and women, over the age of twenty-one.

Article 3

The Government is hereby authorized to issue complementary regulations for the compiling of the register of voters and the execution of the present law.

 **NOTES**

Preface

1. M. de Cuendias and V. de Féréal, *L'Espagne pittoresque, artistique et monu-mentale* (Librairie Ethnographique, Paris, 1848), p. 1.
2. R. Fernández Carvajal, 'El gobierno entre el Jefe del Estado y las Cortes', *Revista de Estudios Políticos*, nos. 183–4, May–August 1972, p. 5.
3. J. J. Linz, 'From Falange to Movimiento-Organización', in S. P. Huntington and C. H. Moore (eds.), *Authoritarian Politics in Modern Society* (Basic Books, New York, 1970), p. 191.

1. Introduction

1. This ratio would be based upon the partial figures given by the Marqués de Hoyos, *Mi Testimonio* (A. Aguado, Madrid, 1962). His figures, incomplete as they were, give 22,150 monarchist councillors and 5,875 republican ones. For a complete analysis of the results, see J. J. Linz, 'The party system of Spain', in S. M. Lipset and S. Rokkan (eds.), *Party Systems and Voter Alignments* (Free Press, New York, 1967), p. 231 ff. Linz summarizes the elections by saying (pp. 235–6): 'The main conclusion that one can draw from the 1931 municipal elections . . . was that the country was Republican, but not very Socialist, and

that the Monarchy had even lost areas that would vote Conservative in the 1933 and 1936 elections. The change of regime was inevitable . . .'.

2. José María Gil Robles was one of the outstanding right-wing figures during the Second Republic, as leader of the Catholic party CEDA (Confederación Española de Derechas Autónomas). He published his political memoirs in 1968 under the title of *No fue posible la paz*.

3. The bibliography on the Second Republic and especially the Civil War is plentiful. For contrasting views see: M. Tuñón de Lara, *La España del siglo XX* (Librería Española, Paris, 1966); G. Jackson, *The Spanish Republic and the Civil War* (Princeton University Press, 1965); S. de Madariaga, *España: ensayo de historia contemporánea*, 7th edition (Editorial Sudamericana, Buenos Aires, 1964); R. Carr, *Spain, 1808–1939* (Oxford University Press, 1966); R. de la Cierva, *Historia de la Guerra Civil Española: antecedentes, 1808–1936* (Editorial San Martín, Madrid, 1968).

4. M. Tuñón de Lara, *La España del siglo XX*, p. 237.

5. Cf. decree of the provisional government of the Republic, published in the *Gaceta de Madrid*, 15 April 1931.

6. The national elections held on 28 June 1931 gave the following results: Left, 263 deputies; Centre, 110 deputies; Right, 44 deputies. The largest group in the leftist block were the socialists with 116 seats in Parliament (M. Tuñón de Lara, *La España del siglo XX*, p. 255). The results of these elections vary from author to author – due to the complex electoral system introduced by the Republic and to the lack of definition of many parties and groups – but they do not alter the balance between parties to any noticeable extent.

7. The adjective Catholic is used here in a broad sense, covering all those who, to a greater or lesser degree, could be said to be members of the Church of Rome. Catholicism is still the religion of the majority of Spaniards, even though there are considerable differences between social groups and between geographical areas.

8. S. de Madariaga, *España*, p. 389.

9. The example usually quoted in this respect is that of the Jesuits. Their Order was disbanded by the Republic, but the Jesuits, since they were no longer members of the official Church, were still able to run their schools. Two republican aims – to get rid of the Jesuit Order and to loosen the grip of the Church on education – cancelled each other out, partially at least.

10. Article 3 of the 1931 Constitution.

11. Manuel Azaña, *Obras Completas* (Ediciones Oasis, Mexico City, 1966), vol. 2, p. 52.

12. cf. J. Vicens Vives, *Historia social y económica de España y América* (Teide, Barcelona, 1959), vol. 4.2, p. 429.

13. See on this point M. Tuñón de Lara, *La España del siglo XX*, p. 273 ff. He describes the uprising of 10 August 1932, led by General Sanjurjo, as '*militar, aristocrático y terrateniente*'.

14. 800,000 according to José Peirats, *Los anarquistas en la crisis política española*, (Editorial Alfa, Buenos Aires, 1964), p. 72.

15. Peirats (*Los anarquistas en la crisis política española*, p. 73), on the other hand, blames some of the republican laws for the enmity between CNT and the Republic.

16. Even to this day historians are debating the reasons that motivated the socialist change of attitude. Other factors, like the need to match anarchist violence, or the personality cult in the case of Largo Caballero, cannot be discounted.

17. S. de Madariaga, *España*, p. 458.

18. The elections held under the Second Republic, in spite of all the criticisms directed at them, were the most democratic elections Spain has ever known. See on this subject J. Becarud, *La Segunda República Española* (Taurus, Madrid, 1967), originally published in French in 1962. See also Javier Tusell, *Las elecciones del Frente Popular*, 2 volumes (*Cuadernos para el Diálogo*, Madrid, 1971).

19. See Chapter 5.

20. The term revolution does not necessarily imply violence. It is used here as the antonym of evolution, to signify a break in continuity, a radical change of direction, a rejection of basic principles.

21. M. Fraga Iribarne, *Horizonte Español 1966* (Madrid, 1966), p. 18.

22. F. Franco, *Franco ha dicho* (Madrid, 1947), p. 160.

23. The following words of Carrero Blanco, President of the government, published in 1950 under the *nom de plume* Juan de la Cosa, may serve as an illustration: 'During the five years of the Republic – which were five years of undescribable chaos – while freemasons were trying hard to turn the people against Catholicism, by means of sectarian laws, wicked abuses and duress, communism, always seeking to further its own interests, beat them at it.' (*España ante el mundo: proceso de un aislamiento* (Ediciones Idea, Madrid, 1950), p. 218).

24. José L. Otaño, *Geografía e historia de España* (Ediciones S. M.—— Madrid, 1964). This text book was still being used in some Spanish schools during the academic year 1970–71.

25. See M. Tuñón de Lara, *La España del siglo XX*, p. 418, and H. R. Southworth, *El mito de la cruzada de Franco* (Ruedo Ibérico, Paris, 1963).

26. See R. de la Cierva, *Historia de la Guerra Civil Española*, pp. 708–9. This author calls the false documents 'purely anecdotal', and produces some others, which he considers as definitive proof, but when carefully read, they tell us a great deal about the nature of the Communist Party and very little about its conspiratorial plans, and even less about its strength and ability to implement any of those plans. After all, de la Cierva himself admits that on 18 July 1936 the Spanish Communist Party had no more than some 25,000 members.

27. A good example was provided by Carrero Blanco, President of the government, when he addressed the Cortes in February 1969, on the declaration of a

state of emergency: '... student minorities encouraged from abroad with purely subversive aims; because one of the weapons used by communism, both Russian and Chinese communism, is subversion, for the purpose of weakening those countries it wishes to dominate'. (Text of speech in *Pueblo*, 7 February 1969).

28. The collective letter of the Spanish Episcopate was issued on 1 July 1937, but there is a more recent reprint of it in Cardenal Isidro Goma y Tomás, *Pastorales de la Guerra de España* (Rialp, Madrid, 1955).

29. In a joint conference of bishops and priests held in Madrid from 13 to 18 September 1971. See *Asamblea conjunte de obispos y sacerdotes* (Editorial Catolica, Madrid, 1971).

30. The word *Cruzada* appears in the promulgatory formula used in the Law on the Principles of the National Movement and in article 2 of the Law on the Cortes. The crusading image of the Civil war has been played down in recent years, without disappearing altogether as can be seen in this passage taken from official sources: 'The Church lined up behind the national flag and, whether we like it or not, the Civil War became, *de facto* and *de jure*, the last of the crusades.' (R. de la Cierva, *Los documentos de la primavera trágica* (Secretaría General Técnica, Ministerio de Información y Turismo, Madrid, 1967), p. 608.

31. This argument was used by Sr López Bravo, Spanish Foreign Minister for several years, in an interview with Malcolm Muggeridge in the programme 'The Question Why', shown on BBC-1, 31 January 1971.

32. cf. Alfonso Ortí Benlloch, 'El caso Español: la diacronía estructural de la modernización', an excellent introductory essay to *Anuario político español, 1969* (*Cuadernos para el Diálogo*, Madrid, 1970). In it Ortí Benlloch discusses at some length the problem of uneven development affecting Spanish society at present.

33. Prepared by the Comisaría del Plan de Desarrollo and published by the *Boletín Oficial del Estado* in November 1971.

34. cf. J. L. Sampedro, 'Le Plan de développement espagnol dans son cadre social', in *Revue Tiers-Monde*, special supplement on economic development in Spain, vol. 8, no. 32, October–December 1967. Professor Sampedro points out (pp. 1034–5) that the word 'social' did not appear in the earlier drafts of the first plan, and it was added later without any significant changes in the plan's content.

35. *The Economic Development of Spain* (International Bank for Reconstruction and Development, Johns Hopkins Press, Baltimore, 1963). See an assessment of this report in a work prepared by a team of Spanish economists: Enrique Fuentes Quintana (ed.), *El desarrollo económico de España* (Revista de Occidente, Madrid, 1963).

36. *Tercer plan de desarrollo*, p. 17.

37. 1960 and 1970 figures from *Tercer plan de desarrollo*, 1965 figures from *Anuario Estadístico*, 1970.

38. *Tercer plan de desarrollo*, p. 25.

39. Figures from *Anuario Estadístico*, 1968, 1970, 1971.
40. Even the economic weight of these invisibles has not been sufficient to close the trade gap some years – 1965 and 1966 were years with a deficit in the balance of payments, leading eventually to a devaluation in autumn 1967.
41. Spanish reserves were at 1,730 million dollars on 31 December 1970: *Estudio económico, 1970* (Banco Central, Madrid, 1971), p. 63.
42. *Tercer plan de desarrollo*, pp. 136–7.
43. See in particular Ramón Tamames's *España ante el segundo plan de desarrollo* (Nova Terra, Barcelona, 1968). For a more favourable appraisal, see G. Hill, *Spain* (Benn, London, 1970), pp. 304–37.
44. Laureano López Rodó, *Política y desarrollo* (Aguilar, Madrid, 1970), pp. 238, 246.
45. cf. FOESSA, *Informe sociológico sobre la situación social de España, 1970* (Euramérica, Madrid, 1970). The authors, a team of young Spanish sociologists who have carried out the most profound and thorough investigation of present-day Spanish society, express this opinion in the 'Síntesis del informe', p. 96 – an opinion fully supported, more recently, by the well-known economist R. Tamames, 'El otoño de la economía española', *Cuadernos para el Diálogo*, October 1975, p. 21.
46. The effects of migration are, of course, multiple: depopulation of certain areas of the country, uneven regional development, great human suffering for the emigrant and his family, formation of new employment patterns, etc. but I am only giving consideration to those with greater relevance for this problem.
47. In 1970 some 23 million Spaniards, more than two-thirds of the population, were under the age of 45, and therefore did not take part in the Civil War.
48. *Anuario estadístico 1971*, p. 357.
49. Ramón Tamames, *Introducción a la economía española* (Alianza Editorial, Madrid, 1972), p. 45. The Madrid daily *Ya* estimated (12 July 1972) that approximately one million Spanish workers, including their families, live in the nine countries of the EEC.
50. The minimum daily wage was fixed at 280 pesetas (£2.30 approximately). Official estimates put the number of workers receiving this amount at somewhere between 500,000 and 700,000. Unofficially, it has been estimated, at times, to be as high as two million. cf. *Cuadernos para el Diálogo*, no. 105, June 1972.
51. Ministry of Education and Science, *Bases para una política educativa* (Madrid, 1969).
52. *Ley general de educación y financiación de la reforma educativa* (4 August 1970).
53. The initials stand for Sindicato Español Universitario, a falangist student union founded in 1933 and later adopted by the regime as the one and only union to which all university students had to belong.
54. In the third development plan, the unfairness of the income tax system is admitted. It relies heavily on indirect taxation, it does not help to share out

wealth and there is a great deal of tax evasion, confess naïvely the authors of the plan (*Tercer plan de desarrollo*, p. 83). But, then, practically nothing is programmed in the third plan to correct the situation!

55. Juan J. Linz and Amando de Miguel, 'Within nation differences and comparisons: the eight Spains', in R.L.Merrit and S.Rokkan (eds.), *Comparing Nations* (Yale University Press, New Haven, 1966), p. 290.

56. Dionisio Ridruejo, *Escrito en España* (Losada, Buenos Aires, 1964), p. 56. Ridruejo, a poet himself, takes the expression *macizo de la raza* ('the hardcore of the race') from Machado to convey the idea of solidity and reluctance to change.

57. In Old Castile they find 'the core of Franco's support', J.J.Linz and A.de Miguel, 'Within nation differences and comparisons', p. 313.

58. D.Ridruejo, *Escrito en España*, p. 31.

59. In a survey carried out by the Institute of Public Opinion, 78 per cent of nearly 2,000 young Spaniards confessed to little or no interest in politics (*Revista de Opinión Pública*, no. 15, January–March 1969, p. 278).

60. L.López Rodó, *Política y desarrollo*, p. 256.

61. Though the book containing the text of all the Fundamental Laws is now printed and distributed by the Ministry of Information with the title *La constitución española* on the cover.

62. The preamble of the Charter of the Spanish People in its original version of 1945 used the expression 'fundamental law'. And since their creation in 1943 the Spanish Cortes have had a special Fundamental Laws Committee.

63. D.V.Verney, *The Analysis of Political Systems* (Routledge & Kegan Paul, 1961), p. 83.

64. *Constitutions et documents politiques* (Presses Universitaires de France, Paris, 1964), p. 596. It must be pointed out, however, that the first edition of this work came out in 1957. More recently, M.Duverger has classified the Spanish regime as pseudo-fascist in *Institutions politiques et droit constitutionnel*, 11th edition (Presses Universitaires de France, Paris, 1970), p. 495.

65. *Institutions politiques et droit constitutionnel* (Dalloz, Paris, 1963), p. 168.

66. R.Fernández Carvajal, *La constitución española* (Editora Nacional, Madrid, 1969), p. 81, also applies this label *dictadura constituyente* to the Spanish regime as well as that of *dictadura de desarrollo*. Reference is made to this point in the following chapter.

67. C.F.Friedrich and Z.K.Brzezinski, *Totalitarian Dictatorship and Autocracy* (Harvard University Press, 1965), p.9.

68. S.E.Finer, *Comparative Government* (Allen Lane, 1970), p.578.

69. cf. R.Aron, *Democracy and Totalitarianism* (Weidenfeld & Nicolson, 1968), p. 56; R.G.Neumann, *European and Comparative Government* (McGraw-Hill, New York, 1960), p. 660.

70. J.Ynfante, *La prodigiosa aventura del Opus Dei* (Ruedo Ibérico, Paris, 1970), p. 297.

71. J. J. Linz, 'An authoritarian regime: Spain', in E. Allardt and Y. Littunen (eds.), *Cleavages, Ideologies and Party Systems* (Westermack Society, Helsinki, 1964), pp. 291–341.

72. The expression 'façade democracy' is used by S. E. Finer, *Comparative Government*, although he does not consider this expression to fit the Spanish regime, which he prefers to classify as a military regime.

2. The Head of State

1. G. Brenan, *The Spanish Labyrinth* (Cambridge University Press, 1967), p. 84. This book was originally published in 1943. Brenan was to express a contrasting opinion a few years later: 'Spain for some time to come needs to live under an authoritarian regime'. (Preface, *The Face of Spain* (Turnstile Press, 1950)).

2. Franco's words to the crowds gathered at the Plaza de Oriente in Madrid on 1 October 1971.

3. He was born on 4 December 1892.

4. The decree of the Nationalist Junta handing over all its powers to Franco is dated at Burgos on 29 September 1936, and the actual ceremony of investiture took place there two days later.

5. On the choice and appointment of Franco as Head of State, see the latest version of the episode provided by R. de la Cierva in *Francisco Franco: un siglo de España*, a biography of Franco published in weekly pamphlets by the official Editora Nacional. (cf. pamphlet no. 22, pp. 506–12).

6. The inclusion of Franco's name in the Fundamental Laws creates a curious constitutional problem. The quoted article is not stated anywhere to be transitory, but human life is. This means that when Franco dies the text of the Law on the Succession and some other Fundamental Laws will have to be altered. Will this be done automatically, or will a referendum be necessary, since any change in the Fundamental Laws requires approval by the people?

7. They vary from sycophantic eulogies to political libel and insult. Several biographies published in this country in the last few years have attempted a more balanced picture, though their efforts have been partly marred by the non-availability of some essential sources. A number of these are in the biographical list at the end of this book.

8. S. Agesta, *Derecho constitucional comparado*, 3rd edition. (Editora Nacional, Madrid, 1968), p. 490.

9. Both laws deal with the administrative organization of the State.

10. Organic Law of the State, transitory provision, 1.2.

11. R. F. Carvajal, *La constitución española* (Editora Nacional, Madrid, 1969), p. 81.

12. cf. Diego Sevilla Andrés, *Historia política de España* (Editora Nacional, Madrid, 1968), p. 546.

13. R. F. Carvajal, *La constitución española*, p. 87. In fact, between the time when the Law on the Cortes was first promulgated and 1970, Franco has made use of

his special powers to legislate on six occasions: twice in March 1943 when he issued two ordinary laws dealing with the police and probation of prisoners, and four times at constitutional level: the Law on the Referendum (1945), a law of 9 March 1946 altering the composition of the Cortes, the Law on the Principles of the National Movement (1958), and the Organic Law of the State (1967).

14. They are both dated 3 April 1970. One gives the National Council of the Movement power to initiate legislation, and the other transfers all the property owned by FET y de las JONS to the National Movement.

15. Laws of 14 July 1972, one concerned with the coordination of the functions of the government, the Cortes and the Courts of Justice; and the other with the appointment of the future President of the government.

16. Preamble of the Law on the Referendum.

17. *Ibid.*, article 1.

18. Law on the Succession, article 10.

19. See, for instance, R. F. Carvajal, *La constitución española*, p. 22 ff, and D. Sevilla Andrés, *Historia política de España*, p. 538.

20. C. F. Friedrich and Z. K. Brzezinski, *Totalitarian Dictatorship and Autocracy*, 2nd edition (Harvard University Press, 1965), p. 8.

21. *La Nueva España* (Asturian newspaper), 1 July 1947.

22. From a poster at the time of the 1966 referendum.

23. Issue no. 39, December 1966, of the monthly *Cuadernos para el Diálogo* did express certain views against the Organic Law of the State and particularly against the unilateral nature of the propaganda campaign. But this magazine is a rather learned publication and only read by an intellectual minority. This expression of dissent and some others like it, together with a few illegal pamphlets distributed by clandestine organizations, can hardly be said to amount to a campaign of propaganda against the Law.

24. *Anuario Estadístico*, 1947.

25. Figures published by all national newspapers.

26. As reported in *La Nueva España*, 15 December 1966.

27. SP, a newspaper which has since disappeared.

28. See *Ley Jurídica de la Administración del Estado*, 26 July 1957, article 2.

29. Preamble to the Law on the Principles of the National Movement.

30. Organic Law of the State, article 8.

31. The first two prerogatives are included in article 6 of the Law on the Succession, and the final one in article 13.

32. R. F. Carvajal, *La constitución española*, p. 44.

33. E. Kirkpatrick, 'El jefe del Estado en la ley orgánica', *Revista de estudios políticos*, no. 152, March–April 1967, pp. 33–55.

34. Figures published by *Arriba*, 23 July 1969.

35. As reported in *Ya*, 23 July 1969. The *procurador* was Fernando Mateu de Ros, Councillor of the National Movement and member of the Cortes for Valencia.

36. M. Weber, *Economy and Society*, G. Roth and C. Wittich (ed.) (Bedminster Press, New York, 1968), p. 215 ff.

37. *Bases de la democracia española* (Ediciones del Movimiento, Madrid, 1962), p. 59.

38. cf. Francisco Javier Conde, *Contribución a la doctrina del Caudillaje* (Vice-secretaría de Educación Popular, Madrid, 1942); and Pascual Marín Perez, *El caudillaje español* (Ediciones Europa, Madrid, 1960).

39. We find this even in the speeches of the members of the more recent governments, many of whom have reputations as politically neutral technocrats. López Rodó, for several years minister in charge of development and later in charge of foreign affairs, when presenting the second development plan to the Cortes, referred to Franco with the following words: 'We count on the leadership of the Caudillo. Let us not forget that the decisive factor for the take-off of any economy is the existence of an exceptional man, of a man capable of awakening the latent energies of his people and of giving them confidence. Thanks to the Caudillo we Spaniards have regained our confidence.' (*Pueblo* 7 February 1969).

40. *Arriba*, 1 October 1968, front page.

41. M. Weber, *Economy and Society*, p. 242.

42. Law on the Succession, article 3.

43. *ibid.*, article 8.

44. Definitive in purely legal terms. One cannot forecast a stable monarchy, which is highly unlikely.

45. The only peculiarity in the hereditary rights established is the fact that females are excluded from the throne.

46. A study of the dynastic struggle for the Spanish throne is not included in this work. There are a number of books on the subject, some listed in the Bibliography.

47. Law on the Principles of the National Movement, principle 7 and article 1.

48. cf. R. A. H. Robinson, 'Genealogy and function of the monarchist myth of the Franco regime', *Iberian Studies*, vol. 2, no. 1, 1973, pp. 18–26.

49. He was born in Rome on 5 January 1938.

50. Law on the Succession, article 9, lists the conditions to be fulfilled by the King.

51. Organic Law of the State, article 6.

52. *ibid.*, articles 8 and 9. The Ley de Régimen Jurídico de la Administración del Estado, had already established that all decrees must be signed by the Head of State and counter signed by the Minister concerned or, if the decree affected several Ministries, by the Head of Government.

53. This conclusion is reached, from different standpoints, by R. F. Carvajal, *La constitución español*, pp. 51–7; and J. de Esteban *et al*, *Desarrollo político y constitución española* (Ariel, Barcelona, 1973), p. 44 ff.

54. M. Herrero, *El principio monárquico* (Edicusa, Madrid, 1972), *passim*.

55. R. F. Carvajal, *La constitución español*, p. 52.

56. J. de Esteban *et al*, *Desarrollo político y constitución española*, p. 81.

57. M. Herrero, *El principio monárquico*, *passim*.

58. Organic Law of the State, article 15, and Law on the Cortes, article 7, III.

59. Organic Law of the State, article 17.
60. *ibid.*, articles 7 and 13.
61. See, for instance, editorial in the *Guardian*, 18 July 1969.
62. *Cartas a un príncipe* (Editorial Magisterio Español, Madrid, 1970), p. 142.
63. Organic Law of the State, article 10(d).
64. *ibid.*, article 6.
65. It is not strictly correct to speak of separate executive, legislative and juridical powers in Spain. The principle is not accepted. There is 'unity of power with diversity of functions'. Nevertheless, the three powers are often mentioned separately for the sake of methodology and clarity of exposition.
66. Law on the Cortes, article 17.
67. At the beginning of this century there were more than twenty monarchies in Europe. Only six remain, all completely different from the Spanish monarchy.
68. Law on the Succession, article 4, in its original version of 26 July 1947.
69. *ibid.*, article 4, 1967 version.
70. Leaving aside the *ex-officio* members, at the beginning of 1973, the Council included the following: José Antonio Girón, ex-Minister of Labour and National Councillor, appointed by Franco; Miguel Primo de Rivera, National Councillor, appointed by Franco; Rodolfo Martín Villa, Secretary-General of the Syndical Organization; Carlos Arias Navarro, Mayor of Madrid and National Councillor, appointed by Franco; Juan María de Araluce, President of the *Diputación* of Guipúzcoa; Pío Cabanillas, ex-Under-Secretary in the Ministry of Information and Tourism; Enrique de la Mata, Director General for Social Security; José Botella Lluisá, Rector of Madrid University; Iñigo de Oriol y Urquijo, President of the Chamber of Commerce and Industry and nephew of the Minister of Justice.
71. cf. Miguel A. Medina Muñoz, 'El consejo del Reino', *Revista de Estudios Políticos*, no. 181, January–February 1972, p. 110.
72. Law on the Cortes, article 17.
73. Organic Law of the State, article 7.6.
74. *ibid.*, articles 14 and 58; Law on the Cortes, article 7.
75. Organic Law of the State, article 10. For a more detailed list, consult Organic Law of the Council of the Realm (23 July 1967), article 17 ff.
76. R. F. Carvajal, *La constitución español*, p. 68.
77. Although article 3 in the Law of the Principles of the National Movement could possibly be considered as the first step in such a direction: 'Any law or disposition of whatever kind which violates or impeaches the principles proclaimed in this Fundamental Law of the Kingdom shall be null and void.'
78. Law of Contrafuero, dated 5 April 1968.
79. cf. J. L. Sanlúcar, 'El control de la constitucionalidad de la ley y el recurso de contrafuero', in *Cuadernos para el Diálogo*, vol. 17, p. 16.
80. *Reglamento de régimen disciplinario de los funcionarios de la administración civil del Estado*, dated 16 August 1969.
81. Decree of 22 June 1970. See in *Boletín Oficial del Estado*, 6 July 1970, pp.

10606–11, the text of this decree giving a step-by-step account of the legal process of this appeal.

3. The Government

1. A. Guaita, *El Consejo de Ministros* (Escuela Nacional de Administración Pública, Madrid, 1967), pp. 15 ff.
2. The Junta de Defensa Nacional was a temporary and purely military body; the Junta Técnica del Estado, although it had the resemblance of a government, was no more than a group of experts who advised Franco in his early days as Head of State.
3. One only has to think of the extensive bibliography of men like Fraga Iribarne, Fernández Miranda, Villar Palasí, Fernández de la Mora or Carrero Blanco.
4. An idea repeatedly expressed by R. Calvo Serer in *Franco frente al Rey* ([Paris], 1972).
5. M. Gallo, *Histoire de l'Espagne franquiste* (Gerard, Viviers, 1969), pp. 362–3.
6. In summer 1962 118 Spaniards, representing various sectors of the opposition, held a meeting in Munich. They passed unanimously a resolution stating that Spain could not become part of Europe until she adopted democratic institutions. This motion was later put to and approved by the General Assembly of the European Movement. On the Munich affair see I. Fernández and J. Martínez de Castro, *España, hoy* (Ruedo Ibérico, Paris, 1963), pp. 235–56.
7. Only six months previously, in December 1962, Franco had suffered a serious accident during a hunting party.
8. Under the law of 14 July 1972.
9. R. Fernández Carvajal, 'El gobierno entre el Jefe del Estado y las Cortes', *Revista de Estudios Políticos*, no. 183–4, May–August 1972, p. 9.
10. *ibid.*, p. 11.
11. Pío Cabanillas, Minister of Information and Tourism, and Alejandro Fernández Sordo, Minister of Syndical Relations.
12. Article 13 of the 1957 Law on the Administration of the State gives a long list of the President's powers, and it should be read in conjunction with Title III of the Organic Law of the State.
13. Organic Law of the State, article 16.
14. Law on the Cortes, article 2 (a). The name 'blue bench' given to the seats occupied by the members of the Government in the Cortes comes from the colour of the material with which they are upholstered.
15. Decree-law of 13 May 1955.
16. Organic Law of the State, article 13, II.
17. Article 10.
18. Law on the Cortes, article 13.
19. J. Zafra, in his *Régimen político de España* (EUNSA, Pamplona, 1973), – overall very favourable to the regime – is forced to admit (p. 442) that 'the taking of

extraordinary legislative functions by the Government on grounds of urgency has become one of the most common features of the Spanish regime'. He adds in a note that, between 1960 and 1972, 293 decree-laws of this nature have been promulgated.

20. On this question read the penetrating article by J. R. Parada Vázquez, 'E Poder sancionador de la administración y crisis del sistema judicial penal', *Revista de Administración Pública*, no. 67, January–April 1972, pp. 41–93.

21. A. Carro Martínez, 'Relaciones entre los altos órganos del Estado', *Revista de Estudios Políticos*, no. 152, March–April 1967, p. 17.

22. M. Herrero, *El principio monárquico* (Edicusa, Madrid, 1972), and J. Esteban *et al*, *Desarrollo político y constitución española* (Ariel, Barcelona, 1973).

23. M. Herrero, *El principio monárquico*, p. 73.

24. *ibid.*, p. 72.

25. It seems necessary to point out – and this in no way detracts from the seriousness and scholarly nature of the work – that this book was written at the request of and financed by an anonymous group of Spaniards who wanted scientific proof of the possibility of achieving a democratic solution without altering the present constitutional structure.

26. J. de Esteban *et al.*, *Desarrollo político y constitución española*, pp. 101–5.

27. J. J. Linz, 'An authoritarian regime: Spain', in E. Allardt and Y. Littunen (eds.), *Cleavages, Ideologies and Party Systems* (Westermack Society, Helsinki, 1964), p. 330 ff.

28. The amount involved was in the region of 10,000 million pesetas (£83 million). For a detailed account of the economic aspects of the affair, see Juan Muñoz *et al.*, *La economía española, 1969* (Edicusa, Madrid, 1970), pp. 51–261.

29. He was the president of Catholic Action when he was invited by Franco to join his Government. Before accepting, Martín Artajo requested the advice of Cardinal Pla y Daniel, head of the Catholic Church in Spain at the time. J. Linz ('An authoritarian regime', p. 332) classifies Martín Artajo as a right-wing Christian democrat.

30. The *Ley de ordenación universitaria*, 29 July 1943, made it compulsory for all university students to become members of the SEU and, at the same time, entrusted the SEU with the task of 'instilling the falangist spirit into university students'.

31. According to the list compiled by Jesús Ynfante (Ruedo Ibérico, Paris, 1970), the number of *opusdeistas* who have been in the Government is considerably higher; it includes twelve militant members and sixteen sympathizers, that is to say, the majority of all ministers since 1957 (twenty-eight out of a total of forty-five).

32. This matter is discussed at greater length in Chapter 9.

33. However, it was paradoxical that one of the most ardent defenders of the technocratic myth, Gonzalo Fernández de la Mora, the man who wrote 'it is no longer possible to recruit leaders from amongst those given to popular

rhetoric, nor from amongst political dilettanti, but from amongst professionals' (*El crepúsculo de las ideologías*, Rialp, Madrid, 1965, p. 121) should have become Minister of Public Works, having, as he does, a diplomatic and literary background.

34. If only as a curiosity it is worth consulting the biographical sketches of ministers published by Spanish newspapers whenever there is a change of government.

35. Text of the whole speech and assessment of its contents in all Spanish papers on 13 February 1974.

36. Names given by V.Ortega, 'Vida política y asociativa', *Suplemento al informe FOESSA*, no. 11, 1973, p. 6. There is not always agreement amongst the 'experts'. An editorial article in the right-wing magazine *Avanzada*, no. 51, July 1973, gives the names of J. Solís and J. A. Girón.

37. E.Romero in the appendix to the latest edition of *Cartas al Rey* (Planeta, Barcelona, 1974).

38. In an interview with E.Romero, published in *Pueblo*, 7 February 1968. These same words were repeated in his first speech to the Cortes as President of the Government on 20 July 1973.

39. Apart from the possibility of Franco taking on once again the duties of Head of Government suggested by several newspapers, the names more often quoted were those of Fernández Miranda, who as Vice-President to Carrero Blanco was discharging the duties of President, López Rodó, López Bravo, Fraga, Solís, and some military men like General Castañón de Mena, General Díez-Algería, or Admiral Nieto Antúñez.

40. Here too, newspaper prognosticators erred. Only small changes had been expected. '*Será sólo una minicrisis*' ('It will be no more than a small reshuffle') read the front headline of Barcelona's *El Noticiero Universal* on 3 January 1974.

41. On this point see Chapter 9.

42. The professional requirements to become a minister are discussed in a jocular but scholarly style by A. de Miguel, 'Apuntes sociólogicos sobre los ministros de Franco', epilogue to E. Álvarez Puga *et al.*, *Los 90 ministros de Franco* (Dopesa, Barcelona, 1970), pp. 521–7.

43. The whole text of this speech appeared in all national newspapers on 16 June 1974.

44. Mgr Añoveros, bishop of Bilbao, published in February a pastoral letter defending in very mild terms the rights of the Basque people. The Government's reaction to it went as far as putting the bishop under house arrest and led to a serious confrontation between Church and State.

45. Pío Cabanillas, Minister of Information and Tourism, was dismissed on 29 October 1974, for proving too liberal in easing the restrictions on the Spanish press.

4. The Spanish Cortes

1. J. A. Christophesen, *The Meaning of Democracy, as used in European Ideologies from the French Revolution to the Russian Revolution: An Historical Study of Political Language* (Institutt for Statsvitenskap, Oslo, 1966).

2. From an interview given to *News Service* in November 1937, in F. Franco, *Franco ha dicho* (Madrid, 1947), p. 73.

3. F. Franco, *Discursos y mensajes del Jefe del Estado 1960–63* (Madrid, 1964), p. 448.

4. One of the best known amongst them, Calvo Sotelo, offers in his writings and speeches plenty of examples. cf. E. Vegas Latapié, *El pensamiento político de Calvo Sotelo* (Cultura Española, Madrid, 1941), p. 127 ff.

5. J. M. Ortí Bordás, 'Representación orgánica', *Arriba*, 4 December 1968.

6. Speech at the Teatro de la Comedia, in Madrid, 29 October 1933, in *Textos de doctrina política*, 5th edition (Delegación Nacional de la Sección Femenina, Madrid, 1970), p. 66.

7. *ibid.*

8. Title I, Chapter 2, of the Charter of the Spanish People lays down the general principles for the protection of the family. More indirect references to the same question can be found in other articles of the same Fundamental Law and in the Labour Charter.

9. Luis Sánchez Agesta, *Principios de teoría política* (Editora Nacional, Madrid, 1967), p. 160.

10. *Noticias con acento* (Alfaguara, Madrid, 1967), p. 69.

11. *España invertebrada* (Revista de Occidente, Madrid, 1962), p. 25.

12. See Chapter 6.

13. Approximately 70 per cent of the members of the Cortes are now elected.

14. These figures correspond to the electoral register of 1967.

15. The original Spanish says '*no sufrir inhabilitación política*'.

16. M. Fraga Iribarne (*El reglamento de las Cortes Españolas* (SIPS, Madrid, 1959), p. 31), suggests that in the absence of legal definition of '*inhabilitación política*', it might be identified with the forms of disqualification for public office, covered by articles 27 and 30 of the Penal Code.

17. M. Duverger, *Institutions politiques et droit constitutionnel*, 11th edition (Presses Universitaires de France, Paris, 1970), p. 126.

18. cf. W. J. M. MacKenzie, *Free Elections*, 2nd edition, (Allen & Unwin, 1964), p. 47.

19. As M. Duverger (*Institutions politiques et droit constitutionnel*, p. 134) says: 'In general, the indirect suffrage is less democratic than the direct one; the action of the governed in the election of the one who governs is more remote in the former than in the latter.'

20. W. J. M. MacKenzie, *Free Elections*, p. 50.

21. In the local sector, however, an absolute majority is required in the first ballot. If it is not achieved, there is a second ballot between the two candidates with the highest number of votes in the first one.

22. Law on the Cortes, Article 2, II.
23. For a detailed and critical analysis of the electoral rules, see the three articles by José María Gil-Robles y Gil-Delgado, in *Cuadernos para el Diálogo*, nos. 92, 93 and 94, May, June and July 1971.
24. *Ley de Representación Familiar en las Cortes*, dated 28 June 1967.
25. *Cuadernos para el Diálogo*, no. 50, November 1967, p. 24.
26. 'One would have to wield a pen as skilfully as Azorín to express, in fewer than five hundred words, an opinion on all the great problems facing the nation.' (Editorial in *Cuadernos para el Diálogo*, Nos. 47–8, August–September 1967).
27. The requirement of prior censorship was imposed by a Government decree dated 20 July 1967, articles 15 and 17.
28. In the 1967 elections, one of the successful candidates, don Eduardo Tarragona, claimed to have spent in his campaign in Barcelona upward of £12,000 (exactly 2,037,049 pesetas) according to the accounts published in *Cuadernos para el Diálogo*, no. 50, November 1967, p. 22. In the 1971 elections similar complaints were expressed by Madrid candidates (*Ya*, 25 and 26 October). Eduardo Tarragona's expenses for these elections exceeded £40,000 (6,975,000 pesetas), *Ya*, 12 November.
29. For a clear analysis of electoral results during the Second Republic, see Jean Becarud, *La Segunda República Española* (Taurus, Madrid, 1967).
30. Electoral Law of 8 May 1931, article 6.
31. In 1967 there were 108 *procuradores* in the family sector, but they were reduced by four, when two of the African provinces, Fernando Poo and Río Muni, were granted independence in October 1968, to become Equatorial Guinea.
32. In fact, the final official figure for the turnout of voters in 1971 was 43.2 per cent, a decrease of 16 per cent in relation to the 1967 elections. (B. Díaz-Nosty, *Las Cortes de Franco* (Dopesa, Barcelona, 1972), p. 156).
33. All the percentages have been calculated on the basis of the provisional results published in *Ya* and *Arriba*, on 30 September 1971, and may show some variations from the final figures produced by the Junta Central del Censo.
34. Under article 29 of the Electoral Law of 8 August 1907, elections did not have to be held when the number of candidates equalled the number of posts to be filled. This article was applied so frequently to elections during the earlier part of this century that it has become part of the Spanish language with a pejorative meaning (*ser elegido por el artículo 29*). However, although the 1907 law is still in force, article 29 is no longer applied, and elections take place whatever the number of candidates.
35. The list of candidates used was the one published by *Ya*, 10 September 1971.
36. The figures and percentages given must be taken as approximate – but always on the low side – since it has proved impossible to determine the status of some candidates.
37. The posts of mayor, president of a provincial council and civil governor are incompatible with that of family representative (decree of 20 July 1967) and to

become a *procurador* the holder of one of those posts has to give it up. This does not, however, detract from the fact that such a person has a clear political affinity with the regime.

38. *Cuadernos para el Diálogo*, no. 50, November 1967, p. 26. See, too, a careful analysis of the socio-political background of Spanish *procuradores* in Equipo Data, *Quién es quién en las Cortes, Los Suplementos*, no. 7 (Edicusa, Madrid, 1969).

39. It happened, for instance, in Gerona in the 1971 election. There were four candidates, two inside and two outside the official circle. The latter two won.

40. Election results for this sector in *Arriba*, 6, 7 and 8 October 1971.

41. Quoted in *Anuario Político 1970*, p. 560.

42. *La Voz de Asturias* (a provincial newspaper published in Oviedo), 23 September 1970.

43. 562 is the maximum possible number, but since some are members in more than one group (several ministers, for instance, are also national councillors of the Movement appointed by Franco and both posts entitle them to a seat in the Cortes), the actual number is slightly lower.

44. 'The Government has changed during the life of the present Cortes, especially in the last nine months (that is to say, since the big ministerial reshuffle of October 1969), *nearly one hundred procuradores* whose seat was dependent on a political appointment' (*Ya*, 3 August 1970).

45. At the time of writing the Spanish Government has announced a system of incompatibilities for *procuradores*, whose details are not yet known.

46. See Organic Law of the State, transitory provision 1.

47. Law on the Cortes, article 1. A subtle change was introduced in this article in 1967. The main function of the Cortes was until then 'the elaboration and preparation of the laws', and it became 'the elaboration and approval of the laws'. Important as it may seem, this change has so far had no noticeable effect.

48. Diego Sevilla Andrés, *Historia política de España* (Editora Nacional, Madrid, 1968), p. 563.

49. Manuel M. Fraile, *Comentario al reglamento de las Cortes* (Instituto de Estudios Políticos, Madrid, 1973), p. 41.

50. M. Fraga Iribarne, *El reglamento de las Cortes Españolas* (SIPS, Madrid, 1959), p. 75.

51. This is the case with the Cortes Standing Committee (composition established by Reglamento) or the special committee foreseen in article 12 of the Law on the Cortes.

52. The powers mentioned only represent a small – though the most important – part of his total authority. Article 19 of the Standing Orders, for instance, which deals specifically with the powers of the President of the Cortes has twenty-three separate sections.

53. See Law on the Succession, articles 3 and 4.

54. On the failed attempts of these itinerant *procuradores*, the 'nomadic Cortes', see B. Díaz-Nosty, *Las Cortes de Franco*, p. 77 ff.

55. The new Standing Orders say that the initiative belongs to both Government and Cortes except in budgetary matters, but this change in principle has not been accompanied by the necessary radical changes in procedure.

56. One such case occurred in the summer of 1970. In June, fifty-four *procuradores* submitted a bill suggesting some changes in the electoral rules of family representatives to make these representatives less dependent on the executive. A month later the Standing Committee of the Cortes rejected the proposed Bill, indicating that it was discriminatory with respect to the members in the other sectors, and that it went against some of the basic principles contained in the Fundamental Laws.

57. During the debates on the Education Reform Bill, only some 40 per cent of the *procuradores* who submitted amendments turned up to defend them (*Anuario Político Español, 1970*, p. 443).

58. *Ya*, 29 October 1971.

59. The discriminatory nature of this situation is obvious. It is necessary to have private means in order to become a member of the Cortes.

60. Law on the Cortes, article 10, lists all the kinds of Bills which have to be submitted to plenary session.

61. According to the new Standing Orders, a group of fifty *procuradores* can request that a vote be taken on one or more articles, but it is left to the President of the Cortes to decide whether such action is appropriate.

62. Even a Bill as controversial as the one dealing with educational reform was passed in the plenary session of 28 July 1970 with only one vote against.

63. The new Standing Order allows the questioner another ten minutes to reply, and the minister finally closes the debate.

64. For detailed information about the questions asked by *procuradores* during the period 1967–70, see *Anuario Político Español, 1969*, pp. 343–50, and *1970*, 574–7 respectively.

5.   The National Movement

1. The expression National Movement was used for the first time, according to R. de la Cierva, during the spring of 1934 in Seville. See *Historia de la Guerra Civil Española* (Editorial San Martín, Madrid, 1968), p. 554.

2. Franco, opening speech to the Cortes on 8 July 1964.

3. Rodríguez de Valcárcel speech delivered to the National Council of the Sección Femenina in Gerona on 12 January 1966. The whole text of this speech, together with other writings and speeches of Rodríguez de Valcárcel, were published under the title *Una etapa política* (Ediciones del Movimiento, Madrid, 1969).

4. 'This movement, which is not a party but a movement – it could almost be called an anti-party – is neither right wing nor left wing.' (J. A. Primo de Rivera, speech delivered in the Teatro de la Comedia in Madrid on 29 October 1933, in *Textos de doctrina política* (Delegación de la Sección Femenina del Movimiento, Madrid, 1970), p. 65).

5. In *Fundamentos del nuevo estado* (Ediciones de la Vice-Secretaría de Educación Popular, Madrid, 1943), p. 95, we find this note in which National Movement is used as the equivalent of Civil War: 'Before the final one there were other drafts of the Statutes (of FET y de las JONS) issued *during the National Movement* by the decree of 4 August and 26 November 1937.'

6. 'Our Falange is not a party, it is a Movement for all Spaniards.' (F. Franco, *Textos de doctrina política, 1945–1950* (Publicaciones Españolas, Madrid, 1951), p.4).

7. 'We must make very clear what the Movement is. The Movement is simply a series of fundamental principles, which form the constitutional basis of our system. Not to accept the Movement, therefore, is not to accept the Constitution, our Constitution . . .' (Rafael Ruiz Gallardón (at one time head of the Department for Political Action and Participation), in *Destino*, 22 May 1971, p. 17).

8. '*Falange Española* and *Requetés*, with their existing services and units, shall form, under my leadership and on a national basis, one single political entity, which shall, for the time being, be known as Falange Española Tradicionalista y de las JONS' (Decree of Unification, 19 April 1937, article 1).

9. *Escrito en España* (Losada, Buenos Aires, 1964), pp. 120–21. Curiously enough, Stanley Payne uses the same image in *Falange: A History of Spanish Fascism* (Stanford University Press, 1967), p. 193: 'At the war's end, they [the Carlists] simply returned to the mountains they had left in the summer of 1936.'

10. From a little note published by J. A. Primo de Rivera in the Spanish press on 19 December 1934 (*Textos de doctrina política*, p. 395).

11. J. A. Primo de Rivera, in a speech in the Teatro Calderón, Valladolid, on 4 March 1934 (*Textos de doctrina política*, pp. 194–5).

12. These are the opening words of R. Ledesma Ramos ¿ *Fascismo en España?*, first published in 1935, under the pseudonym of Roberto Lanzas. This work was recently reprinted (Ariel, Barcelona, 1968).

13. Ricardo de la Cierva, official historian of the regime, in his book *Historia de la Guerra Civil Española: Antecedentes*, devotes a whole chapter – Chapter 12 – to the 'Birth and development of Spanish fascism' and he deals primarily with FET y de las JONS. In that chapter we find some very significant paragraphs: 'Primo de Rivera himself declared . . . that his movement was not a fascist movement. But it was. It was not, of course, a purely imitative fascism, though initially it might have been partly so . . .' (p. 533).

14. S. Payne, *Falange*, p. 81. R. de la Cierva, *Historia de la Guerra Civil Española: Antecedentes*, p. 575, accepts the figure given by Payne. But Maximiano García Venero, *Historia de la Unificación* (Madrid, 1970), p. 47, has great reservations as to its accuracy. Whatever the exact figure, there is no doubt that the Falange was a minority party.

15. S. Payne, *Falange*, p. 212.

16. No one has accepted and confessed this change of attitude with greater sincerity than Dionisio Ridruejo in *Escrito en España*.

17. This argument is used by J.J.Linz: 'Such a policy [a totalitarian one] ultimately was not acceptable to Franco and did not fit with his own conception of society and politics, with his own mentality and political style.' ('From Falange to Movimiento-Organización', in S.P.Huntington and C.H.Moore (eds.) *Authoritarian Politics in Modern Society* (Basic Books, New York, 1970), p. 146.

18. J.Weiss, *Fascist Tradition: Radical Right-Wing Extremism in Modern Europe* (Harper & Row, New York, 1967), p. 65 ff.

19. In a speech to the Fourth National Congress of the Frente de Juventudes (Youth Front), on 18 January 1945, at the University City in Madrid. In F.Franco, *Textos de doctrina política (1945–1950)* (Publicaciones Españolas, Madrid, 1951), p. 4.

20. Serrano Suñer confesses to have drafted the Decree of Unification: *Entre Hendaya y Gibraltar* (Ediciones y Publicaciones Españolas, Madrid, 1947), p. 31.

21. *ibid.*, p. 31. The references to the *partido* and *partido único* are numerous throughout the book.

22. M.Duverger, *Political Parties*, 2nd English edition (Methuen, 1964), p. 255 ff.

23. See Statutes of FET y de las JONS, Chapter 2, dated 31 July 1939. Prior to this draft of the Statutes, there were two others, 4 August 1937 and 26 November 1937.

24. Chapter 1, article 1.

25. See C. Ollero, *Revista de Estudios Políticos*, no. 92, May–June 1958, p. 31.

26. See *Nuevo horizonte del Movimiento Nacional* (Vice-Secretaría General del Movimiento, Ediciones del Movimiento, Madrid, 1970), p. 378.

27. See Elías Díaz, *Estado de derecho y sociedad democrática* (Edicusa, Madrid, 1966), pp. 31–3.

28. Law on the Principles of the National Movement, article 1.

29. Point 25 of Falange's doctrine reads:
'Our Movement incorporates into its national reconstruction a Catholic meaning on account of its glorious tradition of its predominance in Spain.
'Church and State shall coordinate their respective powers, but no interference or activity that undermines the dignity of the State or national unity shall be allowed.'

30. J.Antonio, speech delivered in the Cine Madrid on 19 May 1935, in *Textos de doctrina política*, p. 567.

31. For a contrast of the falangist and carlist attitudes to this Law, see J.L.de Arrese, 'Anotaciones a la Ley de Sucesión', in *Treinta años de política* (A. Aguado, Madrid, 1966), pp. 1109–15, and the speech delivered by Esteban de Bilbao to the Cortes on 7 June 1947, in *Discursos* (Editora Nacional, Madrid, 1970), pp. 9–25.

32. See Principle VII and article 1 of the Law on the Principles of the National Movement. The immutable nature of the Principles is considered as inseparable

from the very existence of the regime: 'The Principles are the basis of legitimacy and the support of continuity and political order. That is why they cannot be modified without introducing substantial alterations in the regime. What is beyond the Principles is nothing but revolution.' (Manuel Fraga Iribarne, 'El articulado de la Ley Fundamental de 17 de mayo de 1958', *Arbor*, no. 152 July–August 1958, p. 517).

33. The first and only Minister to hold both posts was José Solís Ruiz. See Table of Ministers on page 78.

34. The number of decrees mentioned is not exhaustive. Only a few major examples have been selected with a view to highlighting the general trend in the development.

35. As Jacques Georgel, for instance, seems to do in *Le Franquisme: histoire et bilan* (Editions du Seuil, Paris, 1970), p. 126.

36. The Law on the Cortes, in its original version of 1942, stated in its article 2(b) that the National Councillors of Falange Española Tradicionalista y de las JONS were members of the Cortes.

37. See article 4, Organic Law of the State, where the National Movement is entrusted with the task of 'promoting political activity', or article 25 which uses the expression 'National Leader of the Movement'.

38. This line of argument is used by Licinio de la Fuente, at present Minister of Labour, in 'El Consejo Nacional en la Ley Orgánica del Estado', *Revista de Estudios Políticos*, no. 152, March–April 1967, pp. 121–35.

39. *Ley Orgánica del Movimiento y de su Consejo Nacional*, dated 28 June 1967.

40. *Estatuto Orgánico del Movimiento*, approved by decree of 20 December 1968.

41. These figures are taken from J. Bardavío, *La estructura del poder en España* (Ibérico-Europea de Ediciones, Madrid, 1969), pp. 117–18. They were presented to a plenary meeting of the National Council of FET y de las JONS on 9 March 1963.

42. Figures quoted in an interview published by the Madrid daily, *Pueblo*, on 29 January 1972.

43. According to some sources the number of members whose ties with the party are simply bureaucratic or functional is in the region of 30 per cent *Anuario Político 1969* (Edicusa, Madrid, 1970), p. 411.

44. See Law on the Succession, article 2, and Organic Law of the State, transitory provision, 1.III.

45. The Statutes of FET y de las JONS were modified in this respect twice in the years after the Civil War, by decree of 31 July 1939, and by a further decree of 23 November 1942.

46. Decree of 3 March 1955.

47. Decree of 22 April 1964.

48. See Organic Law of the State, article 22.

49. There are forty-seven provinces in peninsular Spain; the Balearic Islands form one province and the Canary Islands two; the Spanish Sahara counts too as a

province; and the two garrison towns of Ceuta and Melilla in North Africa, just across the Straits of Gibraltar, each elect a member of the National Council.

50. The candidate must meet one of the following conditions:

  (a) to be or to have been a member of the National Council;
  (b) to be proposed by five members of the National Council;
  (c) to be proposed by ten members of either the Provincial Council or the Local Councils of the Movement.

51. The results of the elections were published in all the national press. The figures here are based on the results published in the Madrid daily *Arriba*, 26 October 1971.

52. In the 1967 elections 38 out of 55 held posts of this kind (*Cuadernos para el Diálogo*, no. 50, February 1967, p. 28). In the more recent elections of 1971, and taking as a basis the list published in *Arriba*, 26 October 1971, the proportion is 34 out of 53. This is a conservative estimate, since most of the others also have or have had some kind of link with the governmental structure at national, provincial or local level.

53. The list of National Councillors appointed by Franco, which was published in *Arriba*, 7 November 1971, includes eleven Ministers, five ex-Ministers, the Mayor of Madrid, the National Vice-Secretary of the Movement, the Director-General for Secondary Education, the President of the Cortes, the Director-General for the Press, the Director of the Institute of Syndical Studies and many other 'well-known personalities in the political life of the country', as *Arriba* puts it.

54. See articles 21 and 23 of the Organic Law of the State.

55. See page 56 on the appeal of *contrafuero*.

56. This theory is put forward by Roberto Reyes Morales in 'El Consejo Nacional del Movimiento y los derechos y libertades reconocidos en las Leyes Fundamentales', *Revista de Estudios Políticos*, no. 152, March–April 1967, pp. 267–76.

57. See, for instance, the article signed by Oscar Alzaga Villamil in *Las asociaciones políticas en España* (*Cuadernos para el Diálogo*, Suplementos, no. 25, Madrid, 1971).

58. Law of Association, 24 December 1964, articles 1 and 3.

59. Organic Law of the State, article 4.

60. *ibid*, article 21(e).

61. Decree of 20 December 1968.

62. *Cuadernos para el Diálogo*, no. 62, November 1968, p. 9.

63. This plan was named in Spanish legal terminology: Anteproyecto de Bases del Régimen Jurídico Asociativo del Movimiento.

64. Oscar Alzaga Villamil in *Las asociaciones políticas en España* and A. Fernández Sepúlveda (Bib. 10) gives the names of eleven such associations. The names of the promoters indicate that in most cases only the people already inside the organization of the Movement showed any interest.

65. Session held on 15 December 1969. See in *Anuario político español, 1969*

(Edicusa, Madrid, 1970), pp 427–34, some of the reactions expressed in the Spanish press at the time.

66. Anteproyecto de normas sobre Asociaciones de Acción Política en el Movimiento, published by all national dailies on 26 May 1970.

67. For a comparison between the text of the two Bills, see F. Prieto, 'Proyectos reguladores de las asociaciones del Movimiento', *Revista de Fomento Social*, no. 100, October–December 1970, pp. 355–73.

68. Articles 2, 3, 9, 17, 19, 20, 21, 26, 27, 43 (twice).

69. The first one appeared in *ABC*, on 11 January 1970; the second at a press conference held in Oviedo on 25 August 1971; and the third was published in *Pueblo*, on 29 January 1972.

70. From the interview in *ABC*.

71. *Indice*, no. 292–5, August 1971, p. 9.

72. Decree published in the *Boletín Oficial del Estado*, 23 December 1974.

6. The Syndical Organization

1. The term syndicate, and its derivatives, have been used, rather than the more common trade union, for two reasons: to show linguistically the difference between two in many ways opposite realities, and to keep in English the link that joins in Spanish the syndicate and the syndical organization to their doctrinal base, national–syndicalism.

2. *SP*, 15 December 1968.

3. Quotations to testify it are abundant: 'Fascism, National–Socialism and National–Syndicalism are children of the same mother, Spiritualism; and therefore brothers, twin brothers if you wish, but not Siamese twins.' (J. L. de Arrese, 'La revolución social del Nacional–Sindicalismo', in *Obras Completas* (Afrodisio Aguado, Madrid, 1966), vol. 1, p. 37).

4. The brief resumé which follows is based on the writings and speeches of J. A. Primo de Rivera and J. L. de Arrese, though the label national–syndicalism was coined by R. Ledesma Ramos (S. G. Payne, *Falange: A History of Spanish Fascism* (Stanford University Press, 1967), p. 12). It should be pointed out that the adoption of national–syndicalism as official dogma found complementary support in the widespread acceptance by many of Franco's followers of Catholic corporativism, particularly fashionable in the thirties and forties.

5. J. A. Primo de Rivera, in an article published in *El Fascio*, no. 1, 16 March 1933.

6. *FE*, a falangist newspaper. The first issue appeared on 7 December 1933.

7. A falangist economist like J. Velarde Fuertes recognizes that such was the case: 'The lack of intellectual development in the economic policies of the movement founded by José Antonio meant that his references to tax reform, nationalization of banks, and agrarian reform were buried beneath a heavy tombstone of granite rhetoric' (*Sobre la decadencia económica de España* (Tecnos, Madrid, 1966), p. 20).

8. *Bases de la democracia española* (Ediciones del Movimiento, Madrid, 1962), p. 19 ff.

9. Labour Charter, 1938 version, declaration III, paragraphs 4, 5, and 6.

10. *ibid.*, declaration XI.

11. *ibid.*, declaration XIII, paragraph 4.

12. *ibid.*, paragraph 5.

13. *ibid.*, paragraph 1.

14. Law on Syndical Unity, dated 26 January 1940.

15. Basic Law of the Syndical Organization, dated 6 December 1940.

16. Law on Syndical Unity, article 1.

17. Preamble to the Basic Law of the Syndical Organization.

18. Basic Law, article 12: 'The head of each national syndicate shall be appointed by the authorities of the National Movement, at the proposal of the National Syndicate Delegate.' And article 13: 'The head of each syndicate, to whom all authority and responsibility belong, shall be assisted by the officers determined in the ordinances. They shall all be appointed by the Secretary-General of the Movement . . .'.

19. J. J. Bellod, 'La organización sindical', in *El nuevo estado español* (Madrid, 1961), p. 333.

20. C. Iglesias Selgas, *La vía española a la democracia* (Ediciones del Movimiento, Madrid, 1968), p. 234.

21. The *enlaces sindicales* are roughly the equivalent of the British shop stewards, though they lack the backing of independent unions. Their position is further weakened by the fact that neither their functions nor their rights are clearly defined. The *jurados de empresa* are committees set up in firms with more than fifty employees. A number of workers, dependent on the size of the firm, are elected to them, and they are presided over by the employer or his appointee. For a recent analysis of the role of these *jurados*, see J. Amsden, *Collective Bargaining and Class Conflict in Spain* (Weidenfeld & Nicolson, 1972), Chapter 6.

22. Decree of 18 August 1947.

23. A member of a *jurado* holds his post for eight years, since the elections held every four years only affect one half of the membership.

24. J. M. Maravall, *Trabajo y conflicto social* (Edicusa, Madrid, 1967), p. 134.

25. Decrees of 2 June 1966 and 23 July 1971 respectively.

26. These decisions can be taken by the syndical hierarchy or by the special labour courts (Magistraturas del Trabajo).

27. Labour Charter, 1938 version, declaration III, paragraph 4.

28. In accordance with two decrees on incomes policy, one of 1944 and the other of 1948, any increases over the official level had to be approved by the authorities. This restriction was removed for individual firms in 1956.

29. Law on Syndical Collective Agreements, dated 25 April 1958. The system of collective bargaining was updated, without any major alteration being introduced, by a law of 18 December 1973.

30. J. M. Maravall, *Trabajo y conflicto social*, p. 165.

31. Ample statistical evidence on all these points can be found in J. Iglesias Fernández, *Convenios colectivos, ¿ofensiva del sistema capitalista?* (Edicusa, Madrid, 1974).

32. Basic Law of the Syndical Organization.

33. In Spanish *línea política* or *línea de mando*.

34. Ley sobre clasificación de sindicatos, dated 23 June 1941.

35. They are the following: miscellaneous activities; health; water, gas and electricity; foodstuffs and colonial products; sugar; banking, stock market and savings; cereals; fuel; building, glass and ceramics; teaching; entertainment; fruit and horticultural produce; livestock; hotels and tourism; chemical industries; wood and cork; merchant navy; metals; olive; paper and graphic arts; fisheries; hides and skins; press, radio, television and advertising; insurance; textiles; transport; wine, beer and beverages. And finally the so-called Brotherhood of Farmers and Stockbreeders is also considered a syndicate.

36. International Labour Organization, *Report of the Study Group to Examine the Labour and Trade Union Situation in Spain* (Geneva, 1969), paragraph 672.

37. *ibid.*, paragraph 632.

38. *Solidaridad Nacional*, 21 June 1966.

39. Declarations II, III, VIII, XI, and XIII.

40. J. N. García Nieto *et al.*, *La nueva ley sindical* (Estela, Barcelona, 1970), p. 13.

41. ILO Report, paragraph 729.

42. This document was drawn up by a special commission of bishops (Comisión Episcopal de Apostolado Social) approved by a general meeting of the Episcopal Conference on 21 July 1968, and made public through the Spanish press three days later under the title *Principios cristianos relativos al sindicalismo*.

43. There are authors, like J. N. García Nieto, a priest himself, who feel that the opinions expressed by the Spanish bishops represent a compromise with the *status quo*, and are far removed from basic Christian principles (J. N. García Nieto *et al.*, *La nueva ley sindical*, pp. 15–16).

44. See Law on the Principles of the National Movement, principle II.

45. E. Romero, in *Pueblo*, 26 July 1968. In September 1969 *Pueblo* and the Catholic daily *Ya* maintained a very interesting debate on the validity of, and the weight to be given to, the document issued by the Spanish bishops.

46. The Spanish bishops made it quite clear in October 1970 (*Ya*, 31 October 1970) when the text of the syndical Bill was already known, that it did not conform with the principles they had laid down in their first document. For the official reaction to the bishops' attitude see C. Iglesias Selgas, *Comentarios a la Ley Sindical* (Cabal, Madrid, 1971), p. 73.

47. 1160 amendments were tabled by the members of the Cortes, but the differences between the Bill and the Act are so slight that the proposed amendments seem to have had very little effect.

48. ILO Report, paragraph 66.

49. At the time when Franco changed his cabinet in October 1969, the post of Minister of Syndical Relations was separated from that of Minister-Secretary-General of the National Movement, offices held jointly by the same person until then. Without now judging the widsom or otherwise of that decision, it is worth pointing out that it affected one of the major points of the syndical Bill, at a time when it was about to be discussed by the Cortes. The Cortes were thus presented with a *fait accompli*, and were unlikely to go against Franco's decision, even if they had wanted to in the first place.

50. Article 4 of the new syndical law.

7. The Judiciary

1. R. David and J. E. C. Brierly, *Major Legal Systems in the World Today* (Stevens, 1968) *passim*.

2. J. H. Merryman, *The Civil Law Tradition* (Stanford University Press, 1969) *passim*.

3. *ibid.*, p. 2.

4. Ley Orgánica del Poder Judicial, dated provisionally 23 June 1870, and finally promulgated on 15 September of the same year.

5. Organic Law of the State, article 2.II.

6. J. Zafra, for instance, says of it: 'it is not precisely a model of clarity and exactitude', in *Régimen Político de España* (EUNSA, 1973), p. 368.

7. Thus section V of the Organic Law of the State is simply headed La Justicia and the new law on the judiciary is entitled Ley Orgánica de la Justicia.

8. Quotations from pp. 2 and 71 of *Justicia y política: España 1972*, a pamphlet anonymously produced and published by a group of Spanish judges, magistrates and lawyers.

9. They are situated in Albacete, Barcelona, Burgos, Cáceres, Granada, Corunna, Madrid, Oviedo, Pampeluna, Palma, Las Palmas, Seville, Valladolid, Valencia and Saragossa.

10. Law of 20 December 1952.

11. Law of 17 July 1945, law of 20 December 1952, and a decree of 11 December 1952.

12. See article 33, Organic Law of the State.

13. For a fuller and more detailed description see L. Prieto-Castro, *Tribunales españoles: organización y funcionamiento* (Tecnos, Madrid, 1973).

14. Quoted by A. Hernández Gil, 'La justicia en la Ley Orgánica del Estado', *Revista de Estudios Políticos*, no. 181, January–February 1972, p. 40.

15. The words are those of a famous Spanish jurist. M. de la Plaza. Quoted by M. Jiménez de Parga, 'La independencia del poder judicial', *Cuadernos para el Diálogo*, 17, December 1969, p. 18.

16. We are here using the dual classification of judicial independence established by L. Martínez Calcerrada, *Independencia del poder judicial* (Revista de Derecho Judicial, Madrid, 1970), p. 38.

17. International Commission of Jurists, *Spain and the Rule of Law* (Geneva, 1962), p. 30 ff.

18. *España, estado de derecho* (Instituto de Estudios Políticos, Madrid, 1964).

19. The norms applying to the organization of the judicial career, to the magistrates of the Supreme Court, and to the office of Public Prosecutor were approved by decrees issued on 28 December 1967 and 27 February 1969.

20. It is not possible to give any bibliographical details about this publication since neither editor, nor author, nor even place of publication are mentioned. The same anonymous authors previously published a similar pamphlet, *El gobierno y la justicia en 1971*.

21. *ibid.*, p. 3.

22. The first section of chapter 6 – pp. 65–71 – deals specifically with the independence of the judiciary.

23. A. Hernández Gil, 'La justicia en la Ley Orgánica del Estado', could be taken as an example of this nature.

24. Organic Law of the State, article 58.

25. *Justicia y política, España 1972*, p. 65.

26. All the rules and norms pertaining to judges and magistrates, from which the examples given are extracted, are to be found in the Reglamento Orgánico de la Carrera Judicial.

27. L. Prieto-Castro, 'La administración de justicia', in M. Fraga (ed.), *La España de los años 70: el estado y la política* (Moneda y Crédito, Madrid, 1974), vol. 3, p. 401.

28. R. Dahrendorf, *Society and Democracy in Germany* (Weidenfeld & Nicolson, 1968), p. 239.

29. On the socio-political background of judges and magistrates in Spain see J. J. Toharía, 'Notas sobre el origen social de la judicatura española', *Sistema*, no. 7, October 1974.

30. For example in 'Coloquio sobre la reforma de la justicia', *Revista de Fomento Social*, no. 96, October–December 1969, pp. 373–87, all the experts consulted appear obsessed with the subject of special courts.

31. J. J. Toharía, *Modernización, autoritarismo, y administración de justicia en España, Los Suplementos*, no. 51 (Edicusa, Madrid, 1974).

32. Organic Law of the State, article 31.

33. The list appears in *Crónica de la codificación española: organización judicial* (Ministerio de Justicia, Madrid, 1970), pp. 342–3.

34. *ibid.*, p. 341.

35. *Pueblo*, 17 January 1969.

36. A. Zaragoza, *Abogacía y política* (Edicusa, Madrid, 1975), p. 43.

37. The main document coming out of this Congress – held from 15 to 20 January 1970 – can be consulted in *Anuario político español, 1970*, p. 634 ff.

38. Point VII.

39. All the legal provisions concerning military courts are contained in the Code of Military Justice of 17 July 1945.

40. The most famous case in recent times was the Burgos trial, held in December 1970, against a group of Basque members of the separatist movement ETA, accused of a number of terrorist activities. The various books published about this case (see Bibliography), offer a good picture, from contrasting standpoints, of the way military courts function in Spain.
41. As expressed in the preamble to the law establishing the Public Order Court, dated 2 December 1963.
42. *Boletín oficial de las Cortes*, 20 December 1973. At the time of concluding this chapter – summer 1975 – the Cortes have not yet passed the Bill.
43. Article 32.
44. Decree-law on the prevention of terrorism, dated 27 August 1975.
45. Published originally in *S P*, and reproduced in *Anuario político español 1969*, pp. 374–5.

8. Spaniards and their Rights

1. L. Sánchez Agesta, *Derecho constitucional comparado* (Editora Nacional, Madrid, 1968), p. 525.
2. The International Covenants of 1966 on economic, social, cultural, civil and political rights represent an attempt to overcome the inadequacies of a mere Declaration of Rights by replacing it with legally enforceable documents. But so far national states have shown marked reluctance to ratify the covenants adopted by the United Nations.
3. Montesquien, *De l'esprit des lois*, in *Oeuvres complètes* (Librairie Gallimard, Paris, 1951), vol. 2, p. 395.
4. *España invertebrada*, 12th edition (Revista de Occidente, Madrid, 1962), pp. 5–6.
5. 'Neither teachers nor students have expressed their opinion about the White Paper or the Bill on Education. Students were totally excluded: as for teachers, only a few were consulted individually and secretly. This was all the interest shown by the Ministry of Education and Science to find out the opinion of the Faculties and Technical Schools of Madrid.' From a document signed by a group of lecturers at Madrid University, reproduced in *Anuario político español, 1970*, p. 445.
6. Law on Associations, dated 24 December 1964. Prior to this date, associations had been subject to a law of 1887 and to a decree of 25 January 1941.
7. Law on Associations, article 1, paragraph 3.
8. See International Commission of Jurists, *Spain and the Rule of Law* (Geneva, 1962), pp. 44–6. This book should be read in conjunction with the arrogant reply by the Spanish government through the offices of its Institute of Political Studies: *España, estado de derecho* (Servicio Informativo Español, Madrid, 1964).

9. The most important is an ordinance dated 20 July 1939, issued to complement a law of 1880 regulating the freedom of assembly, which is still applicable.

10. Only Catholic processions and the normal meetings of officially approved associations are excluded. In the latter case, the associations must inform the authorities of the holding of their general meetings seventy-two hours beforehand, and the authorities may, if they consider it necessary, send a representative to be present at the meeting.

11. Ley de Prensa, issued by decree of 22 April 1938.

12. The preamble of the law made this clear: 'Present circumstances do not allow the drawing up of definitive regulations, and therefore government action must initially be limited to the first few steps . . .'.

13. The directives extended even to sports news. Some rather amusing examples of this kind of official guidance are quoted by Manuel Fernández Areal, *La libertad de prensa en España, 1938–1971* (Edicusa, Madrid, 1971), p. 41 ff.

The International Commission of Jurists, *Spain and the Rule of Law*, p. 49, quotes this *consigna* issued by the Ministry of Information on the occasion of the death of Ortega y Gasset in 1955: 'Each newspaper may publish up to three articles relative to the death of Ortega y Gasset: a biography and two commentaries. Every article on the writer's philosophy must underline his errors in religious matters. It is permissible to publish photographs of the mortuary on the front page, of the death mask or body of Ortega, but no photographs made during his lifetime.'

14. G. Arias Salgado, *Política española de la información* (Secretaría General Técnica del Ministerio de Información y Turismo, Madrid, 1957–8), vol. I, p. 56.

15. *ibid.*, p. 112.

16. *ibid.*, p. 156.

17. The gestation of the law was painfully slow. Its origins go back to 1959 when Arias Salgado set up a committee to prepare the first draft of a law to cover the whole field of information. Fraga Irbarne preferred to have a series of laws to deal with the various facets of information; the Press Law being one of such laws. See on this question M. Fraga Iribarne, *Horizonte español* ([Madrid], 1965), p. 273 ff.

18. '. . . the system established by the law of 1938 was practically in force until the new law became applicable on 9 April 1966' (M. Fernández Areal, *La libertad de prensa en España, 1938–1971*, p. 47). Fernández Areal has a direct knowledge of the situation since as editor of *Diario regional*, a Valladolid newspaper, he was prosecuted, in the early sixties, for 'offences' such as the omission of one of Franco's speeches, and the use of '*Nuestro campo se muere*' ('Our countryside is dying') for a heading on the front page of his newspaper.

19. Press Law, article 2.

20. Thus, for example, the suspension for two months of the Barcelona weekly *Destino*, and the fine of 250,000 pesetas on the editor, Néstor Luján, for the publication in October 1967 of a reader's letter in which the decision to teach

the Catalan language in schools was criticized is, by any standards, a real outrage.

21. Although the obligation to hand in at the offices of the Ministry of Information and Tourism a certain number of copies before the publication is circulated to the public (ten copies, and half an hour are the requirements for daily papers) could still be interpreted as a prior censorship, since on some occasions it has led to the confiscation or withdrawal of publications by Ministry officials. A case in point was that of the April 1972 issue of the magazine *Cuadernos para el Diálogo*. It was stopped by the authorities before it reached the public, and later allowed to appear minus eight of its original articles and a cartoon.

22. Law of 8 April 1967 altering article 165 of the Penal Code, and adding two new articles: 165 bis (a) and 165 bis (b).

23. Ley sobre Secretos oficiales, dated 5 April 1968.

24. *ibid.*, article 2.

25. The number of prosecutions under the present Press Law runs into several hundreds. The official figures used to be given every year in the publication of the Ministry of Information and Tourism, *Crónica de un año de España*. In the 1969 issue, for example, it is stated that during the period 9 April 1968–9 April 1969, the authorities initiated proceedings against 201 publications and finally sanctioned 118. The figures for other years are even higher.

26. A quantitative analysis of *Ya* and *ABC* carried out by Guy Hermet shows the effects the Press Law has had on these two Madrid newspapers. 'La Presse espagnole depuis la suppression de la censure', in *Revue Francaise de Science Politique*, vol. 18, no. 1, February 1968, pp. 44–67. For a wider survey, covering eighteen newspapers over a period of six months, following the Press Law, see *Revista de Opinión Pública*, no. 10, October–December 1967, pp. 171–259.

27. One should by no means assume that reporting on this type of issue is now free. For the most part it takes the form of a 'neutral' note from some news agency or other – to give but one example, *Pueblo*, a newspaper published by the official syndicates always sends a special envoy to any part of Spain where a *crime passionel* takes place, to report all its lurid details in full, but never publishes more than a carefully worded agency note on a strike or other forms of labour unrest.

28. '. . . we see that in Spain there is no newspaper which could be included in the "left": as for the magazines in circulation only a few go beyond the limits of a middle-of-the-road programme to take a moderate leftist line'. This is the opinion expressed by L. González Seara, Professor of Sociology at the University of Madrid: 'Los medios de comunicación de masas y la formación de la opinión pública', in *La España de los años 70, 1: la sociedad* (Editorial Moneda y Crédito, Madrid, 1972), p. 769.

29. What has been said about television could equally be applied to radio. Radio is not a state monopoly, as regards ownership, but the regime has total control over news bulletins and political information.

30. Words written by Manuel García Morente in 1942. In M. de Iriarte, *El*

profesor García Morente, Sacerdote (Espasa-Calpe, Madrid, 1953), p. 277.

31. cf. R. Duocastella *et al.*, *Análisis sociológico del catolicismo español* (Nova Terra, Barcelona, 1967); J. M. Vázquez, *Realidades socio-religiosas de España* (Editora Nacional, Madrid, 1967).

32. Quoted in Alfonso C. Comín, 'L'Espagne, pays de mission (la jeunesse ouvrière et l'église)', *Esprit*, February 1964, p. 317.

33. J. M. Vázquez, *Realidades socio-religiosas de España*, p. 109.

34. R. Duocastella *et al.*, *Análisis sociológico del catolicismo español*, p. 52.

35. Principles of the National Movement II; and Law on the Succession, article 1.

36. International Commission of Jurists, *Spain and the Rule of Law*, p. 55.

37. For some examples of the treatment meted out to protestants, see International Commission of Jurists, *Spain and the Rule of Law*, pp. 55–6; and Benjamin Welles, *Spain: The Gentle Anarchy* (Pall Mall Press, 1965), Chapter 6.

38. See in Javier Rupérez's *Estado confesional y libertad religiosa* (Edicusa, Madrid, 1970), p. 185 ff., a detailed account of Castiella's initiative, and the opposition to it.

39. *Dignitatis Humanae*, no. 2.

40. Ley regulando el ejercicio del derecho civil a la libertad en materia religiosa, dated 28 June 1967.

41. The number of Protestants in Spain is difficult to assess, but it has been officially put by a Protestant body – Comisión de Defensa Evangélica – at the round figure of thirty thousand. For an analysis of this estimate and a detailed study of the geographical distribution of Protestants in Spain see Juan Estruch, *Los protestantes españoles* (Nova Terra, Barcelona, 1968).

42. Law on the Principles of the National Movement, article 2.

43. See the various articles published in *Cuadernos para el Diálogo* during 1967 (particularly issues nos. 42–6) expressing the opinions of a number of Catholic writers: Laín Entralgo, Aranguren, Ruiz-Giménez, Jesús Aguirre, etc.

44. A. F. Carrillo Albornoz makes a critical assessment of the contents of the law in the light of the Vatican Council's Declaration on religious freedom in 'Interpretación española de la declaración conciliar sobre libertad religiosa', *Cuadernos para el Diálogo*, special issue no. 6, July 1967, pp. 40–46. For an assessment more favourable to the official position see C. Corral Salvador, 'El ordenamiento jurídico español de libertad religiosa', *Revista de Estudios Políticos*, no. 158, March–April 1968, pp. 77–98.

45. J. Jiménez, *La objeción de conciencia en España* (Edicusa, Madrid, 1973), gives a complete list of the conscientious objectors imprisoned in Spain with the length of their sentences, pp. 217–52.

46. *ibid.*, Chapter 4, gives a detailed account of the committee debates on the two bills. They provide a further proof of the point made elsewhere in this book that the Cortes have often been more reluctant to change than the government.

47. J. de Esteban *et al.*, *Desarrollo político y constitución española* (Ariel, Barcelona, 1973), p. 426.

48. For the text of this law see *Boletín oficial de las Cortes Españolas*, no. 1.308, 14 December 1973, pp. 31929–31.

49. Some of their reactions are quoted by Javier Rupérez, *Estado confesional y libertad religiosa*, p. 251 ff.

50. Víctor Manuel Arbeloa, *Sobre la iglesia en España* (*ZERO*, Madrid, 1968), p. 60.

51. Declaration XI, 2.

52. Article 222, in its 1944 version, specifically stated that workers who took part in strikes would be punished for sedition.

53. Jose María Maravall, *El desarrollo económico y la clase obrera* (Ariel, Barcelona, 1970), p. 45 ff., discusses this question at some length.

54. The regulations are contained in the law on collective bargaining and agreements of 24 April 1958.

55. Public Order Law, 30 July 1959, article 2.

56. Decree on Banditry and Terrorism, 21 September 1960, article 2. This article was repealed in 1963 and subsequently put back into effect, once again by decree, on 16 August 1968.

57. Decree of 20 September 1962.

58. Article 222, as amended by law of 21 December 1965. It now reads:
    'The following shall be considered guilty of sedition:
    Public officials, employees and individuals responsible for rendering any public or essential service, who, by ceasing their activity, disrupt such services, or in any way impair their regularity.
    Employers and workers who, with the object of endangering the security of the State, of damaging its authority, of disturbing its normal functioning, or of seriously disrupting national production, stop work or impair its regularity.'

59. The Second Development Plan was approved by a law of 7 February 1969, whose article 11 states: 'A coherent basis shall be established for the proper settlement of collective labour dispute, including the stoppages resulting from them, under the authority of the Ministry of Labour and the syndical organization.'

60. Decree of 20 May 1970.

61. This law was passed by the Cortes at their plenary session of 18 December 1973. For an assessment of its contents see J. Muñoz *et al.*, *La economía española 1973* (Edicusa, Madrid, 1974), pp. 278–94.

62. Excellent works on this subject are J. M. Maravall, *El desarrollo económico y la clase obrera*, which covers the period up to 1967, and for the more recent years the annual publication on Spanish socio-economic problems referred to in note 61. One can find in them a wealth of statistics and graphs that space does not allow us to reproduce here.

63. *Informe sobre conflictos colectivos de trabajo, 1970* (Ministry of Labour, 1971).

64. J. A. Peredo, 'Política social-laboral', in *Anuario político español, 1970*, p. 369.

65. J. Muñoz *et al.*, *La economía española, 1971* (Edicusa, Madrid, 1972), p. 206.

66. Sentence of 22 November 1967, passed on the appeal raised on behalf of the workers of a Basque firm (Laminado de Bandas en Frío, Echevarri, Bilbao) who had been on strike.

67. Constitution drafted by the Second Vatican Council and issued on 7 December 1965, Section 68.

68. A number of recent cases show that the regime will use any methods to stop unwanted strikes. In July 1970 three building workers were shot dead by the police, at a demonstration held outside the Syndicate headquarters in Granada. In the same month, a strike of the Madrid Underground was swiftly brought to an end when the Council of Ministers issued an ultimatum to strikers threatening to draft them all into the army, and bring them under military jurisdiction. In October 1971 the police entered the Seat car factory at Barcelona to clear the strikers who were inside the premises; in the events which followed, one worker was killed and a number of them injured. More recently, on 9 March 1972, the police, trying to disperse a shipbuilding-workers' demonstration at El Ferrol, opened fire, killing two demonstrators and injuring more than thirty others.

69. Paragraphs 941 to 943.

70. Charter of the Spanish People, article 33.

71. *ibid.*, article 35.

72. Constitution of the Second Republic, article 42.

73. Speech published by all the national press on 7 February 1969. A similar argument is used by the Institute of Political Studies in their reply to the 1962 report on Spain by the International Commission of Jurists, *Spain and the Rule of Law*, p. 137.

74. *La Vanguardia*, 25 January 1969.

75. The note of the Ministry of the Interior was published in all newspapers on 25 March 1969.

76. *Boletín Oficial de las Cortes*, 22 April 1969.

77. International Commission of Jurists, *Spain and the Rule of Law*, p. 60.

78. The Public Order Law was first promulgated on 30 July 1959. Several of its articles were amended by a new law passed by the Cortes on 21 July 1971.

79. Article 20 as amended in July 1971.

80. Carlos García Valdés, 'Aplicación de la Ley de Orden Público', in *Cuadernos para el Diálogo*, special issue no. 30, May 1972. See in this article some cases exemplifying the way in which the Public Order Law is being applied after its amendment in 1971.

81. Penal Code, article 164 bis (a). This article and the following one, also concerned with offences against the National Movement, were inserted in the Penal Code, together with other restrictive provisions, by a law of 8 April 1967.

82. The title of the poem is *A la muerte del Maestre de Santiago don Rodrigo Manrique, su padre*.

83. *Cuadernos para el Diálogo*, no. 94, July 1971, p. 5.

312

9. Political Forces, Pressure Groups and Opposition

1. 'On civil war in Spain', a review of G. Jackson's book *The Spanish Republic and the Civil War 1931–1939*, in *Government and Opposition*, vol. 1 (2), February 1966, p. 265.
2. A Spanish term, without a suitable correlative in English, applied to those who cunningly try to secure for themselves an inheritance or legacy.
3. 'Panorama político', in the collective work *España, perspectiva 1973* (Guadiana, Madrid, 1973), p. 25.
4. For a more detailed, but no-names-given, dissection of political forces in Spain see J. J. Linz, 'Opposition in and under an authoritarian regime: the case of Spain', in R. Dahl (ed.), *Regimes and Oppositions* (Yale University Press, 1973), pp. 171–259. Interesting too are the attempts of Amando de Miguel at establishing a logical set of categories to classify the opposition in Spain: *España, marca registrada* (Kairós, Madrid, 1972), pp. 249–55.
5. M. Jiménez de Parga, *Las monarquías europeas en el horizonte español* (Tecnos, Madrid, 1966), p. 196.
6. See article 37, Organic Law of the State.
7. See Principle II, Law on the Principles of the National Movement.
8. At least they do so in public, though it has been suggested that in private their comments can be quite different! R. Calvo Serer, 'La politique intérieure dans l'Espagne de Franco', *Ecrits de Paris*, September 1953, p. 14.
9. One has the impression that the number of Spaniards, both inside and outside the regime, who would like a republic rather than a monarchy is considerable, but this is obviously a point open to speculation.
10. Who, from amongst the monarchists, supported Prince Juan Carlos rather than his father was not always clear, but it is now common knowledge that the two main advocates of the young prince were the deceased Carrero Blanco and López Rodó.
11. To understand Calvo Serer's position it is imperative to read his recent works *Franco frente al Rey* (Paris, 1972), and *La dictadura de los franquistas* (Paris, 1973). More recently, after the assassination of Carrero Blanco he published an article in *Le Monde*, 29 January 1974, 'Juan Carlos après son père?', suggesting that Prince Juan Carlos should step down in favour of his father and await his turn on the legitimate line of descent.
12. 'Politically naïve, the carlists, formerly ultra-conservative, and reactionary Catholic, have now launched a new political programme which is basically left-wing with, of course, a constitutional carlist monarch presiding over a social democratic state' (B. Cemlyn-Jones, *Guardian*, 6 July 1972). This kind of move is partly motivated by a sincere desire to update the traditionalist doctrine, but it arrives as a late and desperate attempt as the carlist pretender and his supporters see their claim turning into a totally lost cause.
13. Speech of Rodrigo Royo, published in *SP*, 15 July 1972, p. 24.
14. Girón's speech was given wide coverage by many newspapers (*Ya* allocated

to it 1½ pages, *Arriba* 2½ and *Pueblo* 2) and treated as an event with national repercussions. But in spite of its length (the speech lasted two hours) and the fiery style of the speaker (he was described by *Pueblo* as a 'hurricane'), the content of the speech is rather ambiguous and very little in it can be considered new.

15. *Arriba*, 28 April 1974. The article was reproduced in full by *S P*, August 1974, pp. 57–9.

16. In March 1974 eleven different groups, remnants of the old Falange (Joven Guardia de Franco, Vieja Guardia, Círculos Ruiz de Alda, Club 401, Antiguos miembros del SEU, etc.) gathered in Madrid at a meeting called by the Círculos Doctrinales José Antonio, to discuss what is permanent and what incidental in José Antonio's doctrine. *Ya*, 27 March 1974.

17. For a more complete list of falangist-orientated groups in present-day Spain it is worth consulting 'La Falange de ayer a hoy', *Dossier-Mundo*, no. 22, June 1973. For the opinions of older and younger falangists see M. Veyrat and J. L. Navas-Migueloa, *Falange, hoy* (G. del Toro, Madrid, 1973).

18. M. Cantarero del Castillo, *Ideas actuales: testimonio de una comparecencia política* (Coslada, Madrid, 1970), can be taken as representative of the views of the whole group.

19. *ibid.*, p. 226.

20. *ibid.*, p. 223.

21. The 1966 entry for Opus Dei in the *Anuario pontífico* gives as its main objective: 'to spread amongst all social classes, and especially amongst intellectuals, the search for evangelical perfection in the world'. Quoted by D. Artigues, 'Qu'est-ce que l'Opus Dei?', *Esprit*, no. 365, November 1967, p. 708.

22. The number of works on Opus Dei is now fairly considerable. The most condemnatory of them all is J. Ynfante, *La prodigiosa aventura del Opus Dei: génesis y desarrollo de la Santa Mafia* (Ruedo Ibérico, Paris, 1970). The most valuable part of this book is the fantastic mass of information the author has been able to accumulate, as well as the inclusion of the text of the secret Opus Dei constitutions. But far more damning for the organization is a more recent publication of an ex-member, A. Moncada, *El Opus Dei: una interpretación* (Indice, Madrid, 1974).

23. This book was first published in 1934 as *Consideraciones espirituales*. According to Opus Dei sources, *Camino* has sold some 2.5 million copies and has been translated into more than thirty different languages. Rafael Gómez Pérez, 'Encontrarse siendo cristiano', in *Doctrina y vida* (Ediciones Palabra, Madrid, 1971), p. 78.

24. For an assessment of the contents of *Camino* see J. L. Aranguren, 'La spiritualité de l'Opus Dei: à propos d'une controverse', *Esprit*, April 1965, p. 762; and *P B*, 'Significación religiosa, económica y política del Opus Dei', in *Horizonte Español 1966* (Ruedo Ibérico, Paris, 1966), vol. 1, p. 225.

25. This is, of course, the overall impression of the work. Given its lack of method

and the metaphorical allusions, one can find amongst its 999 aphorisms quotations to suit all tastes. As the organization has developed, the deficiencies of *Camino* have become more and more evident, and the official position now is that *Camino* does not contain *all* the spirituality of Opus Dei. See J. Ynfante, *La prodigiosa aventura del Opus Dei*, p. 136.

26. López Rodó, 'Spain and the E E C', in *Foreign Affairs*, vol. 44, no. 1, October 1965, p. 129.

27. This was not always possible in the past. J. L. Aranguren's article, 'La spiritualité de l'Opus Dei', was written for publication in the Spanish magazine *Revista de Occidente*, and although approved by the ecclesiastical censor was banned by the government. A work in Catalan by Father J. Dalmau, *Contrapunts al camí de l'Opus Dei*, was also forbidden by the authorities.

28. D. Artigues, *El Opus Dei en España* (Ruedo Ibérico, Paris, 1971); J. Ynfante, *La prodigiosa aventura del Opus Dei*; A. Moncada, *El Opus Dei*.

29. The article was published in *Madrid*, 11 October 1971. Calvo Serer says that two ministers at least, Mariano Navarro Rubio and Gonzalo Fernández de la Mora, were promoted in that way. For contrasting views on the *Madrid* affair see *Dossier-Mundo*, no. 6, February 1972, and R. Calvo Serer, *La dictadura de los franquistas: el 'affaire' Madrid y el futuro político* ([Paris], 1973).

30. J. Busquets, *El militar de carrera en España*, 2nd edition (Ariel, Barcelona, 1971), p. 140.

31. *ibid.*, p. 180 ff.

32. *ibid.*, p. 224.

33. Lieutenant-General M. Diez-Alegría, in his speech on becoming a member of the Royal Academy of Moral and Political Sciences, published with some other works of his under the title *Ejército y sociedad* (Alianza Editorial, Madrid, 1972), p. 50 ff.

34. The dismissal of General Diez-Alegría, in June 1974, from his post as Chief of Staff could have been equally motivated. His attitude was too liberal and enlightened for the old guard to digest. He was said to have been in contact with S. Carrillo, Secretary of the Spanish Communist Party (*Guardian*, 12 June 1974). The reason given for his dismissal was a breach of discipline: while on a private visit to Romania he had an unofficial meeting with President Ceaucescu.

35. From a speech made by General Pérez Viñeta at Mérida (Caceres) in December 1970. *Anuario político español 1970*, p. 249.

36. From a speech of General Iniesta Cano, delivered at El Ferrol, Franco's birthplace. *Ya*, 25 August 1972.

37. For an overall assessment of the dialogue between christians and marxists in Spain, together with ample bibliographical guidance, see E. Díaz, *Pensamiento español 1939–1973* (Edicusa, Madrid, 1974), pp. 222–6.

38. In the spring of 1968 there was an interesting exchange of correspondence between the Pope and Franco. The Pope in a carefully worded letter suggested to Franco that the time had come to give up his right to intervene in the appoint-

ment of bishops. The reply of the Spanish Head of State, written in the same diplomatic style, reminded the Pope that perhaps he ought to think too of renouncing the privileges enjoyed by his Church in Spain. See the text of both letters in *Anuario político español 1970*, pp. 792–4.

39. Secretaría Nacional del Clero, *Asamblea conjunta obispos-sacerdotes* (Editorial Católica, Madrid, 1971). See in particular the first paper entitled: 'Iglesia y mundo en la España de hoy'.

40. This was the figure in 1969.

41. The results of the survey are published in *Asamblea conjunta obispos-sacerdotes*, p. 643 ff.

42. This opinion was clearly expressed by the Minister of Justice, who is the official link between Church and regime, in an interview published in *Pueblo*, 3 June 1969. The subject has also been recurrent in Franco's speeches during the last few years.

43. *Las '100 familias' españolas*, compiled by a team of young economists, in *Horizonte Español 1966*, vol. 1, p.47.

44. See the work mentioned in the previous note; R. Tamames, *Los monopolios en España* (Zyx, Madrid, 1968); or the special issue of *Cuadernos para el Diálogo*, no. 8, April 1968, on 'La Banca'.

45. For example, during the course of the first Development Plan, 1964–8, the number of firms controlled by the six major private banks increased considerably. Arturo López and Jose L. García, *Crecimiento y crisis del capitalismo español* (Edicusa, Madrid, 1968), p. 160.

46. See J. Ynfante, *La prodigiosa aventura del Opus Dei*, p. 229 ff.

47. See the revealing article of J. Velarde Fuertes, 'Conexiones entre nobleza de sangre y capitalismo español', *Mundo Social*, no. 35, August 1966. Also his prologue to J. Muñoz, *El poder de la banca en España* (Zyx, Madrid, 1970) in which he lists the economic interests of the monarchists in Don Juan's Private Council.

48. For the size and nature of U.S. investment in Spanish industry, see A. Cabello Moya, 'Las inversiones industriales norteamericanas en España', in *Cuadernos para el Diálogo*, no. 75, December 1969. Or the more recent publication, M. Vázquez Montalbàn, *Le penetración americana en España* (Edicusa, Madrid, 1974).

49. R. Aron, in L. Schapiro (ed.), *Political Opposition in One-Party States* (Macmillan, London, 1972), pp. 17–18.

50. This has become a very popular form of publication in the last few years. In the Bibliography several of these works have been included.

51. This is the expression applied to them by one of the members of that generation, Luís García San Miguel. J. Jiménez Blanco *et al.*, *Las ideologías en la España de hoy* (Seminarios y Ediciones, Madrid, 1972), p. 37.

52. The text of the document submitted to Franco was published in *Ibérica*, vol. 18, no. 1, January 1970. The document was also printed by some Spanish

papers in a shortened version, without the reference to political prisoners. The reaction of *Pueblo* could well exemplify the official reply. According to this syndicalist newspaper (27 December 1969) most of the demands contained in the document had already been met; besides, the paper says, the signatories should have put them through their representatives (the *procuradores* presumably).

53. One of the men who signed the document, Professor Tierno Galván, considers himself 'a marxist socialist'. S. Paniker, *Conversaciones en Madrid* (Kairós, Barcelona, 1969), p. 280.

54. In a survey carried out in Spanish universities in 1970 to the hypothetical question of how they would vote if there were free elections, 27 per cent of the men and 22 per cent of the women opted for socialism, the second largest single group after the Christian democrats. Results of the survey partially reproduced in *Ya*, 19 November 1970.

55. In connection with the dilemma facing Spanish socialism see the illuminating work by P. de Vega, 'Perspectivas del movimiento socialista', in *España: Perspectiva 1973* (Guadiana, Madrid, 1973), pp. 215–41.

56. Both these Alliances were formed at the beginning of the sixties. The ASE included the CNT, the UGT and the STV (Solidaridad de Trabajadores Vascos). The ASO was set up as a splinter group in 1962, by anarchists and socialists too, most of them from the Catalonia area; some Catholic trade unionists were also part of it.

57. César M. Lorenzo, *Les Anarchistes espagnols et le pouvoir 1868–1969* (Éditions du Seuil, Paris, 1969), p. 396. For an official view – from the regime's side – of those negotiations, the list of representatives who took part in them, and a copy of the resulting document, see E. Romero, *Cartas al rey* (Planeta, Barcelona, 1973), pp. 279–84.

58. S. Carrillo, *Después de Franco, ¿qué?* (Éditions Sociales, Paris, 1965), p. 89. See in his book, and also in his *Problems of Socialism Today* (Lawrence & Wishart, 1970) an explanation of how the PCE plans to arrive at a socialist Spain.

59. One of the most recent, the so-called Junta Democrática, was announced at a press conference in Paris at the end of July 1974. *Le Monde*, 31 July 1974.

60. S. Carrillo *Después de Franco ¿qué?*, p. 108.

61. See for instance the critique of S. Carrillo's *Después de Franco ¿qué?*, by F. Claudín, an expelled member of the PCE, 'Dos concepciones de la vía española al socialismo', in *Horizonte Español 1966*, vol. 2, pp. 59–100.

62. G. Hermet, *Los comunistas en España* (Ruedo Ibérico, Paris, 1972), p. 111.

63. C. M. Lorenzo, *Les Anarchistes espagnols et le pouvoir 1868–1969*, p. 391.

64. See the workers' commissions' documents in *Cuadernos de Ruedo Ibérico*, no. 25, June–July 1970, 'Ante el futuro del sindicalismo' and 'Declaración de las commisiones obreras de Madrid', pp. 20–25.

65. These were the APE (*Asociaciones Profesionales de Estudiantes*), in two versions (1965 and 1966), and a decree on students' associations of 14 September 1968.

For an analysis of all these regulations see M. J. Farga, *Universidad y democracia en España* (Era, Mexico City, 1969), pp. 78–84, 95–101, and 149–53.

66. *Anuario estadístico de España 1972*, p. 345. The *Informe sociológico sobre la situación social de España 1970*, p. 963, estimates that by 1975 there will be well over 300,000 university students in Spain.

67. 'Students' opposition in Spain', *Government and Opposition*, vol. 1, no. 4, 1966, p. 484. Professor Tierno Galván, together with two other professors, Aranguren and García Calvo, were deprived of their chairs for life for leading a peaceful student demonstration in 1965.

68. For an assessment of the regional question with a socio-historical perspective see J. J. Linz, 'Early state-building and late peripheral nationalisms against the state: the Case of Spain', in S. N. Eisenstadt and S. Rokkan (eds.), *Building States and Nations* (Sage, Beverly Hills, 1973), vol. 2, pp. 32–116.

69. In 1942 only 4 books in Catalan were published in Spain, by 1968 the number had gone up to 500. A. Figueruelo, *Cataluña: crónica de una frustración* (Guadiana, Madrid, 1970), p. 227.

70. Iker, 'Nacionalismo y lucha de clases en Euskadi: V y VI asambleas de ETA', *Cuadernos de Ruedo Ibérico*, no. 37–8, June–September 1972, pp. 15–36.

10. Personal Conclusion

1. *Indice*, no. 345, January, 1974.
2. *Le Monde*, 31 March, 1972.

BIBLIOGRAPHY

This select bibliography has a twofold aim: the first is the customary one, to let the reader see the main body of the material which has been used and consulted in the preparation of this work. The second one, even though this work does not pretend to be a text-book, is more of a pedagogical nature. My years of teaching Spanish politics in a British university have convinced me that the major difficulty encountered by students is to obtain reliable bibliographical information, due largely to the peculiar political situation in Spain and the neglect of the subject of Spanish politics since the Civil War.

Given the nature of this book most of the works mentioned refer to the more recent years of the Franco regime. On the earlier period only a handful of titles of special interest has been included.

The reader's guide, ordered by subjects, should facilitate further reading and study. The numbers in the guide refer to the articles and books in the bibliography itself.

Reader's Guide

Books and Articles

1. M. AGUILAR NAVARRO, 'Les Chrétiens espagnols et la démocratie', *Espri*, October 1965, pp. 433–45.

2. I. ALBIOL MONTESINOS, 'El ámbito de aplicación del decreto del 2/6/1969 *Revista de Política Social*, no. 86, April–June 1970, pp. 87–125

3. J. M. ALMANSA PASTOR, 'La huelga laboral en España tras la modificació: del artículo 222 del Código Penal', *Revista de Política Social*, no. 72, October December 1966, pp. 49–94

4. M. ALONSO BAQUER, 'La defensa nacional', in M. Fraga Iribarne (ed.), *L España de los años 70: el estado y la política* (Moneda y Crédito, Madrid, 1974) vol. 2, pp. 1051–93

5. M. ALONSO GARCIA, 'Notas sobre el Fuero del Trabajo', *Revista de Trabajo*, no. 2, June 1963, pp. 73–87

6. M. ALONSO GARCIA, 'La vida sindical', in M. Fraga Iribarne (ed.), *La España de los años 70: el estado y la política* (Moneda y Crédito, Madrid, 1974), vol. 1, pp. 625–93

7. E. ALVAREZ PUGA, *Historia de la Falange* (Dopesa, Barcelona, 1969)

8. E. ALVAREZ PUGA *et al.*, *Los 90 ministros de Franco* (Dopesa, Barcelona, 1970).

9. O. ALZAGA, 'Asociaciones políticas. El anteproyecto', *Revista de Fomento Social*, no. 100, October–December 1970, pp. 343–54

10. O. ALZAGA and A. FERNANDEZ SEPULVEDA, 'Las asociaciones políticas en España', *Los Suplementos*, no. 25 (Edicusa, Madrid, 1971)

11. J. AMODIA, 'El asociacionismo político en España: aborto inevitable', *Iberian Studies*, vol. 3, no. 1, 1974, pp. 9–15

12. J. AMSDEN, *Collective Bargaining and Class Conflict in Spain* (Weidenfeld & Nicolson, 1972)

13. C. W. ANDERSON, *The Political Economy of Modern Spain: Policy-Making in an Authoritarian System* (University of Wisconsin Press, 1970)

14. J. ANGULO URIBARRI, *Documentos socio-políticos de los obispos españoles (1968–1972)* (PPC, Madrid, 1972)

15. 'Año diez de las Comisiones Obreras', *Cuadernos de Ruedo Ibérico*, no. 31–2, June–September 1971, pp. 53–67

16. J. L. ARANGUREN, 'La spiritualité de l'Opus Dei, à propos d'une controverse', *Esprit*, April 1965, pp. 762–71

17. J. L. ARANGUREN, *El problema universitario* (Nova Terra, Barcelona, 1968)

18. J. M. DE AREILZA, *Escritos políticos* (Guadiana, Madrid, 1970)

19. J. M. DE AREILZA, *Cien artículos* (Revista de Occidente, Madrid, 1970)

20. G. ARIAS SALGADO, *Política Española de la información* (Ministerio de Información, Madrid, 1957–8)

21. T. ARONSON, *Royal Vendetta: The Crown of Spain 1829–1965* (Oldbourne, 1966)

22. J. L. DE ARRESE, *Treinta años de política* (A. Aguado, Madrid, 1966)

23. F. DE ARTEAGA, *ETA y el proceso de Burgos* (A. Aguado, Madrid, 1971)

24. D. ARTIGUES, *El Opus Dei en España: su evolución ideológica y política 1928–1962* (Ruedo Ibérico, Paris, 1971)

25. J. BARDAVIO, *La estructura del poder en España* (Ibérico-Europea de Ediciones, Madrid, 1969)

26. J. BARDAVIO, *La crisis: historia de quince días* (Sedmay, Madrid, 1974)

27. *Bases de la democracia española* (Ediciones del Movimiento, Madrid, 1962)

28. G. BAYON CHACON, 'La interpretación dinámica del Fuero del Trabajo', *Revista de Trabajo*, no. 2, June 1963, pp. 31–69

29. G. BAYON CHACON, and E. PEREZ BOTIJA, *Manual de derecho del trabajo* (M. Pons, Madrid, 1970)

30. J. BENEYTO PEREZ, *El nuevo estado español: el régimen nacional-sindicalista*

ante la tradición y los sistemas totalitarios (Biblioteca Nueva, Madrid, 1939)

31. E. BILBAO EGUIA, *Discursos* (Editora Nacional, Madrid, 1970)

32. J. BLANC, 'Las huelgas en el movimiento obrero español', *Horizonte Español 1966*, vol. 2, pp. 249–74

33. E. DE BLAYE, *Franco ou la monarchie sans roi* (Stock, Paris, 1974)

34. J. M. BOQUERA OLIVER, 'El valor jurídico de las leyes ordinarias', *Revista de Estudios Políticos*, nos. 169–70, January–April 1970, pp. 137–60

35. J. C. DE BORBON, *Por España con los españoles* (Doncel, Madrid, 1973)

36. R. BORRAS BETRIU *et al*, *El día que mataron a Carrero Blanco* (Planeta, Barcelona, 1974)

37. A. M. BRASSLOFF, 'Church–State relations in Spain since the Civil War', *Iberian Studies*, vol. 2, no. 2, 1973, pp. 88–92

38. I. BRAVARD, 'L'Economie de l'Espagne', *Notes et Études Documentaires*, no. 3, pp. 788–9 (La Documentation Française, Paris, 1971)

39. F. G. BRUGUERA, *Histoire contemporaine d'Espagne, 1789–1950* (Ophrys, Paris, 1953)

40. R. BULNES, 'Del sindicalismo de represión al sindicalismo de integración', Horizonte Español 1966, vol. 2, pp. 285–325

41. J. BUSQUETS, *El militar de carrera en España* (Ariel, Barcelona, 1971)

42. J. J. CABALLERO, 'Clase obrera y relaciones de trabajo', in S. del Campo (ed.), *La España de los años 70: la sociedad* (Moneda y Crédito, Madrid, 1972), pp. 593–753

43. J. C. CABANNE, 'La situacion actuelle du Mouvement Nationale en Espagne', *Revue des Sciences Politiques*, no. 23–4, 1970, pp. 9–113

44. R. CALVO SERER, 'La politique intérieure dans l'Espagne de Franco', *Ecrits*, September 1953, pp. 9–18

45. R. CALVO SERER, *España ante la libertad, la democracia y el progreso* (Guadiana, Madrid, 1968)

46. R. CALVO SERER, *Franco frente al Rey* ([Paris], 1972)

47. R. CALVO SERER, *La dictadura de los franquistas* ([Paris], 1973)

48. J. L. CALLEJA, *Don Juan Carlos, ¿por qué?* (Editora Nacional, Madrid, 1972)

49. M. CANTARERO DEL CASTILLO, *Ideas actuales: testimonio de una comparecencia política* (Coslada, Madrid, 1970)

50. S. CARRILLO, *Después de Franco, ¿que?* (Éditions Sociales, Paris, 1965)

51. S. CARRILLO, *Problems of Socialism Today* (Lawrence & Wishart, 1970)

52. S. CARRILLO, *Libertad y socialismo* (Éditions Sociales, Paris, 1971)

53. A. CARRO MARTINEZ, 'Relaciones entre los altos órganos del Estado', *Revista de Estudios Políticos*, no. 152, March–April 1967, pp. 7–18

54. J. A. CASTRO FARIÑAS, *De la libertad de prensa* (Fragua, Madrid, 1971)

55. I. CAVERO, 'Perspectivas del Movimiento Demócrata-Cristiano', in *España: perspectiva 1973* (Guadiana, Madrid, 1973), pp. 179–211

56. P. CEPEDA CALZADA, *Reflexiones sobre la estabilidad política ante la compleja alma hispánica* (Fomento de Cultura, Valencia, 1969)

57. J. CERON, 'Las comisiones obreras entre la táctica y la estrategia', *Cuadernos de Ruedo Ibérico*, no. 15, October–November 1967, pp. 97–106

58. 'Las cien familias españolas', *Horizonte Español 1966*, vol. I, pp. 47–119

59. R. DE LA CIERVA *et al.*, *Francisco Franco: un siglo de España* (Editora Nacional, Madrid, 1972–3)

60. R. DE LA CIERVA, 'Franco y el franquismo', in M. Fraga Iribarne, *La España de los años 70: el estado y la política* (Moneda y Crédito, Madrid, 1974), vol. I, pp. 159–219

61. C. L. CLARK, *The Evolution of the Franco Regime* (n.p., n.d.)

62. F. CLAUDIN, 'Dos concepciones de la vía española al socialismo', *Horizonte Español 1966*, vol. 2, pp. 59–100

63. F. CLAUDIN, 'La crisis del Partido Comunista de España', *Cuadernos de Ruedo Ibérico*, nos. 26–7, August–November 1970, pp. 51–82

64. J. C. CLEMENTE, *Conversaciones sobre el presente y el futuro político de España* (Juventud, Barcelona, 1972)

65. J. C. CLEMENTE, *Conversaciones con las corrientes políticas de España* (Dopesa, Barcelona, 1971)

66. M. CLEMENTE DE DIEGO, *El futuro político de España* (n.p., 1968)

67. J. CLEUGH, *Spain in the Modern World* (Eyre & Spottiswoode, 1952)

68. COMISARIA DEL PLAN DE DESARROLLO, *III Plan de Desarrollo* (Boletín Oficial del Estado, Madrid, 1971)

69. 'Declaraciones de Comisiones Obreras de Madrid', *Cuadernos de Ruedo Ibérico*, no. 8, August–September 1966, pp. 64–8

70. F. J. CONDE GARCIA, *Contribución a la doctrina del caudillaje* (Vicesecretaría de Educación Popular, Madrid, 1942)

71. J. M. CORDERO TORRES, 'La administración consultiva del Estado en la Ley Orgánica del Estado', *Revista de Estudios Políticos*, no. 152, March–April 1967, pp. 21–30

72. C. CORRAL SALVADOR, 'El ordenamiento jurídico de libertad religiosa', *Revista de Estudios Políticos*, no. 158, March–April 1968, pp. 77–98

73. J. CORTES ORMAZABAL *et al.*, *Derecho de huelga* (Zyx, Madrid, 1965)

74. J. CORTS GRAU, 'Sentido español de la democracia', *Revista de Estudios Políticos*, nos. 25–6, January–April 1946, pp. 1–42

75. B. CROZIER, *Franco: A Biographical History* (Eyre & Spottiswoode, 1967)

76. DATA, EQUIPO, *Quién es quién en las Cortes*, *Los Suplementos*, no. 7 (Edicusa, Madrid, 1969)

77. J. M. DESANTES, *Hacia el realismo político* (Dopesa, Barcelona, 1969)

78. P. DESSENS, 'La loi organique de l'état espagnol', *Notes et Études Documentaires*, no. 3, 400 (La Documentation Française, Paris, 1967)

79. J. DIAZ DE VILLEGAS, 'Los ejércitos como salvaguardia de la integridad de la Patria', *Arbor*, nos. 151–2, 1958, pp. 347–64

80. B. DIAZ-NOSTY, *Las Cortes de Franco: 30 años orgánicos* (Dopesa, Barcelona, 1972)

81. J. M. DIEZ-ALEGRIA et al., *Concordato y sociedad pluralista* (Sígueme, Salamanca, 1972)

82. M. DIEZ-ALEGRIA, *Ejército y sociedad* (Alianza, Madrid, 1972)

83. G. DUEÑAS, *La Ley de Prensa de Manuel Fraga* (Ruedo Ibérico, Paris, 1969)

84. R. DUOCASTELLA et al., *Análisis sociológico del catolicismo español* (Nova Terra, Barcelona, 1967)

85. W. G. EBENSTEIN, *Church and State in Franco Spain* (Princeton University, 1960)

86. RAFAEL ENTRENA CUESTA, *Curso de derecho administrativo* (Tecnos, Madrid, 1971)

87. RAMON ENTRENA CUESTA, 'La jefatura del estado', in M. Fraga Iribarne, *La España de los años 70: el estado y la política* (Moneda y Crédito, Madrid, 1974), vol. I, pp. 975–1026

88. J. I. ESCOBAR Y KIRKPATRICK, 'El jefe del Estado en la ley orgánica', *Revista de Estudios Políticos*, no. 152, March–April 1967, pp. 33–55

89. *España: perspectiva 1974* (Guadiana, Madrid, 1974). Yearbook published regularly since 1968

90. J. ESPERABE DE ARTEAGA, 'Perspectivas constitucionales de una evolución parlamentaria', *Revista de Fomento Social*, no. 101, January–March 1971, pp. 85–96

91. J. ESPERABE DE ARTEAGA, 'La necesaria reforma del Reglamento de las Cortes', *Revista de Fomento Social*, no. 102, April–June 1971, pp. 121–35.

92. J. ESPERABE DE ARTEAGA, 'Entorno y contorno de un Reglamento', *Revista de Fomento Social*, no. 105, January–March 1972, pp. 9–16

93. M. ESPINAR, *Una democracia para España* (Edicusa, Madrid, 1967)

94. J. DE ESTEBAN, 'Desarrollo político y régimen constitucional español', *Sistema*, no. 2, April 1973, pp. 77–99

95. J. DE ESTEBAN et al., *Desarrollo político y constitución española* (Ariel, Barcelona, 1973)

96. J. ESTRUCH, *Los protestantes españoles* (Nova Terra, Barcelona, 1967)

97. M. J. FARGA, *Universidad y democracia en España* (Era, Mexico City, 1969)

98. M. FERNANDEZ AREAL, *La política católica en España* (Dopesa, Barcelona, 1970)

99. M. FERNANDEZ AREAL, *La libertad de prensa en España* (Edicusa, Madrid, 1971)

100. M. FERNANDEZ AREAL, *El control de la prensa en España* (Guadiana, Madrid, 1973)

101. R. FERNANDEZ CARVAJAL, *La constitución española* (Editora Nacional, Madrid, 1969)

102. R. FERNANDEZ CARVAJAL, 'La potestad normativa de las Leyes Fundamentales en España', *Revista de Estudios Políticos*, nos. 169–70, January–April 1970, pp. 63–77

103. R. FERNANDEZ CARVAJAL, 'El gobierno entre el jefe del Estado y las Cortes', *Revista de Estudios Políticos*, nos. 183–4, May–August 1972, pp. 5–21

104. R. FERNANDEZ CUESTA, *El 18 de julio* (Doncel, Madrid, 1962)

105. I. FERNANDEZ DE CASTRO, 'La Iglesia de la Cruzada y sus supervivencias', *Horizonte Español 1966*, vol. 1, pp. 207–23

106. I. FERNANDEZ DE CASTRO, *De las Cortes de Cadiz al Plan de Desarrollo* (Ruedo Ibérico, Paris, 1968)

107. I. FERNANDEZ DE CASTRO and J. MARTINEZ, *España, hoy* (Ruedo Ibérico, Paris, 1963)

108. T. FERNANDEZ MIRANDA, 'El Fuero del Trabajo en la constitución del Estado español', *Revista de Trabajo*, no. 2, June 1963, pp. 11–28

109. G. FERNANDEZ DE LA MORA, *El crepúsculo de las ideologías* (Rialp, Madrid, 1965)

110. A. FIGUERUELO, *Cataluña: crónica de una frustración* (Guadiana, Madrid, 1970)

111. FOESSA, FUNDACION, *Informe sociológico sobre la situación social de España 1966* (Euramérica, Madrid, 1966)

112. FOESSA, FUNDACIÓN, *Informe sociológico sobre la situación social de España 1970* (Euramérica, Madrid, 1970)

113. A. FONTAN, 'Présent et futur politique de l'Espagne: un point de vue monarquiste', *Revue des Sciences Politiques*, no. 17, September–November 1967, pp. 7–21

114. D. FORMENTOR, 'Universidad: crónica de siete años de lucha', *Horizonte Español 1972*, vol. 2, pp. 179–235

115. M. FRAGA IRIBARNE, *Así se gobierna España* ([Madrid], 1949)

116. M. FRAGA IRIBARNE, *El reglamento de las Cortes Españolas* ([Madrid], 1959)

117. M. FRAGA IRIBARNE, 'El articulado de la Ley Fundamental de 17 de mayo de 1958', *Arbor*, no. 152, July–August 1958, pp. 515–22

118. M. FRAGA IRIBARNE, *Horizonte español* ([Madrid], 1965)

119. M. FRAGA IRIBARNE, *El desarrollo político* (Grijalbo, Barcelona, 1971)

120. M. FRAGA IRIBARNE, *Legitimidad y representación* (Grijalbo, Barcelona, 1973)

121. M. M. FRAILE CLIVILLES, *Comentario al Reglamento de las Cortes* (Instituto de Estudios Políticos, Madrid, 1973)

122. M. M. FRAILE CLIVILLES, 'Las Cortes Españolas', in M. Fraga Iribarne (ed.), *La España de los años 70: el estado y la política* (Moneda y Crédito, Madrid, 1974), vol. 1, pp. 1097–1164

123. F. FRANCO, *Franco ha dicho* ([Madrid], 1947)

124. F. FRANCO, *Textos de doctrina política (1945–1950)* (Publicaciones Españolas, Madrid, 1951)

125. F. FRANCO, *Discursos y mensajes del Jefe del Estado 1968–1970* (Dirección

General de Cultura Popular, Madrid, 1971). Published regularly since 1951

126. J. M. DE FRUTOS ISABEL, 'Decreto-ley y recurso de contrafuero', in *Estudios en homenaje al Profesor López Rodó* (CSIC, Madrid, 1972), vol. 2, pp. 53–71

127. A. DE FUENMAYOR, 'Estado y religión: el artículo 6 del Fuero de los Españoles', *Revista de Estudios Políticos*, no. 152, March–April 1967, pp. 99–120

128. L. DE LA FUENTE, 'El Consejo Nacional en la Ley Orgánica del Estado', *Revista de Estudios Políticos*, no. 152, March–April 1967, pp. 121–35

129. L. DE LA FUENTE, *Trabajo, sociedad, política* (Ministerio de Trabajo, Madrid, 1974)

130. E. FUENTES, 'La oposicion antifranquista de 1939 a 1955', *Horizonte Español 1966*, vol. 2, pp. 1–28

131. J. FUEYO, 'El principio de representación', *Arbor*, no. 151–2, 1958, pp. 418–30

132. *Un futuro para España* (Ebro, Paris, 1967)

133. F. J. GALVEZ MONTES, 'El control de la constitucionalidad en España', in M. Fraga Iribarne (ed.), *La España de los años 70: el estado y la política* (Moneda y Crédito, Madrid, 1974), vol. I, pp. 1291–369

134. M. GALLO, *Histoire de l'Espagne franquiste* (Gerard, Viviers, 1969)

135. O. GAMO, 'La informacion sobre las huelgas en España: un ejemplo de la manipulación de la noticia por la prensa', *Horizonte Español 1972*, vol. 2, pp. 103–27

136. E. GARCIA, 'Los periódicos de Madrid al primer año de la Ley de Prensa', *Cuadernos de Ruedo Ibérico*, no. 12, April–May 1967, pp. 37–42

137. M. GARCIA, 'Los ex-ministros de Franco en el mundo de las finanzas', *Cuadernos de Ruedo Ibérico*, no. 10, December–January 1967, pp. 75–84

138. J. GARCIA ABELLAN, *Derecho de conflictos colectivos de trabajo* (Instituto de Estudios Políticos, Madrid, 1969)

139. J. GARCIA ABELLAN, *Derecho sindical español: estudio sistemático de la Ley Sindical de 1971* (Servicio de Información y Publicaciones Sindicales, Madrid, 1972)

140. L. GARCIA ARIAS, 'Las fuerzas armadas en la Ley Orgánica del Estado', *Revista de Estudios Políticos*, no. 152, March–April 1967, pp. 137–55

141. E. GARCIA DE ENTERRIA, *La administración española* (Alianza, Madrid, 1972)

142. J. GARCIA NIETO et al., *La nueva ley sindical: análisis de una protesta* (Estela, Barcelona, 1970)

143. L. GARCIA SAN MIGUEL, 'Estructura y cambio del régimen político español', *Sistema*, no. 1, January 1973, pp. 81–106

144. L. GARCIA SAN MIGUEL, 'Para una sociología del cambio político y la oposición en la España actual', *Sistema*, no. 4, January 1974, pp. 89–107

145. F. GARRIDO FALLA, 'The constitutional background and implications of the

new Spanish trades union Act', *International Labour Review*, vol. 105, no. 3, March 1972, pp. 261–73

146. J. GARRIGUES, *Tres conferencias en Italia sobre el Fuero del Trabajo* (Editora Nacional, Madrid, 1939)

147. J. GEORGEL, *Le Franquisme: histoire et bilan, 1939–1969* (Éditions du Seuil, Paris, 1970)

148. R. GIBERT, *El Consejo del Reino* (BO del E., Madrid, 1961)

149. J. M. GIL ROBLES, *Cartas al pueblo español* (A. Aguado, Madrid, 1967)

150. J. M. GIL ROBLES, *Por un estado de derecho* (Ariel, Barcelona, 1969)

151. J. GIMENEZ, 'Temática de la revisión del Concordato español', in *La institución concordataria en la actualidad* (CSIC, Salamanca, 1971), pp. 467–510

152. S. GINER, 'The Structure of Spanish society and the process of modernization', *Iberian Studies*, vol. 1, no. 2, 1972, pp. 53–68

153. S. GINER, 'Spain', in M. Scotford Archer (ed.), *Students, University and Society* (Heinemann, 1972), pp. 103–26

154. *El gobierno informa* (Editora Nacional, Madrid, 1964)

155. I. GOITIA, 'Referéndum', *Cuadernos de Ruedo Ibérico*, no. 10, December–January 1967, pp. 41–53

156. I. GOITIA, 'Algunas precisiones sobre Euzkadi', *Cuadernos de Ruedo Ibérico*, no. 25, June–July 1970, pp. 39–52

157. R. GOMEZ ACEBO, 'El ejercicio de la función legislativa por el Gobierno: leyes delegadas y decretos-leyes', *Revista de Estudios Políticos*, no. 69, November–December 1951, pp. 67–97

158. L. GOMEZ DE ARANDA, *El tema de las ideologías* (Ediciones Europa, Madrid, 1966)

159. L. GOMEZ DE ARANDA, 'La filosofía política de la Ley Orgánica y las ideologías contemporáneas', *Revista de Estudios Políticos*, no. 152, March–April 1967, pp. 157–72

160. L. GOMEZ DE ARANDA, *Conferencia sobre el X aniversario de la Ley de Principios Fundamentales del Movimiento* (Ediciones de Movimiento, Madrid, 1968)

161. J. A. GONZALEZ CASANOVA, *El régimen político de la televisión* (Nova Terra, Barcelona, 1967)

162. J. A. GONZALEZ CASANOVA, 'El derecho constitucional y las instituciones políticas en España', in A. Haurion, *Derecho constitucional e instituciones políticas* (Ariel, Barcelona, 1971), pp. 855–928

163. F. GONZALEZ-DORIA, *¿Franquismo sin Franco . . .?* (Cunillera, Madrid, 1974)

164. J. M. GONZALEZ PARAMO, *Política de prensa* (Grijalbo, Barcelona, 1972)

165. L. GONZALEZ SEARA, 'Los medios de comunicación de masas y la formación de la opinión pública', in S. del Campo, *La España de los años 70: la sociedad.* (Moneda y Crédito, Madrid, 1972), pp. 759–806

166. J. GRAU *et al.*, *Treinta mil españoles y Dios* (Nova Terra, Barcelona, 1972)

167. A. GUAITA, *El Consejo de Ministros* (Escuela Nacional de Administración Pública, Madrid, 1967)

168. V. A. GUILLAMON, 'Sindicalismo', in *España: perspectiva 1969* (Guadiana, Madrid, 1969), pp. 75–92

169. G. HERMET, 'La Presse espagnole depuis la suppression de la censure', *Revue Française de Science Politique*, vol. 18, no. 1, February 1968, pp. 44–67

170. G. HERMET, 'Les Espagnols devant leur régime', Revue Française de Science Politique, vol. 20, no. 1, February 1970, pp. 3–36

171. G. HERMET, *Les Communistes en Espagne* (A. Colin, Paris, 1971)

172. G. HERMET, *La Politique dans l'Espagne Franquiste* (A. Colin, Paris, 1971)

173. J. HERNANDEZ, 'Aproximación a la historia de las Comisiones Obreras y de las tendencias forjadas en su seno', *Cuadernos de Ruedo Iberico*, no. 39–40, October–January 1973, pp. 57–79

174. A. GIL HERNANDEZ, 'La justicia en la Ley Orgánica del Estado', *Revista de Estudios Políticos*, no. 181, January–February 1972, pp. 35–48

175. M. HERRERO, 'El asociacionismo', in *España: perspectiva 1970* (Guadiana, Madrid 1970), pp. 231–46

176. M. HERRERO, *El principio monárquico* (Edicusa, Madrid, 1972)

177. M. HERRERO, 'El rey legítimo: ensayo inocuo en torno a Max Weber', *Sistema*, no. 6, July 1974, pp. 119–24

178. F. HERRERO TEJEDOR, 'El estado de derecho en las Leyes Fundamentales', *Revista de Estudios Políticos*, no. 152, March–April 1967, pp. 175–205

179. G. HILLS, *Franco: The Man and his Nation* (Hale, 1967)

180. G. HILLS, *Spain* (Benn, 1970)

181. G. HILLS, 'ETA and Basque Nationalism', *Iberian Studies*, vol. I, no. 2, 1972, pp. 83–9

182. D. IBARRURI et al., *Historia política del Partido Comunista de España* (Editora Política, Havana, 1964)

183. J. IGLESIAS FERNANDEZ, *Convenios colectivos, ¿ofensiva del sistema capitalista?*, *Los Suplementos*, no. 47 (Edicusa, Madrid, 1974)

184. C. IGLESIAS SELGAS, *Los sindicatos en España* (Ediciones del Movimiento, Madrid, 1966)

185. C. IGLESIAS SELGAS, *La vía española a la democracia* (Ediciones del Movimiento, Madrid, 1968)

186. C. IGLESIAS SELGAS, *Un régimen social moderno* (Fomento Social, Bilbao, 1969)

187. C. IGLESIAS SELGAS, *Comentarios a la Ley Sindical* (Cabal, Madrid, 1971)

188. C. IGLESIAS SELGAS, *Las Cortes Españolas* (Cabal, Madrid, 1973)

189. IKER, 'Nacionalismo y lucha de clases en Euzkadi: V y VI asambleas de ETA', *Cuadernos de Ruedo Ibérico*, nos. 37–8, June–September 1972, pp. 15–36

190. INSTITUTO DE ESTUDIOS POLITICOS, *España, estado de derecho* (Servicio Informativo Español, Madrid, 1964)

191. INSTITUTO DE OPINION PUBLICA, 'Encuesta sobre la juventud española', *Revista Española de la Opinión Pública*, no. 15, January–March 1969, pp. 231–337

192. INSTITUTO DE OPINION PUBLICA, 'Análisis del contenido de la prensa diaria', *Revista Española de la Opinión Pública*, no. 10, October–December 1967, pp. 171–259

193. INTERNATIONAL COMMISSION OF JURISTS, *Spain and the Rule of Law* (Geneva, 1962)

194. INTERNATIONAL LABOUR ORGANIZATION, *Report of the Study Group to Examine the Labour and Trade Union Situation in Spain* (Geneva, 1969)

195. J. JIMENEZ, *La objeción de conciencia en España* (Edicusa, Madrid, 1973)

196. F. JIMENEZ ASENJO, *Organización judicial española* (Revista de Derecho Privado, Madrid, 1952)

197. E. JIMENEZ ASENJO, *Ley de Orden Público de 30 de julio de 1959* (Instituto de Estudios Políticos, Madrid, 1961)

198. J. JIMENEZ BLANCO, 'Desarrollo económico, desarrollo político', in *España: perspectiva 1972* (Guadiana, Madrid, 1972), pp. 153–78

199. J. JIMENEZ BLANCO et al., *Las ideologías en la España de hoy* (Seminarios y Ediciones, Madrid, 1972)

200. M. JIMENEZ DE PARGA, *Noticias con acento* (Alfaguara, Barcelona, 1967)

201. M. JIMENEZ DE PARGA, *Atisbos desde esta España* (Guadiana, Madrid, 1968)

202. P. JOBIT, *L'Église d'Espagne à l'heure du Concile* (Spes, Paris, 1965)

203. JUSTICIA Y POLITICA, two volumes, written by a group of Spanish lawyers and magistrates (n.p., 1971, 1972)

204. K. KIRBY, 'Borraka: la lutte des Basques', *Esprit*, February 1974, pp. 336–59

205. P. LAIN ENTRALGO, *El problema de la universidad* (Edicusa, Madrid, 1968)

206. R. LEDESMA RAMOS, *¿Fascismo en España?* (Ariel, Barcelona, 1968)

207. L. LEGAZ LACAMBRA, *Introducción a la teoría del estado nacional-sindicalista* (Bosch, Barcelona, 1940)

208. L. LEGAZ LACAMBRA, 'Ideología y principios fundamentales', *Revista de Estudios Políticos*, no. 175, January–February 1971, pp. 5–16

209. S. LEON, 'Notas sobre el movimiento estudiantil en España', *Horizonte Español 1972*, vol. 2, pp. 157–77

210. P. H. LEWIS, 'The Spanish ministerial elite, 1938–1969', *Comparative Politics*, vol. 5, no. 1, October 1972, pp. 83–106

211. J. J. LINZ, 'An authoritarian regime: Spain', in E. Allardt and Y. Littunen (eds.), *Cleavages, Ideologies and Party Systems* (Westermack Society, Helsinki, 1964), pp. 291–341

212. J. J. LINZ, 'The party system of Spain: past and future', in S. M. Lipset and S. Rokkan (eds.), *Party Systems and Voter Alignments* (Free Press, New York, 1967), pp. 197–282

213. J. J. LINZ, 'From Falange to Movimiento-Organización: the Spanish single

party and the Franco regime, 1936–1968', in S. P. Huntington and C. H. Moore (eds.), *Authoritarian Politics in Modern Society* (Basic Books, New York, 1970), pp. 128–203

214. J. J. LINZ, 'Opposition in and under an authoritarian regime: the case of Spain', in R. Dahl (ed.), *Regimes and Oppositions* (Yale University Press, 1973), pp. 171–259

215. J. J. LINZ, 'Early state-building and late peripheral nationalisms against the State: the case of Spain', in S. N. Einsenstadt and S. Rokkan (eds.), *Building States and Nations* (Sage Publications, Beverly Hills, 1973), vol. 2, pp. 32–116

216. J. J. LINZ and A. DE MIGUEL, 'Within nation differences and comparisons: the eight Spains', in R. L. Merrit and S. Rokkan, *Comparing Nations* (Yale University Press, 1966), pp. 267–319

217. A. LLOYD, *Franco* (Longman, 1970)

218. A. LOPEZ, *La Iglesia desde el Estado* (Editora Nacional, Madrid, 1972)

219. J. LOPEZ MEDEL, 'Declaración XIII del Fuero del Trabajo y Ley Sindical', *Revista de Estudios Políticos*, no. 182, March–April 1972, pp. 5–31

220. A. LOPEZ MUÑOZ and J. L. GARCIA DELGADO, *Crecimiento y crisis del capitalismo español* (Edicusa, Madrid, 1968)

221. A. LOPEZ MUÑOZ, *Capitalismo español: una etapa decisiva, 1965–1970* (Zyx, Madrid, 1970)

222. L. LOPEZ RODO, *Política y desarrollo* (Aguilar, Madrid, 1970)

223. C. M. LORENZO, *Les Anarchistes espagnoles et le pouvoir, 1868–1969* (Éditions du Seuil, Paris, 1969)

224. T. LUCA DE TENA, *Crónicas parlamentarias* (Prensa Española, Madrid, 1967)

225. S. DE MADARIAGA, *España: ensayo de historia contemporánea* (Edit. Sudamericana, Buenos Aires, 1964)

226. J. MAESTRE ROCA, 'Los nombramientos episcopales y las circunscripciones eclesiásticas dentro de la problemática que plantea la revisión del Concordato español de 1953', *Revista de Estudios Políticos*, no. 191, September–October 1973, pp. 171–92

227. J. M. MARAVALL, *Trabajo y conflicto social* (Edicusa, Madrid, 1967)

228. J. M. MARAVALL, *El desarrollo económico y la clase obrera* (Ariel, Barcelona, 1970)

229. J. M. MARAVALL, 'Modernization, authoritarianism, and the growth of working-class dissent: the case of Spain', *Government and Opposition*, vol. 8, no. 4, 1973, pp. 432–54

230. J. MARICHAL, *El nuevo pensamiento político español* (Finisterre, Mexico City, 1966)

231. P. PEREZ MARIN, *El caudillaje español* (Ediciones Europa, Madrid, 1960)

232. P. PEREZ MARIN, 'La administración de justicia en la Ley Orgánica del Estado', *Revista de Estudios Políticos*, no. 152, March–April 1967, pp. 215–49

233. V. MARRERO, *La consolidación política* (Punta Europa, Madrid, 1964)

234. C. MARTIN, *Franco: soldado y estadista* (F. Uriarte, Madrid, 1965)

235. E MARTIN LOPEZ, 'Informe sobre los conflictos colectivos de trabajo 1963–65', *Revista de Trabajo*, no. 13, pp. 141–210

236. I. MARTIN MARTINEZ, 'La libertad religiosa en la Ley Orgánica del Estado', *Revista de Estudios Políticos*, no. 182, March–April 1972, pp. 181–211

237. I. MARTIN MARTINEZ, 'Presencia de la jerarquía de la Iglesia católica en organismos políticos del estado español', in *El fenómeno religioso en España* (Instituto de Estudios Políticos, Madrid, 1972), pp. 349–96

238. L. MARTIN-RETORTILLO, *Libertad religiosa y orden público* (Tecnos, Madrid, 1970)

239. R. MARTIN VILLA, 'The Spanish trades union Act and the ILO constitution', *International Labour Review*, vol. 105, no. 3, March 1972, pp. 275–93

240. L. MARTINEZ-CALCERRADA, *La independencia del poder judicial* (Revista de Derecho Judicial, Madrid, 1970)

241. M. MARTINEZ CUADRADO (ed.), *Cambio social y modernización politica: Anuario político 1969* (Edicusa, Madrid, 1970)

242. M. MARTINEZ CUADRADO (ed.), *Anuario político, 1970* (Edicusa, Madrid, 1971)

243. M. MARTINEZ CUADRADO, 'Representación. Elecciones. Referéndum', in M. Fraga Iribarne (ed.), *La España de los años 70: el estado y la política* (Moneda y Crédito, Madrid, 1974), pp. 1371–439

244. C. MARTINEZ ESTERUELAS, 'Las funciones del Consejo del Reino', *Revista de Estudios Políticos*, no. 152, March–April 1967, pp. 251–66

245. M. MARTINEZ SOSPEDRA, 'El Consejo del Reino', in M. Fraga Iribarne (ed.), *La España de los años 70: el estado y la política* (Moneda y Crédito, Madrid, 1974), pp. 1241–90

246. H. MATTHEWS, *The Yoke and the Arrows: A Report on Spain* (Braziller, New York, 1961)

247. L. MAYOR MARTINEZ, *Las ideologías dominantes en el sindicato vertical* (Zyx, Madrid, 1972)

248. M. DEL MAZO et al., *Los cenocentristas: radiografía política de unas cenas* ([Bilbao], 1970)

249. K. MEDHURST, 'The Political presence of the Spanish bureaucracy', *Government and Opposition*, vol. 4, no. 2, 1969, pp. 235–49.

250. K. MEDHURST, *The Basques* (Minority Rights Group, 1972)

251. K. MEDHURST, *Government in Spain: The Executive at Work* (Pergamon, 1973)

252. M. A. MEDINA MUÑOZ, 'Los consejeros nacionales del Movimiento según la Ley Orgánica del mismo y el Reglamento del Consejo', *Revista de Estudios Políticos*, no. 171–2, May–August 1970, pp. 117–39

253. M. A. MEDINA MUÑOZ, 'El Consejo del Reino', *Revista de Estudios Políticos*, no. 181, January–February 1972, pp. 105–30

254. J. MEYRIAT, 'Changement politique en Espagne?', *Revue de Défense National*, no. 25, January 1969, pp. 64–84

255. A. DE MIGUEL, *España, marca registrada* (Kairós, Barcelona, 1972)

256. A. DE MIGUEL, *Manual de estructura social de España* (Tecnos, Madrid, 1974)

257. MINISTERIO DE INFORMACION Y TURISMO, *Anuario de la prensa española 1970* (Editora Nacional, Madrid, 1970)

258. MINISTERIO DE JUSTICIA, *Crónica de la codificación española: organización judicial* (Madrid, 1970)

259. C. MOLINERO, *La intervención del estado en la prensa* (Dopesa, Barcelona, 1971)

260. A. MONCADA, *El Opus Dei: una interpretación* (Indice, Madrid, 1974)

261. A. MONTOYA MELGAR, 'La jurisdicción laboral y el Fuero del Trabajo', *Revista de Trabajo*, no. 2, June 1963, pp. 213-31

262. J. M. DE MORAL, *Pensamiento y política* (Ediciones del Movimiento, Madrid, 1967)

263. R. MOSS, *Between Past and Future: A Survey of Spain* (*Economist*, 1973)

264. MOVIMIENTO NACIONAL, Un cuarto de siglo del, *Revista de Estudios Políticos*, no. 119, September-October 1961, pp. xxxv-lvii

265. C. MOYA, *Burocracia y sociedad industrial* (Edicusa, Madrid, 1972)

266. J. MUÑOZ, *El poder de la banca en España* (Zyx, Madrid, 1971)

267. J. MUÑOZ et al., *La economía española 1973* (Edicusa, Madrid, 1974). Published yearly since 1968

268. D. NICHOLL, 'Religious liberty in Spain: a survey to 1968', *Iberian Studies*, vol. 1, no. 1, 1972, pp. 4-14

269. E. NIETO, 'Introducción al Opus Dei', *Cuadernos de Ruedo Ibérico*, no. 3, October-November 1965, pp. 87-96

270. J. M. NIN DE CARDONA, *Las ideologías socio-políticas contemporáneas* (Reus, Madrid, 1971)

271. *El nuevo estado español: 25 años de Movimiento Nacional 1936-1961* (Instituto de Estudios Políticos, Madrid, 1961)

272. OECD, *Spain: Economic Survey*. Published yearly

273. E. OLCINA, *El carlismo y las autonomías regionales* (Seminarios y Ediciones, Madrid, 1974)

274. C. OLLERO, 'Desarrollo político y constitución española', in M. Fraga Iribarne (ed.), *La España de los años 70: el estado y la política* (Moneda y Crédito, Madrid, 1974), vol. 1, pp. 1441-66

275. V. ORTEGA, 'La nueva regulación de los conflictos colectivos de trabajo', *Revista de Fomento Social*, no. 100, October-December 1970, pp. 375-87

276. V. ORTEGA, 'Nueva ley sindical', *Revista de Fomento Social*, no. 101, January-March 1971, pp. 15-36

277. V. ORTEGA, 'Problemática laboral y sindical', *Revista de Fomento Social*, no. 105, January-March 1972, pp. 31-43

278. V. ORTEGA, 'Problemática laboral y sindical', *Revista de Fomento Social*, no. 109, January-March 1973, pp. 23-34

279. J. M. ORTI BORDAS, 'El Movimiento y su Consejo Nacional', in M. Fraga

Iribarne (ed.), *La España de los años 70: el estado y la política* (Moneda y Crédito, Madrid, 1974), vol. 1, pp. 1165–239

280. M. ORTUÑO, 'Opus Dei', *Cuadernos Americanos*, vol. 126, no. 1, January–February 1963, pp. 40–66

281. J. PABON, *La otra legitimidad* (Prensa Española, Madrid, 1969)

282. S. PANIKER, *Conversaciones en Madrid* (Kairós, Barcelona, 1969)

283. J. R. PARADA VAZQUEZ, 'El poder sancionador de la administración y la crisis del sistema judicial penal', *Revista de Administración Pública*, no. 67, January–April 1972, pp. 41–93

284. PARTIDO COMUNISTA DE ESPAÑA, *VIII Congreso del PCE* (Bucharest, 1972)

285. S. G. PAYNE, *Falange: A History of Spanish Fascism* (Stanford University Press, 1967)

286. S. G. PAYNE, *Politics and the Military in Modern Spain* (Stanford University Press, 1967)

287. S. G. PAYNE, *Franco's Spain* (Routledge & Kegan Paul, 1968)

288. S. G. PAYNE, 'In the twilight of the Franco era', *Foreign Affairs*, vol. 49, no. 2, January 1971, pp. 342–54

289. S. G. PAYNE, *El nacionalismo vasco: de sus origenes a la ETA* (Dopesa, Barcelona, 1974)

290. PB, 'Significación religiosa, económica y política del Opus Dei', *Horizonte Español 1966*, (Ruedo Ibérica, Paris), vol. 1, pp. 225–52

291. JU. PEMARTIN SANJUAN, *Teoría de la Falange* (Editora Nacional, Madrid, 1941)

292. JO. PEMARTIN SANJUAN, *¿Qué es lo nuevo? Consideraciones sobre el momento español presente* (Espasa-Calpe, Madrid, 1940)

293. A. PEÑA, 'Veinticinco años de luchas estudiantiles', *Horizonte Español 1966*, vol. 2, pp. 169–212

294. L. PEREÑA VICENTE, *La objeción de conciencia en España* (PPC, Madrid, 1972)

295. J. PEREZ LLANTADA, 'La Ley 44/1967 y los derechos civiles individuales de libertad religiosa', in *El fenómeno religioso en España* (Instituto de Estudios Políticos, Madrid, 1972), pp. 306–48

296. A. PEREZ VOITURIEZ, 'Las Leyes Fundamentales ante el derecho internacional', *Revista Española de Derecho Internacional*, vol. 22, no. 2, 1969, pp. 248–79

297. E. PINILLA DE LAS HERAS, 'España una sociedad de diacronías', *Horizonte Español 1966*, vol. 1, pp. 1–12

298. M. PIZAN, *El poder y la oposición* (Dopesa, Madrid, 1970)

299. J. PRADOS ARRARTE, *El plan de desarrollo en España, 1964–1967* (Tecnos, Madrid, 1965)

300. F. PRIETO, *España política, 1969* (Fomento Social, Bilbao, 1970)

301. F. PRIETO, 'Proyectos reguladores de las asociaciones del Movimiento',

Revista de Fomento Social, no. 100, October–December 1970, pp. 355–73

302. F. PRIETO, 'Instrumentalización del liderazgo carismático de Franco', *Revista de Fomento Social*, no. 104, October–December 1971, pp. 401–7

303. L. PRIETO-CASTRO, *Tribunales españoles: organización y funcionamiento* (Tecnos, Madrid, 1973)

304. L. PRIETO-CASTRO, 'La administración de justicia', in M. Fraga Iribarne (ed.), *La España de los años 70: el estado y la política* (Moneda y Crédito, Madrid, 1974), pp. 371–410

305. J. A. PRIMO DE RIVERA, *Textos de doctrina política* (Sección Femenina, Madrid, 1970)

306. *Quién es quién en las Cortes* (Documentación española contemporánea, Madrid, 1971)

307. C. M. RAMA, *La crisis española del siglo XX* (Fondo de Cultura Económica, Mexico City, 1962)

308. L. RAMIREZ, *Francisco Franco: historia de un mesianismo* (Ruedo Ibérico, Paris, 1964)

309. M. RAMIREZ JIMENEZ, 'Modernización política en España', *Revista de Estudios Sociales*, no. 5, May–August 1972, pp. 107–31

310. E. F. REGATILLO, *El Concordato español de 1953* (Sal Terrae, Santander, 1961)

311. R. REYES MORALES, 'El Consejo Nacional del Movimiento y los derechos y libertades reconocidos en las Leyes Fundamentales', *Revista de Estudios Políticos*, no. 152, March–April 1967, pp. 269–76

312. D. RIDRUEJO, *Escrito en España* (Losada, Buenos Aires, 1962)

313. R. A. H. ROBINSON, 'Genealogy and function of the monarchist myth of the Franco regime), *Iberian Studies*, vol. 2, no. 1, 1973, pp. 18–26

314. A. RODRIGUEZ DE VALCARCEL, *Una etapa política* (Ediciones del Movimiento, Madrid, 1969)

315. C. RODRIGUEZ DEVESA, 'Ordenación jurídica vigente de los conflictos colectivos', *Revista de Política Social*, no. 99, July–September 1973, pp. 129–44

316. J. M. RODRIGUEZ DEVESA, *Derecho penal español: parte especial* ([Madrid], 1971)

317. J. RODRIGUEZ MARTINEZ, *Impresiones de un ministro de Carrero Blanco* (Planeta, Barcelona, 1974)

318. M. RODRIGUEZ-PIÑERO, 'El Fuero del Trabajo y la carta social europea', *Revista de Trabajo*, no. 2, June 1963, pp. 123–62

319. F. RODRIGUEZ RODRIGUEZ, 'Los conflictos colectivos y el Fuero del Trabajo', *Revista de Trabajo*, no. 2, June 1963, pp. 165–78

320. J. ROIG, 'Veinticinco años de Movimiento Nacional en Cataluña', *Horizonte Español 1966*, vol. 2, pp. 117–30

321. M. ROMAN, *The Limits of Economic Growth in Spain* (Praeger, New York, 1971)

322. E. ROMERO, *Cartas a un Príncipe* (Magisterio Español, Madrid, 1970)

323. E. ROMERO, *Cartas al pueblo soberano* (A. Aguado, Madrid, 1965)

324. E. ROMERO, *Los gallos de E. Romero* (Planeta, Barcelona, 1968)

325. E. ROMERO, *Cartas al Rey* (Planeta, Barcelona, 1973)

326. J. ROS HOMBRAVELLA *et al.*, *Capitalismo español: de la autarquía a la estabilización (1939–59)* (Edicusa, Madrid, 1973)

327. C. RUDE, *La Phalange: Histoire de fascisme en Espagne* (Édition Spéciale, Paris, 1972)

328. C. RUIZ DEL CASTILLO, 'Las entidades sociales en el estado nacional', *Arbor*, no. 151–2, 1958, pp. 384–92

329. J. RUIZ-GIMENEZ, 'Reflections on the new Spanish trade union Act', *International Labour Review*, vol. 105, no. 3, March 1972, pp. 203–40

330. J. RUPEREZ, *Estado confesional y libertad religiosa* (Edicusa, Madrid, 1970)

331. R. SALABERRI, *El proceso de Euskadi en Burgos* (Ruedo Ibérico, Paris, 1971)

332. F. SALVA MIQUEL, *Francisco Franco: historia de un español* (Ediciones Generales, Barcelona, 1959)

333. L. SANCHEZ AGESTA, 'La representación política en nuestras Leyes Fundamentales, *Arbor*, no. 151–2, 1958, pp. 405–17

334. L. SANCHEZ AGESTA, *Derecho constitucional comparado* (Editora Nacional, Madrid, 1968)

335. L. SANCHEZ AGESTA, 'El recurso de contrafuero y la protección del orden constitucional', *Revista de Estudios Políticos* no. 181, January–February 1972, pp. 5–31

336. J. SANZ OLLER, *Las comisiones obreras de Barcelona: entre el fraude y la esperanza* (Ruedo Ibérico, Paris, 1972)

337. J. SANZ OLLER, 'La larga marcha del movimiento obrero español hacia su autonomía', *Horizonte Español 1972*, vol. 2, pp. 87–102

338. F. SANZ ORRIO, *Los sindicatos españoles* (SIPS, Madrid, 1948)

339. J. SAUNIER, *L'Opus Dei* (Grasset, Paris, 1973)

340. H. F. SCHULTE, *The Spanish Press 1470–1966* (University of Illinois Press, 1968)

341. C. SECO SERRANO, *Historia de España: época contemporánea* (Instituto Gallach, Barcelona, 1968)

342. SECRETARIADO NACIONAL DEL CLERO, *Asamblea conjunta obispos-sacerdotes* (Editorial Católica, Madrid, 1971)

343. J. SEMPRUN, 'La oposición política en España 1956–1966', *Horizonte Espanol, 1966*, pp. 39–55

344. I. SERRANO SERRANO, *El Fuero del Trabajo* ([Valladolid], 1939)

345. R. SERRANO SUÑER, *Entre Hendaya y Gibraltar* (Ediciones y Publicaciones Españolas, Madrid, 1947)

346. SERVICIO DE ESTUDIOS Y DIFUSION DOCTRINAL (Vice Secretaría General del Movimiento) *Nuevo horizonte del Movimiento Nacional* (Ediciones del Movimiento, Madrid, 1970)

347. D. SEVILLA ANDRES, 'La defensa de la constitución en la Ley Orgánica',

Revista de Estudios Políticos, no. 152, March-April 1967, pp. 279–302

348. D. SEVILLA ANDRES, *Historia política de España 1800–1967* (Editora Nacional, Madrid, 1968)

349. J. SOLE-TURA, *Introducción al régimen político español* (Ariel, Barcelona, 1970)

350. R. SOLER, 'The new Spain', *New Left Review*, no. 58, November-December 1969, pp. 3–27

351. J. SOLIS, *Nuestro sindicalismo* (SIPS, Madrid, 1955)

352. F. SOSA WAGNER, 'Las medidas excepcionales en el ordenamiento constitucional, español', *Revista de Administración Pública* no. 66, September-December 1971, pp. 256–82

353. E. de la SOUCHERE, *An Explanation of Spain* (Random House, New York, 1964)

354. H. R. SOUTHWORTH, 'Qu'est-ce que le fascisme?', *Esprit*, no. 379, March 1969, pp. 421–38

355. R. F. STARR (ed.), 'Spain', in *Yearbook of International Communist Affairs* (Stanford University Press, 1972), pp. 220–25

356. F. SUAREZ GONZALEZ, 'El sindicalismo vertical y el Fuero del Trabajo', *Revista de Trabajo*, no. 2, June 1963, pp. 235–44

357. R. TAMAMES, *Centros de gravedad de la economía española* (Guadiana, Madrid, 1968)

358. R. TAMAMES, *España ante un segundo plan de desarrollo* (Nova Terra, Barcelona, 1968)

359. R. TAMAMES, *Los monopolios en España* (Zyx, Madrid, 1968)

360. R. TAMAMES, *Introducción a la economía española* (Alianza, Madrid, 1972)

361. R. TAMAMES, *La república. La era de Franco* (Alfaguara, Madrid, 1973)

362. A. TARDIO BERZOCANA, 'Relaciones del Estado español con la Iglesia a la luz del Concilio Vaticano II' *Revista de Estudios Políticos* no. 178, July–August 1971, pp. 147–73

363. A. TELLEZ, *La guerilla urbana en España* (Belibaste, Paris, 1972)

364. J. J. THIERRY, *L'Opus Dei: mythe et réalité* (Hachette, Paris, 1973)

365. H. THOMAS, 'The balance of forces in Spain', *Foreign Affairs* vol. 41, no. 1, October 1962, pp. 208–21

366. E. TIERNO GALVAN, 'L'université espagnole', *Esprit*, October 1965, pp. 414–21

367. E. TIERNO GALVAN, 'Students' opposition in Spain', *Government and Opposition*, vol. 1, no. 4, 1966, pp. 467–86

368. E. TIERNO GALVAN, 'Some Comments on the Spanish trade union Act of 17 February 1971', *International Labour Review* vol. 105, no. 3, March 1972, pp. 245–60.

369. J. J. TOHARIA, 'Modernización, autoritarismo y administración de justicia España', *Los Suplementos*, no. 51 (Edicusa, Madrid, 1974)

370. J. TOMAS VILLARROYA, 'El Gobierno', in M. Fraga Iribarne (ed.), *La*

España de los años 70: el estado y la política (Moneda y Crédito, Madrid, 1974), vol. I, pp. 1027–82

371. J. R. PERIS TORREGROSA, *La juventud española: conciencia generacional y política* (Ariel, Barcelona, 1972)

372. L. TORRES, 'The Spanish Left: illusion and reality', in R. Miliband and J. Saville (eds.), *The Socialist Register 1966* (Merlin Press, 1966), pp. 66–85

373. TRABAJADORES DE LAMINACION DE BANDAS (Echevarri), *Nuestra huelga* (n.p., 1968)

374. J. W. D. TRYTHALL, *Franco* (Hart-Davis, 1970)

375. M. TUÑON DE LARA, *El hecho religioso en España* (Ebro, Paris, 1968)

376. M. TUÑON DE LARA, 'Le Problème universitaire espagnol', *Esprit*, no. 381, May 1969, pp. 842–58

377. TXABI, 'ETA y la cuestión nacional vasca', *Horizonte Español 1972*, vol. 2, pp. 77–86

378. J. USCATESCU, 'Filosofía de la libertad en la Ley Orgánica', *Revista de Estudios Políticos* no. 152, March–April 1967, pp. 305–17

379. F. de VALDESOTO, *Francisco Franco* (A. Aguado, Madrid, 1943)

380. J. VALYNSEELE, *Les Prétendants aux trones d' Europe* ([Paris], 1967)

381. J. M. VAZQUEZ et al., *La iglesia española contemporánea* (Editora Nacional, Madrid, 1973)

382. M. VAZQUEZ MONTALBAN, *Informe sobre la información* (Fontanella, Barcelona, 1971)

383. M. VAZQUEZ MONTALBAN, *El libro gris de televisión española* (Ediciones 99, Madrid, 1973)

384. P. DE VEGA GARCIA, 'Perspectivas del movimiento socialista', in *España: Perspectiva 1973* (Guadiana, Madrid, 1973), pp. 215–41

385. P. DE VEGA GARCIA, 'Fuerzas políticas y tendencias ideológicas en la España del presente', in M. Fraga Iribarne (ed.), *La España de los años 70: el estado y la política* (Moneda y Crédito, Madrid, 1974), vol. I, pp. 569–624

386. J. VELARDE FUERTES (ed.), *La España de los años 70: la economía* (Momeda y Crédito, Madrid, 1973)

387. J. VELARDE FUERTES, *El nacional-sindicalismo cuarenta años después* (Editora Nacional, Madrid, 1972)

388. M. VEYRAT and J. L. NAVAS-MIGUELOA, *Falange hoy* (G. del Toro, Madrid, 1973)

389. D. VIDAL, *Nosotros los protestantes españoles* (Marova, Madrid, 1968)

390. J. VIDAL, 'Iglesia y sociedad en la España franquista', *Cuadernos de Ruedo Ibérico* no. 36, April–May 1972, pp. 9–23

391. S. VILAR, *Cataluña en España* (Ayma, Barcelona, 1968)

392. S. VILAR, *Protagonistas de la España democrática: la oposición a la dictadura 1939–69* (Librería Española, Paris, 1969)

393. J. M. VILLAR ROMERO, *Siete cartas al Príncipe de España* (Editorial Católica, Madrid, 1970)

INDEX